Literary Mobile

10th Anniversary Edition

A Revision of the 2003 Publication
Literary Mobile

Literary Mobile

10th Anniversary Edition

10th Anniversary Edition Edited By

Rachael Alex

First Edition Edited By

John Hafner

Mary M. Riser

Sue B. Walker

First Edition Foreword By

Ann Bedsole

Negative Capability Press • Mobile, Alabama

A Negative Capability Press Book

Published in the United States of America by
Negative Capability Press
62 Ridgelawn Dr. East
Mobile, AL 36608

Text and cover design by Brittany Hawkins Davis

Printed in the United States of America

Literary Mobile First Edition

ISBN 0-942544-57-9

Literary Mobile 10th Anniversary Edition

ISBN 978-0-942544-78-7
LCCN 2012940520

Dedicated to the Citizens of Mobile

TABLE OF CONTENTS

FIRST EDITION FOREWORD

Ann Bedsole, President, Mobile Tricentennial, Incorporated

O wad some Power the giftie gie us
To see ousels as ithers see us!
It wad frae monie a blunder free us,
An' foolish notion.
Robert Burns

This book, originally the brainchild of three Mobile writers, attempts to answer, from different perspectives, the questions we Mobiles are asking and have asked for three hundred years.

Like standing too close to the trees and not seeing the forest, it is always hard to see your hometown as it really is. You are, at once, too critical and too defensive. You see, but you don't see. The changes may not be apparent, until one day, you ask "Who is this stranger?"

What is Mobile really like? How does this city that seems to be so beautiful and yet so commonplace look to others? Is it just an ordinary small southern city like so many others? Or is it a place that nurtures creativity to the point that people say—and they do say, "It must be something in the water?" Can it be that the magnolias bloom longer here, that the gardenias smell sweeter; can it be that the grass is greener? Were Mobile's founding fathers braver and nobler than the pilgrims and other early Americans? If Mobile is different, how it this so—and why?

The Mobile Tricentennial, the city's 300th birthday, offered a lens through which to look at the city—its past as well as its present. The celebrations were designed to discover not only who we are, but why we are here, how we got here, and most importantly, where we go from here. Among the goals of the events that were produced was the idea of bringing about a Renaissance for our city. Mobile has long been a city where theater was vibrant and the latest plays were regularly performed by outstanding actors and actresses. During the 19th century, many of the best minds in America often gathered in Mobile at Madame Octavia LeVert's French-style salon.

How do others see us? We ask visitors to describe Mobile, and we get some very insightful answers. A response that I especially like is "laid-back elegance." This anthology enables us to see ourselves as others see us. The city of Mobile owes much to those who have compiled this review. We thank them for choosing the essays, stories, and poems that preserve the literature of a great southern city on the bay.

REVISED ANNIVERSARY EDITION

This edition owes its inspiration and editing of content to Rachael Alex Fowler, a student of creative writing and anthropology at the University of South Alabama. Rachael chose to revise this book as a creative writing project.

EMBRACING LITERARY MOBILE

But the spell holds unbroken, and those who would know the long-forgotten tales must trace them, bit by bit, in the iron runes intricately woven in grilles of gates and galleries.

—Annie Shillito Howard, from *Iron Lace*

MOBILE'S HAUNTED BOOK SHOP

Cammie East

Born in the embrace of "Literary Mobile," I was fortunate to spend my earliest years, in the late 1940s, in the company of those who valued books and written words. I have a sense that the era was an edge of time in downtown Mobile—the last great glow of a community of souls who read books rather than computer screens, who cherished leather-bound books as sources of learning as well as opulent displays, of children for whom a bedtime story was better than any Disney movie, no matter how showy. In it I enjoyed a childhood that built a trust in those who share such care and such values. In it I enjoyed a kind of community nurturing of the mind and soul, I believe, that too many young Mobilians miss today. The scale was human then, and even that which was larger than life was no larger than could be comprehended by the human imagination.

My parents were Cameron and Mary Francis Plummer, proprietors of The Haunted Book Shop. I entered the scene, in November of 1945. Founded by my father and his partner, Adelaide Marston (Mrs. Edward Trigg)—long a saint in Mobile's iconography of booklovers and genuine kind souls—the shop then had what could be called "a staff." They were gentle people, as were "the haints," that fellowship of friends of the bookshop who frequented the place and made my days lively and loving.

Some were people who wanted technical treatises. Others simply loved books that fired their imaginations, or took them on fantasy trips. Many had particular interests—when the salesmen visited, with their multiple loose-leaf binders promising titles in the new lines, my parents could know that Mrs. Smith would like this one, or Mr. Jones would want that one, or five copies would be right.... And usually there was a copy of the latest Nancy Drew or Hardy Boys title waiting for me, as well. I loved the lap-sitting, the looking over the shoulder, the listening to the planning. All were part of the preparation for the season—mainly Christmas—and I think it was there that I learned first and best the joy of choosing something that a friend will take to pleasure.

There were aspiring authors, who stopped by for conversation and coffee. Writing a book was an effort of often unrewarded dedication in those days—and releasing it to the efforts of a "vanity house" was a sort of resigned admission that the work was less than completely successful. By contrast, gaining the label of a recognized house—which the Haunted Book Shop stubbornly insisted upon remaining—was a seal of worthiness, a mark of acceptance in a world larger than the one we knew.

There were those who made that cut, and Mobilians enjoyed celebrating their triumphs. Harnett Kane of New Orleans was shameless in his appeal to his readers, including pages and pages of acknowledgements at the end of most of his books, so that everyone whose name was listed in print would want to own a copy, preferably inscribed. But his books had substance, if only that of popular history, and they sold. His publishers brought them out regularly, and he was unfailing in his gracious care of his readers.

William March, author of *The Bad Seed*, frequented the store, although I was too young to remember much of him. Borden Deal became an author in those days, and later, his wife Babs did, as well. So did Paul Darcy Bowles—not to be confused with the other Paul Bowles of Mobile and Moroccan connections.

Caldwell Delaney's many books told tales of Mobile's history that would today be lost, I am certain, had he not recorded them. He, too, seemed to know that he stood on a corner of the city's progress, and that what went unrecorded would not survive a generation's memory.

There were others—a Mid-European ship captain, whose work on a novel went on and on—he sought and received my father's editorial counsel, and eventually, I believe, the book was published. A postal retiree's war novel had many difficulties, but carried the seeds of greatness, my pop believed.

Many Mobilians fancied themselves poets, some worthy of the title, and others more or less adept at rhymes. One of my father's favorite ploys when pushed indelicately hard for an evaluation, was to reply, "My, yes! That IS a book!"

Poetry has hardly ever been a commercial enterprise, except for a few enormously successful writers with great gifts. But the shop, and its publishing business, was intended to be one. I learned that early when, by the time I was five, I'd become a bookseller-proprietress of the "Rive Gauche Bookshop," so named by my father, Cameron Plummer. Still unready for school, I was bored in the summer heat of downtown Mobile.

"What can I do, Daddy?" I whined, with the monotony of a mosquito. "I'm boooored."

In exasperated response, he picked up a stack of otherwise worthless books and a wooden apple crate, and took me out to the sidewalk in front of the Rapier House, the building at 56 S. Conception St. that then was home to the bookshop. He got me a chair, and said, "Here. Sell these."

To his amazement, the books sold in about 15 minutes, and I was back asking for more…

In those days, it was still a relatively safe proposition to set a cute kid up on a downtown sidewalk without close supervision. I'd learned enough to count the money and hand the nice people the books and say thank-you, and the Rive

Gauche was a success. In the best spirit of the takeover mentality, however, my prescient pop knew a good thing when he saw it, and soon there were carts on wheels, with locks and waterproofing, bearing shelves full of books for prices from a dime to a dollar. Even without the cute kid, the books sold, and many Mobilians found the browsing worthwhile and the pleasure cheap in the sidewalk book bins at the Haunted Book Shop.

The book business, my parents often said, was an interesting indicator of the city's economy. They knew booms—when people ordered new and expensive books, or bought things regarded as luxuries, such as the handsome art books that sold, maybe, for $25 a volume. They knew busts—when people brought in boxes and boxes of used books for sale. And everything else they could think of, as well. We bought and sold coins. We bought and sold postage stamps, for numismatists. We bought and sold bottles—and sometimes almost anything else. In the era of "Urban Renewal," when the East Church Street historic district met the bulldozers in the name of "progress," all sorts of things were unearthed, and for a time there was even what I was told was the antique pelvic structure of an adult woman—eventually someone stole it.

Thieves were part of the business. They were the reason I hated the coin business. There's something about something shiny and glittery that attracts sticky fingers. Curiously enough, there's also something about religious books that attracts sticky fingers—they were the ones that most often went missing. Perhaps those who walked out without paying for them were the ones most in need of redemption, and knew it. One of the things I most regret losing, though, was the letter written by Christopher Morley to the partners establishing the infant Haunted Book Shop. They took the name from one of the novels by Morley, and wrote him to ask his permission. He assented readily, warning, though, that everyone who had tried had gone out of business in economic distress. Nonetheless, the two courageous partners braved the enterprise, and Morley's note was posted in the shop for almost half a century. And then someone made off with it.

The place was one in which not only were books treasures, but the essentials of life itself. A child, I will always believe, could have no finer heritage than the one given me by "literary Mobile."

Literary Mobile? The city has inspired some powerful writing, I believe, and it has had many citizens who cherish what words and shared knowledge can do for the mind. Authors as diverse as Henry Miller and Albert Murray have found inspiration here.

We have moved into new modalities today. I write on a computer, rather than a typewriter, or a yellow pad. But this city has been a town that took time for its traditions, a city where books have been known, enjoyed, read, and studied.

I was invited to write here, I am sure, because I am the child of the Haunted Book Shop. Maybe even the main ghost surviving, at this point. If I am proud of anything the bookshop and my parents did, it was the encouragement they gave to the exchange of thought and memory by being both a publishing house and a bookselling house. The financial risks they took were enormous. The rewards they garnered were, by many measures, small. But I measure them great in terms of the contribution they made to the city. Shared knowledge, I will always believe, is stronger than any one person's insight. And booksellers, book buyers, and those who read, by their very nature, encourage such sharing.

THE LEGACY OF THE HAUNTED BOOK SHOP

Jack Shearer

The spirit of the Plummer's Haunted Book Shop lived on, in and through the establishment of Jack Shearer and Mary May Miller's HB Publications that began with a spectacular tribute to "Miz" Plummer.

When we would have special events, First National signings, and regular book signings at the Haunted Book Shop in downtown Mobile, our staff headed by Manager Blake Wood would say, "the literati and the glitterati have turned out!"People would come to see, meet and touch such authors as: George Plimpton, Winston Groom, Eugene Walter, Vivian Smallwood, Jay Higginbotham, Virginia Greer, Emily Staples Hearin, the writing couple Terry Cline and Judith Richards, Alabama's Poet Laureate, Ralph Hammond and some of the poets featured in *Alabama Poets.* And they would come to pay tribute to Mary Francis (yes, 'is'), the legendary "Proprietress" of the Haunted for 44 years. They also wanted to meet and chat with Adelaide Marston Trigg, the cofounder of the Haunted Book Shop with Cameron McGee Plummer. The Plummers' literary heritage lives on in 2002 through their daughter, Cammie East, the noted journalist for the *Mobile Register.*

In the early days of the Haunted Book Shop, persons would come to have their books signed by Harper Lee, Evelyn Waugh, Harnett Kane, William March and Julian Rayford. And, of course, to rub elbows with "the ghosts of all great literature!"

Such gatherings continued after the HBS changed hands, when Jack Pendarvis and his friends would bring such young writers as Mark Childress, Charles McNair, Carolyn Haines, Tommy Franklin and Frank Daugherty. Jack's friend Ben Harper would entertain with poetry and music at "Sunday Punch" gatherings where established writers such as Sue Walker would present selections from her poetry and writings printed in *Negative Capability.*

Mary May Miller, my partner from Pensacola, was the guiding light in reorganizing the Shop and adding the Book Nook, first occupying the ATM space for AmSouth Bank in the Riverview Plaza Hotel that was ably managed by the brilliant and delightful Margaret Everhart. Margaret had been seduced to Mobile by her good friend, author and community leader, Gay Caffee. Thus a new imprint, HB Publications, was inaugurated with "The Hants Gala" at the Riverview Plaza Hotel on October 31, 1988. Our Director of Publications, Steven Mason, President of the Ingram Book Group, the largest distributor of books and tapes in the world, helped bring greetings from the Company, headquartered in Nashville. Winston Groom was present with his lovely wife, Anne Clinton, just before *Forrest Gump* hit it big as a book and movie. Inspiring and entertaining were Eugene Walter, one of the cofounders of the *Paris Review* and Dr. Jerry Alan Bush, concert pianist and much honored Professor at USA. Mary Cox Powell and Rod Jackson., and all sorts of writers, community leaders and officials celebrated and joined in the feast. The favors for all present were three new publications: Walter's *Jenny the Watercress Girl*, a reprint; *Iron Lace*, a reprint by Annie Shillito Howard, illustrated by her husband William in 1934; and a double issue of our literary quarterly, book list and reviews called, of course, *Downtown*. Tom Mason, PR Director, came up with a new slogan for HB: "Books of local interest and national importance."

In the last paragraph of his history of the HBS, Pendarvis left us with a prophecy: "As for downtown Mobile and for the bookshop itself, well, it is a common piece of knowledge in these parts that all good ghosts reappear when they are least expected. Let us keep watch." Russ Adams has resurrected its spirit in his antiquarian bookstore in downtown Mobile, aptly named Bienville Books.

ON SHERWOOD ANDERSON

Walter Rideout

Around February 9th (1918), [Sherwood Anderson] took the little side-wheel steamer Apollo across the Bay to Mobile. This quiet, untouristed Southern city was just what he was looking for. Quickly he found a place to hold up in, an old roominghouse at 351 St. Michael Street inhabited by dockworkers from the nearby wharves on the Mobile River. For only $3.50 a week he had a large, low-ceilinged room with "quaint little windows and a fire place." As he would recall it, that first evening he walked about the city streets in a warm, gentle rain and by luck found a wallet with $140 in it and no indication of its owner. This, added to his savings, was the key to a long stay in the South. Walking on through a Negro section, hearing the quiet voices of the blacks in the soft night, he felt the tensions of Chicago and the business whirl leaving him. The North was like this, he told himself, making a hard fist; the South was like this, he said aloud, letting his hand "lie open and relaxed before [him]." For the first time in months he felt fully happy.

...[H]e rose gladly each morning, made his own breakfast, and wrote undisturbed by anyone until ready to stop for the day. Afternoons he walked about Mobile, which he thought charming with its fine old houses and its sleepy air.

WAUGH REVISITED

J. Franklin Murray, S.J.

So in the late forties the British novelist Evelyn Waugh came up with a best seller, *Brideshead Revisited.* He sold the movie rights to M.G.M., but later cancelled the contract when he could not accept their interpretation of the sexual acrobatics in the novel. During the litigation he distracted himself by visiting Forest Lawn Cemetery in Los Angeles, where he became fascinated with the peculiar variety of funeral rituals in practice there. In the summer of '43 he gathered his observations into an outrageously funny little novel called *The Loved One*, which rocketed him into national attention.

On receiving notice that Waugh was available for a lecture tour of American Catholic colleges, I began negotiations to bring him to Spring Hill College. He arrived in Mobile, March 7, 1949, for three days of lectures and conferences. I met him and his wife at the old L & N station in the early afternoon. His first remark was that his name was not pronounced "Ev-lyn," but "Eve-lyn." He was much shorter than I had expected and looked somewhat ridiculous under his bowler hat. His charming, aristocratic wife suffered from neglect and found it hard to keep up with his long strides.

Newspaper reporters were excited about Waugh's visit to the city and had arranged for an interview with him at the Admiral Semmes Hotel. On the way to the hotel I asked Mr. Waugh to meet the press and got the curt answer that he would ignore all reporters except one from the Catholic paper. At the hotel three reporters were waiting for him. He brushed aside two of them and began a conversation with Mr. John Will of the *Mobile Press Register*, whom he judged to be the Catholic reporter. Waugh spent a good hour with Mr. Will and gave him his philosophy of life, his theory of government, and his opinion of American civilization. All of this appeared with a large picture on the front page of the *Mobile Register* the next day. Waugh was immensely pleased by this publicity and commented that Mr. Will was one of the few intelligent and honest reporters he had ever met.

That evening Waugh and his wife were my guests at a dinner at Constantine's, then on Royal Street. Mr. Fred McCaffrey, a young Jesuit English teacher, accompanied us to dinner. In a quiet, dark little booth in the rear of the restaurant, Waugh ordered an Old Fashioned and a cheese soufflé noting that this was a day of fast and abstinence in Lent. The Old Fashioned arrived with ice and triggered Mr. Waugh into a vehement protest about the barbarous American custom of ruining drinks with ice. He asked the waitress for a "styner." Puzzled at first, I told the waitress that

Mr. Waugh wanted to strain the ice from his drink. She shrugged her shoulders and shortly returned with a warm drink.This round was followed by another. By this time the cheese soufflé had arrived. Waugh looked at it from several angles and asked the waitress what it was. She replied that it was the cheese soufflé he had ordered.

"Whatever resemblance this has to a cheese soufflé is minimal. The best restaurants of Paris would never recognize this as a cheese soufflé." The embarrassed waitress was forced to call the manager to calm him down. After another insult or two, Waugh ordered a shrimp dish and a bottle of California burgundy. As the meal progressed, he made away with most of the wine, which he praised highly. He became quite animated in his description of the absurdities of Forest Lawn Cemetery in Hollywood. His order of another bottle of burgundy frankly disturbed me. Since he was doing most of the drinking, I feared that his coming lecture on "Chesterton, Belloc, and Graham Greene" might wander far afield. Meanwhile, he regaled us with short bursts of song, jests, and imitations of cockney, which I could not fully appreciate.

Looking nervously at my watch, I insisted that we should get underway to the auditorium although the time of the lecture was three-quarters of an hour off. He polished off the meal with a brandy while I paid the check. Mrs. Waugh left us to see a western at the old Saenger Theatre.

Waugh's lecture was to be given at the auditorium of Toolen High School. I spent half an hour driving around in various directions to kill time, hoping that the spring breezes would clear his head for a coherent lecture. In the lobby of the high school Mr. Cameron Plummer, owner of the Haunted Book Shop, had arranged a large display of Waugh's novels. Mr. Plummer greeted us warmly at the door and asked Waugh to autograph some of the books on display. Waugh refused indignantly and mumbled a few expletives which I did not understand. Plummer protested, saying, "I only want to help you sell your books." Waugh retorted, "They will sell without your help."

At this point a lady approached Waugh waving a copy of *Time* in his face with the request that he autograph *Time's* review of *The Loved One*. Waugh brushed her aside rudely with the remark that *Time* was an obnoxious little rag, incapable of reviewing anything objectively. The lady retired somewhat abashed and flustered.

By this time the auditorium had filled up. I led Mr. Waugh out of the lobby and down the front steps to go around the building. A high school girl reporter tagged along behind us trying to get Waugh's attention. He stopped suddenly and asked me what that remarkable perfume was. It was magnolia frescati, a flower with a strong banana oil odor. Waugh plucked some of the flowers from a shrub and stuck them in his pocket. Meanwhile, the young lady worked up enough courage to question Waugh. "Mr. Waugh, what do you think is the future of the Catholic novel in America?"

"Brilliant, I would say. Brilliant. It has no past nor present. Therefore, it must have a future." Somewhat crestfallen, the reporter fell behind us as we entered the rear of the building.

Still concerned about which course the lecture would take, I adjusted the microphone, tested the PA system, and introduced Waugh briefly and nervously. The full house pleased me because it meant that Waugh's fee would be met. I took a seat at the rear of the auditorium. Waugh's lecture was incredibly sober. He commented brilliantly on the literary exploits of Chesterton and Belloc, but spent most of his time on Graham Greene, then popular because of his character "Scobie" in *The Heart of the Matter*. Waugh made much of the Catholicism of these three authors to the point of chauvinism. At times I shuddered at his comments about the Anglican establishment, fearing that our Episcopalian brethren would be offended, and they were. But at the end of the lecture the audience gave him a good hand, feeling perhaps that insults by a celebrity should be politely tolerated.

Waugh's ardent admirers among Mobile's literati had insisted on a reception for him at the Kirkbride Club. A friend of the college, Mrs. Leila Sauer, had agreed to serve as hostess, but was unhappy because the President of the college had vetoed alcoholic punch during Lent. She made many delicate little sandwiches and prepared a large bowl of fruit punch.

"Waugh's not going to like this. Englishmen like their liquor," she said. How right she was! In the lobby of the club Waugh handed me his coat and headed for the punchbowl. As Mrs. Sauer was filling his glass, he commented that sandwiches were out of place among Catholics since this was Lent, a time of fast. She handed him the glass of punch without reply. He sipped it gingerly, made a horrible face, and spat it out in a potted plant on the window sill mumbling, "Where can I find some Cutty Sark?" He disappeared into a patio lounge in the rear while his admirers were waiting to meet him in the front rooms of the club. I was unable to persuade him to leave the bar and greet his audience. Chattering among themselves in a half-hearted fashion, they left one by one. About eleven o'clock Waugh came out from the bar in the courtyard looking for me. "Where is my Jesuit chauffeur?" Mrs. Waugh joined us at this time, having just come in from the cinema. As soon as we got in the car, Waugh began reciting a poem in a high-pitched voice. I recognized it shortly as Chesterton's poem "In Praise of Wine." At the entrance to the hotel Mr. McCaffrey and I waited for him to finish the poem, wondering what the next day would bring.

In the morning Waugh announced that he wanted to visit the old cemeteries in Mobile. The first on the list was the one behind the Mobile Public Library. Waugh took big strides from one grave to the next while Mrs. Waugh made chirping little remarks about the Anglo-Saxon names on the tombstones. I managed to get in a few remarks like calling attention to the location of the grave of Joe Cain, the founder of Mobile Mardi Gras. Walking through cemeteries is not my favorite pastime. By the time we had covered the Magnolia Cemetery on Virginia Street, I was tired of hearing Waugh's running commentaries. At the Catholic Cemetery he stood strangely silent before the grave of Admiral Semmes, the naval hero of the Confederacy. Suddenly he blurted out, "How on earth do you put up with all of these Protestants sects?"

"I hadn't thought of putting up with them," I said. "They are a major part of the American scene. We get along well enough together, and besides nearly all of them came from your 17th century England, didn't they?"

"Well, yes," he said, "but we had nothing like these dreadful Christian Scientists and Mormons."

Next in order was an excursion to Bellingrath Gardens, now at the height of its beauty. Visitors are usually enthusiastic about the great variety of camellia and azaleas there. Not so the Waughs. Not once during the two or three hours we spent in the Gardens did either of them comment on a single flower. Once Waugh went up to an old live oak tree and plucked some moss off the bark. He beckoned to his wife who went running to see what he had found. "My dear," he said, "this reminds me of the forests in Abyssinia."

As we walked by a flowing artesian well, Waugh asked me where we could find something to drink. I made the terrible mistake of leading him to a nearby coke stand. The lecture I received on the destructive qualities of Coca-Cola silenced me for a good many minutes. Waugh had no other choice but to drink water.

As we walked along, I made bold to reopen the conversation. "How does this large lawn compare with some of the English gardens I have heard so much about?" Waugh looked at me intensely, batted his eyes several times, pulled his bowler hat down a little tighter on his head, and walked about forty feet out on the lawn, ignoring the "Keep Off the Grass" sign. Then, to the amazement of the onlookers, he got down on all fours and crawled around, first in this direction and then in that. He plucked up blades of grass here and there and cast them aside. Then he got up and strode toward us. "It's full of weeds," he said. "My backyard at home is better than this."

On the way back to the city Waugh asked to stop several places, one of them called the "Treasure House." It had a number of museum pieces and objects of art in it. He looked them over carefully and remarked to me, "All of these are from Europe. Have you Americans nothing of your own?" By this time I had had about enough and was happy to leave the Waughs at their hotel to dine alone.

I returned to pick them up about 7:30 for a visit to the college. Waugh had promised to speak to the young Jesuit seminarians in their recreation room. Before we arrived, Waugh plied me with several questions. "Do American Catholics ever confess any sins except those against the sixth commandment?"

Taken aback, I replied, "Surely you must know that confessional matters are not open to discussion!" He went on commenting about the bad influence of Irish puritanism on American Catholics.

The better Waugh came out in his talk to the scholastics. He analyzed the themes of *Brideshead Revisited.* He called it a failure because he had tried to do too many things in it. "I tried to show how grace operates in the souls of different types of people. I collected these people all into one family, and that was a mistake," he admitted. Waugh pleased the scholastics by praising three eminent Oxford Jesuits: Broderick, D'Arcy, and Martindale. He attributed his conversion to them. For refreshments the scholastics served coke and cookies.

After the talk, we toured the campus. Passing the old dining room in the Quadrangle, Waugh asked me, "What do the students have to drink with their meals?"

"Oh, a number of things," I said. "They like milk and iced tea. For breakfast they have fruit juices and coffee." And before I could catch myself, I added "coke" to the list.

"You should never let them drink that vile stuff," he said. "It will ruin their livers."

"I should think you would give them a spot of rum with their meals," chirped Mrs. Waugh, "as they do in the British Navy."

"I doubt whether their parents would approve a spot of rum with their meals," I replied.

"I should think this repressive policy would drive them to the stews," Waugh added.

"Possibly," I said, "but I am sure that those who want something stronger than milk or coke find ways of getting it off campus."

At the library Waugh asked to see the archives and rare books. I apologized for our lack of a significant collection because of a fire in 1909, which destroyed the entire library.

"Small wonder that you have all of these fires. You Americans overheat all of your buildings. I have been gasping for air ever since I've been here." Waugh did not know that I had heard how he was evicted from the Ponchartrain Hotel in New Orleans because he threatened to put a chair through a window which would not open.

Next morning I arrived at the hotel a few minutes early to put our distinguished visitors on the train for St. Louis and got this unsolicited bit of advice from Mr. Waugh: "Promptness does not consist in arriving early or late. Promptness means arriving at the time specified."

We drove off to the old GM&O railroad station where the Rebel was waiting on the tracks. Waugh tipped the porter lavishly and made up somewhat for his crusty and crotchety behavior by a gracious leave-taking. He even consented to autograph his photograph. Mrs. Waugh waved to me from the platform of the pullman. Breathing a sigh of relief, I headed for home in deep meditation about the value of hobnobbing with celebrities.

First published in *The Motley: Spring Hill College Literary Magazine*, Spring, 1972.

ON THE ROAD
Jack Kerouac

I drove through South Carolina and beyond Macon, Georgia, as Dean, Marylou, and Ed slept. All alone in the night I had my own thoughts and held the car to the white line in the holy road. What was I doing? Where was I going? I'd soon find out. I got dog-tired beyond Macon and woke up Dean to resume. We got out of the car for air and suddenly both of us were stoned with joy to realize that in the darkness all around us was fragrant green grass and the smell of fresh manure and warm waters. "We're in the South! We've left the winter!" Faint daybreak illuminated green shoots by the side of the road. I took a deep breath; a locomotive howled across the darkness, Mobile-bound. So were we. I took off my shirt and exulted. Ten miles down the road Dean drove into a filling station with the motor off, noticed that the attendant was fast asleep at the desk, jumped out, quietly filled the gas tank, saw to it the bell didn't ring, and rolled off like an Arab with a five-dollar tank full of gas for our pilgrimage.

I slept and woke up to the crazy exultant sounds of music and Dean and Marylou talking and the great green land rolling by. "Where are we?"

"Just passed the tip of Florida, man—Flomaton, it's called." Florida! We were rolling down to the coastal plain and Mobile; up ahead were great soaring clouds of the Gulf of Mexico. It was only thirty-two hours since we'd said good-by to everybody in the dirty snows of the North. We stopped at a gas station, and there Dean and Marylou played piggyback around the tanks and Dunkel went inside and stole three packs of cigarettes without trying. We were fresh out. Rolling into Mobile over the long tidal highway, we all took our winter clothes off and enjoyed the Southern temperature. This was when Dean started telling his life story and when, beyond Mobile, he came upon an obstruction of wrangling cars at a crossroads and instead of slipping around them just balled right through the driveway of a gas station and went right on without relaxing his steady continental seventy. We left gaping faces behind us.

STARS FELL ON ALABAMA
Carl Carmer

"Mobile and the Bayou Country"

Mobile stays in the heart, loveliest of cities. I have made many journeys down the Black Warrior and I have always found happiness at its mouth. And so I summarize my impressions rather than tell the story of a visit. Few travelers "pass through" Mobile. The old city rests apart, remembering the five flags that have flown over her. Spain and France and England and the Old South, grown harmonious through the mellowing of time, are echoes in the streets. But since only people who "are going to Mobile" are her visitors, her charms have been less exploited than those of any of the other sea cities of the South…

Mobile is a city of intimacies that have stood the test of time. On Government Street the houses shaded by magnolias and cape jasmines shelter families whose grandfathers and great-grandfathers were friends. Along the azalea-strewn road to Spring Hill, the old Episcopal college, today as a hundred years ago, a black cook bears a gift of wine and jelly from her white folks' kitchen to the white folks next door. Affections are strong in this place, for they have been long depended on.

Even the heat of summer drives but few of the people of Mobile northward. Point Clear "across the bay" or Biloxi on the Gulf Coast a few miles away are pleasant enough for vacations. Country houses on the picturesque Dog River are usually filled with gay parties on week-ends throughout the year. At midday the city's homes are cool refuges and streets are empty. In the evening thousands of automobiles line Mobile Bay while a breeze from the moonlit waters blows inland and little sailboats scud about silhouetted against the shining surface.

It is easy to become adapted to the rhythm of this city. Acquaintances gradually become friends. The processes of earning a living are slow and comparatively unimportant to the living itself. Dignity and charm and gayety permeate life there. Mobile is a city of the lotos—bringing forgetfulness of everything except the pleasant passing of the hours.

COTTONMOUTH

Julian Lee Rayford

Mobile lies beside that tawny river. Swamps lie along that golden-red muddy-green-yellow river. Swamps as individual, each one, as the people on their outskirts. Some grim, some bitter, some smelly, some sweet and full of a sharp fragrance, some inviting, some harmless, and some brooding and waiting like the glowering eyes of a wildcat. Wildcats are in there, coons, possums, rabbits, squirrels, bear, deer, alligators... to this day, that section, along with Baldwin County, which has spots that are virtually unexplored, is one of the finest hunting grounds in the United States...

Allen got himself one of those little cars, there weren't many cars in Mobile at that time, and Allen cut quite a figure in his red roadster with the buddy top. Right back of the driver's seat was a little box on which two people could sit. It would have made a swell lovers' seat, because two people had to sit so close together.

Paul loved it, chugging into town in that little red car. One day, Allen took him to work with him. Carried him down to his shack on the wharf, where he was watchman, and he kept Paul with him all the whole day. Nick always called Allen "Peggy" because of his leg, but to Paul he was always Mist' Allen. And all day, there on the wharf, it was "Mist' Allen, what's this?" and "Mist' Allen, what's that?"

Allen took him up to the banana warehouse, a block away, and said, "Here, this little boy wants some bananas, don't you, Pauly!" And he got bananas for him. Paul saw the coast guard cutter tied up to the wharf, and the tugboats, and the little white fruiters, that's what they called the banana boats. Across the river was the "graveyard for ships," where, next to the island, rotting old schooners were.

The next week, Allen got the notion maybe he'd like a motorcycle better than a car. He didn't sell his car, he just rented a motorcycle for a couple of days, to give it a tryout. He brought it out to the house, said he wanted to show it to the boys before he did any special riding. They thought it was fine

First one to get a ride was Ed. Ed sat on the saddle over the mudguard, behind Allen. They rode west over to Michigan Avenue, past Magnolia Cemetery, and down to the main part of town. Down to Bienville Square. They began to go round and round the Square.

A policeman was standing there on the corner of Dauphin and Conception. He waved at Allen the first couple of times around.

Allen waved back and rode on to St. Francis and east to St. Joseph and south to Dauphin and west to Conception. Then he'd make the circuit again. Next time he came around, the cop shouted, "Caint you stop that damn thing?"

Allen flew on past him, with Ed squealing happily. But when he passed the cop again, he said, "No. I don't know how. I forgot!"

Allen was a moody man; he'd got to brooding there on that motorcycle, and damn if he didn't forget all about how to shut off the engine. He just went circling round and round the Square. And Ed didn't care, he just laughed. For more than an hour they went round and round the Square till the thing gave out of gas.

By that time people had gathered along the sidewalks to watch, wondering what it was all about. All the firemen in Number Four, on St. Joseph Street, came out and stood there, watching. When the gas ran out and the motor stopped, people jammed around and the policeman said, "What's the idea, couldn't you stop it?"

"Nope, I forgot how to."

"Then why didn't you drive out to another part of town?"

"Cause I thought I might get too far away from where they sold gas, that's why."

EXCUSE ME, MA'AM

Eugene Walter

Mrs. Mountjoy was not truly a mean lady; just nervous. Like take that time she spent all morning fuming with not the best results.

She had just moved into a grand new mansion her husband had built for her in Spring Hill. She was striding about the elegant parlor, changing the position of ashtrays—she smoked ferociously. There were ashtrays everywhere. She lit a cigarette, snapped her lighter lid closed with a bang, and strode to the window. Now, she paused to study her new blonde wig in the Venetian mirror. Impulsively she picked up the phone by the mirror. She dialed the beauty parlor.

"This is Mrs. Mountjoy," she croaked. "Give me Miss Maybelle."

Maybelle came quickly, slightly shaken. She had barely gotten out the "Hell-" in "Hello" before the other end attacked.

"Maybelle, the way you did the wig is all wrong… I mean it's too flat over the ears and the bangs are too fluffy… now, I'm paying you to get things right so why didn't you? I mean—"

"Oh, Mrs. Mountjoy, I'm real sorry… look, honey, Alice is going to the hospital like she does every Saturday to do old Miss Muncie and I'll tell her to come by your place first. She'll be there right away."

"Good!" snapped the Châtelaine and hung up. Puffing energetically, sending out little nervous clouds, she went to the window and lifted the lace curtain to gaze at a tall young man who was raking leaves.

"Oh, God!" she said, and rang a little enamel push-button on the desk. She had only puffed twice before a nervous middle-aged cleaning lady rushed into the room.

"Yes, ma'am?"

"Beulah, run out there and tell that idiot Jerkins to come in here to me… right away?"

"Yes'm," said Beulah and hurried out, crossing herself in the hall as she returned to her work.

Mrs. Mountjoy dialed a number.

"Happy Day Nurseries," came a jovial middle-aged voice over the phone.

"Mr. Waggett," growled the lady. "I've just been standing at my window looking out at the things you planted yesterday. I was in town, you know, checking on that fool cabinet-maker, so I didn't see how you planted the crêpe myrtles… all wrong! All wrong! When they've grown some, in about three years from now, I won't be able to see the fountain at all. I want you out here tomorrow morning early to move them all about six yards toward the east, you hear me?"

"Well, I planted them where Mr.Mountjoy showed me he wanted 'em," replied the nurseryman quietly.

"Bill doesn't have any idea about where to place a tree!" she howled. "You get out here tomorrow morning!"

"Yes ma'am," said the nurseryman as he thought of how he'd paid the bill.

She dialed another number. She puffed and puffed until someone replied at the other end.

"Grace," she stormed, eying the lace curtains, "one of these curtains is at least six inches shorter than the others. I want you to come take it down and do it right and get it back here for my party on Tuesday. You hear me?"

"Sure," said Grace and hung up. Mrs. Mountjoy looked out the window and rapped on the glass. The room was full of smoke. She stubbed it out and lit another. She saw that the gardener had not heard her and banged harder on the pane, then screamed. He looked up calmly, tipped his hat, looked puzzled, then put down his rake and started toward the house. Smoke everywhere. She opened a window a bit. The gardener cracked the door and smiled.

"Come in here, Jerkins," she said. "I want you to… "

"Oh, Mrs. Mountjoy!" he said nervously but she broke in.

"Look out of this window! Those perennials! How come they're in groups of six and eight at this end of the bed and all spaced out, two or three to a foot, at the other end … "

"Oh, listen, ma'am!" he said with a nervous gesture.

"Don't interrupt me! Where are your manners? Now, I want you to—"

He shouted. "Please, Mrs. Mountjoy, listen to me!" He started toward her.

"Why should I? We pay you to do a good job. I can't stand sloppiness. I insist that—"

The young man asserted himself, with a scowl. "Goddam it, you listen to me!"

She interrupted with a gasp, coughing, but he stopped her.

"Shit, lady, I'm trying to tell you that your wig is on fire!"

And it was, too. He grabbed it off her head just as she began to feel the tickle on her scalp. But the lace curtains were on fire, too. Then the wooden window frames. He ran for help, for water. She collapsed.

Well, of course, the house burned down. Mr. Mountjoy, nagged by her, was in the cellar with the plumber where he'd been for several days. They called the fire department, but the lady from the beauty parlor had stalled in the drive and the fire engine couldn't make it in time. Mr. Mountjoy had been so busy with her last minute instructions that the new insurance contract was still on his desk, unsigned.

Later, the Mountjoys moved to Idaho.

from JENNIE THE WATERCRESS GIRL
Eugene Walter

This fable follows the life history of Jennie Heynonny from Broad Street in Mobile, to the stage of The Metropolitan Opera House, where Jennie triumphs as a ballerina—before returning to Mobile.

On Broad Street, in Mobile, in the early nineteen-twenties there was born to the Jasper Heynonny household a fat pink baby girl who was christened Jennie after her grandmother on her mother's side. All the family were a little crazy, some more than others, but they enjoyed life and the quiet pleasantries of Southern living. Jennie herself grew up right there on Broad Street, under the oaks, an ordinary locust-chasing, dam-in-the-gutter building, grimy-cheeked pink and white little girl who went in at four for a bath and then sat on the steps and strung four-o-clocks on grass stems until supper.

Her early life was rather usual. She was good, she was bad, she was spanked, she was rewarded, and finally reached the age of seven and regarded herself as a subdeb.

But the year was 1929, and everything that goes up must come down, and the stock market did, like a runaway elevator, and the unfortunate Jasper Heynonny was caught in the general down-draft and ruined.

"Ruined!" was all that he said, and put his head on the table, and did his damn-dest to look that way.

"Well, I declare," snorted Jennie's mother, "Don't you know where the victuals will come from now. Guess we really are pure-dee ruined."

"I'll dance barefoot in the snow for pennies," said Jennie.

"Hell's bells, there's no snow in Mobile," said her mother. "Besides, people here don't give a loon's whistle for the arts. Art just ain't profitable here, not artfulness either. Mobilians like something they can eat, or something in the gadget line."

"Well, I'll go to Biloxi and be a real Biloxi shrimp-picker."

"What? No daughter of mine is going to—."

"Well," interrupted Jennie, "I'll tell you what. I'll take me a little old basket and I'll pluck me watercress in Wragg Swamp by the light of the full moon, and I'll sell it downtown."

Jennie's mother was breathless with admiration...

"Watercress, watercress, who'll buy my watercress?

"Watercress sweet and shy,

"Watercress wet and dry,

"Oh, who buy my watercress, watercress buy?"

from THE LOOKING GLASS

William March

"And please stop calling her The Goodwife!" said old Mrs. Wentworth in her baritone, aggressive voice. "She's got a name like you and me and everybody else! For your information, her name is Virginia Dunwoody Owen. Please call her that! Call her Miss Virginia, if you want to! Call her Miss Owen, if that pleases you better! But stop calling her by that sickening name which the people of this town have tied to her!"

Then, in a more conciliatory voice, she continued: "I've got an old picture of Virginia in my album, taken when we were girls together. Wait a minute, and I'll show it to you. You'll see then what I mean."

The photograph was of four girls grouped together. Three of them were standing with their arms around one another's waists. The fourth was sitting in a chair which had been draped with a photographer's shawl. Mrs. Wentworth said: "I'm one of the girls standing up: the one on the left. It's a miserable photograph, isn't it? It makes me look as if I had a mustache."

Minnie examined the photograph and glanced again at her hostess. She smiled noncommittally and shook her head, but to herself she said: "But you have got a mustache, old girl! You've got as nice a little mustache as there is in Reedyville!"

"The two girls standing with me," continued Mrs. Wentworth, "are Anne May Kimbrough, who later married Ralph Porterfield, and became the mother of the peerless Robert that you admire so much, and a girl from Montgomery, who was visiting the Kimbroughs at the time. Her name was Effie something-or-other. Silly-looking, isn't she? Anyway, she made a good marriage, I understand. He was very rich, and they went about everywhere; but he was a Northerner, from New York, so of course nobody expected him to be quite a gentleman."

She shrugged and went on: "Oh, yes! That's Virginia Owen sitting in the chair. You didn't recognize her, did you? You had your mind set for something that resembled an old, moulting buzzard, didn't you, my dear?"

Minnie examined the old photograph more carefully. The girls who were standing gazed hopefully above the head of the unseen photographer, their mouths fixed in coy and unconvincing smiles, their faces struggling to register, at his insistence, that sparkling gaiety which he felt was expected of them, as handsome young ladies of quality; but Virginia's face, in its frame of silken ringlets, was resigned and melancholy. Her beautiful hands lay languidly in her lap, and her eyes looked outward into space with a concentrated intensity.

"Well, Minnie!" thundered old Mrs. Wentworth. "What do you think of her now? Are you satisfied? Was she a beautiful girl, as I said, or was she not?"

Minnie learned much that afternoon, enough to fill many pages in her current ledger. The Goodwife, it seemed, had been born, not in Reedyville, as was commonly thought, but in Mobile, on Conception Street—a name which had always struck Mrs. Wentworth as being in the worst possible taste—in one of the old, red brick houses there: a dark red house with balconies and slender iron pillar, and webbed lavishly with intricate, lacy grillwork.

TO OCTAVIA
Edgar Allan Poe

Addressed to Octavia Walton, who would marry and become Madame Octavia LeVert, this unsigned poem was written in the hand of Edgar Allan Poe.

[TO OCTAVIA]

When wit, and wine, and friends have met
And laughter crowns the festive hour
In vain I struggle to forget
Still does my heart confess thy power
And fondly turn to thee!

But Octavia, do not strive to rob
My heart, of all that soothes its pain
The mournful hope that every throb
Will make it break for thee!

from BELLE OF DESTINY
Evelyn Dahl

Belle of Destiny is a fictional account of Octavia Walton's life. She married to become Madame LeVert, hosted the first salons of America, was commanded by Queen Victoria to a State Ball, and wrote a set of books, "Souvenirs of Travel." From the 1830s to the 1850s, she lived in Mobile and entertained influential politicians and literary figures.

The haze of the October day was made up of pungent odors from many bonfires of sycamore leaves that were already falling, the salty tang from nearby waters, and the earthy dankness of dreamy bayous. It hovered over coastal Mobile, sifting across the Spanish, French, and English architecture that reflected more than a hundred years of growth.

At the Southern Club on St. Francis Street a doctor's natty hansom stood between the conveyances tied to the hitching rail at the curb under the shade of a fern-grown oak. The spirited black horse attached to it switched his tail angrily at the flies that annoyed his midday siesta. Propped against the five-foot base of the tree the plump black driver slept with his master's cast-off Panama hat over his eyes, and in his hand a forgotten handout from the kitchen.

Echoing in sharp relief to the somnolence of the day, the clack of horses' hooves and the accompanying rattle of the accoutrements of a stylish carriage drawn swiftly by a pair of English thoroughbreds over the flagstone surface of the street came through the open window of the exclusive Southern Club. Two ladies dined near the French porticoed aperture, and a female voice, almost as in answering mockery to the tempo of the day, exclaimed, "What a beautiful gown you are wearing, Octavia, my dear! I expect it cost your father a pretty penny!"

"He didn't seem to mind, Cousin Clarissa," replied Octavia Walton, dropping her heavy dark lashes over her blue eyes to keep from showing that she understood the implied criticism of the older woman. A slender hand reached up to her soft brown coiffure of cascading curls and charming bonnet; then abruptly it fell. She wondered if it would have been more tactful if she had said, "Oh, I've had this old thing forever."

Mrs. Peak leaned across the table, overemphasizing her words with a pointed forefinger, "I suppose Cousin George didn't mind—with all his money! You've always had anything you wanted. Thank heavens, your father is an exception to our frugal Mobilians."

"Oh, come now, Cousin Clarissa, what's a new gown more or less!" Octavia toyed with her glass of ice water.

The ice had been shipped down the Mississippi River from the North in February of that year 1835 and stored in a sawdust ice-house to bring comfort to the long summer.

"I suppose it would mean nothing to you," said Mrs. Peak. "Your last year's clothes would be new to us. But what could we expect, you've never known privations and sorrows as Ameria and I, or you wouldn't be so extravagant. No one can say though that I don't bear my lot cheerfully."

"Indeed you do, Cousin Clarissa," soothed Octavia, intent on being polite. She was thinking: how ridiculous Cousin Clarissa is when she's far from penniless. No matter what she says, she indulges her daughter Ameria as much as most girls her age.

Mrs. Peak remorselessly went on to say, "Remember, you want people to like you, not envy you, Octavia. I've already heard you called pampered and extravagant."

Octavia reflected: Why do people always criticize me? I had hoped that here in Mobile it would be different. She forgot the oysters à la poulette on her plate as she looked around at the others in the room. For the first time since her family had brought their wealth and their flawless background and immense success to Mobile two months before, she began to wonder what impressions they were exchanging about her. Her eyes rested a moment on the blond gentleman who had arrived in the carriage drawn by the English horses, barely conscious of him before she looked elsewhere.

from IRON LACE

Annie Shillito Howard

Such magic is in the name MOBILE!

MOBILE! Heard in distant places it works its varied charm. Far inland it is the sound of murmuring waters; for the snowbound it conjures up visions of high green canopies swaying above multitudinous blossoms of rose and white and amethyst and flame; for the lonely exile it is transmuted into the pressure of a friendly hand.

Mobile is more than a place name. It is a long-used vase remembering a thousand fragrant guests; it is an aureole that warms as it brightens; it is a bit of melody, doubly sweet because the audible notes drifting upward are merged with the harmony that turns the stars and beats in the pulses of men.

For the city itself is enchanted. On all sides are evidences of the spell. Fruits and flowers, centuries old, yet unblighted by frost or sun, hang above entries in frozen perfection. Ancient lanterns glow with lights too mystic for the current that feeds them. Ageless as the progress of the seasons, tiny figures maintain tireless vigil about windows and galleries waiting patiently for the signal that will release them from their bonds.

One who has walked intimately among these things is charged with a vague excitement. His spirit is on tiptoe. He feels himself caught in some rare interlude that may be broken at any moment—perhaps by the arrival of a princely liberator, or perhaps by the recovery of a talisman that will set in motion the arrested beauty of another age.

Then, like buried jewels brought into the sunlight, the roses and daffodils, the forget-me-nots and bleeding hearts, will burst their iron husks, wreathing doorways and balconies with color and fragrance; and the white fire of the lilies will burn away the crust of time. Dewdrops, suspended for a hundred years in stark opacity, will melt under the gracious influence, falling in crystalline showers on grapes and plums and pomegranates, no longer dull and motionless, but surging with red and purple wine. Acorns and leaves of alien oaks' long fixed stillness, will be lustered with bronze and emerald, and tremble with joyous whisperings. Nor will supporting trellises content themselves as base metals, but touched by the moment of transformation, brackets and spirals and lattices will flash a golden salutation to the sun.

In the streets there will be soft stirrings, breezes of tinkling laughter rounding the corners, and echoes of dancing feet, as the elfin prisoners are freed at last to take up their interrupted festivals.

What stories they could tell of That Other Mobile lying like the lost painting of an old master under the lively scene that is Today!

But the spell holds unbroken, and those who would know the long-forgotten tales must trace them, bit by bit, in the iron runes intricately woven in grilles of gates and galleries.

from THE AIR-CONDITIONED NIGHTMARE
Henry Miller

"My Dream of Mobile"

The Mobile I knew was thoroughly imaginary and I wanted to enjoy it all by myself. It gave me a great pleasure, I might say, to secretly resist [my friend Alfred Perlès'] prying curiosity. I was like a young wife who delays telling her husband that she has become a mother. I kept Mobile in the womb, under lock and key, and day by day it grew, took on arms and legs, hair, teeth, nails, eye-lashes, just like a real foetus. I would have been a marvelous accouchement, had I been equal to it. Imagine a full-fledged city being born out of a man's loins! Of course it never came off. It began to die in the womb, from lack of nourishment, I suppose, or because I fell in love with other cities—Dômme, Sarlat, Rocamadour, Genoa, and so on.

How did I visualize Mobile? To tell the truth, it's all quite hazy now. Hazy, fuzzy, amorphous, crumbling. To get the feel of it again I have to mention the name of Admiral Farragut. *Admiral Farragut steamed into Mobile Bay.* I must have read that somewhere when a child. It stuck in my crop. I don't know to this day whether it's a fact or not—that Admiral Farragut steamed into Mobile Bay. I took it for granted then, and it was a good thing I did probably. Admiral Farragut has nothing more to do with the picture than that. He fades out instanter. What is left of the image is the word Mobile. Mobile is a deceptive word. It sounds quick and yet it suggests immobility—*glassiness.* It is a fluid mirror which reflects sheet lightning as well as somnolent trees and drugged serpents. It is a name which suggests water, music, light and torpor. It also sounds remote, securely pocketed, faintly exotic and, if it has any color, is definitely white. Musically I would designate it as guitarish. Perhaps not even that resonant—perhaps mandolinish. Anyway, pluckable music—accompanied by bursting fruit and thin light columns of smoke. No dancing, except the dancing of mote-beams, the evanescent beat of ascension and evaporation. The skin always dry, despite the excessive humidity. The slap-slap of carpet slippers, and figures silhouetted against half-drawn blinds. Corrugated silhouettes.

I never once thought of work in connection with the word Mobile. Not *anybody working.* A city surrounded with shells, the empty shells of by-gone fiestas. Bunting everywhere and the friable relics of yesterday's carnival. Gaiety always in retreat, always vanishing, like clouds brushing a mirror. In the center of this glissando Mobile itself, very prim, very proper. Southern and not Southern, listless but upright, slatternly yet respectable, bright but not wicked. Mozart for the mandolin. Not Segovia feathering Bach. Not grace and delicacy so much as anaemia. Fever-coolth. Musk. Fragrant ashes.

In the dream I never pictured myself as entering Mobile by automobile. Like Admiral Farragut, I saw myself steaming into Mobile Bay, generating my own power. I never thought I would pass through places like Panama City, Apalachicola, Port St. Joe, or that I would be within striking distance of Valparaiso and Bagdad, or that by crowning Millers Ferry I would be on the way to the Ponce de Leon Springs. In their dream of gold the Spaniards had preceded me. They must have moved like fevered bedbugs through the swamps and forests of Florida. And when they hit Bon Secour they must have been completely whacky—to give it a French name, I mean. To cruise along the Gulf is intoxicating; all the water routes exfoliative, if one can put it that way. The Gulf is a great drama of light and vapor. The clouds are pregnant and always in bloom, like oneiric cauliflowers; sometimes they burst like cysts in the sky, shedding a precipitate of mercurium chromide; sometimes they stride across the horizon with thin, wispy legs of smoke. In Pensacola I had a crazy room in a crazy hotel. I thought I was in Perpignan again. Towards dusk I looked out the window and saw the clouds battling; they collided with one another like crippled dirigibles, leaving steamers of tangled wreckage dangling in the sky. It seemed as though I were at a frontier, that two wholly different worlds were fighting for domination. In the room was a monstrous poster that dated back to the days of the sewing machine. I lay back on the bed and before my eyes there passed in review all the screaming, caterwauling monstrosities of the poster art which had assaulted my innocent vision when a child…

I had never anticipated an appetizing banquet like that when dreaming of sailing down Mobile Bay. It was like being in limbo, a levitation act on the threshold of the dream. A day or two before we had crossed the Suwanee River. In Paris I had dreamed of taking a boat and sailing right into the Okefinokee Swamp, just to trace the river to its source. That was a pipe dream. If I had another hundred years to live, instead of fifty, I might still do it, but time is getting short. There are other places to visit—Easter Island, the Papuan Wonderland, Yap, Johore, the Caroline Islands, Borneo, Patagonia—Tibet, China, India, Persia, Arabia—and Mongolia. The ancestral spirits are calling me; I can't put them off much longer. *"When Henry Miller left for Tibet…"* I can see my future biographer writing that a hundred years from now. What ever happened to Henry Miller? He disappeared. He said he was going to Tibet. Did he get there? Nobody knows… That's how it will be. Vanished mysteriously. Exit with two valises and a trunkful of ideas. But I will come back again one day, in another suit of flesh. I may make it snappy, too, and surprise everybody. One remains away just long enough to learn the lesson. Some learn faster than others. I learn very quickly. My home work is all finished. I know that the earth is round, but I know also that that is the least important fact you can mention about it. I know that there are maps of the earth which designate a country called America. That's also relatively unimportant. Do you *dream*? Do you leave your little *locus perdidibus* and mingle with the other inhabitants of the earth? Do you visit the other earths, whatever they be called? Do you have the stellar itch? Do you find the aeroplane too slow, too inhibited? Are you a wanderer who plays on muted strings? Or are you a coconut that falls to the ground with a thud? I would like to take an inventory of man's longings and compare it with his accomplishments. I would like to be master of the heavens for just one day and rain down all the dreams, desires, longings peculiar to man. I would like to see them take root, not slowly through the course of historical aeons, *but immediately*, God save America! That's what I say too, because who else is capable of doing the trick?...

I am back in the fourteenth arroundissement and the cot on which I am lying is steaming into Mobile Bay. The exhaust pipe is open, the tiller is at the till. Below me are the crustaceans of the zinc and tin age, the omnivorous anemones, the melted icebergs, the oyster beds, the hollyhocks and the huge hocks of ham. The Lufthansa is conducting a pilgrimage to Hattiesburg. Admiral Farragut has been dead for almost a century. In Devachan most likely. It is all so familiar, the ricocheting mandolins, the ashen fragrance, the corrugated silhouettes, the glassy stare of the bay. Neither toil nor spin, neither bubble nor trouble. The cannons look down on the moat and the moat speaks not. The town is white as a sepulcher. Yesterday was All Souls Day and the sidewalks are peppered with confetti. Those who are up and about are in white ducks. The heat waves make their ascent slantwise, the sound waves move seismographically. No rataplan, no rat-a-tat, but slap-slap-slap-slap. The ducks are floating up the bay, their bills all gold and iridescence. Absinthe is served on the verandah with scones and bursting paw-paws. The caw, the rook, the oriole gather up the crumbs. As it was in the time of Saul, as were the days for the Collossians and the nights for the Egyptians. East, west, clock, counter-clock, Mobile revolves like a torpid astrolabe. Men who knew the shade of the baobab swing lazily in their hammocks. Haunched and dehaunched the boneless bronzed women of the Equatorial regions amble by. Something Mozartian, something Segovian, stirs the air. Maine contributes her virginity, Arabia her spices. It is a merry-go-round standing stock still, the lions affable, the flamingos poised for flight. Take the milk of aloes, mix clove and brandywine, and you have the spiritual elixir of Mobile. There is no hour when things are different, no day which is not the same. It lies in a pocket, is honeycombed with light, and flutters like a plucked cat-gut. It is mobile, fluid, fixed, but not glued. It gives forth no answers, neither does it question. It is mildly, pleasantly bewildering, like the first lesson in Chinese or the first round with a hypnotist. Events transpire in all declensions at once; they are never conjugated. What is not Gog is Magog—and at nine *punkt* Gabriel always blows his horn. But is it music? Who cares? The duck is plucked, the air is moist, the tide's out and the goat's securely tethered. The wind is from the bay, the oysters are from the muck. Nothing is too exciting to drown the pluck-pluck of the mandolins. The slugs move from slat to slat; their little hearts beat fast, their brains fill with swill. By evening it's all moonlight on the bay. The lions are still affably baffled and whatever snorts, spits, fumes and hisses is properly snaffled. *C'est la mort du carrousel, la mort douce des choux-bruxelles.*

from STATE OF THE NATION

John Dos Passos

"GOLD RUSH DOWN SOUTH: MOBILE, ALABAMA, MARCH, 1943"

The man in the seat beside me sits hunched up holding a cigarette in the strained fingers of a hand that hangs limp between his knees letting the ash drop on the scruffed toe of his fancy pointed shoe. He wears a thin sunfaded suit of some cottony material worn at the elbows and knees but his white shirt is clean. He has wavy brown hair and deepset eyes in a sallow slightly pock-marked face. Suddenly he begins to talk very low staring down at his cigarette. "Went down an' got me a job down there, 'spector, 'spectin' ammunition before it goes on board ship… I got me a certificate that'll find me a job any time I want one… Been workin' in a cotton mill up home, not so bad… good people to work for, company gives you a nice house, sells you coal cheap, used to give you vacations down to the shore… all you had to pay was a dollar a day, before transportation got so tight; company's all right but there ain't no money in it. They don't pay no wages. My wife she works there too. I'm goin' to leave her home so that she kin keep the house. I wouldn't carry her down here where I'm goin'. I'm lucky to git a place to stay. A nephew of mine down there, he's goin' to board me for seven dollars a week. That's cheap but he kinda likes me. I'll git home once a month or fix it so my wife kin come down an' see me. Couldn't do it oftener. This trip wears a man out… Company's helped a lot of folks build up homes. They lend 'em the money for the materials an' some fellers build their houses theirselves… One of these days I'm goin' to build me a house. I always thought I'd like to build me a log house out in the woods. I'd buy me a piece of land an' cut down the trees to build the house with."

We have left the lightcolored frilly country behind and for miles now have been grinding down long straight stretches through pinewoods. All you can see on each side of the road are the tall longleaf pines scarred by the slashing cuts the turpentine gatherers make. After a while strings of washing fluttering in the wind begin to appear among the pines, then brown tents with scaly old cars parked beside them, tarpaper shacks kneedeep in tin cans and old papers and cartons, occasional battered trailers at perilous angles. On the door of a corrugated iron barn far gone in decrepitude is a sign 'Housekeeping Rooms.' Back of a fillingstation a row of white tourist cabins festooned with laundry is lost behind dense ranks of trailers shining in the sun. The road dips down into a broad expanse of salt marshes and crosses a dyke along the edge of a broad brown bay. On every stump and snaggled log sticking up out of the shallow muddy water sits a brownishgray gull.

"A world of mullet out there," says one of the men behind me to the other.

Startled by the roar of the bus, a white heron rises out of the dry reeds of the salt marsh and flies with slow wingflaps landward. Now, all along the horizon across the bay from out of a smudge of smoke begin to appear the tall derricks and the crossed.arms of cranes and the hoists and the great steel cradles of the shipyards. Along the sandspit in front of the yards as far as you can see, parked cars sparkle endlessly in the sun.

The man beside me is sitting up looking out of the window with dialated nostrils. "I didn't tell the company I was gittin' me this other job… Thought I'd better see how I liked it first. They just think I'm off for a couple of days. I'll be makin' three times what I made up home. Might save some money this way… for that log house."

A Town Outgrows Itself

We are in the city now. The bus is swinging out of the traffic of the crowded main street round the low gray building of the bus station and comes to a stop in the middle of a milling crowd: soldiers, sailors, stout women with bundled up babies, lanky backwoodsmen with hats tipped over their brows and a cheek full of chewing tobacco, hatless young men in lightcolored sport shirts open at the neck, countrymen with creased red necks and well-washed overalls, cigar smoking stocky men in business suits in pastel shades, girls in bright dresses with carefully curled hair piled up on their heads and high-heeled shoes and blood-red fingernails, withered nut-brown old people with glasses, carrying ruptured suitcases, broad-shouldered men in oil-stained khaki with shiny brown helmets on their heads, negroes in flappy jackets and pegtop pants and little felt hats with turned-up brims, teenage boys in jockey caps, here and there a flustered negro woman dragging behind her a string of white-eyed children. Gradually the passengers are groping their way down the steep steps out of the bus and melting into the crowd.

Out on the streets every other man seems to be in work clothes. There are girls in twos and threes in slacks and overalls. Waiting for the light at a crossing a pink-faced youth who's dangling a welder's helmet on a strap from the crook of his arm turns laughing to the man who hailed him. 'I jes' got tired an' quit.' Ragged families from the hills and the piney woods stroll staring straight ahead of them along the sidewalks towing flocks of little kids with flaxen hair and dirty faces. In front of a window full of bright-colored rayon socks in erratic designs a young man with glasses meets two girls in slacks. "We missed you yesterday," they say. "I was sick. I didn't go in. Anyway, I've got me a new job… more money."

The mouldering old Gulf seaport with its ancient dusty elegance of tall shuttered windows under mansard roofs and iron lace overgrown with vines and scaling colonnades shaded by great trees, looks trampled and battered like a city that's been taken by storm. Sidewalks are crowded. Gutters are stacked with litter that drifts back and forth in the brisk spring wind. Garbage cans are overflowing. Frame houses on tree shaded streets bulge with men in shirtsleeves who spill out onto the porches and trampled grassplots and stand in knots at the street corners. There's still talk of lodging-houses where they rent 'hot beds.' (Men work in three shifts. Why shouldn't they sleep in three shifts?) Cues wait outside of movies and lunch-rooms. The trailer army has filled all the open lots with its regular ranks. In cluttered backyards people camp out in tents and chicken houses and shelters tacked together out of packing-cases.

In the outskirts in every direction you find acres and acres raw with new building, open fields skinned to the bare clay, elevations gashed with muddy roads and gnawed out by the power shovels and the bulldozers. There long lines of small houses, some decently planned on the 'American standard' model and some mere boxes with a square brick chimney on the center, miles of dormitories, great squares of temporary structures are knocked together from day to day by a mob of construction workers in a smell of paint and fresh-sawed pine lumber and tobacco juice and sweat. Along the river for miles has risen a confusion of new yards from which men, women, and boys ebb and flow three times a day. Here and there are whole city blocks piled with wreckage and junk as if ancient cranky warehouses and superannuated stores had caved in out of their own rottenness under the impact of the violence of the new effort. Over it all the Gulf mist, heavy with smoke of soft coal, hangs in streaks, and glittering the training planes endlessly circle above the airfields.

SHOO-FLY BLUE IN TENNESSEE

for John Sledge. 2007

Celia Lewis

I.

No this isn't
this isn't about a jar.

II.

Georgia Cottage, 1868.
Mobile, Alabama.
I, Augusta Evans Wilson radiate
from the floor boards of this porch.
A certain distance. A shade of myself,
to you.

III.

A young boy at your daddy's feet.
But you are not yet born. Wait.
It will come to you.

IV.

Your grandfather calls
from among the camellias.
It's December and time
for Christmas. We are at war.
But your father is not your father.
He is on the road from Peleliu.

V.

He doesn't speak to you.

VI.

You study mortise and tenon
in Tennessee, a reference

a shade, a hue, a way of windows
framed and roof lines: a turn
of phrase set in cedar shakes,
dog trots, shotguns and hound dogs.
Everywhere ghosts roam, you are.

VII.

Down every overgrown path of sweet olive
your mother's there. Augusta Wilson is there.
Your grandfather is there calling from among
the roses or is it the camellias
or the rank weeds of the garden?
They are all
you coming forward into your own.

VIII.

Shoo-fly blue in Tennessee:
crucibles the living set in graveyard stones,
in wood. And paint. And hues
and shades of you.

IX.

He'll not speak to you:
only of the path to Peleliu.

X.

You took all that isn't to Tennessee
into a shade, a hue of shoo-fly blue
hoping that somewhere he waits for you
without mortise and tenon,
without the pitch line of a roof,
without the terrible need to make all
in a body of wood: a breathless man,
a man willing to speak
to only you.

MOBILE SPORTS: SETTING RECORDS

You could walk in there blindfolded and take one whiff and you would know where you were, because nothing smells quite like an old gymnasium.

—Paul Hemphill, from *The Good Old Boys*

from I HAD A HAMMER

with Lonnie Wheeler

Henry Aaron

The day I left Mobile, Alabama, to play ball with the Indianapolis Clowns, Mama was so upset she couldn't come to the train station to see me off. She just made me a couple of sandwiches, stuffed two dollars in my pocket, and stood in the yard crying as I rode off with my daddy, my older brother and sister, and Ed Scott, a former Negro League player who managed me with the Mobile Black Bears and scouted me for the Clowns. When we got to the station, Mr. Scott handed me an envelope with the name Bunny Downs on it. Downs was the business manager of the Clowns, and when I arrived at their camp in Winston-Salem, North Carolina, I was to hand him the envelope unopened.

My knees were banging together when I got on that train. I'd never ridden in anything bigger than a bus or faster than my daddy's old pickup truck. As we pulled out of the station and Daddy and Sarah and Herbert Junior and Mr. Scott kept getting smaller and smaller, I never felt so alone in my life. I just sat there clutching my sandwiches, speaking to nobody, staring out the window at towns I'd never heard of. It was the first time in my life that I had been around white people. After a while, I got up the courage to walk up and down the aisle a few times. I wanted to see what a dining car looked like, and I needed somebody to tell me where I wasn't allowed to go. Then I sat back down, listened to those wheels carrying me farther away from home, and tried to talk myself out of getting off at the next stop and going back.

I've never stopped wondering if I did the right thing that day. I was barely eighteen at the time, a raggedy kid who wore my sister's hand-me-down pants and had never been out of the black parts of Mobile. I didn't know anything about making a living or taking care of myself or about the white world I'd have to face sooner or later. I didn't know what I wanted to be doing when I was forty or any of the other things I needed to know to make a decision that would affect the rest of my life—except for one. I know that I loved to play baseball. And I had a feeling that I might be pretty good at it.

I suppose that's reason enough for an eighteen-year-old boy to board a train and set off on his life's journey, and I suppose it's time I stopped second-guessing myself. But I'm not eighteen any more, and two generations later I'm still living with a decision I made back when JFK was starting out as a senator. I live with the fact that I spent twenty-five of the best years of my life playing baseball. Don't get me wrong; I don't regret a day of it. I still love baseball—Lord knows, it's the greatest game in the world—and I treasure the experience. God, what an experience. But sometimes I have to wonder just how far I've really come since I took that envelope from Mr. Scott and walked onto the L&N. How far can a guy really go playing baseball? I guess that's what I wonder about. I can only thank God that I played the game well enough that maybe it meant something. Maybe in the end, I can do as much good, in my way, as say, a teacher. That's what Mama wanted me to be.

With all of my wondering, I don't doubt for a minute what baseball has done for me. Let me put that another way: I don't doubt what my ability to play baseball has done for me. I realize that if I hadn't been able to hit the hell out of a baseball, I would have never been able to lay a finger on the good life that I've been fortunate to have. Playing baseball has given me all that a man could ask for—certainly a lot more than a timid little black kid like me ever dared to dream about. I've traveled the world, met Presidents, had my share of fortune and more fame than I ever wanted. I even have a place in history, if only for hitting home runs. The fact is I have every reason to be content. My kids have all been to college. I don't know how I managed to stumble onto the great woman who is my wife. Everything is just about perfect. I don't even hear much about Babe Ruth anymore, thank goodness…

from THE GOOD OLD BOYS

Paul Hemphill

The place is in a musty old two-story brick building on a narrow one-way street. Conti Street, stuck between an aging resident hotel and a place that sells carpets and drapes, and the only identification is a flaking white sign hanging over the sidewalk with red lettering that says Littleton's Gymnasium. It has been there for at least 40 years and it has changed very little. On the first floor there are metal lockers and massage tables and an exercise bike, and upstairs there is a steam box and a large room full of punching bags and barbells and mirrors. You could walk in there blindfolded and take one whiff and you would know where you were, because nothing smells quite like an old gymnasium.

At noon, Tommie Littleton had it all to himself. The businessmen would not be in until mid-afternoon for their massages and steam baths and light workouts, and the only customer was a muscled-up weightlifter who sat on one of the tables upstairs and ran a hand through his greasy black hair while he read a comic book. Tommie Littleton dropped a dime in the pay phone, dialed a number and then waited, scratching his chest through a white T-shirt imprinted on the front with UNIVERSITY MILITARY SCHOOL in washed-out maroon letters.

"Hello," he was saying. "I want to talk to Tillman… Tillman, the one's brother's a fighter… yeah, that's him… Oh. Tomorrow?… No, I'll call back tomorrow…"

Littleton hung up and said, "He's off today."

"His brother's pretty good, you say."

"Good kid. Good puncher. Only about 20."

"Are there any other fighters in town?"

"You kidding? He said. "Nobody fights anymore."

Mobile used to be a good fight town, 30 or 40 years ago, when boxing had some respectability as a sport. For one thing it was a tough shipping town, meaning there were always a lot of seamen around who would pay good money to watch a fight. For another, there were enough Negro kids and poor white and sailors hungry enough to fight for a buck. So Mobile, in the 1920s and 1930s, had a lot of gyms around and they were busy every day with young fighters who would work out during the week and then ride to New Orleans or even Tampa to fight on the weekends. Or they would stay and fight right here. Tommie Littleton remembers when 1,000 people would crowd into the upstairs room at his gym to watch the fights.

Littleton was a part of it then. He was born on the west side of New York City in a tough neighborhood where "you had to fight to stay even," and he fought his first professional fight when he was 14. He wound up in Mobile in the late 1920s, when he was about 35 years old, and he fought in towns all over the South. He ran the gym and fought and was boxing coach at Spring Hill College, and his last fight was when he was 40 years old and Jack Dempsey brought a stable of boxers into town for a show. Since there was nobody else around to fight Dempsey's light-heavy weight, Tommie Littleton volunteered and decked the heavier and younger man in the sixth round. "We were trying to get me a fight with Young Stribling in Macon," he remembers, "but I guess he figured he had everything to lose by fighting me and that was it."

Those days will never come back, of course. Boxing is dead here and everywhere else. Gamblers and television helped kill it, and nobody wants to fight for a living anymore because it isn't worth it. There are fights in New Orleans on Monday nights that draw up to 2,000 fans, but that's it for the Gulf Coast. Now and then there will be fights in an armory in Mobile, but they don't amount to much. About the only fighter left in Mobile is a 20-year old kid named Jack Tillman, whose father was a good one in Mobile until boxing died and he had to take a job on a garbage truck. Tillman works out at the fire station where his brother works, and he has won 17 of his first 18 fights. Beyond that, there is nothing.

"Amateur boxing, that's what you've gotta have first," said Tommie Littleton. He was leaning on a parking meter in front of his place now, soaking up the bright noon sun, well preserved at 75 with only a trace of cauliflower ear to show for the years of fighting. "You gotta start with amateurs and bring 'em along before you can have professionals. It's a nucleus."

"What're the chances?" he was asked.

"Of what?"

"Getting amateurs going."

"Nothing," he said. "The gamblers ruined it. Them, and the way things changed. Nobody'll fight anymore. You get some hungry kid to fight, soon as he gets the wrinkles out of his stomach he quits. Nobody's hungry anymore. Maybe that's good." Then Tommie Littleton wandered back inside to tidy up his place. He does a pretty good business, he said, with businessmen who come around every afternoon to keep their bodies in shape.

*Jack Tillman was a former Sheriff of Mobile County.

REFLECTIONS OF MOBILE

I believed, until now, that all cities in America had decayed into crammed concrete jungles, but Mobile sparked a growing hope about cities that I had never had before.

—Peter Jenkins, from *A Walk Across America*

from THE SEVEN LEAGUE BOOTS

Albert Murray

Not that Mr. B. Franklin Fisher was ever dogmatic about literal application but his world of secondary education was the realm of pragmatic fundamentals, the world of carefully monitored drill sessions and the elements of grammar, mathematics, science, and the precise documentation of historical events and geographical relationships.

Which was entirely consistent with the all too obvious fact that at the Mobile County Training School it was almost always as if the highest premium was placed on meeting the precise standards of eligibility required by the occupations and professions that added up to social, economic, and political betterment as such. Nor could anything have been more consistent with community expectations, not only in general and in accordance with conventional ancestral imperatives that book learning was assumed to be about, but also with the specifics of what they had expected of him in the first place.

I can remember them talking and speculating about him all that summer before he came. It was also the summer before I was to be in the third grade and carry my books strapped onto my wide *First Year Geography* instead of a primer grade book satchel, and everywhere you went sooner or later somebody would mention something about the coming school year and the fact that there was going to be a new principal. There were sermons and prayers about it at church and discussions and arguments about it in Papa Gumbo Willie MacWorthy's barbershop, and you heard no end of gratuitously avuncular signifying about what he was going to be like as you moved around the neighborhood and during swing porch visiting time at home.

They tell me that new principal, that Professor B. Franklin Fisher is supposed to be rolling in town the day before Labor Day, and they say he is a natural born pistol. They say he has a way of just cutting his eyes in the direction of any kind of naughtiness that'll make these young rascals and freshtails straighten up as fast as cracking a whip; and they also say he got a tongue that can take the hide off a Hog Bayou alligator.

"Lift Every Voice" was already a school bell song along with "My Country 'Tis of Thee" and "Oh, Say Can You See," but when he arrived that Monday morning it also became the anthem that specifically evoked the ancestral imperatives of the Talented Tenth. From then on it was also a school bell song that resonated as if surrounded by stained glass windows. That was a very special day indeed.

We were all there waiting, students, a number of parents, welcoming committees from civic groups as well as churches; and at five minutes before the last bell, the Ford bringing them, Mr Hayes, who was driving, Miss Duval and Miss Lexine Metcalf, turned in and rumbled across the cattleguard and came flivvering on up the drive with two carloads of faculty of staff people following.

Mr. Hayes got out first. He was wearing surveyor's boots and britches, and he was carrying a tricorn folded flag, and on the chain around his neck there was a whistle, which he blew and began lining everybody up, parents and all for the Pledge of Allegiance ceremony. Then he marched us all to the entrance to the Assembly Room, and everybody was thinking that he was the one, until we got inside and found out who was going to speak.

He was standing at the podium wearing a dark blue hand tailored suit, and as soon as people saw him we could tell by the look on their faces that most of them were either mumbling or wondering is that him? That boy? Is that boy the man? Because what he looked like was a boy evangelist. The other teachers except Mr. Hayes who was standing at parade rest in back of the room and Miss Duval who was at the piano, were seated on the stage looking not unlike the evangelical chorus that they in fact turned out to be.

The music Miss Duval had been playing for us to get in step with as we came up to the landing to march into the assembly and find our seats and stand waiting by was a very fancy strutting New Orleans march called "High Society." But I guess that the first number we were going to have to sing together was "Lift Every Voice" because it was already the sound that went with school bell times and classroom smells, but that was the first time it also made you feel like being in church, which is exactly what Mr. B. Franklin Fisher wanted, and somehow even before he opened his mouth to say the first words you knew he was about to begin a sermon. And the first thing he said was that he was beginning an old time revival meeting that was going to last for nine months.

I've come here to these notorious sawmill outskirts of the historic and legendary seaport town of Mobile, Alabama, he began in a voice that was nothing if not that of a boy evangelist, to revive the spirit that that song from the turn of the century was composed to generate. It was first performed by schoolchildren such as you as a part of a celebration of Abraham Lincoln's birthday. But for me it is song of songs. For Mobile County Training School it is to be by my decree the clarion call to excellence.

The spirit of the extended revival meeting which I have come to conduct for this student body is the same that motivated and sustained the fugitive slave on the Underground Railroad, Harriet Tubman, Frederick Douglass, the nonpareil nobility of the magnificent volunteers in young Colonel Shaw's Massachusetts 54th. It was what motivated bondage-born Booker Washington to service and uplift as free-born white youths were inspired to wealth and status by the books of Horatio Alger.

Who knows perhaps the grounds of our campus like those of some of our outstanding universities, colleges, and normal and industrial institutes were once a part of a plantation that our forefathers were bound to. Well true or not, it is in effect another kind of plantation with another sort of overseer. And I intend to raise my kind of crops on it. Yes, I come here to raise crops that will supply this town with the civic nourishment it hungers and thirsts for: Instead of catch as catch can common laborers, expert technicians and skill into the common occupations of life; crops of dedicated professionals with certification second to none and artisans who will prosper by putting brains and along with everything else in every walk of life our people need leadership, leadership, leadership, the potential for which may even now be fermenting in the most lawless and backward seeming corners down in Meaher's Hummock.

Apropos of all of which there was also to be that assembly session that I remember from the term in which I was in the ninth grade. He began naming famous leaders and their historical achievements and calling them our appropriate ancestors and he singled out old Elzee Owens and said Citizen Tom Paine and when old crazy Willy Lee Berry whispered what he whispered to old Elzee about being put in the dozens the assembly which usually lasted from ten to ten-thirty each Wednesday went on until three o'clock with only a twenty minute break at one o'clock.

The dozens, he said. Stand up Willy Lee Berry. So now you're wondering how I heard you. Well, I got twenty-twenty vision as well as absolute pitch, so I didn't have to hear you. All I needed was to see you lean over and I didn't even have to read your lips. The dozens. Boy, I'll tell you something about the dozens. Boy, we were already in the dozens generations before we were born. Boy, they brought the flesh and blood ancestors of our people over here in chains in 1619. Boy, I'm not up here talking about bedsprings and berry thickets. I'm trying to tell you something about history and responsibility. I'm talking about you and your obligations to yourself and your allegiance to the principles on which the United States of America is founded.

If you call that playing the dozens, then I'm going to be playing the dozens with you from now on. All of you. Every last one of you. Boy, Tom Paine is precisely the great-great-great-granddaddy that suits the signifying you seem to think you're already qualified to whisper while your principal is addressing the junior high school student body. Citizen Tom Paine, yes, Citizen Tom Paine. Boy, I forbid you to put your number eleven feet on these grounds that we are in the process of hallowing until you read enough about his life and work to explain why I match you with him. And I'm going to be right here waiting for you at seven-thirty tomorrow morning. We'll all be here at seven-thirty and when we've heard from you we'll hear from your good friend Elzee Owens.

Then before Elzee Owens could figure out whether he also was supposed to stand up, the voice from the podium went on to say: "In fact, I don't think we should slight any one of you, if you know what I mean. I mean I'm going to be standing right here pointing my finger and ready to pat my foot if it takes the rest of the week for every last one of you to testify. I mean I am herewith promulgating my grandfather clause. The Mobile County Training School corollary to the grandfather clause, effective as of tomorrow morning at seven-thirty and appertaining to everybody in the seventh, eighth, and ninth grades. Your homeroom teachers will be right up here on the stage with me tomorrow morning and when they call your name you will answer by giving the ancestor you've chosen for emulation. You may change to someone else later as your aspirations come more and more into focus as you advance to graduation but the ones you select for this exercise had better be suitable. Duplication of choices will be permitted but your reasons must be yours alone. And please don't let me catch you using anybody's name in vain."

At that time I had my own reason for wanting to say Benjamin Franklin, but I knew very well you could never get away with that. And nobody would ever let you live it down. So I said what I said about Frederick Douglass as fugitive slave and said, "For the time being."

That was the instantly legendary Mr. B. Franklin Fisher who had come not only in response to the official call of the school board and community elders but also as answer to the old folks' prayers down through the generations. And yet this was also the selfsame Mr. B. Franklin Fisher who said what he said when I won the award I won in the tenth grade: Note bene, note bene, note bene. Every time some bright-eyed pupil like this comes out of the sawmill bottoms of Gasoline Point and makes straight A's in Latin 1 and 2, not only because he studies his lesson as required but also because he likes the history and the stories that he's able to translate, we are witnessing yet another personification of hope for the survival of the human proposition as such.

AN INTERVIEW WITH TRUMAN CAPOTE
Truman Capote

This is an excerpt from an interview by Pati Hill which was printed in the Paris Review.

Interviewer:

When did you first start writing?

Truman Capote:

When I was a child of about ten or eleven and lived near Mobile.

I had to go into town on Saturdays to the dentist and I joined the Sunshine Club that was organized by the *Mobile Press Register.* There was a children's page with contests for writing and for coloring pictures, and then every Saturday afternoon they had a party with free Nehi and Coca-Cola. The prize for the short-story writing contest was either a pony or a dog, I've forgotten which, but I wanted it badly. I had been noticing the activities of some neighbors who were up to no good, so I wrote a kind of *roman à clef* called "Old Mr. Busybody" and entered it in the contest. The first installment appeared one Sunday, under my real name of Truman Streckfus Persons. Only somebody suddenly realized that I was serving up a local scandal as fiction, and the second installment never appeared. Naturally, I didn't win a thing.

from A WALK ACROSS AMERICA
Peter Jenkins

I walked toward the Gulf and the towns seemed to get friendlier and warmer, with gentle names like Pine Hill, Grove Hill, Jackson and Sunflower. The closer I came to Mobile, the more certain I became: I would stop and get another job.

Fifty-eight miles north of the Gulf Coast city, I smelled a familiar scent, one I had grown up with on Long Island Sound. The hot breezes were coming straight from the south, and they carried with them the scent of the ocean. The excitement of seeing the sea for the first time since I left New York grew as I passed through tiny places like McIntosh, Calvert, Chastang and Creola.

After seven days, I walked down Telegraph Road into downtown Mobile. I didn't know anyone and had no preconceptions about the town. But if I liked it, I would stop and find work. Telegraph Road was straight and so was Pole Cat Bay, just to the east. Pole Cat Bay merged with Mobile Bay and then emptied into the Gulf. Once past the fast-food stores, self-service stations and burger joints, Mobile became a fantasy city. Thousands and thousands of people lived here, somewhere, but every direction I looked was like a park. Everywhere azalea bushes blazed red, white, pink and orange. It was as if Mobile had strung miles and miles of curly puffs of color throughout the city and lit them with neon lights.

Even more than by the psychedelic azaleas, I was moved by the great-grandfather live-oak trees. Multistoried buildings are usually the dominant structures in a city, but here in Mobile the seven-foot-thick oak trees, which twisted and crawled to the sky, dominated the landscape. They were at least two hundred years old and full of wisdom and gray moss beards. Their massive branches stretched outward and sheltered the people and their homes. These trees were symbols of life, protection, and balance. Here, man wasn't the only living thing that mattered. Here, the trees were like kings and to be respected. Their fatherly arms reached over Mobile's four-lane main streets, such as the busy Government Boulevard and Spring Hill Avenue. This was my dream come true. At last I had found a city where man and nature existed in harmony.

I got a job on a Thursday with the City of Mobile and was told to wear a hard hat. Our patients were very old, mostly over a hundred, so we had to rush from place to place to treat them. Our fully equipped ambulance had everything needed to help these arthritically twisted patients. Instead of a scalpel to perform midair operations, we used chain saws.

Being a doctor to these moss-draped trees was very special. Skillfully cutting and trimming with our chain saws was like operating on someone very famous, because people came from all around to watch and make sure their beloved live oaks were being treated with expertise. People dashed out of their homes, stopped their cars and took breaks from yard work to observe and oversee the surgery.

The other guys on my crew were young and treated the old magnificent trees with love and professional care. The head surgeon on our crew was called Bossman. The other surgeons were Dog Boy, Indian, Brother Dale, Big Boy and me. My name was Feet.

With every operation our crew performed, I fell more in love with this shaded city. Mobile made me want to sing and shout! I believed, until now, that all cities in America had decayed into crammed concrete jungles, but Mobile sparked a growing hope about cities that I had never had before.

LIVING AND DYING IN MOBILE

Robert Bahr

In 1994, after living in Mobile about five years, I wrote in the introduction to a collection of short stories by Mobile writers called *Home Again, Home Again*, "We long for community, for people who know us by name and who care, for a place where we belong, where we are rooted. We will make do, if necessary, with a bar called Cheers or even with a gang of brothers in south L.A. But what we seek is home."

By then I was coming to realize that, after fifty years of searching and living in New Jersey, New York, and Pennsylvania I had finally found home in Mobile. Here is a city unique in my experience. It has personality. To quote myself, "We Mobilians realize that, just as we live in this city, this city lives in us."

I know several people who have moved away from Mobile—and then moved back. There really is no place like home if home's Mobile.

Fourteen years ago, when we told our friends in Pennsylvania that we were moving to Mobile, we were asked repeatedly, "Where on earth is Mobile?" But over the years we've had visits from those friends. They all went home happy to know where on earth Mobile is, and I report with some chagrin that they've all been back more frequently than I would like.

Oh, yes, they come for the climate, especially in the winter. I'm writing this in February, 2002, and yesterday wife Alice and I walked around Langan Park dressed in summer clothes. In Pennsylvania it was below freezing.

And they come to see the azaleas that bloom in February instead of May as they do up north, and the camellias, which are still in bloom, and don't bloom at all up north. They come because, as Alice put it when we first arrived on these shores in 1989, "There's so much more sky around here!"

They come for the beaches and the water. My dearly departed friend Joe Wanner climbed a dune with me east of Gulf Shores a few years ago and stared at the water with mouth agape. Then he turned to me, astonished. "What's wrong with this water?" he demanded.

"Nothing. I don't know what you mean."

With the assurance of one who had just caught me in a lie, he informed me, "That water is blue and green. It's supposed to be brown and black like in New Jersey!"

Yes, they come for all those reasons, and they enjoy Battleship Park and Bellingrath Gardens and the Mardi Gras parades and the live oaks along Government Street and the antebellum mansions. But that's not what they talk about, and why they come back. The magic of Mobile is in its people.

All of them—rich and poor, educated and not so educated, blacks and whites. Republicans and Democrats. Young and old, religious and non-believers. It's the whole mix and the balance of that mix, the harmony of it that makes Mobile different from any other town I've known. It's a delicately, perfectly seasoned gumbo, a people-gumbo.

The main ingredient in that gumbo is playfulness, and the ability to believe in the game. Within days of our arrival in Mobile, former neighbor Henry McClary told me of the little people of the deep bayou, only three feet tall and always naked, but rarely seen. "Hardly any left these days," Henry told me solemnly. "They were hunted down for dog meat." I almost believed him. I think Henry almost believed himself.

June, Henry's wife, came straight from the set of *The Glass Menagerie*. She pronounced "again" so that it rhymes with "rain."

Dave Brill, in his early forties, is the best "true" storyteller I ever met. As he talks, his eyes widen with a child's enthusiasm. He gesticulates. He modulates. He's playing.

Uncle Bud: "Uncle Bud was my grandfather's oldest brother. When he was 14, he went off to WWI. He was one of the youngest guys who managed to get into the war by lying about his age. My great grandfather confirmed the lie. He was trying to get rid of Bud because, even in his younger years, he was a scoundrel kind of a kid.

"Well, he came back with a whole bunch of medals for killing the enemy. He was trained as an explosives expert. When he got back to Mobile he was broke and bored, so he blew up the post office in what is now Brookley Field. His plan was to steal money, and if there was no money, take all the stamps he could carry and sell them all over town at a discount.

"Instead, he just blew his eye out and destroyed everything inside the post office along with the building.

"He got a year in jail—it was a different time back then. For one thing, the federal government wasn't very popular in the South. For another, he was a war hero. And before the trial his father died and he inherited the family farm, and the government wanted it to build B. C. Rain School on it, so he agreed to sell it. He made the equivalent of a million dollars today on the sale.

"With the money, he went to the southeastern part of town and bought a large parcel of land—Brill Road runs right through what used to be his property. He opened a little store, did some bootlegging, and was an all-around nefarious dude.

"When I was about six years old, my parents decided that I should learn to do little tasks and chores, so I was made to go to work for him in his store. He had a little meat market in the back where he did the butchering, and groceries in the front. My job was to sweep the floors, clean windows, that sort of thing. Uncle Bud was an old man by then, and not in the best of health, and one day he started coughing really violently—and his glass eye just popped out! It rolled way under the meat counter. So, holding a hand over the empty socket, he yelled, 'Come here, boy!'

"I came running, and he says, 'Get under that counter and get my eye!'

"I get on my hands and knees with a broom—I'm going to use the handle to just knock it out into the middle of the store. So I kneel way down, and peek under the counter, and there it is covered with cobwebs and some red slop, and staring right at me!

"Well, that's just too much for a six-year-old to handle. I mean I just jumped up and yelled, 'Aaahhh!' I ran out of that store, and two years later I still wouldn't go in there. In fact, I was 16 before I went back there."

The Postmaster of Copper Hill: "He was a mean man, Uncle Ben, but he never killed anybody except in war. Now, my wife Beverly had a relative in Copper Hill, Tennessee, who killed a guy in a gun fight. Some guy insulted his wife, called her fat. (Actually, she was fat, but that's not the point.) The local judge wouldn't convict him. A man just can't go around calling another man's wife fat, and if he gets killed it's his own fault.

"So the case went to a federal judge, who convicted him of murder, and instead of hanging him they sentenced him to be the postmaster of Copper Hill, Tennessee. He spent the rest of his life having to admit he was an employee of the federal government."

Dave the Project Manager: "I was working in New Orleans. I was the project manager with a crew dismantling the old Mart Arial Skyway across the Mississippi River. It was supported by two towers that stuck way out over the river. They were each about 400 feet high. One of the men working for me was Bernard Kabody, from the Belgian Congo. He was a brilliant engineer, but he couldn't work in this country because he didn't have a license; he didn't speak any English, except when he saw me he'd go, 'Oh, hello Mr. Dave!' and a few other standard phrases. But he was a good surveyor.

"Bernard volunteered to go up the tower and put some laser targets on it so we could measure stresses as we lowered it to the ground. Otherwise, it could be overstressed and break into pieces, and that could be dangerous.

"Well, he's up there, and the wind's kinda whipping up. He's got this body harness on for safety, and it's fastened to the tower, and I'm talking to him by radio and finally say, 'Bernard, it's getting too windy. Come on down.'

"'No,' he says, 'Two more targets I do, then come down.'

"So I get involved in something else, and a few minutes later Bernard calls over the radio, 'Oh , hello Mr. Dave! I need help please!'

"I tell him, 'No, Bernard, I'm not climbing up there to help you with the targets. I hate heights, scared to death of them. Besides, I told you it's too windy. Just come on down.'

"So Bernard says, 'Oh, hello Mr. Dave! I fall!'

"So I looked up toward the top of the tower, way out over the Mississippi, and there's Bernard swinging back and forth like a pendulum at the end of his safety harness.

"First I asked the rest of the crew for volunteers, but they decided that, since Bernard was a foreigner, and since he didn't even speak English, he wasn't worth dying for. So we called the fire department, and when they came and saw the angle of the tower, and how far out over the water it was and that their ladders would be useless, they reached about the same conclusion as the crew had.

"Nobody was going to get the guy, so, hating myself for ever taking the stupid job, I put on a safety harness and went up the tower. One step at a time, as terrified as I've ever been, a rope over my shoulder, I went up.

"I got just above him, and there he is, swinging back and forth, 15 feet below me. He looks up at me and says, 'Oh, hello Mr. Dave. I so glad see you!'

"Oh, shut up, Bernard," I'm thinking. I'd brought a sharp knife, and for a moment I considered cutting the safety harness and letting Bernard fend for himself. But the risk was too great. So I took the rope I had and made a loop around the safety harness and lowered the loop to Bernard's waist, then climbed back down the tower and pulled him sideways till he was actually able to grasp the tower, and together we got him up. I made him climb down first. I didn't need him falling on me."

Dave Brill is Mobile's version of Mark Twain, especially after a few beers.

I believe we have more amateur, semi-pro and professional sports teams than any city our size in the country. Although we may actually be sitting in an armchair or a bleacher, in our hearts we're out there on the field or down in the rink playing our hearts out.

We'll use any excuse for a party, a festival, a parade. Once a year virtually the whole town gets involved in two weeks of Mardi Gras celebrations. Most people don't know why—and don't care. It's the playfulness that counts.

We bring that spirit even to the biggest transition of our lives since our births-dying. Funerals are pretty much the same north and south. People give eulogies. Mourners walk past the coffin, sometimes closed, sometimes open.

If the pastor is into saving souls, he'll work in his sales pitch about eternal damnation. (That can get touchy if the dearly departed was a non-believer.)

The first Mobilian of my acquaintance to die was Eugene Walter. He was 76 years old. He left the planet on March 29, 1998, although his body resides at the historic Church Street Cemetery. He set the tone for the events to follow when, rushed to the hospital after collapsing in his home, the doctor asked if he had any allergies.

"Yes," Eugene answered, "[our governor] Fob James."

Eugene avoided the darker side of life like the plague.

Perhaps the best paragraph he ever wrote was the one with which he opened his prize-winning novel *The Untidy Pilgrim*: "Down in Mobile they're all crazy, because the Gulf Coast is the kingdom of monkeys, the land of clowns, ghosts and musicians, and Mobile is sweet lunacy's county seat." He lived in a place where children live, where life is the fiction you concoct on the spur of the moment, and, if you have it in you, you persuade others that your fiction is their reality. And so it was with the planning of his wake. Here was the opportunity for the grandest of parties, and Eugene dearly loved a party. Weak and frail with terminal liver disease, he nonetheless threw himself into the details of the event.

The party would be held at the Scottish Temple on Saint Francis Street a few blocks west of Bienville Square. The casket would be placed in the center of the vast open space, surrounded by tables overflowing with food and wine. A few people would make speeches, but mostly there would be laughter and harmless gossip and farewell messages scrawled with felt tipped pens of various colors on Eugene's casket:

"Say hi to Julie Rayford."

"Keep your voice down. The Baptists think they're the only ones up there."

"Keep it up, Eugene!"

"J" Trufant was the second Mobilian I knew who died. She stood out from the crowd because, to begin with, she was pleasant to look at. Slender, pretty, always smiling, she appeared much younger than her late 60's.

"J" was involved in just about every charitable organization in the city. She seemed to have boundless energy, a sparkling personality, and enough charm to melt an iceberg. She served as president of Friends of the Spring Hill College Library.

One morning she was diagnosed with an inoperable brain tumor. She helped plan her wake, then donned a black dress and reclined on the covers of her bed, where she received visitors. Eventually, she could not speak, but still she smiled and grasped hands with the same warmth that she'd shown throughout her life.

About a month after the diagnosis she died.

According to her instructions, "J"'s family rented the Saenger Theater. As the hundreds of guests arrived, they read newspaper clips posted in the foyer telling of "J"'s contributions to the community, photos of her and her family, even letters of recognition from prominent people. Upon entering the theater, they were handed glasses of champagne, and later drank a toast to "J" Trufant's life.

Speakers recalled happy moments. Someone sang a favorite song. Others shared amusing stories. It was a happy time, a celebration.

All things being equal, I'd rather die in Mobile.

At the moment, Alice and I aren't living in Mobile. Blame it on circumstances beyond our control. When all the farewell parties and dinners ended and we approached our last days in the city, we sat in the quiet and cried. Oh, it is a painful thing to finally discover where you are meant to be and then have to leave. Alice still grieves at times. But I look at it this way: It's only a temporary relocation, a mere decade. We'll be back home again and playing at life in Mobile in no time.

You can count on it.

NOSTALGIA

John Hafner

When I remember how I used to stand
Or sit or lie upon a worn-out bed
And listen to the ravings of a friend
Who never quite remembered what he read;
Or reminisce about the times we spent
On beaches where the seagulls dove for bread
While we walked past the cottages for rent
And argued about loathing, fear and dread;
Or better yet, recall the party times
At Korbett's Bar with air as light as lead
From smoke and conversation over lines
Of poetry that we had vaguely read;
Then I regret the movements of the sun
Only a bit. But some of it was fun.

A JUBILEE OF MOBILE MEMORIES

Norman Jetmundsen, Jr.

Mobile—place of my birth and childhood—will always be home, no matter how far I travel. What is Mobile's mysterious charm that forges an enduring and endearing locus in one's heart? A past memory is one attempt to grasp this will-o'-the-wisp.

At dawn on this April morning, I toss and turn, with butterflies of anticipation. Outside, a chorus of crickets and frogs serenade the sunrise. Dashing to the window, I'm relieved to see a clear pink sky and the glittering ripples from a gentle breeze caressing Dog River. Today is the annual sailboat race to Dauphin Island.

My sleepy-eyed friends and I are soon casting off the lines of our Ensign sailboat, christened Skoal. Consistent with Southern family ritual, and despite the fact we're all over the age of majority, my mother has lovingly packed us more food than we could eat in a week ("just in case"), and my dad stands on the point of our property jutting out into Dog River, watching us until he becomes a faint speck. I pretend to be embarrassed, but secretly delight in their care.

As we glide down the river, watched by a lone pelican perched on an abandoned piling, the gurgling of our little outboard motor is the only disturbance of this quiet morning. Long strands of gray Spanish moss hanging from sprawling hundred-year-old oak trees wave gracefully as we pass. Numerous palettes of pink and white flowering azaleas dot the riverbanks. We busily work stowing gear, pulling out sails, and washing down biscuits with steaming coffee. The sun looms over Dog River Bridge as the swift current carries us quickly toward Mobile Bay. Near the mouth of the river a cacophony of sounds emanate from the Mobile Yacht Club harbor, with metal halyards rapping rhythmically against aluminum masts providing the background beat. The sultry air is thick with the smells of salt water, fish, and muddy marshes. A flock of seagulls argue overhead.

Once our boat enters the brackish waters of Mobile Bay, waves send our bow gently up and down, causing us to grab for something to steady ourselves as we hoist the mainsail and Genoa jib. Hundreds of boats swarm into the bay from all directions, each in various stages of dress—some are already under full sail, while others try to get sails up as they rock along unsteadily in the choppy seas. The sparkling ripples on the water denote an easterly breeze that is all too whimsically unpredictable with its continual shifts of direction. As soon as our motor is stopped, the immediate sensation of silence is striking, the only sounds being the water lapping against our boat, and the wind whistling past the stays.

Sailboats, large and small, new and old, fast and slow, zig zag across the bay. Two colorful Hobie Cats slice swiftly through the water, passing a creaking wooden two-masted schooner, with faded white paint and stained canvas sails, as if it were at anchor. Skippers and crews busy themselves with preparations for the start, but friends still take time to wave and shout jovial threats of piracy, as well as wishing one another good luck.

Our sails set, and with a few minutes to spare, I stare at the skyline of downtown Mobile, marking evidence of business and commerce in the Port City. An American flag slapping in the morning breeze atop a tall mast is a reminder of the six flags that have flown over this region since the first French settlement in 1702. One can almost imagine the statue of Raphael Semmes observing us from his downtown perch. A glance to the right reveals the impressive, gray outline of the U.S.S. Alabama. The clear morning air affords a view across the bay of the red cliffs of Montrose, supposedly the highest point on the coast between here and Maine. I ponder what this scene would have looked like to Pineda when he first sailed into the bay over 450 years ago, or what it was like for the Native Americans who preceded the advent of Western civilization.

The sound of the ten-minute gun breaks my reverie, and we begin in earnest to strategize how to start the race. With so many boats it's difficult to maneuver, and shouts of "Starboard Tack" fill the air, as more knowledgeable sailors claim their right of way. (I later learn that one novice sailor thought people were shouting "Starboat Attack!") The minutes elapse quickly, and the starting gun booms in our ears as we pass the committee boat almost right on time, beginning the long journey to Dauphin Island.

A few minutes later, we hear indications of a flurry of activity behind us and look back to see the incredible sight of numerous rainbow-colored spinnakers, like scores of hot-air balloons, gently unfolding, snapping as they fill with wind. The breeze has shifted to the north, and one of our crew dashes below to bring up our carefully-packed spinnaker. Directly behind us, a huge black spinnaker emerges, revealing a large, silver skull and cross bones. This is not the first time a Jolly Roger has been seen near these shores. As the shift reaches us, we drop our jib and hoist the spinnaker, which promptly wraps itself around the mast. The poet, Robert Burns, must have had a sailboat in mind when he wrote, "The best-laid schemes o' mice an' men gang aft agley..."

The tangled mess occupies us for several minutes, but finally Skoal is gaily skipping down the bay. The regal sight of the Grand Hotel, nestled beneath numerous oak trees at Point Clear, comes closer into view. Its stately presence is accentuated by the backdrop of ominous gray clouds. What secrets could this place tell us of the Civil War, gala balls of bygone years, weddings and reunions, hurricanes and jubilees, of dreams and disappointments?

The fickle wind shifts abruptly toward the south, and spinnakers are rapidly gathered in. We watch as the boat next to us seemingly tries to turn their spinnaker into a fishing net when it falls into the water and drags the boat to a halt. We're thankful that our earlier spinnaker snafu is not repeated. Tightening the lines of our sails, we set course for Middle Bay Lighthouse, which we must round in order to complete the race properly.

Almost without warning, the bay suddenly becomes like a boiling pot of green tea as dark clouds rush toward us. A lightning bolt and accompanying blast of thunder announce the arrival of a regular Mobile visitor, a thunderstorm. We have only a few seconds to get ready before the wind howls around us, and a white sheet of rain envelopes us. We do not have time to think about anything but survival, as we fight to keep Skoal from capsizing. A scream and excited pointing from one of my crewman alerts us to another boat bearing down on a collision course with us. The other crew is frantically trying to pull down a large mainsail, which appears to be jammed, and they don't give any indication they see us. I pull the tiller with all my might, and we miss the boat literally by inches. Another heavy gust, however, allows no time for self-congratulations.

After about a half hour, the tempest begins to dissipate, revealing in the mist a ghostly apparition—the hexagonal 1885 white cottage of Middle Bay Lighthouse, sitting atop tall, rusted, metal pilings. How many vessels passing by in the dead of night have been grateful for its light to guide them?

An eerie calm envelopes the bay, in stark contrast to the squall only moments before. Specks of blue sky appear between the swiftly moving gray clouds. Sailboats are now scattered all over the bay—as far as the eye can see—rocking gently in the mirror-like water. The sight brings to mind the words of Coleridge's Ancient Mariner, "as idle as a painted ship upon a painted ocean…"

An old friend of bay sailors soon returns, however, in the form of a steady southeast breeze. Boats ahead of us lurch forward as their sails fill. We hold our breath, waiting for this welcome elixir to reach us. The blazing sun reappears. Countless waves swell with the stiffening breeze, and white caps cover the bay like swirls of icing on a cake. In the distance, another reminder of Mobile's economy and location appears in the form of a massive ocean-going cargo ship making its way up the channel. The blast of the ship's horn sounds a mournful cry. The ship dwarfs two wooden shrimp boats returning to Bon Secour after several days of hard labor. Scores of seagulls accompany the two shrimp boats, testifying to their successful fishing venture. A jet airliner zooms overhead. Past and present in one indelible sight.

Three porpoises leap playfully in the waves off our port bow. Before us is the hazy outline of Dauphin Island. It's now a perfect afternoon for sailing, with a blue sky, several billowing white clouds, and a steady wind. Our boat surges through the waves in a constant rhythm. With the storm only a memory, the crew threatens mutiny unless we break out lunch. What seemed like excessive mounds of fried chicken, potato chips, turkey sandwiches, and chocolate chip cookies quickly disappear. Mom always knows best.

What was once a dim speck is now a large bridge and island, as the southern end of the bay comes into focus. Brilliant white sand accentuates the lush green pine trees blanketing Dauphin Island. Fort Gaines looms over the east end of the island. A lone figure stands on the walls of the fort, hands shading his eyes, anxiously scanning the bay. I don't need binoculars to know it is my Dad, making sure we have arrived safely.

On the other side of the bay's entrance, Fort Morgan adds the corresponding bookend. An exclamation point between these imposing brick forts is the tall, cylindrical Sand Island Lighthouse, which stands on the site where lighthouses have marked the entrance to Mobile Bay since 1838. The island of sand is now only a few rocks, however, serving as a reminder of the fragility and transitoriness of life. It's not difficult to believe that one hears "Damn the torpedoes..." echoing across the watery grave of the Tecumseh. The ghosts of Pineda, Iberville, Bienville, Semmes, Farragut, Hunley—and countless others who have been drawn to this beautiful and romantic setting—surely accompany us today.

The crew of Skoal shouts when we cross the finish line. The day is long from over, however. The gaggle of boats converges on Dauphin Island, some sailing, some motoring, and one even being towed, its broken mast a testament to the mid-day storm. Before long, we enter the harbor, where boats lash onto one another sometimes ten deep. My crew tosses me overboard, but before I can climb aboard to revenge this insubordination, they pop the cork on a bottle of champagne. Assuaged by this gesture, I gleefully join in a toast to St. Brendan, the patron saint of sailors. The gaiety and frivolity in the harbor are tangible, with hundreds of sailors, young and old, tying down sails, jumping from boat-to-boat, or diving in for a cool swim.

Yet another Mobile tradition is under way, a party. Friends and strangers share a beer together, while regaling one another with scuttlebutt from the day's adventures. Somewhere in this mélange of boats, a loud speaker blares out music from Mobile's own patron saint of sailing fun, Jimmy Buffett. Several teens on one boat launch water balloons from a huge elastic band stretched between several stays of a tall mast. Many faces look like boiled lobsters. We don't know if we've won or lost the race, but by now we're not too concerned about that. There's something captivating about the way Mobilians joyfully celebrate life, with gusto and playful revelry. It's no accident that Mobile is the original home of Mardi Gras.

The gulf breeze begins to die down, and the sun, now an orange ball on the horizon, gives a final salute to the day. The Man-in-the-Moon and Orion will have to oversee the end of this day's festivities.

I sit in the stern of Skoal, sipping a beer, looking at the jumble of sailboats bobbing in the water, and drifting into thought. Mobile indeed has a unique ambiance: history, romance, beauty, and Southern hospitality. I've experienced all of that today. Mobile's enchanting allure is something I can't touch, but it's as real as to me as my boat. Its golden threads are woven into the tapestry of my heart and soul.

MOBILE REFLECTIONS
Roy Hoffman

Roy Hoffman, a journalist and novelist, sometimes offers personal observations on passing events and seasonal pastimes. Many of these reflections are gathered in his collection of profiles, personal essays, and narrative non-fiction, *"Back Home: Journeys Through Mobile"* (University of Alabama Press). Others, as these personal essays that appeared originally in the *Mobile Register*, are being reprinted here, in slightly different versions, for the first time.

STUCK IN MOBILE
(on a Bob Dylan concert, Oct. 28, 1997)

Whenever I hear the Bob Dylan song, "Stuck Inside of Mobile With the Memphis Blues Again," I envision the old Greyhound Bus Station in downtown Mobile, travelers hunched over mugs in the coffee shop during layovers, or drifting about with rucksacks over their shoulders at midnight, trying to get home. In many places I've traveled, when I tell people I'm from Mobile, they ask not about azaleas, Mardi Gras or seafood gumbo, but about the title of Dylan's plaintive song.

The old bus station has long been demolished, a new one situated, like much else today, in the western part of town; the Government Plaza rises gleaming where the funky waiting room used to be. Hearing Bob Dylan on Sunday at the Mobile Civic Center puts me in mind of a lot of places I have not seen in many a year: the side of a lonesome highway where I once hitchhiked with friends; the laid-back venue of a rock emporium where a buddy spoke to me like a mystic guru through the tangle of a beard; a college quadrangle where perfect youths wearing tie-dye shirts soared Frisbees into the sunshine, and cannabis filled the air.

Although not a serious devotee of Dylan, I've heard his raspy poetry through a thousand dorm windows. Songs like "Mr. Tambourine Man" or "Like A Rolling Stone," jangly and reflective, are as familiar as worn nursery rhymes, although if I tried to repeat the lyrics I would scramble them. Like the Beatles, moon launches and marches on Washington, Dylan was part of the American landscape of my youth.

"I'm here for a religious experience," a lawyer acquaintance at the concert told me, perhaps only half-joking, admitting that his days of abandon had long passed. "I still have on my shoes."

I came across one cluster of hard-core fans who'd convened in Mobile through a Dylan chat line on the Internet, among them a professor from Knoxville, a construction supervisor from New Orleans and a newspaper employee from Houston.

Of middle years, in academics or computers or business, some of the group were trailing Dylan this whole tour, from Jackson, Miss. right through to Athens, Ga., and Birmingham. "We're like gainfully employed Deadheads," one woman told me, setting Dylan followers a practical cut above the groupies of the Grateful Dead. As they conversed, they made constant references to where they'd first seen Dylan, their favorite albums and songs.

There were Dylan newcomers, too, teen-agers who'd come to Bob through his son, Jakob, and Jakob's '90s rock band, the Wallflowers. They seemed out of time, jumping up and down to the music on the first few rows, waving their hands like Bob Dylan was nothing more than a purveyor of high-octane rock.

All of us, in many ways, have our tastes forever shaped by the music we hear when young, by the fashions in vogue at the time, by the hot movies at the box office. I recognized a lot of people at the Dylan concert, some I hadn't seen in 20 years, still youthful-looking if no longer young, faces touched with experience, and a few more lines.

From where I sat with two men friends, like me in their 40s with desk jobs and families, I could look out over the sea of other silver-heads and bald-heads on the concourse below. I suspect that many were silently singing along to the 57-year-old bard in leather pants and Wyatt Earp tie crooning "Just Like A Woman." A few, I'm sure, saw themselves up there hitting guitar licks and bending into the mike.

If we had been witnessing a Dylan contemporary such as Mick Jagger, we might feel let-loose and raunchy again, just as we did the first time we clutched a beer and danced in the corner with a date to "Satisfaction." If my friends and I had come out to hear James Taylor, chances are our wives, rather than staying home to spend Sunday evening readying themselves for work and our children for school, would have dropped everything and been at our sides. Taylor's sweet Carolina mornings have been around as long as Dylan's Highway 61, and Taylor still makes you want to walk home with your arm around your loved one. Dylan makes you want to jam your hands in your jean pockets and kick down side streets alone.

You can't dance to vintage Dylan, and lovebirds rarely request it at weddings as they do the music of Elton John, but Dylan speaks to heartbreak and confusion. Lose a job, bust up a relationship, go on a bender, watch the stock market slide 500 points, and it may be Dylan, gravelly and comforting, you want to hear. When he pumped out the song lyrics "Everybody Must Get Stoned," hundreds of responsible, middle-aged citizens with multiple dependents and steep house notes forgot Monday morning. I suspect few, if any, were "high." Most would probably be home in bed within the hour, feeling not so much stoned as just plumb tired. But they all sang along, comforted that their rambling days were as close as the dandelion-haired street-poet on stage.

Leaving the concert I turned on the radio—what else but classic rock?—and a kindly DJ, knowing throngs of us would want to join in, was playing Dylan's "Like A Rolling Stone."

"How does it feel / How does it feel / To be on your own / With no direction home / Like a complete unknown / Like a rolling stone?"

I could hear the voices of all the other former 20-year-olds, crying out of their car windows, gritty and Dylanesque, filling Mobile with those Memphis blues again.

LIGHTNING SENSE
(summer 2001)

One stormy night in the summer of 1968, I was a teen-ager with my family at a vacation house on Mobile Bay. The night rocked with the wash of rain, the crackle of lightning and the roar of thunder, but we were tucked away cozily in the house, playing cards and Scrabble, keeping one eye on the television, where the Democratic National Convention in Chicago blasted forward. A new baby, belonging to one of my older sisters, was in her bassinet.

BANG! The room exploded as though a camera flash had gone off in our eyes and a cherry bomb under our chair.

I can still remember the aftershock of the noise, as though cotton were stuffed in my ears, and the after-images of the bright flash: my father, reaching down to feel the electric voltage that had skipped over his ankles, my mother touching her hair, with the lamps to each side of her knocked out, the baby beginning to cry, to howl.

"The TV's on fire!" someone shouted.

It had begun to smoke, the wires smoldering. We yanked it from the room and dragged it into the back yard, where it burst into flame. Lightning, all around us, came zig-zagging down, as though giants, playing a cruel game, were out to incinerate us.

The storm, soon passing, had scored the side of a large pine next to the den. The lightning had left its gash—the force jumped from the sky, to the tree, into the electric sockets, across our feet—before finding its ground.

We escaped unhurt, but forever wary. To this day, I can detect someone who has been in a house or boat once struck by lightning. When the celestial show begins in our late afternoons, they are the first to shout, "Let's head in!"

And the first to get that fretful look in their eyes.

On summer days in coastal Alabama, when skies darken in late afternoon, we regularly behold lightning scissoring the horizon. Bolts flash like carnival lights, silent in the distance. Moments later, as the sky begins to rumble, we take stock of how far away the storm might be. Out over the airport? Sliding past Satsuma? Moving toward us across the Bayway?

No matter where we are—lugging packages from a store or ambling along sidewalks after dinner—we make a random calculation. One-thousand-one…one-thousand-two…one-thousand-three, a mile for every five seconds we count.

Electric currents jumping from thunderheads have a dangerous beauty, like poisonous flowers or snakes. Those of us with "lightning sense" know to seek cover. Umbrellas and raincoats will hardly do.

Not all of us have "lightning sense," of course.

There are those, I know, who will insist on lollygagging at the pool or heading up the sixth fairway, five-iron in hand, despite the warning of 100-million-volt flashes in the sky.

Perhaps they think the odds are still in their favor, that the sledgehammer from above will never crash down on them. Let them get nearly walloped just once, and they'll never dismiss lightning again.

~

Lightning, of course, has become a metaphor for many experiences—of the body, and heart.

White lightning is moonshine liquor.

The 1970s song, "Lightning Striking Again," refers to the pangs of love.

"If I lie, let me be struck dead by lightning," is an oath as solemn as they come.

A young adult novel by Fairhope writer Judith Richards, set in a Florida Everglades with "jagged, ripping flashes of lightning," is titled, *Summer Lightning*.

In the film version of the 1954 novel, *The Bad Seed*, by the Mobile author William March, the diabolical young girl is on a bayside pier in the middle of a storm at the story's conclusion. That's where lightning metes out to her a gruesome fate.

And some see in lightning artistic inspiration.

Until they moved to Wyoming, photographer J.L. Wooden and his wife, Catherine, resided in Mobile for the fundamental reason of its being one of the locales most subject to lightning strikes.

J.L. Wooden once told a *Register* reporter that he loved to photograph lightning and that he was one of only eight such enthusiasts in the nation. The Woodens follow lightning like the characters in the movie "Twister" chased terrifying Oklahoma winds.

"Yes, we are still chasing storms," Catherine Wooden tells me from Wyoming.

The Woodens realize, of course, as do all of us with "lightning sense," that you can chase lightning all you want, but, in the end, it hunts you.

~

In 1987, according to an Associated Press story, lightning hit the launch pad of three NASA rockets, firing them off. Another time, the news told of seven Citronelle oil tanks ignited by lightning.

I know a sweet, older lady who lost a dog to lightning. When she went looking for him in her Spring Hill neighborhood, sorrowfully she found him stretched out in a field.

In May, on a single afternoon in Prichard, one man suffered a lightning strike while heading from his office to his truck—he described the sensation as feeling on fire from head to foot—while another was clobbered using the phone while sitting in a chair inside his barber shop. He came to nearly an hour later in the hospital.

A boy playing baseball. A kid swimming. A man walking down a country road. When we hear about these ordinary people suddenly ripped off their feet, tossed into the air, thrown to the dirt, we are shocked, unnerved.

In its own startling way, lightning is timeless. Just as we would have done 100 years ago or will do 100 years hence, when Earth's canopy begins to spark, all we can do is gaze up in awe—flinch—and hurry on in.

THE PLEASURES OF SUMMER READING
(Summer 2000)

One summer when I was in junior high, the bookmobile came to my family's midtown Mobile neighborhood. A couple of times a week, the long, trailer-like vehicle took up residence and welcomed us as we arrived with our parents by car, or traveled on our own by skates, bicycle or foot. In my family, we were hardly rural dwellers but there was a kind of summertime romance in the notion of thousands of books being hauled, like chickens or furniture, through familiar streets.

I remember climbing up the steps to the packed shelves, heading to the novels marked "adventure," or "science fiction," and leaving with a stack of them under my arm.

One book I hazily recall in its details—a story about a man who traveled from planet to planet, meeting odd creatures at every destination—but I can still sense the delight I took in traveling through language to places I would never see. Since I recall neither the author nor the title, the book is gone forever for me. If I were to discover it today at a garage sale, it could never envelop me again as it did when I was a boy.

Another book I remember more specifically was about an eccentric man who talked to animals and traversed the globe. His name, of course, was Dr. Doolittle, and to this day, when I am feeling wanderlust, I imagine acting as he did. He'd open an atlas at random, plunk down his finger, and wherever he pointed is where he'd go.

Looking back on my bookmobile summer, I realize that travel to exotic places was not so far-fetched at all. That's what we kids were learning to do.

While we believed that the characters in stories were having the adventures, it was really us, journeying via the mind.

~

Summer is officially beginning. Jobs, sports, camp, family vacations, beach-going, hanging out—endless, hot-weather hours will become crowded schedules for some, boredom for others. Some educators believe school year-round would be the best way to spend June, July and August. There's so much to learn, they argue.

But what school rarely affords, given curricular demands, is the chance for young people to read to no end at all except one—sheer pleasure.

Much as we embrace the electronic images of our computers, never will they entice us to curl up with them in a lounge chair or under a tree. And when night comes, a single light illuminating a comfortable chair and silence throughout the rest of the house offers the reader an opportunity to enjoy the charms of the most ancient "laptop" of all.

Were the hours wasted when, during one high school summer, I got lost in the remote landscapes created by Joseph Conrad, or in the English villages brought to life by Thomas Hardy, or on the arid Spanish terrain, courtesy of Miguel de Cervantes, brought right from La Mancha to my den in Mobile?

Some of this reading, thankfully, was directed by teachers who offered summer lists of novels, as was the case with my 11th-grade teacher, Bob Morrell—now an Atlanta stockbroker—who led me to Thomas Wolfe's *Look Homeward, Angel*. When I read this story of an exuberant but alienated youth growing up in a close-knit yet constrictive Southern town, I suspected the book was secretly about me. The fact that my friends knew the novel was really about them only bound us readers closer together.

The capacity of teen-agers to enter the experiences of other teens through reading is one of our greatest resources—for teaching compassion. My wife is a teacher, and when she tells me of the profound responses of middle-school students to reading *The Diary of Anne Frank*, I have hope for a better world.

What responsibility do we have, as parents, to ensure that our children will spend time with books?

Surely our powers of persuasion are limited, especially in this day when pictures on screens—from the TV to the computer—are jazzy, easy and fun. Encouraging reading is like encouraging any other habit: If kids never watch their elders sitting down with a book, then why should they?

And if we never suggest they read books or that these everyday treasures are rich, delightful, moving, intimate, dramatic and solitary, then who is ultimately to blame?

It's easy to despair. In a recent *New Yorker* magazine, the novelist Philip Roth tells an interviewer, "'Every year, seventy readers die and only two are replaced. That's a very easy way to visualize it.'"

But I believe more readers can still be made, and summer is the time to entice them.

What we have to offer is as ancient as the storybook drawings scratched on the walls of caves in France, and as new as the print on the bookstore shelf just this morning. All the cable TV channels and CD-rom entertainment in the world can't compete.

AZALEA TIME
(March, 2001)

No bright symbol of coastal Alabama endures more richly than our azaleas—Pride of Mobile, Formosa, Daphne Salmon—turning ordinary street corners into glorious showplaces shaded red, pink and purple, with splashes of white. Soft and dramatic, the flowers, like silent clocks, signal us that another year has gone round.

When we are kids, we imagine that azalea season goes on forever, like childhood itself. Our growing older, of course, brings the realization that, within a couple weeks after we herald them, the flowers will fade.

This morning, though—look quick!—they burst forth in yards, spill over fences, rise against the walls of the grandest, and humblest, of our buildings.

They can be organized in spectacular displays worthy of tourist destinations, as at Bellingrath Gardens. But they also are resolutely democratic, growing freely wherever planted, in front of the gas station on Scenic Highway 98 in Fairhope, down quiet streets of the DeTonti Square district in downtown Mobile, along Grand Boulevard in Midtown, around Cottage Hill Park.

Wildly, they continue to appear, as on cue, long after those who planted them are gone. In vacant lots where homes once stood, the memory of long-ago occupants is kept alive by the return of their azaleas. When I pass the old, abandoned Point Clear School on Baldwin County Highway 32, I'm fascinated by the azaleas near the cracked doors and broken windows, blooms as rich as any hothouse flower tended by a horticulturist.

Like Mobile Bay and hurricanes and damp heat, azaleas are inseparable from the mythology of our town. Azalea Road, the Azalea Trail, Azalea Trail Maids, the Azalea Trail Run—the names say it all. (The only girl I've ever met who was named Azalea was from…guess where?)

Recently, watching creaky home movies my father made of us growing up, I suspected that many families, like ours, saw azaleas in more than one front yard episode. I find myself, a father armed with a sleek video camera, filming azalea scenes pretty much the same.

The images are imprinted elsewhere, of course, even more deeply. When we travel far from our small curve of planet, we look back, in our best memories, not through rose-colored glasses, but through the wash of hometown blooms.

I don't know what most New Yorkers envisioned while peering at the window display of azaleas in Macy's Department Store in Manhattan many years ago, but I—pressed up there, too—glimpsed the house on Williams Court, where I grew up in Midtown Mobile, where azaleas burst forth against walls of old brick.

In other cities well north of us, when I've noticed azaleas for sale in garden shops, I've thought that, like Southern accents or grits or blues music, these creations were appealing but dislocated.

I know that I am not alone in this, having interviewed folks who grew up in Mobile and live all over the country, from Chicago to Washington to Paris. Azaleas, like seafood gumbo, like Mardi Gras bands, are among the delights they recall. "Want to visit?" we tell our friends from other parts of the country. "Come in March."

The flowers, welcoming us everywhere, also know our sadness.

Within recent weeks I've walked through the azaleas to the funeral of a friend's father in Pinecrest Cemetery in Mobile. In Daphne, just the other night, I drove through towering azaleas to make my way to Mercy Medical, to visit an ailing, elderly friend.

The freighted branches—profuse and beautiful—seemed both a rebuke to human suffering, and an expression of earthly majesty all too soon left behind. There may be ancient lore surrounding lilies and roses and dogwood blossoms, but azaleas have a story, to us, of their own.

As I drove away from Mercy Medical, through the Baldwin County night, the azaleas, rampant at roadside, lining my way, made me realize that we do not require a monumental natural wonder—the Atlantic Ocean or the Grand Canyon—to provoke a sense of awe.

Our azaleas will do just fine.

WELCOME BACK, DAWN
(fall, 2001)

In ancient Rome they called her Aurora—the goddess of the dawn, sister of the gods of the moon and sun. Just this morning, on the Eastern Shore of Mobile Bay, I watched her moving through the pine forests from the east, her gown a pale red light, her face softly illuminating the sky. I know Aurora has been there all summer long, but, from the final school bell of last spring until the first of this year, I'd folded her far away. After all, I count myself among those commonly known as "night people," the folks who run out for a gallon of milk at midnight, who check the overnight news upon arriving back home. The lamp on in my living room at 2 a.m. is not the signal of an insomniac, but of a man who enjoys staying up late, reading when it's quiet, listening to frogs croak in the bushes and owls hoot in the trees.

For those of us with youngsters in the house, though, the school bell changes our schedules. The peeking of the sun over the pines, the cry of a rooster, the buzz of the early-morning news shows—these phenomena become familiar occurrences again. Those of us prone to sleep until the last moment possible before leaping out of bed find ourselves shamed into stumbling up early once more. How can a dad lie lazily abed while the rest of the household is up packing bookbags and readying bag lunches? When "Morning Edition" is purring from WHIL, and Nancy and Don are amiably relaying the news on Fox 10?

Witnessing the first light of day makes me realize how comfortable the morning is in relation to the 97-degree afternoon; that dew is still heavy on the ground; that plenty of neighbors are up already, pouring coffee while poring over newspapers, having gotten a jump on the day.

Morning people and night people. We are of different sensibilities, though we meet in the broad middle of day. My friend William and I have lunch periodically and catch up on each other's family news. When I ask him if he gets up early, he tells me that he rises every day at 4:30 a.m. "Why?" I ask. As a turkey hunter, William explains, he maintains the hunter's clock, whatever the season. I nod, having once been his guest at a hunting lodge. He'd shaken me awake at an hour I'd usually be just turning into bed, enabling me to smear camouflage on my face before hiking a mile under a starry sky, listening for a gobbler. He's hardly alone in his pre-dawn waking. At the gym he visits by 5:30 a.m., he tells me, he and other folks are working out, invigorated at day's start.

Some people believe that waking early is healthier than staying up late. In fact, the morning is traditionally associated with ambition, and possibility, and a full workday ahead; the late night with romance and mystery and crime. A generation ago the only 3 a.m. activities in a town like Mobile—outside of factory or hospital work—might well have been decadent, or even illicit. Yesteryear's late-night was a cloak hiding private lives.

Now, you can drive to a pharmacy on Airport Boulevard that never closes and shop for school supplies for your children at 3 a.m.; you can push your shopping cart up the aisles of a Wal-Mart, filling your basket with groceries for the approaching hour of breakfast. You can visit our most celebrated all-night institution—Krispy Kreme—realizing that you're joining millions of other Americans in fueling one of the hottest investments on the New York Stock Exchange. The image of the brightly-lit, 24-hour doughnut emporium on Government Street in Midtown Mobile, for example, is no longer a window onto forlorn men dipping sugary circles into black coffee in the small hours; it's the symbol of a business with local family ties and Mobile locations since 1953 that's ahead of the nation's business curve.* You can pump gas, or buy a magazine, or eat at IHOP or Denny's or Waffle House. The night people are inching ahead.

When I was a teen-ager I sometimes watched TV on weekends until it signed off. About midnight the screen would show an American flag, or military jets flying in formation, and hum with the stirring strains of the National Anthem. Then it would fill with noisy snow. All through town, living room lights would be shut off. Our collective Taps had been sounded. Now, TV is always going—late shows, and late-late shows, and overnight blending into early-morning shows.

Beyond television, cyberspace has bent the clock all out of shape, like the famous painting of the Spanish surrealist Salvador Dali—a watch, melted like a piece of grilled cheese. Surfing the Internet—or visiting chat rooms—one finds an unsleeping nation of researchers and news junkies and gossips. It's enough to make even Aurora tired as she raises herself up from the bed of darkness to start her sweep through coastal Alabama once again.

THANKSGIVING AROMATHERAPY
(November 2000)

Many years ago, on a late November day when I was a junior in college, I found myself far from the world of Pilgrims and gobblers on a study-abroad program in Aberdeen, Scotland. While enjoying ourselves in the land of bagpipes and haggis, the other American students and I, inevitably, put in a request for turkey and stuffing come the fourth Thursday of the month. At a party coordinated for our suddenly homesick group, we gathered around a table to see what the ruddy-faced Scottish cook, who made tasty fish and chips, had done with the recipe for roast turkey, stuffing and sweet potato pie.

I don't recall the taste, but I remember the aroma: the fat, glistening turkey, the sharp, fruity cranberries. For each of us—one from Dallas, another from small-town Pennsylvania, this one from Mobile—the aromas transported us quickly back home.

Thanksgiving, of course, is a time for gratitude for our health and well-being, and prayers for those who are ill, hungry, and oppressed. It is a time, for many, of travel and yearning for home, often for the dining room table where we gathered as children. Remembering that table can bring melancholy—especially when we envision a chair where a loved one, now departed, used to be—but the memory is sustaining, too.

It is also a time in which we breathe in deeply the air around us, plumped as it is with the scent of the occasion.

Of all the American holidays, Thanksgiving is the one richest for the senses. While there is much to be said for firing the grill and rotating the chicken on the Fourth of July, summer heat and mosquitoes vie for our attention. We have Mardi Gras here, which means king cakes, cotton candy and Moon Pies—food, and their smells, which might buoy us, but hardly are comforting.

By contrast, the drift from pumpkin pie on your mother's table, or the banana mincemeat bread your wife is making in the kitchen, provides the sense of a circle unbroken, good conversation, the promise of a nap.

Beyond turkey on the table is a cornucopia of aromas—cinnamon; ham with cloves; red wine; mulled cider; melted marshmallows; stuffing; roasted pecans; vases festive with roses. Wood smoke, pine needles, maple leaves turned late-autumn-red and crushed underfoot—these smells, outdoors, are in the end-of-November air, too.

In the visual world we inhabit, we too often forget that the most mystical of our five senses is right in front of our noses—no, even closer. The movie theaters this long weekend will be packed with kids and grownups eager to catch the holiday blockbusters, but the scent wafting from the cinematic landscapes will be exclusively that of popcorn. Will anybody give it a second thought?

The recollection of a smell takes you back home more quickly than either a long-distance phone call or a Boeing 747. In New York City one spring day, catching the scent of a Japanese magnolia tree, it took me a micro-second to be transported to the block in Mobile's Midtown neighborhood where I'd grown up.

Walking along the piers of an Atlantic coast town, catching the odor of pitch and fish and saltwater, I was suddenly near the docks of the Port of Mobile.

My wife, far more attuned to the sense of smell than I am (she contends women tend to be, more than men), tells me that each person's house even has a defining scent. I'm oblivious. On a family vacation, in Vancouver, British Columbia, she even led me into a store advertising "aromatherapy." As we uncorked and sniffed sample vials that promised "For Calm," "For Well-Being," "For Harmony," I wondered if I were missing something. As I find in a florist shop, or a perfumerie, all the offerings blend into one.

Perhaps, today, I should hang a sign on our kitchen door: "Real Aromatherapy. Take a whiff."

* Unfortunately, Krispy Kreme closed in 2011.

COMING HOME: IN MEMORY OF ROBERT CROSHON

Frye Gaillard

It was my first encounter with the great southern sin.

I remember it now as a warm and sunny day, though it must have been some time in the fall, for the leaf piles were burning, and the sweet scent drifted through the neighborhood. Robert Croshon was there with his wheelbarrow, and I was five years old and ready for a ride. It was something of a ritual for us by now. Every Saturday on his way to work, Robert would stop to pick up his "helper." That was me—the youngest grandchild in a family for whom Robert had worked for thirty years.

Robert was a black man, a person of indestructible good humor, and then as now, the gentlest soul that I ever met. He was a gardener by trade, scratching out a living for himself and his family, and on the day I'm remembering he was working in my grandfather's vegetable patch, chopping at the weeds and tugging at the meanest clumps of wild onions. My own contributions were a little more random; I chased away the Indians in the bamboo hedges and practiced high-jumping across the collard greens.

It was, however, an exuberant partnership that we had forged, and when it was time for lunch, we headed for the Big House, as my grandfather's dwelling was known in those days. The extended family was beginning to gather, and it was an impressive spread on the dining room table—fried chicken, turnip greens, a platter of biscuits. But as we took our places around the great cluttered feast, Robert found a chair by himself in the kitchen.

To a five-year-old it made no sense. "Robert!" I called. "Come on in here."

I knew immediately that I had made a mistake, for my aunt quickly shot me a look that could kill. "Shame on you!" she said with a hiss. "Shame on you for hurting Robert's feelings."

This was Mobile in 1951, and I remembered that moment as the years went by and the civil rights movement descended on the South. I was a teenager when the movement hit its stride, and for me at least, those festering doubts that began when I was five—the secret suspicions that the world around me didn't make a lot of sense—finally erupted into full-scale rebellion. I went away to college, and I was still in a struggle with the issue of race when Martin Luther King paid a visit to the campus.

It is safe to say that in Mobile, where I had been raised, King was probably the ultimate pariah. My own family had first taken notice of him in the closing weeks of 1955, when he became the spokesman for the Montgomery bus boycott. He was only 26 years old at the time, but despite his youth and relative inexperience, he seemed to be so sure of himself.

"We are not wrong tonight," he declared at the first mass meeting of the Montgomery movement. "If we are wrong, the Supreme Court of this nation is wrong. If we are wrong, the Constitution of the United States is wrong. If we are wrong, God Almighty is wrong… If we are wrong, justice is a lie."

Even down in Mobile, my family and friends were incensed at the impudence of this middle class Negro and his intimations of a shredded status quo. They thought he was the most dangerous man in America. At Vanderbilt, however, where I was a student in the 1960s and first heard him speak, he seemed to be far less frightening than that. He was a smallish man with large, dark eyes that were shaded with sadness, and his manner in conversation was casual and relaxed—none of the pomp that we might have expected from a man who had recently won a Nobel Prize.

Only when King began to speak to the whole student body did the full implications of his presence become clear. It was true enough that he stood as an apostle of reconciliation, holding out the olive branch to white Americans. But he was also making his militant demands—not only for the laws that would end segregation, but for a change of heart and mind in the country that would enable us all to live up to our values.

As an aspiring journalist, working in the summers for my hometown paper, I knew immediately that this was a struggle I would have to write about. But I decided also that I could not do it from the state of Alabama. I tried it for a while. In 1968, as I limped out of college, newly endowed with a degree in history, I returned to Mobile and took a job with the *Mobile Register*. The paper, however, was not especially interested in the civil rights story, and family tensions were still on the rise - too many uncles and cousins and friends who were astonished and angry at the things I was writing.

Searching for a more hospitable climate, I soon moved on to the *Charlotte Observer*, one of the South's most distinguished newspapers, where my first assignment was the busing controversy. It was a landmark case that compelled the community to confront its legacy of segregation. For a while, the city was thrown into turmoil, with racial fighting closing down the schools, adults throwing rocks at children on the buses, a black lawyer's offices burned to the ground.

It was a spectacle you might have seen in Alabama.

But there were other people who stepped forward also, black and white, defending the schools and the idea of integration, appealing to the better instincts of their neighbors. As the community struggled with what it wanted to be, it was, for me, a lesson in the literature of the craft, in the notion that journalists, like their upscale cousins in the world of fiction, could wrestle with the great Faulknerian themes: the human heart in conflict with itself.

All in all, for a writer in search of a place to ply his trade, it was as fine an opportunity as I could imagine. I remained in North Carolina for the next thirty years, never expecting to go home again. But then sometime in the year 2000, I was asked to do a book on the civil rights movement in Alabama, a state that had been at the heart of the struggle. Supported by Auburn University and the University of Alabama, I spent the first three years of the new millennium interviewing the veterans of that history—foot soldiers, mostly, those ordinary men and women who managed for a time to do extraordinary things.

There was Annie Cooper, an old woman now, who was beaten bloody during the Selma protests, but remembered the speech of Martin Luther King when the marchers finally made it to Montgomery. "His eyes were just a'twinklin'," she said. And there was Barbara Cross, who, as a Birmingham teenager, had survived the infamous bombing of her church, but lost four of her closest friends in the blast. J.D. Cammeron faced the cattle prods during a march in Gadsden, and Vivian Malone of Mobile took her stand for dignity as the first black student at the University of Alabama.

When the book came out, telling these stories, I met people all across Alabama who seemed to be fascinated by the history. The University of South Alabama asked me to teach a course on what I had learned, and I was suddenly face to face with an irony: the issue that had driven me out of the state was now on the verge of bringing me home.

I talked to my old friend Robert about it—Robert Croshon, my grandfather's gardener, with whom I had managed to keep in touch through the years. I would drop by to see him on visits to Mobile, talking about old times, and listening also to stories of his family. He was the proud descendant of runaway slaves, people who had fled from a Georgia plantation, but found themselves headed south instead of north when a thunderstorm blotted out the stars.

They decided to make their way to Mobile, where there was a small, but determined community of free Negroes, and I always knew that the great and unruffled dignity of Robert—his equanimity in the face of segregation—was rooted in part in the courage of his forebears.

"It's different today," he said near the end.

He was lying at the time in his hospital bed, a wispy, gray-haired man in his nineties, recently retired from his physical labors, as his heart was slowly giving up the ghost.

"It's better for all of us," I told him, handing him a copy of the book I had written.

Robert took the book and thumbed through the pages. I knew he was probably too sick to read it, but as his mind drifted back to the way it used to be, through the arc of history that had shaped us all, he seemed to be pleased.

My own feeling, as the old man nodded and laid the book at his side, was that in a way I never could have expected, it was good to be home.

NEWCOMER IN MOBILE

Yvonne Kalen

If you were not fortunate enough to have been born in Mobile, you're a newcomer. You can age in Mobile, but you'll never qualify for the designation of "Old Mobilian," but those with established traditions and long-established ancestors are the nicest people in the world. They love Mobile, and they want everyone who visits or moves to the city to love it too.

Mobilians are the most hospitable people on the face of the earth. They invite newcomers to their Krewe's Mardi Gras ball, even if they aren't asked to join. Such an invitation requires having Mobile ancestors. Nevertheless, newcomers are proud guests, and their hosts are the ones paying the dues and the expenses for the evening. Guests need only to enjoy themselves and take note that all of the excitement of Mardi Gras is privately financed.

In Mobile, those who live next door know the meaning of neighborliness. I have lived in a number of cities in the U.S.A. and never have I had a neighbor as thoughtful and kind as the "Old Mobilian" who lives next door. I have opened my door a number of mornings to find surprises in bags or boxes—all edible.

Mobilians pass on to others their appreciation of the many wonderful aspects of the city. I'm so completely sold on Mobile that when I visit another place, I sound as if I had been sent by The Chamber of Commerce. I soon realized that I wasn't just talking myself into the superlatives I was using, I was reflecting how I truly felt about Mobile. I must admit that as a product of a long line of professional Southerners, I didn't have to get used to the language, the customs or the food: the spicy gumbo and the abundance of fresh seafood. That was part of my heritage, and I'm proud of it.

Mobile adds a southern flavor that is particularly its own. It's not just Mardi Gras and an appreciation of the past that marks the city; there is also an interest in making progress and planning for the future.

Old Mobilians are not complainers and make the best of everything. One day I was having lunch with a friend downtown when we came out of the building only to find that the rare snow that falls was coming down in surprising amounts. The going was slow and walking the icy streets was potentially treacherous. My friend, looking around with admiration and forgetting that she could fall, kept repeating: "Isn't Mobile beautiful?"

The city is especially beautiful in spring when the azaleas are in full bloom. Though their splendor lasts for not much more than a week and the plant is an ordinary bush the rest of the time, Mobilians think of it in all of its glory and name countless things in its honor. Azalea may well be one of the first words a child learns right along with Krewe, thank you, and please.

When I first moved to Mobile, I joined a group sponsored by the Welcome Wagon called "The New Mobilians." This organization provides a wonderful introduction to Mobile and enables newcomers to happily adjust to their new home. Mobile is a good place to retire, the climate is mild, and playing golf is preferable to shoveling snow!

After thirty years "The New Mobilians" organization is still going strong and investing in Mobile. Its membership reflects a growing number of newcomers, for once a person becomes involved in the community, there are other established organizations to join; people quickly find their niche. The cultural groups, vital to the city, benefit from the wide-spread interests, talents, and experience of the New Mobilians.

The schools of higher education in Mobile offer a treasure trove of classes for newcomers to enjoy. Of special interest are courses tailored for adults. The "Odyssey" program for seniors that meets at the University of South Alabama is one example. For a modest fee, members enjoy courses all year long. In addition to these classes, there are monthly luncheons for members that feature interesting topics and speakers.

A number of private clubs in Mobile have open memberships and offer additional opportunities for community involvement. The public golf and tennis clubs are excellent, and the mild weather enables them to be open year round. There is something for everyone to enjoy.

Mobile has many opportunities for the Arts. When I came to the city, the Symphony was struggling with a sizeable debt—that happily no longer exists. There is an excellent orchestra playing at the Saenger Theatre. The small ballet that was trying to get established when I first arrived is enjoying success. The Arts Council, then in its infancy, is now an effective voice of the Arts. There are now three museums in Mobile instead of just one, and they offer greatly increased space and exhibits. Russian, Chinese, French and American exhibits have enhanced the cultural stature of the area. All of this has happened during my forty years in Mobile! The city has come of age. Its wonderful and colorful past is deeply revered, and there is also a very promising future.

HONK IF YOU LOVE MOBILE

Patricia Crosby Burchfield

You don't have to be born in Mobile,
In order to love this town.
You don't have to be conceived
Under an azalea bush,
In Bienville square,
During Mardi Gras,
To claim this place as your own.

You can be an upstart, uppity
Baldwin County girl,
Who came to Mobile
Through the sloshing waves
On the causeway,
So many times that
One day she decided to stay.

She filed for citizenship
And became a naturalized Mobilian.
They said:
We'll have to have three names
That we can call for references.
She said:
Disa Stone,
Miss Gladys Baxter,
and the Peanut Man.

They asked:
How long you been comin' here?
She said:
Long enough to have seen Gone With the Wind
At the Roxy, in 1939,
And to ride through the Bankhead Tunnel
On a big yellow school bus,
When it opened, in 1941.

Long enough to have shopped at Hammels,
Downed a co'cola at Van Antwerp's,
And eaten lunch at Morrison's, downtown.
Long enough to remember Mardi Gras parades
With mules and flambeaux,
And no barricades.
That long enough?

They said it was.
Now this Baldwin County girl
Is a card-carrying,
Registered Mobilian,
Driving an SUV,
Sporting a bumper sticker:
Honk, If You Love Mobile.

from ISLE OF JOY

Franklin Daugherty

Concise Guide to the Mobile Accent
By George Belzagui
Linguist (part-time)

When southbound travelers cross the live oak / gumbo line, so close to the Gulf of Mexico, and arrive in Mobile, they may notice that the accent changes, too, into deliquescent vowels and convolute sounds totally different from the upstate twang. It was probably influenced by the many Irish and German immigrants in the nineteenth century, and no doubt by black English as well. The true Mobile accent is spoken in full feather mainly by older people these days, alas, but once you hear it you will not mistake it for any other, north or south.

After many years of research according to strict scientific methodologies, I have ascertained that no one speaks a purer version of this accent than myself. And in a relentless quest for exact observation, I have spent many years—indeed, decades—listening to myself talk, often standing for hours on end in front of the mirror watching my lips, tongue, teeth, and gums articulate these mellifluous and well-crafted phonemes. An exhausting project, yes, but not without its pleasures.

Here are some of the highlights of my research:

THE MOBILE "UI": Most "er," "ur," and "ir" sounds are pronounced "ui." For example: "What on uith did Cuitus luin in chuich?" This is quite different, I assure you, from the New Orleans or New York "oi," as in "New Joisey." The first sound of the diphthong is a short "u."

THE SHORT "A" sounds like "I" of "night," especially, for some reason, when ladies are talking. Thus "half" rhymes with "life," "pass" rhymes with "ice," "grand" with (standard English, not Southern) "grind."...

"AR" AND SOME "AL" SOUNDS sound like "au" or "aw," as in "Paul" or "saw": "Jimmy Cawter tawked about the waw."

THE MOBILE GLIDE: Long "A's" and long "O's" die a lingering death, so that "blame" becomes "blayim," or "suppose" becomes "suppouhs." Not two separate sounds, but a long Louis Armstrong shift in the back of the throat. "Felix ro-uhs from his thro-un."

THE WORDS "ON" AND "WANT" are pronounced "oin" and "woint," especially, for some reason, by younger people: "I cain't believe thatga! You're putting me oin!"

The true old-fashioned Old Mobilian speaks in a deep, low, rich, vibrating, throaty voice, and emphasizes every word slowly and carefully as though he or she were issuing the most important pronouncement ever uttered on the face of the earth.

After seeing these few examples, you will probably feel eager to hear many more of my observations about the way I talk. These are available in my recent work: *Complete Guide to the Mobile Accent*, by George Belzagui. Publlished by Kahil Q. Belzagui Memorial Library, c/o George Belzagui, New Hamilton Street, 3839 pages. $499.99.

Supplies of the book depend on the availability of the Xerox machines at the Commerce National Bank, but chances are good that it will not yet be sold out when you write.

Handy Pronouncing Lexicon
Also by George Belzagui
Historian (part-time)

Readers in California and Vladisvostok and other such far-off places may wonder how to pronounce some of the names that figure prominently in this chronicle, in which, as the author informed me, I was honored to play a small part. As president of the Iberville Historical Society (the esteemed Mrs. Odilia Belzagui, née de la Rochefoucauld, formerly Mrs. O. d.l.R. Chhhighhizola, and myself constitute the bulk of the regular membership), I am in the position to shed some light on the matter.

DE LA ROCHEFOUCAULD: The purist pronunciation, Rosh-foo-COLE, has lately been preferred by Mrs. Odilia and her distinguished niece McCorquodale, the only remaining members of this genteel and refined, though strangely forgotten, French colonial family of Mobile. Despite many hours of research in the genealogical division of the Mobile Public Library, we have been unable to find a connection with the seventeenth-century philosopher, but a breakthrough is expected any day.

The more common pronunciation, however, is ROSHfookle, which has been used for many generations here, and indeed until recently the name was written "Roshfookle." Since "Beroujon" became BERRY-john locally, "Roche" became Roach, and "Huger" became YOO-jee, ROSHfookle, too can be said without fear of stigma.

CHIGHIZOLA: Chhhhig-I-ZOE-luh. Mrs. Odilia's first husband, the late Joe Chighhizola, the bookie at McAlpin's Pool Hall on St. Francis Street (now a parking lot), exemplified all the hard-working virtues of this proud Iberian line.

ODILIA: O-DEEL-yuh. Rhymes with "camellia."

BALLERIEL: Buh-LAYR-I-el. As in Fred "Astaire-I-el," as it were. No introduction is needed to this wealthy and prominent family. Now my grandfather, Raphael Belzagui, remembered Mrs. Harmsworth Balleriel's great-grandfather, old Mr. Theo Parkhurst, when he had nothing but a fruit stand on Front Street.

BELZAGUI: BEL-za-gooey. Until my father retired in 1952 to gather the laurels of a long career in well-deserved repose, Belzagui's Shoeteria on St. Emanuel Street was a Mobile landmark. Wealth has unfortunately eluded us, but the Belzagui men became most prominent in the Knights of Columbus after arriving in Mobile from Lebanon (they were Maronite Catholics!) in the 1880s.

The pronunciation of other names, Anglo-Saxon and Celtic, we trust to the erudition of the reader.

from LET YOUR MIND RUN FREE
Harry Myers

FREDERIC

Great Frederic
Mighty Frederic
Leveler
Neither Oak
Nor Pine, Magnolia
Dogwood or Laurel
Find strength to stand
When Frederic decides
They must bow.

Frederic the leveler
Rich and poor
Young or old
Black or white
All on one level
At Frederic's height
Hoping for mercy.

Some poor trees uprooted
Set straight again
Will make it
The strongest will survive
All in nature's plan,

And how exhilarating
The show of human spirit
To dig out
Lend neighborly hands
Feel compassion,

Then say
This too will pass.

Great Frederic
You bastard
We'll not stay
Down.

from MOBILE, MOBILIANS, AND SOUTHERN WAYS
Joseph Sackett

MOBILIANS

A Mobilian is one who enjoys life at a little slower pace. Deadlines, agendas, and timetables are notional at best.

A Mobilian loves good spices, fresh food from the sea, and a good martini to share with friends. Martini glasses are considered neighborhood property.

A Mobilian is one who dutifully conducts sociological research to document the ways in which other Mobilians interact. That is why Mobile celebrates Carnival for two weeks and why Mobilians throw so many parties the rest of the year.

A Mobilian loves a good story—and is skilled at enhancing said story to make it more seductive the next time it is told.

A Mobilian nurtures all things that bloom—especially midnight backyard azalea cuttings from a neighbor's prized cuttings.

A Mobilian prefers casual dress—except for those occasions that require costume de riguer. A combination of tails, plaid pants, and two-toned suede shoes is considered casual attire, not formal.

A Mobilian loves a good scandal—and secretly encourages scandalous activities by all who are not related through paternal bloodlines.

All female Mobilians over the age of twenty-nine aspire to be a widow of Joe Cain. Each year more and more gender-perplexed Mobilians share those aspirations.

All Mobilians claim one of more adopted descendants in Church Street Cemetery and/or Confederate Rest.

Because lawyers have such a profound presence in Mobile, all Mobilians are intimate friends with a lawyer, have married a lawyer, or are serving time for shooting a lawyer.

So there you have it—all about Mobilians. If a little knowledge is a dangerous thing, you are now armed and dangerous.

AZALEA SPRING

Rob Gray

---

azaleas paint mobile
in a signature sea
of purplish pink
splattered against
greens of early spring

the mossy haggard
reverence of live oaks
drapes this symphony
in quiet subtle dignity
framing the timeless
character of an old city

the azalea trail curves
in endless arrhythmic lines
linking stately mansions
with humble cottages
throughout midtown

when easter comes early
to my front porch
swinging explodes
with significations
while momentary markers
of dying march wither
to trodden mottled nothingness
in still emerging spring

but this splash of sublimity
brings sustenance
for more mundane months
till march returns
with its sea of pink
under the languid live oaks

MARDI GRAS IN MOBILE

...in Mobile, the nights are magic—and there has always been, and there is always, much to ponder in this city of live oaks and uncommon shade.

—Sue B. Walker, *Uncommon Shade*

MOBILE MYSTIC SOCIETIES

Father Abram Ryan

The olden golden stories of the world,
That stirred the past,
And now are dim as dreams,
The lays and legends which the bards unfurled
In lines that last,
All-rhymed with glooms and gleams.
Fragments and fancies writ on many a page
By deathless pen,
And names, and deeds that all along each age,
Thrill hearts of men.
And pictures erstwhile framed in sun or shade
Of many climes,
And life's great poems that can never fade
Nor lose their chimes;
And acts and facts that must forever ring
Like temple bells,
That sound or seem to sound where angels sing
Vesper farewells;
And scenes where smiles are strangely touching tears,
'Tis ever thus,
Strange Mystics! In the meeting of the years
Ye bring to us
All these, and more; ye make us smile and sigh,
Strange power ye hold!
When New Year kneels low in the star-aisled sky
And asks the Old
To bless us all with love, and life, and light,
And when they fold
Each other in their arms, ye stir the sight,
We look, and lo!
The past is passing, and the present seems
To wish to go.
Ye pass between them on your mystic way
Thro' scene and scene,

The Old Year marches through your ranks, away
To what has been,
The while the pageant moves, it scarcely seems
A part of earth;
The Old Year dies—and heaven crowns with gleams
The New Year's birth.
And you—you crown yourselves with heaven's grace
To enter here:
A prayer-ascending from an orphan face,
Or just one tear
May meet you in the years that are to be
A blessing rare.
Ye pass beneath the arch of charity.
Who passeth there
Is blest in heaven, and is blest on earth,
And God will care,
Beyond the Old Year's death and New Year's birth,
For each of you, ye Mystics! Everywhere.

DR. WILLOUGHBY RETURNS
Carolyn Haines

The February wind rattled the slender limbs of the tallow trees on Grand Boulevard, causing a strand of purple beads to chatter. Cissy deMur sat on the steps of the little white cottage and held her head in her hands, her elbows on her knees.

"I hate Mardi Gras," she said to the wind. "Some stupid jerk has been throwing trash in my trees again. Next they'll pee in my yard. It's the same thing every year."

The slender limbs fluttered wildly.

Cissy stared up at the tree. "I have a right to hate Mardi Gras," she said with some belligerence. "I hate the stupid crowds and the mess they leave behind. I hate the way people push and shove for nasty candy, cheap trinkets and those goddawful moon pies. I hate the people who dress up and think they're so la-di-da." She picked up a rock and threw it at the beads hanging in the tree.

She felt the pressure of something against her shin and glanced down to find a black cat staring straight up at her. His golden gaze was unwavering.

Cissy didn't like felines. They were hairy and had claws. "Shoo! Get away from my porch! If you hang around until the parade tonight, you'll probably get hurt."

The black cat put a paw on her foot and gave a sad meow.

"So, you hate Mardi Gras, too?" Cissy felt a sudden kinship with the black cat. "I wish they'd cancel Mardi Gras this year."

"Is that right?"

Surprised by the unexpected male voice, Cissy stared at the elderly gentleman with a shock of white hair and amused blue eyes. "Who are you?"

"Oh, I'm just a representative for the holy order of The Need for More Pleasure and Less Development. That's TNMPLD for short. You can call me Dr. Willoughby."

"I don't talk to strangers," Cissy said, standing up. She felt the pressure of the cat's claws in her calf. Not enough to break the skin, but enough to get her attention. She was right the first time. The cat was a nuisance.

"Have a seat, dahling," the man said. "I have something for you."

"I don't accept things from strangers," Cissy said.

"Oh, what a shame." The elderly gentleman reached into his coat and pulled out a magnificent mask of peacock feathers. "Isn't it lovely?"

Cissy's hand reached out involuntarily for the mask. "It's beautiful. It's the most beautiful mask I've ever seen." Then she remembered. "I don't wear masks. I don't go in for all that Mardi Gras foolishness. Masks! The very idea. As if I had something to hide."

The man held it out to her. "Why don't you try it on?"

Cissy snatched her hand back. "I said I don't accept gifts from strangers." She was ready to go inside. The man was watching her with what seemed to be amused pity. How dare he? She tried to lift her foot but realized she could no longer control her legs. She was stuck to the steps.

"Hey!"

"Don't panic," the man said. "I've come to see you because I want to help you."

"I don't accept help from strangers." She twisted and struggled, but it was as if her shoes and feet had been bonded to the wooden step. How had this happened?

"You're going to accept my help," the man said. "And since you know my name, we're no longer strangers." He held out the mask. "Take it."

"I don't—" To Cissy's surprise, she saw her hand reaching out for the mask. She felt the weight of it in her hand, and she saw it slowly approaching her face as she lifted it to cover her eyes. The feathers tickled her nose a little, and she closed her eyes.

She heard Dr. Willoughby's musical voice as if from a great distance. There was another sound. The tinkling of the Mardi Gras beads in the tallow tree.

"When you open your eyes, Cissy Louise deMur, you'll see many things. I've come to you, in the finest Dickensian tradition, as a gift from the gods. Use what you learn wisely."

Cissy, still fuming from the use of her middle name, opened her eyes and found she was walking in a vast building. Her footsteps echoed, and she stepped over little scraps of brightly colored paper.

In the middle of a huge, empty space was a man sitting on a stool, his back bent in abject despair. When he saw Cissy approaching, he began to talk.

"My design for the floats was brilliant. They would have floated down the streets of Mobile like a dream. 'Oz' was the theme. Can you imagine the Emerald City? Horses of different colors! Munchkins! It would have been magnificent. And now it will never be." The light went out of his eyes and he slumped over again. "The year 2020 will go down in infamy as the year Mardi Gras was murdered."

"What happened?" Cissy was almost afraid to ask.

"The fanatics took control. Instead of parades and dances and parties, all of the folks of Mobile are going to have to recite scriptures and political manifestos."

Cissy's eyes widened. "No floats!"

"None," the float-maker said. "No parades."

"Why?"

"The fanatics decided it was too much fun. They don't like for the masses to get all excited and happy. It makes them want to play instead of work. It's bad for productivity. Some even say it's bad for the soul."

The sound of tinkling beads caught her attention. Before Cissy could say another thing, she saw the man begin to waver and disappear. It was as if a fog swept over her, and soon she had the sense of traveling at a blinding speed. She felt dizzy and closed her eyes, and when she opened them, she was standing on a dirt street with horses and wagons all around her.

A group of men were gathered beneath an oak tree. They looked rag-tag and three of them were limping.

"We'll trick the Yankees and have our Mardi Gras," one of them said. "We're under the boot-heel of the enemy and we can't even have a drink or dance. But we'll show 'em we're not licked. They may kill us, but they can't stop us from having Mardi Gras. No damn law can stop carnival." The men suddenly looked at Cissy.

"Pardon me, ma'am. I wasn't aware a lady was present." He gave a sweeping bow.

"Is it really against the law to have Mardi Gras?" Cissy recognized a few of the buildings—enough to know she was indeed in Mobile, though it was a Mobile long past.

"Indeed it is, little lady," the spokesman said. "But that's going to change. We're going to have a surprise visit from Chief Slacabamorinico. He's going to show our tormenters that we aren't beaten yet. Not by a long shot. Mardi Gras is our way of saying we'll never be defeated."

There was the sound of a horse and carriage driving by, and also the sound of beads rattling in a February wind. The fog began to cover Cissy before she could say anything else. In a moment she felt the strange sense of travel again. When she opened her eyes, she was standing on a familiar street corner in downtown Mobile.

"Mardi Gras is just getting too expensive," a suited man said. "It costs the city a fortune."

"But it brings in a fortune in revenue," another man in a suit replied.

"Perhaps it does, but that's only because no one has sued. The liability is incredible. And all for a good time. I just don't know that it's worth it."

"I see your point. As much as I enjoy the parades, I'm a realist. Perhaps we should move Mardi Gras inside. We could charge an admittance fee. We could restrict those who attended. Keep out the rabble, you know."

"That's an idea," the first man said with some enthusiasm. "We'd have to set the plans in secret. If the people got wind of this..." Both men started walking toward Cissy. Though she tried to get out of their way, she gasped as they walked straight through her.

She'd just recovered her breath when she heard the chink-chink of the beads yet again. She turned around and Dr. Willoughby was standing at her elbow.

"Why are you showing me this?" she asked. "I can see that the floats bring beauty and joy to many people and that Mardi Gras has a lot of history and tradition behind it, but I have no say-so over what happens in Mobile."

"Ah, but that's where you're wrong. You, like everyone else in town, has the power to make Mardi Gras a wonderful tradition, or to cancel it. Mardi Gras is a time for fun and play, a time to dance and party. Lent follows right on its heels, and that's a time for contemplation and sacrifice. Don't you see it's the balance that we need?"

"I'd never thought of Mardi Gras in that way, as part of the balance."

"Mardi Gras is the mirth and fantasy, the dream and delight. It's a time for forgetting your woes and giving yourself to the pleasure of life. If you can't do that, you can't really give yourself to mediation or prayer. Humans need both joy and sorrow. One is sweet only because of the other."

"I see," Cissy said, and suddenly she did. "Mardi Gras is only one part of life's experience." She slowly lowered the mask from her face. "Thank you, Dr. Willoughby."

Turning around in a circle she searched for Dr. Willoughby, but there was no sign of the elderly gent. She was standing on the steps of her Grand Boulevard home with only a black cat for company.

She looked around for Dr. Willoughby once again before she had to accept that she'd been daydreaming. But what a daydream! It was the craziest thing, and just when she'd been thinking how much she dreaded the season. The odd thing, though, was now she felt a desire to attend the parades. She wanted to yell, "Hey, Mister!" and catch the beads and candy that was thrown.

In fact, she wanted to attend at least one ball. She wanted to dance and sing and skip in the streets. Soon the season would be over, the streets swept, and Mardi Gras just another memory. But at least this year, she'd have memories of fun and pleasure.

She began walking into her house when she realized she was holding something in her hand. She looked down to see the most extraordinary mask—a peacock feather mask.

The black cat leaped down the steps and started down the street, running to catch up with the figure of an elderly gentleman who was dancing in the street, purple, green and gold beads ching-chinging as he went.

First printed in the February 12, 2002 *Mobile Register*

NO PUMPKIN, NO GLASS SLIPPER, NO FAIRY GODMOTHER

Steve Joynt

Francine dropped down into the old chair with an audible groan. She fished a Winston Light 100 out of the scrunched pack, lit it, exhaled the smoke with an air of relief and gingerly patted her foot-tall pile of stiffly sprayed hair as if it might fall.

"I tell you what," she said. "I hate this time of year. Really hate it."

"C'mon, Francine. Hate?" Cindy asked, while standing in a corner of the break room with her thin arms folded across her chest. Cindy had heard this one—Francine Tirade Number 327—plenty of times, but it usually amused her to egg Francine on.

"Mardi Gras. Pbbbbbbb. They can have it," she said, following with another long drag on the cigarette. "All of those precious women and their precious daughters, driving their precious cars here to buy their precious gowns for their precious balls. And ugly? Girl, when they fell out of the ugly tree, they hit every branch on the way down."

Cindy tried hard not to smile. "I don't know," Cindy said. "I think it sounds really nice, all of those people dressed up, the fancy masks, the dancing, the…"

"Oh, please," Francine cut in, "they get drunk, they fall down, they think they're having fun. Believe me, I been to a couple of those shindigs, and I was not impressed. There was hardly any food."

"When you get my age, sugar, you'll see how things really are."

Cindy was pretty sure she could already see how things really are. She was 28 years old, married once, divorced, living in a broken-down apartment just outside Mobile with a no-count, jobless, cheating boyfriend. She stretched her skills, talent and experience to the limit to work her job as a sales clerk at On The Town Gowns and made precious little money doing it.

She was quiet and cute, but her looks weren't going to last forever. It was only a matter of time before her boyfriend, Ubie Duncan, was going to knock her or someone else up and leave. She never kidded herself, but she still thought of herself as a romantic. And she really, desperately just wanted to feel her heart beat again.

Then again, Cindy saw Francine pretty well too. Francine Purvis was lazy, crude and selfish. She was burned out on life and her job after selling dresses for 32 years. She never saw her husband anymore, and her kids never visited her.

She could be sweet, sickly sweet, to a customer, then stick out her tongue as soon as the person's back was turned. She was funny, but in a sad way. More than anything, Cindy did not want to become Francine.

"Mardi Gras," Francine sputtered. "Bah, humbug."

There was a noise at the back door, the boom, boom, boom of someone kicking it impatiently. Cindy walked over as if she didn't know who it would be. It was, of course, Ubie.

"Hey, baby," he said, a little slowly and with a little slur. "Hey, I'm goin' with the boys to the Trough, an' I'm a little light. How'bout 20?"

"I'm about to get off work, Ubie; can't you wait for me?" she said, trying to sound annoyed when she was mostly just tired. "Awwwwww, but baby," he started to whine, "the boys're already there an..."

"Here's 10. That's all I got," she said quickly, just wanting the display to be over. He ran off, shakily, and she closed the door.

"Oh, he is a prize," Francine said, chuckling and coughing at the same time. "He's a keeper. Gotta take him home to mama right away."

Suddenly Francine wasn't funny anymore. "Honestly girl," Francine pressed, "what do you see in that good-for-nothin? When he goes to prison or worse, how's that gonna help you?"

Marva, the store manager, stuck her head in the door. "OK, y'all," Marva said in a singsong voice that was just a little too deep. "It's closing time." Cindy was certain that between the linebacker's shoulders and the voice when Marva was born, they didn't exactly put her in a pink bassinet.

"Closing time, hot damn," Francine said. In one swift motion, she grabbed her canvas tote bag and waddled out the back door, never looking back.

"Cindy, can you be a dear and lock up?" Marva asked.

"No problem," Cindy said quietly.

After Marva left, Cindy turned the "Open" sign around, locked the front door and started the cashing out process at the register.

She looked up when there was a knock at the front door and saw a good-looking man, probably in his mid-30s, motioning, asking if he could come in. He had an On the Town Gowns bag in his hands. Oh, yeah, she thought, that's the guy who came in the other day with his girlfriend. They were buying her a gown for the Mystic something-or-other ball.

Cindy walked over to the front door and recalled how the man doted over his girlfriend, who was anything but impressed. Cindy noted that while the girl was far more made-up, she wasn't any better looking than Cindy, and they were both about the same size.

When the girl couldn't make up her mind, Cindy recommended her favorite gown, the dark green one with one shoulder. She brought it out for the man's sake, not the girl's, and he snapped it up while the girlfriend still found reasons to pout.

"I'm sorry, I know you're closed, but I need to return this," the man said from outside. Cindy smiled and flipped the lock open.

He opened the door and walked in as Cindy headed back for the counter.

"Was there a problem with the dress?" Cindy said with concern in her voice.

"No, the dress is great," the man said, "I really love it. It's just that I no longer have a girlfriend to hang it on." He smiled. "She told me she no longer had a need for my services."

Stupid girl, Cindy thought. "Oh, I'm so sorry," she said, trying hard to look sorry.

"Well, you were such a great help to us and so nice, I almost hate to bring it back," he said, "but I don't think it will fit me."

They both laughed, and she went to work filling out a store credit form while they exchanged pleasantries. His name was Dave, and he owned three auto parts shops. In a moment, it was over, and he was heading for the door.

Then he stopped and slowly turned with a pained look on his face, like he was Columbo or something. "You know, I'll bet you've been to a hundred of these Mardi Gras things," he said.

"No," she shook her head, "not a one."

"Really?" he took a step back toward her. "Well, if I knew your name, I could probably invite you to this one."

"Um, uh, Cindy," she said quickly.

"Cindy, would you like to go to the ball with me on Thursday night?" Dave asked, taking another step toward her like she might dart off somewhere. In fact, she was thinking about it.

"I, well, I'd love to," she stammered. "Great," he said, as he tore his store credit form into four pieces and laid it on the dark green dress with one shoulder. "I'll pick you up here at 8."

He turned and left, and she stood and watched, her mouth slightly ajar. Then she distinctly felt her heart slamming hard against her rib cage, and she hugged the green dress just a little.

First printed in the March 10, 2002 *Mobile Register*.

from THE GIRL IN THE FALL-AWAY DRESS
Michelle Richmond

"SLACABAMORINICO"

The Sunday before Fat Tuesday in the port city of Mobile, revelers dance on Joe Cain's grave in the Church Street cemetery. In 1866, Joe Cain rode through the streets of Mobile on the back of a coal wagon, dressed as Slacabamorinico, the legendary Chickasaw chief. Joe Cain and his crew made a general ruckus. An old mule plodded along before them. "Take this," Joe said to the Union troops who occupied the city.

Those who dance on Joe Cain's grave are quick to tell you it all started here, in the streets of Mobile in eighteen and sixty-six. They christen the headstone with beer bottles, water the grass around his grave with straight bourbon and piss. Men dress in women's clothing. Women stand on shifting balconies of old French hotels, lift their shirts for passing floats, bare their breasts to the kindly spirit of Joe Cain. Joe Cain's bones dance a knock-kneed lay-down kind of dance at the sight of the bare-chested happy women. On Joe Cain's grave, teenaged boys get laid for the first time, and the heat of their quick love seeps down into the fertile earth. Slacabamorinico himself is rumored to be buried somewhere on the outskirts of Mobile County, in an unmarked grave near an abandoned skating rink.

The year before Hurricane Frederick, our father took Darlene and Celia and me to the Crewe of Columbus parade. We clambered to catch plastic necklaces and chocolate doubloons, felt the crowd crushing forward as we sang the Moon Pie chant. A big man in overalls nearly knocked me over when he reached out to catch a shower of Jolly Ranchers. He stepped on my foot and sloshed beer on my shirt. On the way home I ate twenty-six Now & Laters and vomited out the window of our Galaxy 500. When we got home our mother was waiting at the front door "You smell like beer!" she said, dragging me inside. I felt grown up and slightly sinful, like the prodigal child come home. My mother was so angry she locked my father out of the house. Late into the evening he paid penance for the debauchery we had witnessed, sitting on the doorstep staring out at the street. Years later I would learn of the infamous Cowbellions, with their rakes and hoes and cowbells, their bovine inclinations, their triumphant march through the streets of Mobile decades before the war. Drunk on whiskey and New Year, they rang their bells and clanged their rakes until the whole city awoke. In their hearts that night there was no inkling of the coming War of Northern Aggression, no thought of the slaves who peered in disbelief from the dim windows of their shanties. Mobilians don't know that the party has long since ended, clinging hardheadedly to the notion that the Confederates won the war.

UNCOMMON SHADE
Sue B. Walker

Ye who read are still among the living, but I who write shall have long since gone my way into the region of shadows. For indeed strange things shall happen, and many secret things be known, and many centuries shall pass away, ere these memorials be seen of men. And, when seen, there will be some to disbelieve, and some to doubt, and yet a few who will find much to ponder upon in the characters here graven with a stylus of iron.
from Edgar Allan Poe's "Shadow: a Parable" (1835).

The city was wrapped in a cloak of fog so thick that the boatman was indistinguishable in the mist. He had been lost for over two hours and had been expected to arrive at the foot of Government Street before 8:00 p.m., in time for those in the vessel behind his punt to disembark and arrive at the Tricentennial Ball celebrating Mobile's 300th birthday and the start of the Mardi Gras season. The visitation had been arranged before the millennium. The entourage would be a total surprise.

It is said that those who leave Mobile always want to return. It is said that perhaps devotion like oxygen is valenced in the water. It is said that Mobile is a city unlike any other, and although it has been described as "crazy," the madness is only another word for love—like "crazy in love," like "madly in love," like the kind of love that endures beyond the grave. As Eugene Walter says, "We're not like other people, here on the Gulf of Mexico. Our mystical realm is founded on phantoms, on long twilights, on friendly demons, and in the evening, we are watchful for our ghosts."

This evening, however, at the beginning of the Mardi Gras season, Mary Dees Dodge was curiously anxious. She had been told that following the Grand Dance, she would call out the names of the dignitaries as they removed the masks shielding their eyes and strode to the center of the ballroom floor. Everyone would sing "Happy Birthday Mobile," and "Mobile" just as Julius La Rosa sang it on the "Ed Sullivan Show" and made it the nation's, as well as Mobile's song. It had been argued that "Cheeseburger in Paradise" should be a featured song, but Mobile wasn't part of the title. The tune was rejected.

Mary had not been apprised of a single moniker prior to the moment the mayor would hand her a decorated scroll with the name of each guest on a tiny tag attached to the ribbon that bound it. He had, in fact, locked the scrolls in the city vault for secrecy.

Ann Bestheart, whose melodious voice lent dignity and grace to any occasion, the mayor himself and other dignitaries who had been at the previous evening's screening of "We Are Mobile: The Spirit of a Place and Its People," were vibrant, splendid, and totally alive as they awaited the moment Mobile would announce at the guests who would later inaugurate a new Mardi Gras Crewe.

As the moment of recognition neared, the tension was almost unbearable. Martin Dawson had been waiting at the Dock for over an hour. He was alarmed at the fog, for he couldn't see a yard out into the bay. Perhaps it was the warmth of the January evening that intensified the mist. "What if all our plans go awry?" the mayor asked.

"Don't worry," Ann Bestheart replied. She had sneaked away from the ball to accompany the mayor to the place where the houseboat and the punt gliding before it would harbor. She was used to coping with any situation and was not the least carfuffled or upset. "Trust," she said. "It will be magnificent."

"You look lovely," the mayor told her.

Suddenly, a voice called out as if on a megaphone. "Halloo."

"Did you hear that?" the mayor asked.

"Of course," Mrs. Bestheart replied.

The boatsman edging into the lamplight, had a long pole he was dipping in and out of the murky water. He was dressed in black, a sort of apparition, and not at all the kind of person anyone would escort to a ball. He stepped from the punt. The Mayor reached out one hand in the attitude of a handshake, the other extending behind him to hold Mrs. Bestheart back if, indeed, all were not well. The man had a sinister appearance.

"We had the devil of a time," the boatsman said. "Weren't expecting fog. Had trouble securing passports, but it's good to be back." The stranger's head was covered, but his skin was pallid and thin. He seemed otherworldly and smelled of musk and decay. A hint of death hovered in his vacant eyes.

"Do we dare take him to the ball looking like this?" Mr. Dawson questioned.

"Trust me," Mrs. Bestheart replied. "It'll be awe-inspiring."

The Mayor had arranged for horse-driven carriages to deliver the guests to the ball, and as the houseboat anchored next to the punt, the guests disembarked and stepped immediately into waiting buggies. The last figure that emerged from the houseboat was dressed as an Indian chief.

~

"My word," the mayor said. The elaborate costumes of the guests were amazing. One woman, who seemed no less than the eighth wonder of the world, held a dance card in her hand and gave it to the mayor who smiled and signed it, not once, but twice. The lady was dressed as Nourmahal, Light of the Harem. Her tightly fitted bodice of silver lamé was covered with a net of pearls. A girdle of glittering gems adorned her waist: topaz, amethysts, emeralds and diamonds. Her dark hair, simply parted upon her white forehead, was gathered beneath a turban of white that featured a diamond crescent of rarest value. Her trousers were silk and fastened by silver anklets that exhibited perfect feet cased in crimson slippers.

The noisy crowd hushed, and every eye turned toward her as she entered the room. Mr. Dodge said he had never seen a visage so lovely, and he let out an audible ahhh. "She is nature's masterpiece," he said.

Only moments later, the lights dimmed, and Mary Dodge stepped up to the microphone. She called the name: "Joe Cain." Drums rolled, and the crowd shouted "Slacabamorinico lives." Mary called out "Madame Octavia Le Vert," and a voice, as if from beyond, intoned:

When wit and wine, and friends have met
And laughter crowns the festive hour
In vain I struggle to forget.
Still does my heart confess they power
And fondly turn to thee!

Some say it was the voice of Edgar Allan Poe. They say he had come to read his love poem once more to Lady Octavia. Some say the boatman was Charon of the River Styx. He had led a houseboat of old Mobilians from the Styx to Perdido River, to Perdido Bay, out into the Gulf of Mexico, and into Mobile Bay to be presented at the Tricentennial Ball. Others doubt this can be, but in Mobile, the nights are magic—and there has always been, and there is always, much to ponder in this city of live oaks and uncommon shade.

First published in the February 2, 2002 *Mobile Register*

MOSTLY HOME

Mary Murphy

Mobile—
the home I intended to leave,
but could never co-ordinate
desire
with time, money, or
a yard sale or U-haul.

Instead, even when traveling,
I wanted to return home
to the place pulled together and apart
by hurricanes, politics, or the paving of roads,
where recipes for gumbo, fish batter, and fried chicken
are heritage as much as name.

Tree limbs scrape the top of cars.
Possoms and raccoons waddle across yards
to raid trash cans undisturbed by barking dogs,
hissing cats, or passing cars.
Dew Drop, Cannon, Old Shell, and Spring Hill,
all have meanings and jokes
few outsiders understand.

Mardi Gras, where people can hide in public,
is condemned by many
and attended by most.

Thunderstorms move across the bay,
chase white caps and dump
twenty-minute floods on the city.
Still on a Sunday morning
at Barnes and Noble, with coffee
and the *New York Times*, horrors of the world
or secluded vacation spots in the Pacific
you can look up from your table
to see people greet each other—
dressed for fishing or church
and oblivious to the social trinity
of this haunted Southern city.

MOBILE AND MUSIC

It's a honeysuckle heaven by the name of Mobile.

—R.Wells and D. Holt, "Mobile"

DUNBAR, WE LOVE THEE

Ariel Williams Holloway

From *Shape Them Into Dreams.* The words and music for "Dunbar, We Love Thee" were written during Ariel Holloway's second year as a teacher at Dunbar High School in Mobile, Alabama, 1933-1944. The song was dedicated to the late Mr. W. A. Caldwell, then principal of Dunbar, and was first used to initiate what continued for years as an annual school musical called "Dunbar Night."

O Alma Mater, Dunbar High,
We love thee, we honor thee.
Our songs we'll raise to sing thy praise
Where'er we be, on land or sea.
Dear classmates, schoolmates, teachers dear,
Our love for thee grows year by year.
And so we'll lift our voices in a cheer
For Dunbar, we love thee.

To him who half a century
Has carried on, has labored on,
We dedicate this word of praise—
This little song, our little song.
To other principals so dear
We pledge our faith from year to year
And so we'll lift our voices in a cheer
For Dunbar, we love thee.

ALL DRESSED UP AND NO PLACE TO GO

Whitney Balliett

I received a telephone call not long ago from an Al St. Clair, inviting me to the fifth annual Mobile Jazz Festival. St. Clair, who lives in Mobile and is a member of the festival committee, says that he has read a piece I have written on the gloomy state of jazz and that I might be cheered by the festival, which is devoted wholly to high-school and college jazz bands. The festival is small, non-profit, and run on a competitive basis by a handful of young jazz-minded Mobilians. This year, twelve high-school bands will compete, as well as fourteen big and small college groups from nine states, most of them Southern. The judges will include Thad Jones (cornet), Larry Ridley (bass), and three Mobilians—Mundell Lowe (guitar) and the brothers Al and Urbie Green (piano and trombone). St. Clair says that the music has been imposing in past years, and should be even better this year. I accept.

My trip, a few days later, on a Thursday, is par for the course. We are an hour late taking off (no plane), and when we stop in Atlanta the end of the left wing slams into a parked food truck. The truck jumps several feet, and a football-size hole is opened in the wing. We are transferred to another airline and another plane, on which I run into Jones and Ridley. Jones, who is tall, thickset, and funny, is a C.B.S. staff man in New York as well as a co-leader of the Thad Jones-Mel Lewis big band, and Ridley, who is younger, smaller, and equally funny, has played a college gig with George Wein's band the night before in Maine and has been traveling ever since. A cloudburst keeps us on the runway for an hour, and we arrive in Mobile four hours late. St. Clair, a patient, quiet man, meets us (he has kept tabs on us, mysteriously, by "calling the computer" in Atlanta) and drives us to the Admiral Semmes Hotel, where the judges meet briefly and are given mimeographed sheets on which they are to grade the categories of Selection, Rhythm, Interpretation, Blend, Precision, and Dynamics. They are also to choose three big-band winners and three small-band winners, and they decide this year to disregard appearances and "presentation," on the basis that the music is what matters. A sliced-turkey-and-baked-potato dinner is held in the hotel for the festival committee, the judges, and the directors of the college bands. I sit between Lowe and Lee Fortier, the director of the Southeastern Louisiana college band. Lowe, who is in his late forties, is gracious and easygoing and lives in Los Angeles, where he is a free-lance composer and arranger. He gave up on New York five years ago, he says, and doesn't understand why he hasn't lived in California all his life. He and Fortier, who is about the same age, appear to have known each other in the old days, when Fortier was a trumpeter with Woody Herman and Hal McIntyre. Fortier is earnest and fast-talking. "I still play an occasional gig," he says. "I subbed for Al Hirt at his place in New Orleans three years ago, but those days on the road are gone for me. I have two daughters and a son and I've put down my roots. I've got a bachelor of music and a master of music from L.S.U., and I'm the musical director at Broadmoor High, which is in Baton Rouge. I started the first high-school stage band in Louisiana nine years ago, and before that I had an all-parish band. I also direct the stage band at Southeastern, which is over in Hammond. The kids I teach in high school have good taste, and they're very choosy. They have to join the concert band first, and we draw the stage band from that. They listen to jazz and they like good rock. I remember one of them bringing me a record by Blood, Sweat, and Tears before the group was anyways known nationally, and saying, 'What do you think of this?' I play a lot of jazz for them—Buddy Rich, the Thad Jones-Mel Lewis band, Don Ellis, Woody, and the old Basie band. And Charlie Parker and Clifford Brown and Coltrane. I play the old Basie records for time. That's the kids' biggest hand-up-time and I'm a nut on the subject. And I recommend Jerry Coker's fine paperback, *Improvising Jazz.* Most of the emphasis in the stage band is on ensemble, but every once in a while a bunch of us sit around with our horns and get some blues going. I write some chords on the blackboard and we go around from instrument to instrument and change key and go around again, and they learn a little about improvising. The kids love the stage band. I could call a rehearsal any time of day or night and they'd be there. And when they graduate they come to me and say, 'Man, I hate to leave high school,' because they may be going to study medicine or engineering at a college where there isn't any stage band. It isn't easy for those that decide to stay in music. It's mostly studio work after college, or teaching, but maybe rock will be the way out. Last year, a bunch of the kids had a rock band with four or five horns and solos and they really had something going."

By eight o'clock we are in the new Municipal Theatre, which has fine acoustics. James Brown is holding forth next door in the Municipal Auditorium, and there are two basketball games on television tonight. Brown and basketball are big in Mobile, and the house is only half full. The judges are seated in a transverse aisle at a table with student lamps. They have their heads together and are laughing. Their faces are lit from below and they look like cowpunchers around a fire. The Glassboro Lab Band, from New Jersey, opens the proceedings, which are devoted to the first half of the college groups. It is nineteen-strong and weak in the knees rhythmically, but it has a good pianist and an interesting bass trombonist. The Ray Fransen Quintet, from Loyola, is made up of trumpet, alto saxophone, guitar, bass, and the leader on drums. The bass player is black—the first for the evening. The group plays Eddie Harris's "Cryin' Blues" in a tight, swinging, Horace Silver way. Fransen is an excellent drummer, and his soloists are commendable post-hop performers. The University of Alabama Stage Band has thirty pieces, and it includes one Negro (on organ) and four girls. It is a show band, with almost no solos, and it, too, has rhythmic problems. The Butler-Farmer-Jackson-Pack—alto, tenor, and baritone saxophones, trombone, piano, bass, and drums—is out of Southern University, and is all black. The saxophonists reveal admiration for John Coltrane, and the group moves capably, in the manner of the Herbie Hancock sextet. The Morehead Stage University State Band, from Kentucky, is surprising. The drummer is tough and sounds like the old Don Lamond, and there is a wild, red-headed alto saxophonist and flutist named Red Clark. In a complicated number, "Concertino," a trombone, a trumpet, and an alto saxophone move to one side of the stage, where they solo and play ensemble figures and are answered by the rest of the band. The gimmick works. The Louisiana State University New Orleans Combo is led by Ben Smalley, a trumpeter and flugelhornist, and has piano, bass, and drums. Smalley, who is diminutive, plays with a sweet, florid precision. The group does "Here's That Rainy Day," "On the Trail," and a Brubeck number. Smalley would have little trouble in any New York or Los Angeles studio. The evening is closed by the University of Southern Mississippi Jazz Lab Band. It hustles, and in one number three soloists play at once, and in another four French horns appear and the saxophone section doubles on a total of twenty instruments. Like the two groups just ahead of it, it is all white.

After the concert, St. Clair drives me to a party at Bill Lagman's house. Live oaks, mossy and thick-trunked, clasp hands across the streets, and the antebellum houses sit back on their plots, their big, elegant windows staring through porches and columns. They are 1830 New England houses, grown fat in an easy climate. Lagman, St. Clair tells me, has led a dance band for thirty years in Mobile and is on the festival committee. A year or two ago, his musical faithfulness was rewarded with the Mr. Mobile Music Award. The guests are mainly involved with the festival. A fine buffet offers shrimp remoulade. After a while, Mundell Lowe, Thad Jones, and Al Green gather in a small room off the kitchen, where there is an upright piano. Lowe has his guitar and Jones his cornet, and Green, a constantly smiling man who taught his extraordinary younger brother, Urbie, sits down at the piano. A local bassist appears. It is the best possible way to hear jazz, and the music is easy and affecting. Jones plays with startling freshness, and Green is a good late-swing pianist. Lowe, who does not perform much anymore, settles slowly into his instrument, and the muscles around his mouth reflect his pleasure. There are blues and ballads, and Lagman gets out his trumpet and joins in. He has the gentle, old-lady tone of the older New Orleans trumpeters, and the contrast between him and Jones, who has a brilliant tone and a nervous, punching attack, is marvelous. I wish that the kids could be there.

I have a late breakfast on Friday with Chuck Suber, the publisher of *Down Beat*. He is an intense, unassuming man in his late forties, and he has spent a good deal of the past fifteen years traveling the country and helping to put the high-school and college stage-band movement on its feet. He hands me a six-page brochure he has written, "How to Organize a School Jazz Festival-Clinic." It is terse and enthusiastic and exhaustive. He talks in much the same way: "Generally, the first music teachers in the public schools in this century were Sousa men, displaced when concerts in the parks and such began to give way after the First World War to the Model T and the movies. The next wave of teachers was made up in large part of dance-band men displaced after the Second World War, when the big bands began to disappear. Gene Hall, an inspired leader and teacher, organized the first college stage-band course in 1947, at North Texas State. He coined the euphemism 'stage band' simply because the terms 'jazz band' and 'dance band' were not acceptable in academic circles. Concurrently, jazz musicians were studying at the Westlake College of Music, on the Coast, and in Boston, at the Berklee School of Music, which has now become a four-year college with an enrollment of nine hundred and fifty. The first high school stage-band festival was held in Brownwood, Texas, in 1952. There were nine or ten bands. I was there, and it excited me tremendously. Gradually Gene Hall graduates began fanning out—getting jobs in high schools and colleges, starting stage bands, fighting for recognition—and their students did the same thing. The Farmingdale High School Dance Band, from Long Island, with Marshall Brown as its director, appeared at Newport in 1957, and became the first high-school jazz band to gain national recognition. In fact, it was something of a sensation. The next year, the International Youth Band, which had kids from all over Europe and the U.S.A., was another Newport success. By 1960, Stan Kenton was hiring sidemen from North Texas State, and the thing had mushroomed. Fifteen or sixteen thousand high schools of all kinds now have stage-band courses, and there are sixty-two regional high-school festivals, some of them with as many as a hundred and twenty-six competing groups. Six colleges offer majors in jazz, or the equivalent of it, and four hundred and fifty colleges have accredited jazz courses. There is also a loose federation of a dozen or so college festivals, held, among other places, in Hamden, Connecticut, and Notre Dame, Little Rock, the University of Utah, San Francisco Valley College, and here in Mobile. Each sends a winning big band, combo, and vocalist to the National Collegiate Festival. The first such festival was held in Miami Beach, in 1967, and the fourth one will be given in Urbana, Illinois, in May."

I ask Suber where this flood of musicians hopes to work after college.

"That's the great problem. Some will try and make it on the road and some will wind up in the studios, but most of them will probably go into teaching, which of course results in a kind of closed-circuit, self-perpetuating system. Another problem is with the blacks. Integration has been slow, and many of the black schools, still hung up on the Negro-middle-class distaste for jazz, have nobody to organize and teach stage bands. But the whole program, despite the cul-de-sac conditions in jazz these days, is well worth it. It teaches the kids about a great, unique form of music. It teaches them a little about improvisation. Most important, it teaches them a valuable form of self-expression in an increasingly repressive and unoriginal society."

Suber is a judge at the high-school competition this afternoon. We get to the Municipal Theatre just before one-thirty. A dozen bands are scheduled. All are from Alabama, with the exception of the Starliners, from Bowie, Maryland, and the Holy Cross Stage Band from New Orleans. It is only the second time the Mobile Festival has included a high-school competition. The house, which is nearly full, is made up largely of the relatives and friends of the musicians. Giggling and squirming are constant, and now and then a row of kids, uprooted by winds of enthusiasm, rises, flows down an aisle, and subsides in another row—pigeons suddenly clouding the air and settling fifty feet away. Solos, numbers, and sets are cheered wildly, and when each band finishes its members file into the audience and sit in a clump. Feeling relieved and possibly heroic, with the eyes of a grateful audience riveted on them, they whisper and elbow one another. If the succeeding band sounds uncertain, the whispering becomes a steady counterpoint, but if the new group is obviously superior they grow still, amateurs digging old pros. Some of the bands are out of tune, some sag rhythmically, and many are marching bands in disguise. They play Neal Hefti, Marshall Brown, Stan Kenton, Blood, Sweat, and Tears, and the Beatles. The afternoon is a tossup between the Holy Cross Stage Band and the Murphy High Band, from Mobile. Both play the Beatles' irresistible "Hey Jude," but Murphy High, warmed by the bosom of local pride, builds a stunning pyramid of sound in its final choruses and brings the house to a boil. The last group is unbelievably old-fashioned ("That Old Black Magic," "I'll Be Around"), and provides a calming anticlimax.

I fall into an ironic reverie, remembering the music scene in my high school, in the early forties. We had a band, or, rather we had two bands—a ten-piece "big" one, which played dreary stock arrangements of the "Johnson Rag" and "Stardust," and a splinter Dixieland group. But it was an underground operation. We had no teacher or director. We were allowed to use a rehearsal room in the basement of the school chapel only when it was not occupied by the longhairs or the marching band. We provided our own arrangements, our own instruments, and even our own raison d'être, by giving illicit, well-attended jam sessions in the chapel basement. (During them, the resident music teacher, high-domed and wearing trousers invariably six inches too short, would poke his head in, and if he didn't throw us out would smirk and slam the door. The glee club, which he directed, was warmly received at neighboring girls' schools.) Most of the musicians were terrible, but the exceptions were memorable. There were a couple of flashy drummers patterned on Gene Krupa, a bass player with the power of Wellman Braud and the precision of Jimmy Blanton, and a musing, gentle cornettist who would play all of Bix Beiderbecke. There was also a tenor saxophonist from Maine, who, though he couldn't speak two coherent sentences, played exactly like Lester Young. But those were champion times. We were Krupas and Blantons and Youngs, and since jazz had reached one of its peaks, our idols were almost always within sustaining reach. Now, jazz has grown lean and withdrawn, but every backwoods high school has a "Good Housekeeping" approved jazz band with school-supplied instruments, arrangements, practice halls, and teachers. A huge army of potential professionals, all dressed up and no place to go.

Another dinner is given before this evening's concert, at which the remaining college groups will play. The festival committee and the judges attend the dinner, and the judges are presented with miniature silver tankards. St. Clair takes me through the Municipal Auditorium on the way to the theatre. It is almost the size of the Houston Astrodome and is packed with dining Shriners. The music tonight at the festival is, by and large, several notches above last night's. The Jacksonville State University Band plays Buddy Rich's version of the Beatles' "Norwegian Wood," and there is a fine, bursting trombone solo in "Summertime." The next group, a quintet from the University of Florida, is made up of semi-ringers, for its members are graduate students. They pump sternly through a couple of free-for-all "new thing" numbers, and sound like an Archie Shepp ensemble, minus the humor. The Loyola University Jazz Lab Band, which I have heard about for several years, plays four swinging precise numbers, one of them Don Ellis's difficult "In a Turkish Bath." It has a Negro bassist. Ray Fransen is on drums, and he makes everything cook. It is the best band we have heard yet. Some comic relief follows. The University Debs, hailing from Ball State University, in Indiana, and made up of eight very assorted girls accompanied by a rhythm section, yoohoo their way through a milky gospel number, some soft rock, and an imitation blues. The Louisiana State University Jazz Lab Band, which boasts the second Negro performer of the evening, is built mainly around the trumpet and flugelhorn of Ben Smalley. A nine-piece group, the Texas Southern University Contemporary Jazz Ensemble, has two whites and seven blacks, and is the first really integrated band at the festival. It is expert. It plays one long three-part number that suggests George Russell. The last band of the evening, Lee Fortier's Southeastern Louisiana College Stage Band, is every bit as good as a Woody Herman band, and three of its numbers, arranged and/ or written by an alumnus, Joe Cacibaudia, are fascinating. They are full of satisfying, teeth-grinding harmonies, a variety of rhythms, and subtle dynamics. The band handles all this without a quaver.

The competition is over, and the judges retire to a dressing room to choose the winners. There is a good deal of badinage, some of it salty. The University Debs are awarded a special prize, since they are in a class by themselves. Not surprisingly, Morehead, Loyola, and Southeastern sweep the big bands, while Ray Fransen's Loyola group, the University of Florida Quintet (the grad students), and Texas Southern (the integrated group) take the small-band honors. Suber and his compeers have already named the Holy Cross band the winner of the afternoon. Tomorrow night, all eight winners will give a display program.

Off to another party with St. Clair, this one at a doctor's house, where a Dixieland band made up of local businessmen is to perform. The living room is built around an indoor garden with small trees, and the music is paunchy and purple-faced. A stocky man in his later thirties tells me that he acts as the group's bandboy. He says the band doesn't take itself seriously. I note the standing microphones in front of the band, the bank of recording equipment beside it, the stacks of tape, and the glistening instruments. Thad Jones sits in against his will—a cheetah pursued by hippos. Suber and I talk of the times when his father, who was head of Local 802, in New York, took him to the Savoy Ballroom to hear Chick Webb.

On Saturday morning, I learn that someone got brutish with Thad Jones at the end of last night's party, and that, on top of that, his horn has been stolen from his hotel room. It is not the horn but the mouthpiece that matters. A trumpeter builds his chops around his mouthpiece, and adjusting to a new one is like starting a new career. I wander over to the theatre, where rehearsals are in progress, to talk with Ray Fransen, who seems the most confident and gifted musician in the festival. I notice that Mobile, like all old Southern towns, comes in warring parts. I'm in the middle of town, but I pass a sagging antebellum house and a field-size lot, full of knee-high grass and gap-toothed shrubbery. Beyond the house, I can see the twelve-story Admiral Semmes and the thirty-three-story First National Bank building. The celebrated Mobile azaleas are in bloom, but the sour, noxious odor that rolled over the town yesterday, compliments of Mobile's two paper mills, still hangs in the air. Blacks seem to make it all right in the public places, but there haven't been many at the parties, and a member of the festival committee has told me when the leaders of N.O.W., a civil-rights group, were invited to the festival, one of them told him that they would attend, so long as they didn't get "rained on" in the Municipal Theatre. The town cherishes its past, but one of its chief diversions is listening in on police calls.

I find Fransen backstage. He is compact and round-faced and bearded. He is also articulate, outspoken, and out of step with his generation, for he has a strong sense of tradition. "I was born in New Orleans, and I've lived there all my life. No one in my family plays an instrument, but I was always exposed to music—to Cole

Porter and Gershwin and even Art Tatum. When I was a kid, I was real fat and introverted, and I used to stay home and listen to the old people's radio station WWL. My father's a Nicaraguan. He's a dentist and a damned good one, and I guess it was he, who, if he didn't lead me into music, allowed me into it. He loves music as art and he loves manual dexterity. I started lessons on drums six years ago, and on the side. I played in rock groups. Both experiences dragged me. I went the whole rudimental route in the drum class, but drum rudiments are just like scales—a means to an end and not an end. I got tired of rock drumming quick; I didn't want to blow my eardrums out. Anyway, that's changing. The rock musicians are stretching out their numbers and getting into solos and other instruments than guitars. I consider myself a percussionist. I've learned most of the percussion instruments, including tympani and vibes. I'm going to do graduate work in ethno-musicology, but my prime interest is in being a performer. I'm not interested in amassing a fortune, but rather than prostitute myself musically I'd sell shoes. Fortunately, with my background, I could probably get a job in a symphonic organization or in jazz or with certain rock groups. The reason the kids ignore jazz is partly because they associate it with parents, with a different era. It's supposed to be acquainted with brothels, and brothels are out. But when they do listen, they hear the excitement. I took my quintet into a small beer lounge on campus a while back, and at first nothing happened. Then it caught on and now the place is packed. But the kids are denying roots. They only want what's now. They say, I don't want to study Dixieland, but I say, Man you don't have to study it, just know what it is. The past is there for a cat to take what he needs from it. Paul Desmond listened to Lester Young and Gil Evans to Brahms, and they wouldn't be what they are if they hadn't. I listen and steal from everybody—Gene Krupa and Sidney Catlett and Chick Webb—and recently I've been listening to Joe Morello and Buddy Rich and Grady Tate. That's the drag about my generation-tossing everything out and replacing it with nothing. It's ridiculous. Everybody hates what's going on, but nobody has any solutions."

There aren't many surprises at tonight's performance. A lot of new material is brought out, though, including numbers by Charlie Mingus, Luis Bonfa, and Clifford Brown, and the Ball State Debs have new hairdos. Everyone plays well. For some reason, the trophies are handed out after the theatre has emptied, but it is good to see the three hundred or so kids cheering the winners and keeping their disappointments to themselves. The judges make the awards—all except Thad Jones, who flew home earlier today.

ON MOBILE BAY
Earle C. Jones

Earle C. Jones is the lyricist of this song. The other people involved were Charles N. Daniels (composer) and Ribe Denmark (arranger). It's preserved in the W.S. Hoole Special Collections Library at the University of Alabama.

On Mobile Bay,
Honey stole my heart away,
Beside the sea,
When she gave a loving kiss to me.

She said, "goodbye"
While the moon was shining high,
On the dreaming, beaming, gleaming
Mobile Bay.

MOBILE
R. Wells, D. Holt

This song was famously performed by Julius LaRosa.

They saw a swallow building nest.
I guess they figured she knew best,
So they built the town around her
And they called it Mobile.
Where's that?
Alabama.

They took a swampland heavy with steam
And added people with a dream.
And the dream became a heaven
By the name of Mobile.

Pretty soon the town had grown
Till they had a slide trombone,
And a man who played piano,
And a swallow who sang soprano.

So if you're wondering where you should go,
It's on the Gulf of Mexico
Where the Southern bells are ringing
And the climate's ideal.
It's a honeysuckle heaven
By the name of Mobile.

MEASURING LIFE
Rachael Alex

Music Literature

Some people listen to Bach, and Mozart, and Beethoven. Some people understand symphonies, and sonatas, and concertos. I'm not one of those people.

In the summer of 2010, I registered for an introductory course on music literature. A night class. Tuesdays and Thursdays. 5:30-7:45. Two hours and fifteen minutes of a stiff, squeaky desk and stale, over-sweetened coffee. An over-filled classroom of non-music majors ready to master musical genius and fulfill a graduation requirement.

A few people fell asleep in the first class. A few people dropped out before the second class. A few people were absent the whole semester. But not me. I attended class, stayed awake, took notes. I listened to every classical recording assigned, but I don't remember any of them.

Only one thing replays in my mind.

It was the second week of the semester when the professor turned his back to the board, facing the class. His ironed khakis didn't move as he checked to make sure his collared shirt was sufficiently tucked in. After tightening his leather belt, he scanned the room as if our faces were the horizon. The clock ticked. Then, he spoke.

"What type of instrument is the piano?"

The clock ticked again.

"By the end of the semester, you should know the answer."

Tempo: Semplice (regular speed)

Do you remember having music class in grade school? At St. Dominic Catholic School, we had music class every other week. The weeks in between, we had art class. Music class meant learning how to play "Mary Had a Little Lamb" on a plastic clarinet called a recorder. Art class meant learning how to cut straight lines with plastic scissors.

There were about sixty kids in every grade. Sixty pairs of oxford shoes. Sixty white button-up shirts. Sixty colds every winter. In a single file line we marched to music class in alphabetical order by last name.

The music room was small, with three straight walls and one rounded wall made of glass bricks. The music teacher was also small. She was round, too. The piano she played had wheels on it because it was rolled to the church every Friday for school mass. We sat Indian style in front of the piano. Boy, girl, boy, girl.

"I want you to lose yourself in the music." The teacher's face wiggled when she talked. The bottom of her skirt danced across the floor. "Lose yourself in the music."

We nodded in agreement, but none of us understood.

If we got really lucky, we wouldn't have to blow into our plastic clarinets. Instead, we practiced church songs for Friday mass. To third graders, singing in mass is exciting.

I was in third grade when I memorized church songs so that I could sing them at home. I always liked "On Eagles' Wings." I sang it like a whisper in the car, on the boat, in my bed. I whispered it during Mardi Gras as I stood on the barricade, trapped by an anxious crowd, impatiently waiting for the next float. I whispered it on the way to band rehearsal in the fifth grade. I whispered it on the way to piano lessons in the sixth grade. That same year, Eminem was on the radio rapping the same line a music teacher preached to some Catholic kids every other week. "You better lose yourself in the music," he said. Maybe that's what I was. Lost on eagles' wings, singing my hushed song.

<u>Tempo: Morendo (fading away)</u>

It was about eighth grade when everyone stopped singing in church. That's also when we didn't have to sit boy, girl, boy, girl anymore. Girls upgraded from plaid jumpers to grey skirts. Boys upgraded from blue shorts to grey pants. Eighth graders sat in the back of the church.

Eight graders were too cool to sing.

There I was. Eighth grade, grey skirt, back of the church.

Not singing.

It was about that same time that I quit the band. No more band practices, band rehearsals, band concerts. I put down my clarinet for good, even though it wasn't plastic. Then, I quit piano lessons.

Soon after that, I sat in the passenger seat of my grandma's SUV. Five o'clock traffic stalled us in the turn lane. I stared at the red light, the air conditioner blowing the hair around my face.

"Why do you want to quit piano?" My grandma gripped the steering wheel, eyes straight ahead.

"I want to focus on sports." I watched the cars passing in front of us.

"You'll regret it."

"I won't."

The Mobile sun blazed through the windshield.

"If you don't use your gifts, you will lose them," she said, turning to me.

The light turned green.

A car honked behind us.

"Green light," I said.

Broken Metronome

Freshman year of high school. A blur.

McGill-Toolen was just a smudge of monogrammed shirts and grey pleated skirts. Snatches of brown from a crucifix in every room. Scrapes of beige from outdated paint and worn stairs. A few slashes of orange and black for school spirit. My world was painted by an angry artist who mixed too many standard colors together and ended up with a grotesque shade of vile. Then, the artist smeared students onto the palette. Sometimes, they talked to me.

"Hey, Rachael. How are you?"

"How did you do on the test?"

"What color is your homecoming dress?"

Sometimes, I talked back.

"I'm fine."

"I did okay on the test."

"I'm not going to the dance."

Sometimes, they didn't talk to me. Just about me.

"She doesn't talk much."

"I heard her mom moved to Texas with her new boyfriend."

"Why is she absent so much? Is she sick?"

"Divorce. That's what I heard."

Those times, I didn't talk back.

The world was tuned to popular music and talk shows, football games and homecoming dances. But I was tuned to nothing.

I didn't want a clarinet, plastic or not. I didn't want the wings of any eagle. I didn't want to play piano.

Silence.

I wanted silence.

People tell me that smell is the quickest way to memory because of the olfactory bulb's location on the brain. My brain is different. I remember by music. Music is my file cabinet. Every memory is attached to a song and filed accordingly. That's why freshman year is still a blur. I wanted silence. I tuned to nothing because some files just shouldn't be made. There are some things you don't want to remember.

Those are the things you experience in silence, because no song deserves to be associated with such memories.

Silence is better.
Silence is better.
Silence is better.

Tempo: Stringendo (pressing forward)

I used to be a poet. I was self-taught, and I wasn't very good at poetry. Well, I was more of a songwriter.

Sophomore year of high school, I sat down one night in front of my piano. Dust rose into the air when I blew on the keys. After ten minutes of sitting in silence, I played a few melancholic chords and wrote the refrain to my first song, "Three Little Words":

Three little words I can't bear.
It's so hard to see you there.
I know it might get better.
Until then, I'll brace the weather.

I was a self-taught poet. A bad one, I know. It was necessary at the time.

There's something about them. Those poems. They pack a punch. Not always with a narrative, but with an emotion. That's why they make sense. A feeling is feeling. It isn't linear like a narrative. It doesn't make sense. Poets. They understand.

Poets know that saying "I love you" is useless when it isn't proven, when it sounds practiced, when it arrives too late. They understand. When I was a poet, I understood too. Three little words can start a poem or even title a song, but they can't heal a wound.

Music Literature

In the summer of 2010, I registered for an introductory course on music literature.

"What type of instrument is the piano?" the professor asked.

At the end of the semester, he told us the answer.

"Percussive," he said. "The piano is percussive."

Measuring Life

The piano is percussive.

The piano keeps the time.

The piano measures the change.

It is the heartbeat of the music.

Some people use clocks to tell the time. Some people use watches. That's how we measure the day. But measuring life is different.

Memories are not numbers from the face of a clock or a watch. Memories have a heartbeat. Plastic clarinets and eagles' wings. Those are memories. A number on a clock is just a reference that tells you time has been lost.

"Lose yourself in the music." This is what we're told.

But music is not something you lose yourself in. Music is a mental file cabinet. A reference with a heartbeat. Music is something you use to find yourself.

One day, I'll run into my music literature professor. "You're right," I'll say. "The piano is percussive. It keeps the time."

"Yes, Rachael," he'll tell me, looking quite pleased with himself.

A clock will tick.

"But music is percussive, too," I'll state. "It keeps my time."

A clock will tick again, but I'll hear Middle C.

Originally published in *Oracle Fine Arts Review 2012*.

THE PURPLE PIANO

Linda Busby Parker

In the middle of July, hot and muggy, there was nothing to do but watch reruns on television and read *Movie Life, Motion Picture or Screen Star* dreaming of Frankie Avalon, Ricky Nelson or James Darren coming to the Saenger Theatre in search of the perfect date, and finding me. I turned fifteen that April of '59, finished ninth grade at Mae Eanes Junior High and would start Murphy High School in September.

In the mornings I slept late, avoiding Mama, which was also a means of escaping housework; I sunned on a towel in the back yard listening to "Will You Love Me Tomorrow" and "Mama Said" by The Shirelles. I sang "Venus," harmonizing with Frankie Avalon's smooth chords coming out of the tiny speakers on my portable radio. I came alive only once in every day—at five o'clock when the teenagers from Philadelphia strolled and bopped across the screen on "American Bandstand." I watched the slow dances with keen interest, especially the way the girls draped their arms around the boys' shoulders and the way they looked into their partners' eyes and smiled, but as soon as Dick Clark's regulars (Bunny, Justine, Eddie, Kenny) said goodbye, I closed the exotic world where teenagers got to rate the record ("it's got a good beat"), where the coolest girls wore wide belts with big buckles and sweaters that buttoned in the back, and I folded up to just me in our little white, wood-framed house in our working-class neighborhood. In the evenings that summer, I settled down in the living room to watch reruns on TV with Mama.

"He's watching that house," Mama said. She held the drape in her right hand, her large backside arched away from the small opening she created in the curtain so she could peer down the street. Her brows raised as her rounded brown eyes peeked past the edge of the window. Mama and I were in the living room, illuminated only by the phosphorescent blue-glow of the television tuned to a rerun of "The Many Loves of Dobie Gillis."

"Who's watching what?" I asked, still reclining on the couch watching beautiful Tuesday Weld tell Dobie she wanted a corsage delivered from the florist, not brought to the house by him. She had that wonderful child-woman voice, high pitched, exasperated, and that blonde hair as charming as Shirley Temple's corkscrew curls had been a generation earlier.

"Mr. Doleman," Mama said. "Mrs. Doleman is divorcing him and he's watching her house."

I came off the couch, planting my feet firmly between the parted curtains. Sure enough, a man stood halfway down the block beside an old car, a black Dodge, about a '49. I knew cars because my older brother, Bobby, breathed cars, probably even dreamed about cars and always shouted out makes and models we passed on the street. The man that Mama watched stood by the passenger side, under a street lamp like he didn't care who saw him. He wore dark pants, a white shirt and a dress hat, the kind my granddaddy donned on Sundays. The Doleman house was four doors from our house, but on the same side of the street; the man in church clothes gazed down the block in the direction of Shirley Doleman's place, a rented house, small, painted white with dark green shutters. When I took a step closer to the window to get a better view, Mama popped me a good one on the shoulder with the back of her hand and it stung like ten fire ants biting at once.

"Why'd you do that?"

"Get back, Rosey!" Mama never gave justification when the backside of her hand made body contact. She considered a swift blow to be shorthand, conveying all kinds of messages in one conservative move.

"You didn't have to hit me!"

"I think the man's crazy. He comes to her house on those metal crutches like he's had polio or something, but look at him now. No crutches. Something's wrong with that man!"

The alarm in Mama's voice told me I wanted another peek. I eased behind her, ducked my head below hers and our four eyes watched him.

He lit a cigarette and stared in the direction of Shirley Doleman's front door. He leaned against the side of the Dodge, his hat tilted slightly on his head and he looked like Joe Friday from Dragnet conducting a stakeout. The black Dodge had a big chrome front grill that looked like hissing teeth and the widespread headlights were eyes, almost comic, but a little mad.

We didn't know the Dolemans well. Mrs. Doleman was a blonde, like Tuesday Weld—shoulder length curly hair, blue eyes, thinner and younger than most of the women in the neighborhood. She had been in the rented house down the block about a year. She worked as a secretary for some lawyers in downtown Mobile and she had a five-year-old daughter named Dixie. When Mrs. Doleman first moved into the neighborhood the last of August, she told Mama she was separated from Mr. Doleman and would file for divorce soon, but Mr. Doleman moved in with her before Christmas and then moved out again in the spring.

Mrs. Buster, our neighbor across the street, came over almost every afternoon. She sat with my mother on the front porch and the two of them drank sweet tea and passed the scuttlebutt between them. Mrs. Buster knew everything about everybody in the vicinity and she told Mama the Dolemans were definitely getting a divorce.

"Didn't work out," Mrs. Buster said. "He's possessive. Didn't want her to leave the house without him." Mrs. Buster put her short, hefty arms under her pendulous breasts and her blue eyes darted across the yard in search of nothing in particular, but lighted on a purple hydrangea, and then she reached for her tea.

She sniffed a long breath and her bosom expanded, stretching the faded fabric of her pink-and-blue-flowered housedress; her stubby feet, in black flip-flops, pushed hard against the porch floor, causing her rocking chair to creak. "Wanted her to quit her job. Said she should stay home and watch Dixie, but he's not earning a penny. Lost his job over a year ago."

"Somebody's got to bring in a dollar and keep the wolf off the doorstep," Mama said.

"He's got some kind of problem though. Something's wrong with his legs," Mrs. Buster said. "He's on crutches."

That was all I knew about the Dolemans, except Mrs. Doleman's house was as clean as the inside of new copper pipe. I'd been in her house several times, once to borrow a couple of eggs for something Mama was cooking, and a couple of other times when Dixie asked me to come in and play with her.

"She doesn't have any brothers or sisters and I don't expect she ever will," Shirley Doleman told me. "If you've got a minute, come on in."

I went inside their house and Dixie got a small red ball out of a cedar chest that Mrs. Doleman used as a coffee table. Dixie and I sat on the floor, spread our legs wide and rolled the ball back and forth between us. It was simple play, but Dixie enjoyed it. Each time, I stayed about half-an-hour and then I told Dixie I had to leave. I could give only a limited amount of time to rolling a little red ball back and forth across a hardwood floor. But while I was there, I looked around again and was amazed at how organized everything was. At our house we left stuff out everywhere—boxes of corn flakes and frosted flakes and a jar of Ovaltine on the kitchen table, salt and pepper shakers on the counter by the stove, two or three pairs of shoes by the front door, dirty socks in the corner of the kitchen, stacks of newspapers by the recliner, old magazines under the coffee table. Mother loved to sew and the trimmed tissue-paper edges of patterns would stay on the floor at our house for a couple of days, and dirty laundry stood in piles on the utility room floor, but at Shirley Doleman's house, there wasn't one thing out anywhere, not one thing. Her house could have been photographed for my mother's *Good Housekeeping* magazines, except she didn't have much furniture and what she did have was like what we had—ordinary.

Mother and I were still watching Mr. Doleman. His figure was a dark silhouette, but when he inhaled, we saw the orange glow of his cigarette and smoke curled toward the streetlight. While the TV flickered behind us, we saw Bobby coming home with his friend Josh Franklin. Bobby was riding in Josh's new truck, a cherry red El Camino, streamlined, with white darts racing down the sides that made the truck look like it was speeding.

Josh was an only child, and he got everything he wanted, including the El Camino, but Bobby was rebuilding the engine of a '49 Mercury that had no class at all. The faded gray Mercury had a rounded roof and a fat body, small windows, a super big front door and looked like a tired, thick-skinned elephant trudging down the street. Bobby planned to have the engine rebuilt by September so he could drive to Murphy High, and I would be riding in that old worn-out beast.

Mr. Doleman jumped back a step when Bobby and Josh drove by. He put his hand on his hip and watched the boys. Sparks flew when he flicked his cigarette toward the curb and walked to the driver's side, got in, and started the Dodge. Josh's El Camino pulled onto the grass in our front yard as Mr. Doleman eased away from the curb.

"Glad he's gone," Mama said.

Bobby and Josh came in the front door, each of them carrying automobile parts wrapped in greasy newspaper which they placed on the floor by the front door.

"Don't put that stuff down," Mama said. "You'll get grease on the floor."

"That's why it's wrapped in newspaper," Bobby said, wiping his hands on his tee shirt and heading toward the kitchen.

"You'll still get grease on my floor," Mama said. "If you do, I'll make you clean it up."

"Bobby got lucky," Josh said. "Found a partially stripped engine at Tanner's."

"Had to go two places," Bobby's voice cut in from the kitchen. "Struck pay dirt at Tanner's."

"Got two pistons, three new rings," Josh said pointing to the greasy newspapers on the floor. He looked like James Darren in his blue jeans and undershirt.

"Got a front door lock too," Bobby said, and we could hear him opening pot lids in the kitchen. "Thought we'd never get that door stripped."

"Well good," Mama said. Anybody could tell she wasn't interested in Bobby's old Mercury out in the garage because her eyes kept glancing toward Dobie Gillis. "You boys hungry?" she asked.

"Man, yeah," Josh said.

Mama raised her voice so Bobby could hear her. "You can't wash up in here. Go out to the garage. Use some of that GoJo to get that grease off your arms. Don't come back in here till you're clean."

That summer, Bobby worked every night out in the garage and Josh came over to help him. They were both sixteen, but Josh had something my brother didn't have—coolness and he was also a little wild. His family went to our church, the little

Baptist church near Broad Street. Josh sat on the back row during the preaching and always engaged in some type of smalltime devilment. If some tiny something happened in youth group that shouldn't have happened, Josh Franklin was responsible or he knew the culprit because he put the poor sucker up to it. Josh was never more than second or third-fiddle from mischief.

His mother, Lottie Franklin, my piano teacher, complained openly that his grades weren't good and his daddy said Josh struggled on account of him being an only child. But Josh was funny, and tall, and he had broad shoulders and big feet, and I thought he liked me at least a little. Josh called me Scooter. He gave me that nickname because he claimed I "scooted" home from school with my nose in the air, my chin high, my three-ring binder tucked under my arm, taking little steps—"scooting along," he said, and he laughed. At fifteen, I was nothing, nobody, nowhere, in the very center of nowhere. But next year I would be in tenth grade and I would join Bobby and Josh at Murphy High and that would establish us as equals.

In the kitchen, Mama held back a plate loaded with food for Daddy. He was working late and probably wouldn't be in until after nine. She knew if she put all the food on the table, there wouldn't be one thing left when Daddy got home because we'd all seen Bobby and Josh go through half a chocolate cake and nearly a gallon of milk for just an after school snack. Mama and I placed a plate of fried chicken, a bowl of potato salad, another of black-eyed peas, and a saucer with sliced loaf bread on the revolving center of the lazy-Susan in the dining room. When the boys came in, Mama went back to the television and I sat at the table with them.

"I want to get those pistons finished up tonight." Bobby said.

"I'd like to play monopoly," I piped in like I was party to their conversation.

"We're not going to play monopoly tonight," Bobby said. "We got work to do."

Josh looked at me with his big brown eyes. "Maybe we can pull those pistons tonight and then we can play monopoly with Rosey. I can come back tomorrow and we can work all day," Josh said and winked at me. I felt my cheeks turn red and I looked over at Mama but she was stretched out in the recliner with her back to me.

"Next year, you gonna scoot to Murphy with those little ole bitty steps or you gonna ride in Bobby's fine car?" Josh asked me.

"She's so dumb," Bobby said. "She fell out of a car once when Daddy picked us up at school. She was running along the road holding on to the door. Daddy looked over and there was dumb ole Rosey racing on the street trying to keep up with the car." Bobby laughed, but Josh didn't.

"That door probably wasn't closed was it, Scooter? Good thing you weren't killed," he said and he looked even more like James Darren sitting at my dining room table eating a workman's supper and the only bad thing about it was that Bobby sat beside him.

After they ate, they went out the back door headed toward the garage. Mama got up from the recliner and I helped her wash the dishes, dry them, and put them in the cabinets. I went to my bedroom and pulled a movie magazine from under my mattress. Mama let me buy the magazines, in fact, she even bought some for me, but I thought if she ever studied what was in them she would fuss about it, and besides if Bobby got his hands on them, he would tease me, showing no mercy.

While I waited for Bobby and Josh to finish in the garage, I read about a girl madly in love with a guy who looked like Troy Donohue—full golden hair, blue eyes, broad shoulders. In the story, the girl tried to decide whether to sacrifice her virginity for the Troy look-a-like. All her girlfriends gave her advice. The boy she loved said she should go all the way because he would love her forever and never leave her and he had a good job unloading fruit at the grocery store, which he planned to turn into a grocery management position one day. "I'm waiting for you baby," he said, "'cause nobody's got what you got."

I stretched out on my bed, with the window opened and the breeze floating in and I could hear Bobby and Josh out in the garage. I loved the sound of their voices—male voices working on an engine, pulled out of the body of the Mercury and hoisted on chains that hung over the rafters.

I read a little more of the story and the girl's friends told her the guy would get what he wanted and would leave her, but the girl in the story didn't believe them. I put the magazine across my chest, closed my eyes and listened again to the sounds of Bobby and Josh. When they came inside, they would have black grease imbedded under the edges of their fingernails, their faces would have a smear or two, and their clothes would smell sweet and stale all at the same time—the Dial soap they had used in the morning mixing with the sweat they generated in the sticky night air.

I started thinking about Troy Donohue and drifted into near-sleep until I heard the backyard gate slam, drawn to a swift close by its short spring and then Bobby opened my bedroom door without knocking. "Come on dummo. We got the monopoly."

Bobby and Josh set-up the card table in the corner of the dining room and opened three folding chairs. It was nearly nine o'clock but we settled down for a long game. With no school tomorrow, Mama didn't care if we stayed up late. I sat between Bobby and Josh and got my favorite piece, the blue train. The boys wanted me to be banker because they didn't want to bother with counting the money, so I lined up all the pink, green and yellow currency in neat stacks in the box lid and placed it beside me in the empty spot at the card table. We no sooner got started than Josh had a stroke of luck and landed on good property and collected rent every time Bobby and I went around the board. But I was most aware of Josh's knees as they touched my thigh; I moved back a full inch but it wasn't long before I felt Josh's knees again, warm against the side of my leg.

Daddy came in a little after nine. His navy-blue work shirt had Rosell Air Conditioning embroidered on the front pocket and he had fuzzy, orange particles of insulation stuck to his right shoulder where he had crawled around in somebody's sweltering attic installing air ducts or cleaning them out. Daddy brought his plate from the kitchen and sat at the end of the table watching the game.

"Went to Tanner's this afternoon. Pulled two pistons, like new. Got three rings too and a new door lock," Bobby said.

"That's good. Maybe I'll have a little time to help on Saturday." Daddy held a cold chicken thigh in his right hand.

"That's okay Mr. R. I can help Bobby get that car on the road."

I liked what Josh said. All the men I knew could fix anything that had gears and moving parts, anything that required a little oil or grease, anything that roared or rumbled, anything that had wheels and shafts and brushes and bearings. A man knew all of these things and Josh, like my own Daddy and my brother, knew the mysteries of motors and engines and the inner workings of moving parts.

"Rosey, I think I found you a piano," Daddy said at the same time he scooped potato salad on his fork. "Finished a job today and the man told me he'd pay me or give me a piano. His daughter's grown and they don't need that piano anymore."

I looked at Daddy. "I sure would like a piano. I could practice at home," I said. I had wanted a piano since I started taking lessons two years earlier. I knew we didn't have the money for one and I hadn't pressed the issue because one of Daddy's favorite lines was, "can't squeeze blood from a turnip."

"My Mama says Rosey's getting good at the piano," Josh said.

"She played at youth group couple weeks ago," Daddy said, still chewing his food.

"I was there," Josh said, turning toward Daddy. "She played fine!"

"Come on," Bobby said. "Who cares about Rosey's dumb piano anyway?"

Mrs. Franklin gave me piano lessons at church on Wednesday afternoons before choir practice. Daddy dropped me off at the church and Mrs. Franklin brought me home. I learned pieces from the hymnal. Other girls at school who played piano bought sheet music from Jesse French or Rutz Music and on Saturdays they performed on the Golden Flake TV show. Me, I was learning "Rock of Ages," "Just A Closer Walk," and "What A Friend We Have in Jesus" and I had no piano at home, but I loved the sounds of the notes when the pad of my fingers struck the keys. I especially enjoyed the piano's tones in the church—rich and full, echoing off the pews, the altar, the lectern, and the stained-glass windows. I wanted to play well, to perform the big pieces, and buy sheet music in a music store, but I practiced only two hours a week on Saturdays when Mama dropped me off at the church and let me play piano while she went to Delchamp's Grocery. And, what neither Daddy nor Josh knew was that I had worked on "When the Saints Go Marching In" for nearly a year before I performed it at youth group. But Daddy thought I was good and he had my career in music planned for me.

Daddy had big dreams and he understood what boys should know and what girls should know; boys should know mechanics and carpentry, even if they turned out to be doctors or lawyers; girls should have nice names and should play the piano. That's why Daddy picked my name and wrote it on the birth certificate before Mama came out of anesthesia—Rose Ann Rosell, a flower and two R sounds, with Ann, his mother's name, in the middle, but everybody called me Rosey.

"We get a piano here at the house and I bet you can play 'The White Cliffs of Dover,'" Daddy said. "Heard a man play that one time in San Francisco." He said this to Josh because Bobby and I had heard the story a thousand times. "That man's fingers moved so fast my eyes could hardly follow them. 'The White Cliffs of Dover,'" Daddy repeated. "You play that, Rosey, and you can start making money."

When Daddy was young, before he met Mama, he hitchhiked to San Francisco and heard some man play "The White Cliffs of Dover" in a bar or a restaurant and Daddy had never gotten over it. Me, I was Daddy's only hope if he was ever to hear "The White Cliffs of Dover" performed in his own home.

"Oh man!" Bobby shouted when he landed on Tennessee Avenue, where Josh had houses and Bobby had to pay up.

Josh was cleaning us out on the monopoly board. He had hotels on Park Place and Pennsylvania Avenue and he owned the Water Works and St. James Place. Bobby was annoyed, but I didn't care if Josh won. I had given up on moving my leg and Josh's knees rested, warm and electric against the side of my thigh.

"Let's get this game over with," Bobby said. "This is a slaughter!"

Daddy finished his supper, stood behind us and watched the game for a few minutes before he went to bed. When Josh put a hotel on Pennsylvania Avenue and one on Marvin Gardens, Bobby forfeited and threw all his money at Josh and the game was over. Bobby and I walked Josh outside.

"Be here tomorrow by lunchtime," Bobby said.

"I can handle it," Josh said in his coolest speech. Then he put his hand on the back of my neck. "Good night, Scooter," and his fingers rubbed gently on the naked skin hidden by my long brown hair. The tips of his fingers were warm and roused something inside me I had never felt before.

The whole bed shook next morning and I thought the rapture was upon us, quick and sure, when I opened one eye and saw Mama shaking my shoulder.

"Rosey, wake up! Wake up! Mrs. Doleman's here and she needs you to baby-sit Dixie. Come on now!"

I rolled out of bed and walked into the living room on my bare feet, still dressed in my nightgown. Shirley Doleman and Dixie stood by the door. Shirley Doleman looked beautiful in a flower printed blue, green and yellow dress with her curly blonde hair pulled back in a matching headband and she smelled heavenly. She studied me in my faded gown.

"I'm so sorry to get you out of bed." Her words sounded sweet, but anxious, as they came past her hot-pink lipstick. "I need you to keep Dixie today if you will. My regular baby sitter telephoned and said she can't work on Tuesdays or Thursdays and now I'm stuck. Dixie likes you and we sure would be grateful if you could take the job."

I didn't say anything because I hadn't made the full trip from sleep to wake.

"I'll pay three dollars a day and that's the same thing I pay her regular baby sitter," Shirley Doleman continued.

"She doesn't do anything but sleep late anyway," Mama said. "It'd be good for her."

That was Mama, stepping right in the middle of my business. I needed a little time to consider this, but standing in the living room, in my old gown, bare feet, no bra, my hair un-brushed, intimidated me into a quick decision. "Sure, I can do it," I said. My response was partly to bring the whole matter to a close, get back to my bedroom and dress, but the money sounded pretty good too. While I dressed I did some quick math on how much money I would earn by the end of August. I already knew what I wanted—new penny loafers and a fuzzy sweater with buttons at the back of the neck, red, if I could find it.

Shirley Doleman left and I went to my room to dress. When I came out, Mama had Dixie standing on a stepstool at the kitchen sink, washing dishes, but mostly playing in the suds. Mama wiped the vinyl cloth on the kitchen table with a damp dishtowel while Dixie blew soap bubbles into the air from her cupped hand. If I had done this, Mama would have popped me a good one, but with Dixie, she hopped around the kitchen breaking the bubbles with her index fingers, looking empty-headed and Dixie nearly fell off the stool from laughing so hard.

After I had breakfast, Mama gave Dixie a spoon, a cup and a saucer to dig in the dirt outside the front door. I sat on the steps and watched her unearth a dark brown worm that flipped and jerked in shock after being brought from darkness to light. This amused Dixie for a solid half hour while I sat in the shade of the porch and read *The Old Man and the Sea*, which I knew I had to read in tenth grade at Murphy High. Then, Dixie and I went to her house. Her mother left me the key in case Dixie needed anything.

Dixie's house was quiet and spooky clean like real people didn't live there, not real people who read magazines and walked around with dirt on their shoes and ate in bed and got toothpaste on the bathroom counter and left the telephone book on the sofa. Shirley Doleman had made the beds before she went to work and the spreads were stretched tight and smooth. Floors had been swept, the broom put away, no towels out by the sink, and even the bathroom basin was dry and looked fresh. A sunbeam cut through the living room and I couldn't see any dust floating in it. Dixie and I got her red ball out of the cedar chest in the living room and we took her favorite doll off the pillow on her bed and we went back to our house because Shirley Doleman's immaculate house was too clean and it made me feel hollow and edgy.

When we got home, Josh and Bobby were sitting at the kitchen table eating Campbell's vegetable soup with saltine crackers. "You girls want some soup?" Mama asked.

"I want the A, B, C kind," Dixie said.

"I got that right here," Mama said and took a red-labeled can out of the cabinet while she engaged Dixie in conversation.

"Your daddy hurt his legs?" Mama asked while she stirred the soup at the stove and Dixie watched her.

"On crutches," Dixie said in a cute way like little children talk, not knowing exactly what they're talking about, but glad when they've got an answer.

"All the time?" Mama asked

"All the time." Dixie said. "He can't walk."

"What happened to his legs?" Josh asked.

"Don't know," Dixie said.

After lunch, I brushed Dixie's hair at the painted-pink vanity table in my room, loving the feel of her hair—thick and blonde, full of curls that fell to her shoulders. Beautiful Dixie would have no trouble getting a boy to notice her when the time came. Sometime in the future if Elvis Presley performed at the Saenger, he would spot a teenage Dixie in the audience and have her come on stage with him; she was that pretty—a blue-eyed blonde with soft peachy skin. I pulled her hair into a ponytail and put a rubber band around it. We went outside where Josh parked his El Camino in front of the open garage door and we sat in the truck bed gently tossing the red ball back and forth to each other. Josh watched us from inside the garage.

Daddy surprised us when he came home early and pulled his old truck in the driveway beside Josh's El Camino. "Decided to go get that piano," he shouted at me before he got out of the truck. "That man may change his mind if I don't bring it on home." Daddy went into the garage and told Bobby and Josh he needed them to go with him to help lift the piano.

"I don't want to go get a stupid piano." Bobby said and tossed a greasy rag on the garage floor.

"We can use the El Camino," Josh said.

"My truck's fine," Daddy said and he went inside to get a couple of old quilts to cushion his truck bed for my piano. If I had been Daddy, I would have accepted Josh's offer to ride in the red El Camino because the finish on Daddy's truck, a rusted-out, dark green, late '40's Ford, looked gray-black, mottled and crackled from baking in the sun so many years. Who would have driven that old thing when a ride in the El Camino was there for the taking? But, to Daddy, a truck was a truck, and wide fins, red exterior with white darts down the side didn't mean a thing.

After Daddy, Bobby and Josh crowded in the front seat of the old Ford and eased out of the yard, I sat on the back steps and watched Dixie take the spoon Mama had given her that morning and excavate more earthworms. I thought about my piano—beautiful cherry wood, glowing warm and rose-toned with white ivory keys that looked heavy and rich, or maybe my piano had a dark mahogany finish, so deep the cabinet had a luster to it. Maybe it would be maple. I didn't want a maple piano, but maple would be okay. I could smell my piano, the fragrance of culture, affluence and good living that opened to the sweetness of heavenly tones and murmuring melodies drifting out of a rich resonant cabinet. Tonight I would sit on the piano bench, finger each key and listen to my piano sing, familiarizing myself with the unique voice of my own instrument and I would rub my hand across the soft smooth wood, so lustrous I could climb inside it and live forever in a charmed life.

Mrs. Buster came over, wearing another of her loose-fitting housedresses, and Mama came outside; they sat a long while at the picnic table under the shade tree in the backyard and I heard Mama whisper to Mrs. Buster about Richard Doleman watching Shirley Doleman's house. "I'll swaney," Mrs. Buster said and her blue eyes flashed bright and round. The emblem, "I'll swaney," waved with the warm breeze fluttering the leaves of the oak tree under which the two women sat, cutting iron-fisted July heat with fresh gossip.

"Something's wrong somewhere," Mama whispered. "I think the man's crazy."

"I'll swaney," Mrs. Buster repeated.

Daddy's old truck rumbled down the street. When it passed me, I saw Josh sitting on one side of the truck bed and Bobby on the other, balancing the piano, a tall old-fashioned upright, a light color. Mama, Mrs. Buster, Dixie and I headed for the front yard. When Daddy backed the truck close to the steps, I got a good view of my piano and I froze in utter shame and defeat—the old instrument had been in existence since before the West was won, and somewhere in its long and troubled life, the pitiful thing had been painted lavender.

As usual, Mama spoke first. "You are not putting that old purple piano in my living room."

"I'll swaney, it is purple," Mrs. Buster said.

"I didn't notice whether it was one color or another," Daddy said. "Rosey needs a piano."

"What the heck difference does it make anyway?" Bobby said. "A piano's a piano. Let's get this thing unloaded. I want to seat those pistons before it gets dark."

Josh stood with his hands on his hips, looking from one of us to the other, waiting for his next instructions. I held Dixie's hand in mine, feeling the warm velvet of her skin, feeling the unshielded vulnerability of five-year-old bones, feeling the certitude she placed in my hand, larger, stalwart.

"That piano is not going in my living room," Mama said. "Purple doesn't match a thing I own."

"It's lavender, Mama, not purple," I said.

"Lavender *is* purple," Mama said.

Daddy wiped sweat from his brow. "That beats all," he said, a tone of frustration in his voice. "Boys, we'll put the piano on one of these quilts and slide it down the hall to Rosey's room."

About five-thirty, Shirley Doleman, who still looked fresh and smelled sweet, came for Dixie. We gathered Dixie's red ball and her doll and before she went out the door, she gave me a big hug around my legs, but I bent and hugged her, pressing her firmly against my body, my open hands extending nearly the breadth of her small back. "See you Thursday," I said.

"Thursday," she said.

That afternoon Mama cooked a simple supper—hotdogs, pork-n-beans, and coleslaw. Daddy stayed home to eat before going out on another job. Josh joined us at the dinner table and dropped a bomb. "Mrs. R.," he said. "You're going to have to cook me a roast beef with rice, potatoes and lots of gravy because my parents are shipping me out. They're putting me in Marion Institute. I'll start in September."

"Oh man!" Bobby said. "You kidding me?"

"Nope. They say Marion Institute's gonna make a man of me."

Marion Institute, outside of Birmingham, was one of the country's finest and oldest military academies; we all knew that, but we also knew it was where parents sent their male children when they could afford it, and when they thought a heavy hand on the shoulder would be to their son's advantage.

"Well," Daddy said and wiped his mouth. "There comes a time when a boy's got to be a man. I left home and hitchhiked to San Francisco, went on to Oregon and worked in the great forest of the northwest. Was a man when I came home. There comes a time," he said.

I hoped he was not going to tell Josh again about the "White Cliffs of Dover." I braced and waited, but Daddy fell silent and into the stillness I felt a restive stir that nearly knocked me off-balance. I looked at Josh, but he loaded more dill relish on his hotdog bun and shoved half of it into his mouth.

By bedtime, the lavender piano had filled my room with a musty odor. Young fingers had once touched these keys, but now the fingers of those hands had turned yellow and grown thick-jointed. I sat at the lavender swivel-bench and touched the crazed ivories finding some keys as loose as a stripped screw and others stiff as old rubber. The F above middle C stuck when I touched it and so did the G two octaves below. In bed I could smell the moldy odor of the colossal lavender upright. In the moonlight coming through my half-curtained window, I could see the primeval thing, casting an eerie purplish glow. I thought I wouldn't be able to sleep with this dinosaur hovering so near my head, but I began to plot ways of spending time with Josh before he left for Marion Institute and I drifted off.

Next morning I stayed in bed, deliberately defying anyone to order me up—me, a working woman with steady income. Mama let me lounge until I rolled out about ten. I leisurely dressed and went into the kitchen for a bowl of frosted flakes when Mrs. Buster knocked at the side door.

I noticed immediately her sallow skin. Her eyes were enormous neon-blue disks, startling. Her fingers flittered between her hands like insects quivering near incandescent light. Her flip-flops made a dull thwack against her calloused feet as she thumped directly to the sink where Mama stood. Her melon-shaped breast rose and sank with each shallow breath. The air made a rasping sound between her teeth before she spoke. "He killed them." She inhaled quickly. "Police are down the street." Mama wiped her hands on her apron and followed Mrs. Buster out the door with me two steps behind them.

Police cars and an ambulance parked on the sidewalk beside Shirley Doleman's house with the flashing blue lights visible in the late morning glare. A crowd gathered on the street. Mouths spoke in words flat and hushed in the grisly presence of this awful act—Richard Doleman shot Shirley and Dixie with his pistol pressed to their heads, then went to the garage to shoot himself.

"Look there," someone said. "See. A bloody handprint on the garage door."

Bobby stood on the curb, no shirt on his back, and I noticed the thinness of his chest, his ribs visible, his belly sunk-in below his waist, his pants low around his hips. He stood barefoot and looked like a kid, not like a young man who would be driving a hulking gray Mercury to Murphy High School. His arms folded across his chest and for once in his life, he was silent.

I can't remember thinking anything except that this was all a mistake, something like an election that needed a recount, an accident for which someone said, "I'm sorry," and everything sprung back to normal, a dream from which a weary sleeper would wake. Somebody would come out of the house and tell us Shirley and Dixie were alive, that Richard Doleman shot himself in the garage, but Shirley and little blonde-headed Dixie were shaken, but otherwise fine.

When ambulance workers began bringing the bodies out, one by one, Mama made us move across the street and stand on the sidewalk. I let a crowd get in front of me. I saw the gurneys draped with white sheets, but only in glances because I did not want to see them in full view.

After a while, Mama, Bobby and I walked home. I cannot say that I thought anything that day because I was too numb, too dazed to organize any rational thought about an irrational act. I did not speak either, because words were not within my grasp. I could not bring them out, down through my head, past the nape of my neck, into my throat, between my teeth and out my lips. I was as delicate as exposed skin in desperate need of a callous rind.

Mama made a pitcher of strong, sweet tea and she and Mrs. Buster sat at the kitchen table.

"Wonder when he came?" Mrs. Buster asked.

"Did she open the door and let him in?" Mama queried. "I would have made him bust the door down." Each woman sipped her tea, not looking at the other.

"I should have told her I saw him watching the house," Mama said.

"She probably knew," Mrs. Buster answered.

"I was going to tell her," Mama said.

"I'll swaney, you can't be worrying about what you did and didn't tell her," Mrs. Buster said. "You didn't marry him, and you didn't shoot anybody, and you did the best you could. If we all start worrying about what we could have done, we'll be in a pretty pickle." The two women sipped more tea and sat in silence consoled by the presence of the other.

After supper that night, Mama washed the dishes and Josh came over to help Bobby in the garage; Mama and I sat in front of the television and watched a rerun of "Hawaiian Eye." The handsome detectives came to the Hawaiian Village Hotel to hear Cricket sing. Things happened like they usually did, but I felt half-blind and half-deaf, encased in the motions of life without experiencing them. In everything I did, in everything I heard, there was the background noise of *Why? Why? Why? Why?*

Before I went to bed, Daddy came into my room. He stood over me and put his hand on my forehead rubbing his palm into my hair. "You could have been down there Rosey." His hand was warm, almost hot against my face and his palm was flat and open when he rubbed my hair. "I'm so grateful you weren't there," he said.

I knew this was Daddy's way of saying I'm sorry this kind of thing happens. I'm sorry you have to know about it. I'm sorry for all the meanness in the world. But he didn't say any of that in words. He bent over and kissed me on the crown of my head. "Try to sleep," he said. "That's all we can do."

Mama came too. "Rosey, I went and bought some Excedrin P.M. You want two of these to help you sleep?" She held her cupped fist out toward me and with her left hand she offered me a small glass of ice water. I took the Excedrin and put them in my mouth.

"Maybe they'll give you a good night's rest." She turned and walked out, closing the door. That was Mama's way of saying everything without saying it.

The next day Mama, Bobby and I were awkward around each other, not wanting to talk about the Dolemans, and yet what had happened was so big in our minds, the whole thing shouting to get out. Late that afternoon, before the sun set, I went to the backyard and sat on the open bed of Daddy's old truck. I let my legs dangle and swing while I watched bullbats catching mosquitoes and gnats, dropping down like they would fall, darting sideways in the air and soaring again, dropping and soaring, dropping and soaring. I could hear Bobby and Josh behind me in the garage working on the old Mercury and in front of me the bullbats squawked an awful noise, a sharp, high-pitched screech.

After a while Josh came out and sat beside me on the truck. He carried with him the smell of Old Spice, but I didn't look at him. I watched the bullbats dive. "Rosey," he said and his voice was soft and mild. "I'm sorry about what happened. I know that hurt you a lot and I'm sorry. If I could make it all okay I would, but nobody can do that. I hope you're not hurt too bad."

And then this enormous aching mass in my chest came up. It came from my heart, up my windpipe, into my mouth, out my nose and out my eyes—tears flowed and I couldn't make a sound until I grabbed a breath of air. Then, I sobbed because little Dixie was dead and because there was so much cruelty in the world and because my neighborhood had as much as anyplace. Josh put his arm around me and pulled me to his chest. He wrapped his other arm around the front of me and he held me, not saying one word. I let all the pain come up in sobs and tears with snot covering the front of Josh's shirt while his big hands rubbed my back.

After a while, I felt some of the heaviness taken out of me. "I messed up the front of your shirt," I said when I pulled my face away from his chest.

"I don't care." Josh said. "I'll get you a rag."

When he came back, he handed me a rag from the garage—one he and Bobby used for car work. "It's clean," he said. "Been washed." I took it, blew my nose and wiped under my eyes. The rag had the distant odor of grease and oil and Tide detergent.

Josh leaned forward and kissed the side of my face. To this day I swear that kiss burned like sunshine on early-spring skin.

"Thank you," I said, and I took his hand.

"Josh, what you doing?" Bobby called from inside the garage. "I need you to hold this light."

"Coming," Josh shouted.

He grinned at me, and he was even more handsome than the boys in my movie magazines. He patted me on the top of my head and winked. With that, he was gone.

Again Mama came in that night and brought me two Excedrin P.M. and a glass of ice water. She held her hand out, opened her fist and the two tablets rested in her palm.

I took them. "I'll put them here," I said and I placed the tablets on my nightstand beside my lamp.

Mama left and came back again. "Let me put a washcloth under this water glass," she said. "I don't want it to ruin the finish on your nightstand."

When Mama closed my door, I switched off my light. My eyes burned from crying and stung too sharply to read. I was glad my room was on the opposite side from where Richard Doleman had committed his horrible acts. Devils may lurk on the other side of our house, but I imagined a whole fleet of angels, hovering in the oak tree outside my window. Brown-headed angels with blue eyes, black-headed angels with soft green eyes, blonde angels with brown eyes, and fierce red-headed angels with sharp green swords and fiery tempers—all hovering in iridescent blues and greens outside my window. But every time I closed my eyes, the face of little Dixie Doleman appeared, and the dark shadowy figure of Richard Doleman stood under the street lamp.

I opened my eyes and the purple piano glowed silvery lilac in the light from the moon. It exhaled an odor as thick as a living, breathing person—moldy and tenacious as time. I got up and sat on the swivel bench; I put my nose close to the keys and smelled the old thing—solid, and stolid as a boulder. I gently rubbed my fingers across the keys. Tomorrow I would ask Mama to call a piano tuner. On Wednesday, I would ask Mrs. Franklin to find The "White Cliffs of Dover" for me.

I got back in bed. The Excedrin were on the nightstand, but I didn't take them. I kept my eyes open in the moonlight and thought about Josh. Marion Institute wasn't that far away, and I was glad he was leaving, and I was sad he was leaving. I wrapped the moonlight around me and did not fight against it.

THE ALBERT MURRAY BLUES
Sue B. Walker

I've got the train whistle, train whistle, Al Murray blues,
I've got the train whistle, train whistle, Al Murray blues.
Leaves a'shakin' in the spy glass tree
And the click-clack track awakening me.

I got the blues, the blues, the Al Murray blues
Like an anapestic locomotive tellin' the news;
Chinaberry blossoms on his chinaberry tree
And the name Jack the Rabbit, Jack the Bear, and he's

Playing train whistle, twelve bar, twelve-string blues,
Right hand pluckin' out the notes he chooses--
And he hangs his hat where he props his feet
That clomp and stomp to the music's beat.

I've got the train whistle, train whistle, Al Murray blues
I've got the train whistle, train whistle, Al Murray blues
Blackberries grow along the track
Way down yonder in Buckshaw Flat:

Location in time, intersection on a map--
Maytime, junebugtime, trees runnin' sap
Along muddy waters and old hollow logs
Along pinetree ridges at Bayou Hog,

I got a guitar, and I pluck the strings,
Recall the pitter-patter, and I'm listening
To the train whistle moanin' way back when,
Telling of the places Al Murray's been.

I can hear after midnight, sounds long and low
The L & N jazzin', the GM&O;
He lives up North , way up where there's snow
But he's an Alabama boy, and it's always so

That trains still move on down the track
And Al Murray's words go clickety clack,
Callin' out, callin:' come back come back
to the spyglass tree, and the railroad track.

I've got the train whistle, train whistle Al Murray blues
I've got the train whistle, train whistle Al Murray blues.

A TASTE OF MOBILE

...we cannot know that time has just left on our plates
a memory more satisfying than cold fried chicken.

—P.T. Paul, "Cold Fried Chicken in Cadillac Square"

RECIPE

Raymond Oliver

Take one fine cluster of associations
And crush them in your mind like Keats's grapes
'Till pungence fills your skull, the echo-chamber,
'Till you are high on foam of images,
Froth of the past, and flecks of fantasy.
For instance Spring Hill College, where Loyola's
Statue exudes its substance on moody air,
Odor of sanctity and sweat like jasmine,
Pervasive. When I taught there, Jesuit-like,
Hot in a black suit and fervently tending
My German roots and compounds, herbalist
Of words, I thought the plaster in the walkway
Seasoned with more than aging rain, my office
Spicy with more than mold. My noontime sandwich,
Its honey squeezed through bread like baklava,
Seemed likewise dense with values. And the church:
On such whiteness of stucco, even shadows
Were bright.
Associations make you drunk,
Yes, but are more complex than grapes, are more
Like okra, shrimp, and rice, ingredients
Of one region that blend when simply mixed,
Like Jesuit tropics, incense, work, decay,
To make a catholic summer Spring Hill day.

A TASTE OF THE PAST

Mary M. Riser

Mobile has its share of restaurants worthy of a visit but if you ask anyone of a certain age who grew up in or around the city, you'll find those special places, located in collective memory, where dining was simply the best. Constantine's Restaurant across from the Battle House Hotel tops almost everybody's list. This was where you went to propose marriage, discuss business, or just enjoy elegant dining under the watchful eyes of the omnipresent Constantine Panayiotou. For lunch, a then home-owned Morrison's Cafeteria waited up the block with a staff like a hair-netted army standing at attention behind huge, steaming metal trays filled with just about any dish your big eyes could desire. Korbets at the Loop was the choice for friendly waitresses, Greek home-style food and drinks in a lounge atmosphere. Fresh seafood from the Gulf of Mexico and Mobile Bay awaited a short, windy drive across the causeway where old shacks perched precariously on shaky wooden stilts over muddy bay water. Here were found Palmer's, the original Blue Gill, and The Sea Ranch. Driving deeper into Baldwin County promised the more remote and therefore more exotic Mimi's and Miss Kitty's. It was worth a trip to Fowl River for a meal at Mary's popular eatery, and near Bellingrath Gardens was Bayley's, home of West Indies Salad. The Toddle House and the Freeman House were the spots for late night short orders and icebox pies.

Mobile laments the closing of The Tiny Diny (2150 Halls Mills Road). The staff referred to it as The Little Tiny Diny. "Miss" Trudy Shackleford bought it in the early 1970s. As a teen, she had been to the Tiny on dates and had prayed, "Lord, why can't I ever have a little restaurant like this?"

Breakfast was served from 5:00 a.m. until 10:00 a.m. with egg platters, omelets, pancakes (for which the Tiny was famous) and flaky, homemade biscuits. The Hungry Man Special would hold you until suppertime and only costs $3.85.

Lunch was Big at the Tiny with politicians (especially anyone running for office), local celebrities and athletes, and people from all walks of life coming together for generous weekday specials like crawfish etoufeé, chicken & dumplings, corned beef and cabbage, baked pork chop and dressing, and beef tips with noodles. Cornbread and three sides chosen from about twenty vegetable dishes accompany the entree. And of course, sweet tea was the nexus of the menu.

For fifty-six years, Alvie ("Miss Bea") Hill arrived every morning at five to prepare her delectable biscuits, tasty homemade soups, and glorious mile high lemon, coconut, chocolate meringue and other pies which graced the counter by noon.

Everything, from her famous short ribs to the banana pudding customers lined up for each Thursday, Alvie Hill made from scratch, and she refused to give out recipes, calling them "ancient Chinese secrets." "Miss Bea" was assisted by a staff of eight other cooks, all of whom helped give The Tiny Diny the reputation it deserved for the best home cooking and the most food for your money in Mobile.

Today a few old-timers can still be visited. They remain alive and well, still serving good food under the caring eyes of local, and often family, management. Dining in these restaurants will walk you back in time because the food is still good and the atmosphere as familiar as your own den. Even the customers look like old friends.

Running continuously since 1882, The Dew Drop Inn is Mobile's oldest restaurant. Located at 565 St. Louis Street, the first Dew Drop was owned by Louis Martin and registered as a saloon. Following his death, Mrs. Mary Martin became proprietress. After a fire, the "sandwich shop" was relocated by its next owner, Mr. George L. Widney, to Ann Street at Government because this was one of Mobile's first paved roads, and without air conditioning and electric lights, everybody came there at night to talk, mingle and rollerskate under the streetlight. Mr. Widney traveled a lot, saw hot dogs at Coney Island, tried sauerkraut in Germany, and met a Mexican housewife who suggested chili with hot dogs. Widney engaged a local bakery to make buns and had regular wienies dyed red because he found the brown color unappealing. Under his guidance hotdogs made their first appearance in Mobile in 1924, and Widney became known as "the Hot Dog King."As his wiener empire grew, Widney moved across from the Old Shell Road School. Then Arthur Reid purchased the business and saw the end of Prohibition as an opportunity to serve beer, necessitating a relocation away from the school, to 1808 Old Shell Road. Beginning as a "curb boy" of twelve, Jimmy Edgar grew to be Reid's partner, purchasing the business at Reid's death.

Mr. Powell Hamlin is the current owner and the restaurant has been in his family for forty years. His mom makes the gumbo. Mr. Hamlin's father bought the place from Mr. Edgar who had many offers but sold to Mr. Hamlin, Sr. because he liked him. It is easy to see that his son has inherited his affable manner.

One of the reasons customers keep coming back—one man ate there twice a day for forty-four years—is the Dew Drop's down-home, friendly atmosphere. It was that way back in the 1960's when the male waiters walked around singing to themselves and a high school Jimmy Buffett ordered chili cheeseburgers, and it is that way today. In fact, the interior hasn't changed since Edgar redecorated in 1967. Local art and old photographs line the walls and neon light streams from a beer sign over the door.

A chalkboard lists the popular lunch menu of catfish, macaroni and cheese, mashed potatoes, tomatoes, rice and gravy, apple pie, and daily specials but the homemade onion rings and hot dogs are what most people keep coming back for. The standard dog has beef chili, sauerkraut, sliced dill pickles, mustard and ketchup. There are hybrids for which the staff has special names: "upside down dog" means the wienie is on top with the kraut and condiments on the bottom; "starved dog" means no kraut, and "female dog" means all the stuff, minus the wienie. Weekday lunches are filled with regular customers jockeying for booths or standing in a long line at the cash register awaiting takeout orders wrapped in thin aluminum foil.

In 1938, J.O. Wintzell began his Oyster House right where it is today with good seafood and a lot of wit. In fact, Wintzell's humor is as much a Mobile tradition as the restaurant itself, and the original owner's favorite sayings ("No Matter What Happens, There's Always Someone Who Knew It Would" or "Come in And Eat B/4 We Both Starve") on hand-printed placards are still stuck all over the walls, guaranteeing chuckles from the customers. J.O.'s politics are plastered everywhere, too, along with autographed photographs of JFK, George Wallace, and former Vice President Spiro Agnew.

Everyday, tourists come in by the busload and members of the armed services as well as public service people eat at a discount. Local residents and downtown working people come in too, enjoying seafood like Mobile's #1 gumbo, fish, crab, and shrimp, as well as oyster stew, Oysters Bienville, Rockefeller, and oysters served in a plethora of other ways. My friend and I had the spicy buffalo shrimp and a pound of boiled shrimp with fried dill pickles and the delicious hoagie rolls, buttered, flattened and grilled that accompany every meal. It was only 11:00 a.m. and a steamy 95 degrees outside, but there were already at least seventy people in the restaurant's main dining room. Jazz played from the sound system, the food was as good as I remembered, and the waitress called me "Ladybug."

The oyster eating championship continues at the bar—the only active oyster bar in the city. It features Mr. Willie Brown who has been shucking oysters at Wintzell's for thirty-two years and Mr. Joe White who has been employed for eighteen. While we were there a young man ate twelve dozen in thirty-five minutes, enough to make him sick but not enough to beat Philip Hahn's 1990 win of twenty dozen in nearly the same amount of time. If you win, there's a twenty-five dollar prize and the oysters are free.

In 1943, Mobile's best soul food was cooked at Jack's Place on Beauregard Street. Jack's expanded into a family of five restaurants owned by Mr. and Mrs. Leroy Roberson. Roberson's Cafeteria Number Two (504 South Wilson Avenue) opened in 1983, and remains a thriving enterprise. After their parents' deaths, the torch passed to the Roberson children. James and Larry run the cafe and their sister, Thelmas, can be found there at lunch most days.

Robertson's is a brick building on a curve that allows it to face two streets at once. One of the brothers runs the pit barbeque smoking in the back beside the drive-up window. Inside red-topped stools in front of a narrow lunch counter transport the visitor back to the happy days of neighborhood diners. The first thing you meet upon entry is a glass display case where steam rises from savory dishes in deep trays. Behind it three women and one man make fast work of ladling food to customers. There are pork chops in gravy, beef tips, beef stew, baby pork ribs, pigs tails in white sauce, rotisserie chicken and chicken gumbo. Vegetables offered are turnips, squash, cabbage, and green salad with tomatoes. We ordered gumbo and each bowl was big enough for three. Huge chunks of chicken floated by okra in thick, savory sauce that was poured over white rice. Two cornbread muffins came with the order and we chose a piece of vanilla cake from the generous slices individually wrapped in cellophane and arranged on a cake plate. Our meal was so large we took some to go and paid under six dollars for two people. At 1:30 the place was still packed with chatting customers.

The spicy, warm, cinnamon and ginger wafting from Pollman's Bake Shop on Broad and Virginia will take you back to Grandmother's kitchen. And it's no wonder since Pollman's has been baking cookies, cakes and breads since 1918. In fact, the plant, at the intersection of Broad and Virginia Streets, was once a little house used for baking. Fred J. Pollman started the business on South Royal and his family continues the tradition at the plant, a small bake shop in AmSouth Bank downtown, and the Spring Hill store at Old Shell and MacGregor. Pollman's is the place for Mobile's original po-boy, bridge party petit fours, birthday cakes with ballerinas, astronauts or cowboys, and delicious small brownies with chocolate icing and all types of cookies.

Three Georges Candy Shop, developed by George Pappaiamprous, George Pope, and George Spar in 1917, has long served Mobile's sweet tooth. The first shop was on the spot that now houses the Saenger Theatre lobby; next it opened on Dauphin and then moved beside the Cawthon Hotel on Bienville Square. In 1972, the store came to its current location on Dauphin Street and is now owned by Scott Gonzales.

The interior of the candy shop is authentic with eighty-year-old, four-foot-high, mirrored cabinets flanking old wooden walls. With endless rows of brightly colored hard candies and miles of differing types of chocolate, this is a candy lover's dream come true. Atop the shelves are huge glass jars filled to the top with sour balls, gum balls, gold coins, malt balls, saltwater taffy and jawbreakers. There are coffee beans, macadamia nuts, and even ginger dipped in milk chocolate. The adventurous may purchase yogurt pretzels, chocolate rats, licorice alligators, hot feet, or bleep bips.

In the back are the sugar barrel, the gigantic mixer and other equipment that George's wife, Euple, used in making pralines, divinity, and hand dipped chocolates.

When you visit you may see two ladies sitting up front in the old ice cream chairs beside the sunny window, making candy on the marble table. If you turn a cartwheel at the sight of all the confection, they will understand.

Thomas Wolfe said you can't go home again, but with Mobile's fine food establishments, you can at least eat like you are back home. Food awakens our senses of taste, smell, sight, and touch. It has the magic to bring back memories, and it can be the catalyst for creating new ones. After all, what is more comforting than food?

A BREAD-MAKER'S GRANDMA

Andrew Saunders

For Ellen Grace who told me the story of making cantaloupe purses with her Grandma Annie Louisa Kenny in old Mobile.

Most houses in the neighborhood, wood or stone, had green shutters. Most were the same dark shade of green. In summer, they were thrown back against the house and latched. Nothing was to block the breeze in summer. At her house on Jackson Street, Grandma attached an old shade pull to the windowsill. This was her signal. When the frayed cord and gold tassel were hanging outside the sill, it was okay for me to come in. But, if the tassel were inside, Grandma would be lying down on her high-poster bed and not to be bothered.

When I rounded the corner to her house, if it were afternoon, I could see the tassel right away shining in the sun. If I spied the shine, I'd be happy, but if the tassel wasn't out, I'd be restless. Usually, I'd wait on the front stoop and pry roly-polies with a twig from cracks in the steps.

I'd try hard to make myself wait longer between times of checking the window. If I checked too often, I'd somehow make noise and wake Grandma. She was never as glad to see me then as she would be if I waited for the all-clear. One trick worked when measuring wait-time—I'd make myself have six roly-polies balled up in my hand before going to check the tassel. It seems I'd never have to pry more than three sixes before the tassel was out, and I'd roll the bugs back near their home on the way up the steps.

No matter what, I was always the same amount of excited every time I went into Grandma's house. She'd be powdery fresh and sweet smelling and praising the virtue of what she called her "beauty rest."

Most times we'd go right away to the backyard. Alongside the high board fence by the chicken yard was the old door on saw-horses that was our drying table. Under the table were pots of squished blueberries from the neighbor's fence and strawberries from the produce wagons, and store-bought dyes that Grandma would allow if they weren't too loud-colored. On the table were hundreds of cantaloupe seeds laid out in careful rows. It would make me breathe in hard to see them gleaming white and proud in the summer haze.

Folks I asked to help by saving seeds at home and in the neighborhood were slower eating cantaloupe than I wished they'd be; still, we almost always had enough seeds to keep working and to fill the orders of the girls who wanted Grandma's evening purses.

We always went about the afternoon the same, according to what Grandma called a "proper rhythm." If there were any fresh seeds, I was in charge of laying them out all by myself. Together we would check the color of the soakers and pick out any that were ready for their final drying.

Next we'd collect the seeds that were ready and take our places on a bench and table under the awning on the back porch. Grandma always had a stack of tiny, plain cloth purses she had sewn and marked with lines "to keep the seeds in a pretty set," as she would say. She'd mix up glue and we'd go to applying. "Keep the seeds snuggled up together. No cloth must show anywhere," she said. This was important, because she said it every time.

We could finish a purse a day and still have time to string four-o'clocks before I had to go home. The summer days were sweet and long.

In winter, things were different. Grandma didn't take her beauty rest as often, and the house had all the shutters clapped shut. Open louvers on the shutters meant "Come-on-in." Closed louvers said "Be quiet." Another difference; I was allowed in the front parlor to wait. I loved to watch the colored dust clouds through the door glass, so waiting was quicker. Somehow Grandma always knew when I was in the parlor and pretty soon, she'd call for me to come in.

When I'd get to her big room, the light bulb would still be swinging overhead since she had just clicked it on. The blue-yellow, blue-yellow flicker of the gas heater was always the same, and the overhead light was weaving circle patterns by bending bedsteads on the walls. We'd get under the covers to keep warm and talk about school and about Momma, but mostly about what we'd do next summer. Grandma would tell me about seeds she'd seen—speckled ones from Grand Bay melons and big brown ones that grow on stalks in the woods. It was fun talk, but I could never stay as long as I wanted.

TWO BLOCKS AND TWENTY BUCKS

Corey Harvard

"What's your strangest flavor?" I asked, feeling adventurous. She surveyed the assortment of gelato until her eyes settled pensively on the floor.

A manager beat her to the punch: "Dark chocolate with chipotles."

"Can I sample a few?" I inquired.

"Many as you'd like."

I was feeling risky. After teasing myself with Biscuit Tortoni, Turkish Roast, and Moon Pie (which captured the exact awfulness of the real MoonPie), I settled on Peanutbutter Cup. The young blonde with eyes still cogitating rolled two respectable scoops into a styrofoam bowl and signaled to my left where the gelato bar became a cash counter.

"Anything else?"

The cash drawer shot open like a starting gate; my investigation was consecrated. Armed with a twenty dollar bill, I had set out to experience an afternoon in downtown Mobile.

"Here you go." She handed me sixteen dollars and some change, and I grinned her a "thank you." Lining the wall opposite the gelato bar was a long, unoccupied booth where I sat to take in the atmosphere. Above the cash counter hung four crimson light fixtures floating like crystalline handkerchiefs—fluid in their stillness. Wall tones of sand and lime matched the airy lightness of the Beach Boys singing from somewhere overhead. There was one area that refused itself the levity of the room. The cash counter angled off into a wine bar. Isolated in its dignity, the wine bar rested against a brick accent wall.

Customers made it easy to deduce that Serda's Coffee Company is a hotspot for young adults. A man likely in his early thirties sat down at the other end of the booth and began shuffling through a newspaper; four students slouched (curled, contorted) their bodies across leather couches at the front of the store, demonstrating the slow torture of their calculus textbooks; a brunette in business clothes talked politics with the bartender. Promotions for singer-songwriter events—another lure for college types—were posted liberally on the store windows.

My stomach started growling. Before I left, I glanced at a menu. Beyond staple coffeehouse drinks (espressos, macchiatos, lattes, iced coffees), Serda's flaunted a variety of paninis, wraps, soups, and salads. I mustered up enough willpower to escape without spending anymore money.

A little wandering and I had found my next piece of Mobile. When I entered, the sweet, smokey aroma that filled my nostrils could have killed me with pleasure. Saliva abounded; the hostess spoke at once: "Welcome to Bienville Books."

Bienville, the only used bookstore in Mobile, was touched with a homegrown charm. Strips of paper were taped to shelves to serve as genre labels. A small number of newly-published hardcovers stood awkwardly amongst a swarm of yellowed mass market and trade paperbacks. Major booksellers see one kind of page—smooth, bright, flawless. Here, age conquers beauty. Fatigue, injury, and scar are met with reverence; cleanliness, with disregard.

The first floor was arranged with utilitarian rigor. Two bookshelves, parallel with each other and with the walls, divided the room into three aisles. I perused the classics before moving to philosophy, and from there I scanned the regional section. On display was a signed copy of *To Kill a Mockingbird*. Ten more minutes passed. Satisfied with my discoveries, I decided to go upstairs.

The steps were large and noisy. A small, solitary room, dimly lit and full of old texts, was built between the two floors. It was difficult to see much of anything, which deepened my curiosity. Were it not for a strange man who kept peering at me from over his shoulder, I might have stayed longer.

They named the second floor The Haunted Loft to commemorate Mobile's long deceased Haunted Book Shop. The underaged were prohibited due to "adult" books; everyone else was greeted with a different kind of warning. Suspended above the loft's cash register was a work of kinetic art: a paper-mache construction of a spider killing a fly. The insects were half the size of humans. Fellow arachnophobes can imagine what I was feeling.

In the loft, the bookshelves made a U, framing lavender walls. Organized stacks of books, found at random intervals, added to the contrast between upstairs and downstairs. It was as though the floors were owned by two rivals; the one, methodical, preferring the familiar, the simple, the straightforward; the other, partial to the peculiar, the calamitous.

Bienville utilized colored dots to price its books. Green-dotted books cost six dollars; blue, four; red, two. I bought a copy of *The Time Machine* and a book on the history of southern Alabama, both marked with red dots. I paid little over four dollars and left the store in search for food. On the corner of the block ahead of me sat a dry erase board. As I approached, I could make out the words "Panini Pete's" with an arrow pointing to the left. In need of no convincing, I obeyed the sign.

Creeping fig covered the entire face of the building, except for the windows.

"Grab a table, sugar," prompted the waitress as I stepped inside.

Beneath a thin layer of glass, the tables were decorated with photos of Panini Pete congregating with locals and Food Network's Guy Fieri. The farthest wall from the entrance was a brick accent wall, much darker than the one at Serda's. The aesthetic success of the place was its natural light. Against the density of the creeping fig and the black of the brick wall, the sun poured its softness into the room.

I wanted a burger. From the moment I stepped out of Bienville, I was mad for ground beef. Now, staring at the menu, I was trying to justify ordering a hamburger in a restaurant called "Panini Pete's." *It has been a long time since I've had a burger. A panini is certainly in the burger family; it has the same basic structure. I'm too hungry for a panini.*

"What can I get ya?" asked the waitress.

"The Rosemary Chicken Panini," I answered. I had folded to the guilt. The panini came with frites, miniature french fries with an unusual twist. I flagged down my waitress. "Is there cinnamon on these frites?"

"Well ain't that the funniest thing!" she giggled, fingers covering her mouth, "An old lady said somethin' like that last week. She said 'These french fries smell like Christmas!'"

After a few bites of the panini, I was thankful I hadn't ordered a burger. Producing the wonderful collage of flavors were baby greens, tomato, aioli, goat cheese, and Boursin on wheat berry bread. After the tip, I had spent ten of my twelve remaining dollars.

One more place, I thought to myself. *One more place and I'll have made an afternoon.* Seven days earlier, I was eavesdropping on the conversation that inspired this search for an experience that was distinctly Mobilian.

"It's such a small city, Mobile. It has nothing to offer. And you know what's worse? What it *does* have to offer is owned by big companies. There's no culture in it." Each place I visited had proved her wrong. Not only were the small businesses themselves part of a broader culture, but within those business were glimpses of a rich history. Bienville books preserved the memory of a haunted Mobile. Serda's celebrated Mardi Gras with its Moon Pie Gelato; green and purple beads ornamented the creeping fig at Panini Pete's. And all of this I had stumbled upon—unpremeditated—within a span of two blocks. I left the restaurant, turned a corner, and found my final stop.

The A & M Peanut Shop opened in 1947. Little is striking about the interior of A & M. Cramped and colorless with unwelcoming overhead lighting, at first you might think that they don't want your business. Giving the store a smudge of character was the peanut roaster, thudding away in unbroken dactyls: CH shh shh CH shh shh CH. I ordered chocolate clustered pecans along with two ounces of creole peanuts. One bite and I understood that I had been fooled. The genius of the peanut shop was its modesty. Its product erased any question of merit. The creole peanuts fumed with salt and fire; the chocolate clusters responded with a cool crunch.

As I passed through Bienville Square on the way back to my car, I was accompanied by four sociable squirrels. I imagined them asking me questions in squirrel-talk: *You from around here? What's your name? What do you think of Mobile?* Halfway through the square, I looked behind me. Every oak in the park must have been emptied; the four had become four hundred. I began to wonder if my bushy-tailed companions might have had motives for amassing their whole community. I glanced down at the half-full bag of creole peanuts in my hand and knew. That mob of squirrels was ready for war. I scurried off without a goodbye.

Upon returning to my Alero, I felt thoroughly satisfied. Under scrutiny, Downtown Mobile had held its own. Perhaps it isn't a very large city. But in three hours, I had grasped a local flavor, something that belonged precisely where it was and could be found nowhere else. *She was wrong*, I declared inwardly. *Mobile has plenty to offer*. And I had only seen two blocks of it.

First published in Vol. 3, Issue 1 of *Sense... Eclectic Intellect for the Soul*

COLD FRIED CHICKEN IN CADILLAC SQUARE
P.T. Paul

Cold Fried Chicken in Cadillac Square
(Dauphin Island, Alabama, Summer circa 1960)

We always roll our Chevy into Cadillac Square
like faithful citizens of France
come to reclaim this part of the island for their beloved Dauphin.

Past the rusted anchor chain, hard right and creak to a stop,
lawn chairs sprung on loamy sand with a "plop".

Mama and Daddy homestead with R.O.C. Cola,
a well-thumbed copy of "Gone With the Wind,"
a radiating basket of cooling fried chicken
and a small black A.M. radio tuned to Redsocks or Grand Ole Opry-
whichever comes in clearest.

Kids in Keds ascend bearded grandfather oaks
like Autumn reversed, in high gear,
with whoops and dares and Tarzan yells
from Johnny Weismuller "wannabe's"
and raspberries from Cheeta critics. *(And everyone's a critic.)*

Future second-string quarterbacks chuck apple cores like pros,
while future prom queens skin their noses.
(Unfortunately, future nurses are not yet
a twinkle in Daddy's eye, so best not to cry.)

It don't take no government agency to tell you
that Spanish Moss makes treacherous Tarzan vines.
(This is the age of common sense;
just a peachfuzz shadow past the age of innocence.)

"Bless this food, Oh Lord, to the nourishment of our bodies
and our souls to Thy service. Amen." *(Lord, let us begin.)*

Sinners of the highest order we aspire to be, (secretly)
as Gluttony and Sloth cast chicken bones for our souls
on the leaf-and-acorn crabboil poured out by last night's rain.

(Wishes are split between locked pinkies,
lost on a pull of the wrist,
then stashed in creaking gloveboxes
to be forgotten like pecking orders when tummies are tight
and all the best pieces are gone, anyway.)

Day bungles forward on the backs of single-minded black ants
plundering bits of knuckle and skin from underneath our dangling feet,
navigating femurs and backbones with the same determination we show
to the intoxicating wine of twilight – they stumble out of reach
just as we stumble toward the back seat.

"Go round, go round, little Alice Blue Gown,
we'll all be together about sundown…"*
(Daddy always mumbles songs that seem appropriate at the time,
but only songs that rhyme.)

Rumbling back to the suburbs of Whistler,
piled up with tangled curls and dirty feet,
while Little Jimmy Dickens on the radio allows
as how at Sunday dinner little kids like us might just as well
*"take an old, cold tater and wait.."***,
we cannot know that time has just left on our plates
a memory more satisfying than cold fried chicken.

* *"Little Alice Blue Gown/Cajon Love Song" - traditional*
** *"Take an Old Cold Tater (And Wait)" - Bartlett, by Little Jimmy Dickens*

MOBILE SANCTUARIES

Quite simply, books are venerated here, for their own sake…

—John Sledge, *Home Alone: A Wish is Granted*

HOME ALONE: A WISH IS GRANTED

John Sledge

It is an incomparable place, beautifully conducive to the solitary acts of reading and reflection. I am speaking of the Thomas Byrne Memorial Library on the Spring Hill College campus. This building's elegant, soaring reading room and closely packed bookshelves are a bibliophile's delight. On many past occasions, I have sought out the peace of this literary sanctuary and spent blissful hours wandering amongst its thousands of volumes.

Those of us with bookish tastes are happiest in such environments. There, free of the demands and annoyances of daily life, thoughts are free to drift where they will. When I was a student, I did not so fully appreciate college libraries, being often pushed to finish some particular academic exercise not of my choosing. Since I have been out in the workaday world, however, I have grown to cherish all the more these scholarly cloisters dedicated to the life of the mind. While on a recent visit to the Thomas Byrne Library, I was suddenly seized with a strong desire to spend the night there and write about the experience. Perhaps at that moment I crossed over the fine line that divides bibliophile from bibliomaniac, but the idea immensely appealed to my imagination. I was fascinated to know how the reading room (if left unlit) would appear at different hours of the night, what sort of campus views those wonderful towering windows would reveal as the evening progressed, and I wondered to which volumes I would be drawn if I had an unimpeded run of the book-jammed stacks. Are such fantasies not normal for booklovers? Did not Shakespeare have Prospero say, "My library is Dukedom large enough?"

Following this whim, I contacted Dr. Alice Bahr, director of the library, and asked if it might be possible. I emphasized that in order to write something impressionistic, something beyond mere reportage, isolation would be important. There must be an absence of interruptions and distractions like ringing telephones and bustling staff and students. I wanted to be left alone in that magnificent temple of learning for a very personal intellectual journey.

Dr. Bahr graciously agreed to this unusual request and promised almost all the comforts of home—refrigerator, microwave oven, soft drink machine, a few overstuffed chairs and a worn couch. Therefore, on a recent Friday, minutes before the library's 5 p.m. closing, I appeared at the doors, notepad and frozen dinner in hand. Those students still inside were eager to wrap up their studies and get on with their weekend activities, while I couldn't wait to be locked away from the world. Here then, are my dispatches from that perfect warren of knowledge.

A Night in the Library

6:00 p.m. It is growing dark around me. I am standing in the reading room of the Thomas Byrne Memorial Library. This is, beyond compare, the finest space devoted to reading in our city. As the day fades, I take the measure of this magnificent chamber: fully 100 feet in length, 50 wide and capped off by a soaring cathedral ceiling over 25 feet high, supported by heavy timber trusses. The wooden ceiling itself is constructed of alternating dark and blond boards, making it seem to rest lightly overhead. The walls are gray stucco, scored to resemble stone blocks. Gigantic wood-framed Palladian windows march around the room, affording splendid views of the surrounding campus. As it grows darker, the windows reveal less of the outside and reflect more of the interior.

The carpeted floor is arranged with wooden tables and chairs, a few study carrels, low shelves full of reference books and several overstuffed chairs at the front (west end) of the room where the current magazines and newspapers are kept. Along the walls, between the windows, are more shelves as well as the ancient cast-iron steam heating pipes. Toward the rear of the room is a series of computers, then a low open banister that looks for all the world like a chancel railing, then the reference desk and the sliding double wooden doors leading into the lighted stacks. A marble staircase with a wrought iron railing descends to the ground floor from the reading room.

As I survey this layout, I am struck by its similarity to that of a church. The reading room corresponds to the nave, where the people gather. Then, set off by the banister (chancel rail), is the reference desk where the pulpit would be, with the stacks, or altar, behind. Given that this library was to serve a Catholic college, and a Jesuit one at that, it is perhaps not unreasonable to suppose that the architect purposefully designed the interior with such referents in mind, a literal cathedral of learning.

The interior is now a crazy chiaroscuro of fading objects and deepening shades. I peer out one of the windows. To the south and east the men's dorm, Mobile Hall, looms as a dark mass punctuated by yellow rectangles. Several cars idle at the front steps and a knot of students stands around them. To the north, I can see the headlights of cars traveling Old Shell Road. Though the library is visible from there, it is set so far back that most people don't notice it. Indeed, surprisingly few Mobilians are aware of this cultural treasure in their midst. "We're unknown," the library director, Dr. Alice Bahr, told me at one point.

My reverie is interrupted by the sound of a key turning a heavy lock downstairs. One of the library employees, Richard Weaver, has left something in his office and is returning for it. We speak briefly before he goes into his office to retrieve the forgotten article. As he passes by on his way out, he says, "You're in the Jesuit equivalent of a sensory deprivation tank," and I laugh. He stops halfway down the stairs, turns, and we chat a bit about isolation and the human mind. He is an interesting man, thoughtful and well spoken, but in a hurry to get home. I am sorry to see him go.

It was built out of love. In 1929, Mrs. Nora Byrne gave $100,000 to Spring Hill College for a new library to be constructed in memory of her recently deceased husband, Thomas. The Byrnes were from Chicago originally, but had long maintained a winter residence in Mobile. They were enthusiastic supporters of Spring Hill College, and sent three of their sons to the school. One of these boys, Peter David, was tragically killed in a train accident some years before his father's death. Mrs. Byrne wished for Peter David to be remembered as well, so his name is listed on the library's cornerstone and his photograph hangs over the entrance to the stacks.

Plans called for the library to be finished in time for the college's Centennial celebration in 1931. George Rogers was chosen as the architect. Administrators asked that the new edifice be colonial, to match Mobile Hall (1927, C.L. Hutchisson Sr., architect) and several other proposed buildings (never constructed because of the Depression). With his superior design sense and attention to detail, Rogers (1869-1945) was the perfect man for the job. He had been practicing architecture in Mobile for nearly 30 years and his previous commissions included the Van Antwerp Building (1906) downtown and the Mobile Public Library (1926) on Government Street. He would subsequently design the Bellingrath Gardens and Home (1935).

Rogers took his charge seriously and found inspiration in one of the most important classical buildings in America, Thomas Jefferson's Virginia Statehouse (1789). In planning the latter building, Jefferson had copied a famous first century Roman temple, the Maison Carrée in Nîmes, France. According to Jefferson, the Maison Carrée, with its raised base and Corinthian columns, was "one of the most beautiful, if not the most beautiful and precious morsel of architecture left to us by antiquity." In his drawings for the Statehouse, Jefferson substituted the Ionic order for the Corinthian and, of course, added windows. Rogers' design for the Thomas Byrne Memorial Library is a scaled-down version of Jefferson's interpretation, with some original touches. His inclusion of large Palladian windows was his own stroke of genius, perfectly suited for a building in need of lots of exterior light. As it stands, the Thomas Byrne Memorial Library is a sophisticated edifice with one of the most distinguished architectural pedigrees in the city.

The completed structure pleased everyone. The campus newspaper, *The Springhillian*, admiringly noted that, "Viewed in the light of the setting sun, the library is a poem of architectural beauty." The paper described the reading room as "lofty, spacious, well lighted." Sadly, Mrs. Byrne died two months before the building's dedication. Oil portraits of her and Mr. Byrne, painted by their daughter, were placed just inside the student entrance on the ground floor, where they remain to this day.

The Thomas Byrne Memorial Library was built to hold 150,000 volumes. Today it is filled nearly to bursting, with 156,000 books, as well as 600 journal subscriptions and 191 CD-ROM titles. On the ground floor are a rare books room (open by special appointment), an oversized books room, archives, classrooms and offices. There is absolutely nowhere to expand, and a new library is a must. Dr. Bahr showed me drawings of the proposed building (estimated to cost $10 million dollars), and I was reassured, as the new design is respectful of the old. Dr. Bahr anticipates that the Thomas Byrne Library will eventually be devoted to rare books and the archives, a suitable semiretirement for the venerable pile.

8:00 p.m. The reading room is dark. It's time to go into the stacks and plumb this extraordinary collection. The stacks were considered something of a marvel in 1931. In its March 17 issue of that year, *The Springhillian* described their heavy-duty construction and compared them to the stacks recently installed in the Vatican by "The Librarian Pope," Pius XI. The paper rightly concluded that the Byrne Library's shelving assemblage was "on par with that of most modern libraries of the world."

The stacks consist of six levels from basement to roof, and are entered from the reading room at the fourth level through the sliding wooden doors. Access to the books was originally restricted. From 1931 until 1966 the stacks were closed and students had to present their requests to the librarian. In 1966, the shelves were opened to the student body, and remained so until 1996, when they were again closed, this time by order of the Fire Marshal.

When I enter this bookish realm, the first thing I notice is the smell, a rich mingling of old paper and leather. It's also warmer by several degrees than the reading room, given the low ceiling height and the bare light bulbs. The shelves are spaced closely together and reach from floor to ceiling. A narrow staircase enclosed in wire mesh runs up through the center of the stacks. As I descend, my footsteps are muffled, their sound absorbed by a surfeit of literature. Adjacent to the staircase is an electric dumbwaiter, a blessing, no doubt, for the staff.

The second level proves to be the most interesting, not so much for its titles as for an unusual feature. Set off to one side here is "the cage," a room with a heavy wire door that formerly housed books that the Catholic Church once considered dangerous. When Dr. Bahr had told me of this curiosity, she had laughed and said, "All the great French novelists were in there." A brief perusal of the Index of Prohibited Books (1930 edition) confirms her statement. Included on this forbidden list are Gustave Flaubert, Honoré de Balzac, Anatole France and, of course, Voltaire (he would have been delighted). The Index informs me that these men's works are "impious and unclean and apt to excite lascivious passions or flatter spiritual pride." These days, however, "the cage" houses harmless periodicals. Its door is always open. The works of the irascible French novelists are now freely available.

After an hour or so of browsing, I choose two volumes to take back to the reference desk, where I can sit in a comfortable chair and employ the services of a lamp. My selections are a 1910 edition of John Ruskin's *The Seven Lamps of Architecture* (originally published in 1849) and an 1840 copy of *Memoirs of the Court of England During the Reign of the Stuarts, Including the Protectorate* by John Heneage Jesse. The latter is a beautiful leather-bound volume with marbled endpapers. As night deepens, these books engross me. Ruskin writes, "Architecture is the art which so disposes and adorns the edifices raised by man, for whatsoever uses, that the sight of them may contribute to his mental health, power and pleasure." Such a test this building certainly passes, I muse. Jesse is equally adept with the pen, and typically British when he writes, "The reign of James the First is eminently deficient in matters of stirring and general interest. A timid Prince, a people not discontented, a long peace abroad, and a tolerably submissive Parliament at home, supply but meagre materials to the historian." I am riveted nevertheless as Jesse weaves his tale.

Again and again I venture through the sliding doors, seeking other titles—theology, science, travel, Spanish literature, whatever my heart desires. I sit at the desk and read, the cavernous darkened reading room before me, lighted magical stacks behind.

Midnight and I am tired. I make one more foray, and return with several issues of *The American Scholar* to send me into dreamland. I stumble downstairs to the staff lounge, stretch out on the old sofa, which is not at all uncomfortable, and am quickly lost in slumber.

Dawn. I awaken a little stiff, wolf down a doughnut and climb the main staircase to the reading room. A hard rain is drumming against the windows, smearing the view. The campus appears deserted. After nearly 15 hours alone in the library, it is time to go home. My appreciation for this place and its wonderful staff has deepened as a result of this experiment and now approaches something close to awe. In an age when libraries cull their old books and sell them for trifling sums, the Byrne Library's enduring commitment to its many circulating antique volumes commands respect. Quite simply, books are venerated here, for their own sake, as nowhere else in the city. It is a noble mission, nobly carried on.

from AS SUMMERS DIE

Winston Groom

Mobile appears as Bienville in Winston Groom's novel about the career and turmoil of James Payton "Beau" Gunn.

The land, looking from its highest point, stretched westward and south, rolling fields of broom grass and blackjack oak that glistened in the autumn dew, and a few scrubby pines and thistle bushes, and except in the draws where narrow swampy streams gurgled and tall hardwoods rose from the thickets, it was a harsh, unyielding place, long since timbered out and farmed out—aside from some truck vegetable patches that had been kept by the Negro families. Forty miles to the south, if it had been possible to see that far, lay the great blue-green Gulf of Mexico and the brackish waters of Mississippi Sound through which the original Holt ancestor sailed, took notice of the shoreline, landed and in time established himself as a functionary for the Spanish king, collecting taxes and tariffs.

Years later he was rewarded for this service with these very same acres and many more through a custom of the time call a thumb grant—that being the amount of land a man could cover with his thumb on a map of the day.

This Holt ancestor, Don Miguel Estaban, apparently was blessed with an exceptionally large thumb or a very small map to put it on, since his gratuity extended westward clear into what is now the state of Louisiana, and east to the edge of a great forbidding swamp, and southward to the shores of the Gulf, passing through most of the present riverport-seaport of Bienville.

from CHICKEN BONE PARK II

Tut Altman Riddick

Cries From the Itchy Press

I want to live in a town where someone has chickens,
I want to live where the post man knows my name,
I want to live where an eccentric cuts her lawn with scissors.
and where I can hear the sound of a train.
I want to live in a place where there's a dog named Buddy.
I want to live where there's a home called Termite Hall.
I want to live where a neighbor makes tomato aspic,
keeps up fences but is there when you call.
I'd like to shop where you're offered a liqueur
where stores deliver chicken and blackeyed peas,
where arrows and signs to the town are removed from the highway,
and folks get up early or late as they please.

I want to live where the people sing by the fountain
near a book store with a place to sleep on the third floor,
where kindred spirits are invited on the first meeting
to a gathering where the guests make you soar.
I want to live where every house is not fixed up,
where the hotel has a resident cat,
has been decorated by time, not designers,
where the chef wears gloves and a hat.
This poem could go on forever.
In fact I'm quite sure it will.
Mobile keeps evolving in memory
maybe time and dreams can fulfill.

HEALING WALLS
Elisabeth A. Doehring

My grandfather terrified me. The lone haunting photograph showed a towering man in a dark suit. Two intense owl-like eyes seemed to stare at me from behind a pair of thick wire-rim glasses. With his scowl and tensely drawn, narrow lips he would never be mistaken for Captain Kangaroo. Sinister-looking brows formed two bristly arch-shaped caterpillars above his eyes. Someone once told me that he had leaned over and dropped silver dollars in my crib. Not much of a memory for a child to hold on to. But then I only thought that I knew Eric Theodore Doehring.

The ground was cold and damp, but the air too warm for snow. Old buildings were set against a lifeless sky. The heavy, saturated clouds did not hold the familiar magic of a white Christmas. My senses transported me to past celebrations along the East Coast. The awe of the lights on the National Christmas Tree, the skating at Rockefeller Center, and the ambiance of Biltmore decked out in its holiday finery swirled around in my head.

A bell chimed. The deafening sound riffed through the air. I looked up at the massive clock tower. Three more chimes rang out and then faded away into the vaporous air. Rotten wet leaves stuck like self-adhesive postage stamps to the soles of my designer leather shoes. We continued to amble along the uneven brick walkway, careful to avoid the crevices with our high heels.

My childhood friend, Susan, led the way along the stone-paved walk towards the front door. A white cross atop the rusticated stone chapel caught my eye.

Slinging off another leaf, I stared at the back of Susan's head. Here I was on Christmas Day at the Visitation Monastery. Was I dreaming? Had I actually accepted my buddy's half-baked invitation? I was about to meet some ancient cloistered nun who had wanted to talk with me about my humbug grandfather.

The heavy door closed like a solid seal behind us. Fidgety, I jingled the brass knob on the oak portal. The handle looked old. I drew my palm to my nostrils and inhaled the strong acidic scent of oxidized metal.

"You will really like her," Susan said softly, her voice nearly echoing in the vacant lobby.

I nodded politely. My temples began to throb. Buying into the materialistic dreams of the eighties had depleted my emotional reserves. Twelve years in upstate New York, DC, and the Carolinas and an unfulfilling marriage had bought only a false sense of security.

All roads had led me back here, to my home of Mobile, Alabama. Just a month earlier I was listening to a North Carolina mountain man, who told me, "We go back to our childhood to pick up the future that we left behind." His words back then seemed about as clear to me as the fog that creeps in and settles along the Mobile Bay causeway. But, now I was living them.

We entered the parlor. Several low wattage bulbs burned above us. My eyes adjusted to the murkiness and I stared down at the century-old pine floors. Tall ceilings seemed to rise to the heavens. Religious art hung from paneled walls and statues of saints surrounded us.

How many times had I driven past the high limestone walls along Springhill Avenue and wondered just who lived behind them? Like others, I had envisioned a community veiled in total secrecy.

The mysterious residence undoubtedly housed tall stoic women, draped in black from head to toe. From their waists hung hefty ropes of rosary beads, walloping enough to be designated as lassoing weapons of war. The pious strands doubled as instruments of prayer, equally used for saving lost souls or for seeking deliverance from hopeless causes. Entrance into the place was granted only to those who personally knew the saints or the Pope, himself.

While I took a seat in one of the handcrafted pieces of monastic furniture, I sensed my own trespasses creeping up on me. The cane-back chair's unforgiving fibers and brittle back felt as stiff as my own knotted neck. My eyes stared straight ahead at the bars, wondering just what sort of prisoners that they held.

The cloistered door opened and a short woman came into the room. Clad in black, a humble strand of rosary beads swayed from her waist. Her bright hazel eyes immediately met our faces.

She moved like a deer in the woods weaving around the congested path of furniture, finally settling into a padded leather chair. Sister Mary Paulette's cherub face made her look more like a sixty-year-old rather than a woman in her late eighties. Her speech had an unmistakable Texas drawl. She chattered about Christmas activities and her own family back home in central Texas.

Sister Mary Paulette leaned forward, slid her arm through the bars, and reached out to touch my hand. "Your grandfather, Dr. Eric Doehring, took care of me and the other Sisters back in the forties, fifties, and sixties. He was a fine doctor and a good man. Back then there were more than thirty of us living here. We were from all over the place, the United States, Mexico, and Europe. Dr. Doehring would drive up in his Lincoln and make his weekly rounds in the morning at nine o'clock sharp. The Sister on door duty would greet him and lead him up to the examination room. He used those stairs," she said, pointing to a side spiraling staircase.

Sister Mary Paulette scooted her chair forward and leaned her wrists against the interior railing, "You see, back then our physician's room was very primitive. All that we had was an old white dentist's chair. The good doctor always walked into the room with his trusty leather bag."

The nun held up her hands and stretched her fingers apart. "And," she smiled, "he had surprisingly massive hands for an eye, ear, nose, and throat doctor. One of the other Sisters had lovingly laughed and told me, 'He has hands like hams!' But she was right. Still with those large hands and stubby fingers he was able to perform the most delicate of surgeries."

"Our examination room was on the second floor. It faced the northeast along Springhill Avenue, and took in the morning sun. We had no fans, much less air-conditioning back then. The humidity could be stifling, even in the morning. Yet, your grandfather always looked distinguished in his starched shirt, dark coat, and tie.

"We also had an infirmary located in the back. Dr. Doehring would check on patients from time to time. To reach the clinic he would walk quietly along the upstairs porch and enter the hallway outside the infirmary, moving past the arched alcoves of statues of our founders, St. Francis de Sales and St. Jane Frances de Chantal. Above the infirmary door hung a small cross. Windows inside the room overlooked our private interior courtyard. Your grandfather would look out and view the gardens below.

"Our Sisters looked forward to his visits. He was a master Scrabble player and could play the game in five different languages. He taught us how to play Scrabble, often bringing over books and his latest tricks of the trade. We exchanged new words with him. He loved to try to match words with us. One day he showed up and surprised us with a new Scrabble game. This became our first board. We played with it non-stop during our daily recreational hours.

Sister Mary Paulette suddenly laughed, threw her head back, and clapped her hands, "Oh, and back in the fifties your grandfather sent us the most original dessert. Seems that he had gotten wind of our upcoming Scrabble tournament and to mark the event, he had a cake secretly commissioned. The multiple layer torte was created in the shape of an actual Scrabble board. Atop the thin layer of icing were individual tiles made of marzipan. The good doctor meticulously designed the board and the tiles himself.

"Years later he told the Mother Superior, 'I am planning to remarry and I know how the Catholic Church feels about divorce. If you no longer wish my services, I will understand.' Our Mother Superior was touched by his sensitivity. He remained our doctor for many more years.

"A lover of art, your grandfather commissioned a number of works on the saints. In addition to doctorates in nuclear physics, physiology, and medicine, he studied theology, but he was not Catholic nor was he even a religious man. Yet he had a fascination and deep respect for the saints. One of his own personal pieces, an original of 'Jesus Being Taken Down From the Cross,' hangs in our art studio today. He presented this painting as a gift to us right before he died."

The nun shifted in her chair. Her eyes grew wide. "But, my dear," she said, her voice nearly at a whisper, "I still have yet to tell you the most incredible story about your grandfather. It happened here in the early sixties. And it was a miracle, no less. Sister Mary Lourdes was our Mother Superior back then. Everyone tiptoed around her. But she shared a special bond with your grandfather and revered his practice of medicine.

"One day Mother needed emergency surgery on her nose. Dr. Doehring was set to arrive here at nine o'clock. Fastidious with time, he never ran late. Even though our own clock rang out the hour, he still frequently checked his own Patek Phillippe gold pocketwatch, a gift from his wife, Julie.

"While Mother sat in the dental chair, I posted myself as the lookout. You see, I was an Army medic, a sergeant in World War II, and I always felt honored that he asked me to assist in surgery. Now, neither my watch nor the clock in the tower was working that day. I sat there, waiting for what felt like an eternity, gauging the time by the movement of the sun, but he never showed up. We all worried at what might have happened, speculating that most likely a dire emergency had come up.

"At breakfast the next morning the phone rang. I will never forget the meal, much less the call. We were eating blueberry pancakes when Dr. Doehring's nurse telephoned. She was emotional and apologetic; and she told us that your grandfather had suffered a massive heart attack and had died the day before."

Sister Mary Paulette pointed her crooked finger through the bars. "But," she said, pausing, her voice now as soft as a dove, "the most amazing thing about this whole story, my child, is that from that day forward the Mother Superior never needed surgery. And, her nose—well—it never once bothered her again for the rest of her life."

I felt my arms and shoulders cave into the chair. Sister Mary Paulette looked straight at me. A wall-to-wall silence lingered in the parlor and I gazed back down at the floor.

The older woman casually glanced at her watch. She shifted quickly in her chair and yanked her sleeve back over her wrist. "Oops...I am sorry, but I need to go," she announced. "The time is nearly five and I mustn't be late for vespers."

Susan stood up and shook Sister Mary Paulette's hand. I inched my chair back slowly and wiggled my hand through the bars. The woman from Texas squeezed my hand and vanished behind the door.

I scanned the outer lobby and pictured my grandfather, a black medical bag at his side. Pausing at the stairs, I traced my fingers around the hand pegs and the fluid carved design adorning the base. The staircase had a wide and handsome banister. I ran my hand along the rich oak surface, all the while vicariously following in his path. Two steps up the staircase, the wood creaked beneath my feet. I giggled softly. At the third step I noticed an alcove, a guardian angel peering out.

"Glad that you could meet her," Susan said, as I descended the stairs.

"Me, too. Thank you very much," I answered, my eyes fixed to the railing. I slid my palm along the smooth pedestal and peered at the top of the spiraling staircase.

Susan opened the front door. I followed her outside. We stood on the steps admiring the expansive grounds.

A car whizzed along Springhill Avenue, a muffler rumbling in its wake. I stared at the front entrance and imagined a dark 1956 Lincoln pulling up the drive, stopping by the front door, and a man in a dark suit and thick glasses getting out of the car.

I descended the steps with my friend. We strolled along in silence and I noticed a wet leaf stuck to my shoe.

Susan unlocked the doors to her SUV.

I pulled out my ignition key and walked to my car. A clock rang out five times. I smiled heavenwards at the old white tower.

Lifelong downtown merchants and semi-retired Morrison's Cafeteria employees seemed to spring out of the woodwork. During the next few years, old-timers would stop me at the Weinacker's Delchamps or at the Dauphine Shoeteria on Conti Street to chat about my grandfather. They, along with a few of his retired nurses and patients, told collective stories about his downtown daily routine and medical practice.

In the thirties, patients began flocking to Dr. Doehring's medical office on the eighth floor of the Merchants National Bank Building. Mrs. Greene would arrive and unlock the door every morning at nine o'clock. She would be greeted by early birds already standing or squatting out in the hallway. The former TWA stewardess' soft-spoken voice and gentle manner immediately made her a favorite with the patients. A devoted nurse, she served as the doctor's valuable assistant for many years.

My grandfather always greeted his patients in a freshly starched white double-breasted jacket with a mandarin collar. The physician would treat patients from the moment he walked in the door until the last one was seen, frequently closing the office at eleven o'clock at night. Needing larger quarters, he moved to the fourth floor of the First National Bank Building annex, where he kept the same work pace and long hours.

He treated Mobilians of every race and creed. Especially fond of music, he would pause from his practice and listen to the sounds of sweet "spirituals" filtering through his waiting room doors. Many patients were not charged, such as one anemic woman who pulled out money for her visit. My grandfather immediately returned her payment and instructed her to go out and buy a meal of chicken and vegetables.

The Mobile office was open six days a week. Sunday mornings were dedicated to the folks of Baldwin County. Many of the locals from Fairhope, Daphne, and Montrose worked long weeks and Sunday was their only day off.

Long lines wrapped around the porch of my grandparents' "Happy Landing" (now known as "Sans Souci") residence in Montrose. The townspeople would sip coffee and wait along the veranda. Others waited in the living room, perhaps admiring the hand-hewn pine rafters.

A deep stone pond was located on the side grounds near Rock Creek. The pool was stocked with koi, and two young neighbors, Todd and Miles Jones, began eyeing the big goldfish. Armed with their cane poles and worms, the boys wandered over. They set their lines in the water, determined to snag a fish, much to my grandfather's amusement.

Epiphany was a special day in Montrose. Residents dragged their Christmas trees behind them and walked down to "Happy Landing." Frazier firs and evergreens were piled high on my grandparents' beach. Once the stack ignited, a bonfire roared along the Bay. People laughed, held their mugs, and took soothing sips of hot buttered rum as the holiday music of Frank Kearley's cello filled the air.

Eric Theodore Doehring's noon routine was pure and simple—Spanish mackerel at Morrison's Cafeteria downtown. He would walk over to the St. Francis and Royal Street restaurant, a first edition copy of the Mobile Press always in his hand. Henry, the venerable waiter, carried his tray. My grandfather ate alone in the corner and read his newspaper.

A thrifty man, he shopped at downtown Metzger's and bought his size 48 suits right off the rack. His standard buys were dark wool for winter and blue seersucker for summer.

The Sisters of the Visitation had what my grandfather termed a "sweet tooth." He would frequently dash into the downtown Walgreens' Drug Store on Dauphin and St. Joseph Streets and grab a box of Whitman's Samplers candy before heading over to the Monastery.

A German immigrant, my grandfather had a passion for the game of bridge. Twice in the late thirties he was named state champion. Bridge marathons were commonplace at my grandfather's home. Father Robert L. Anderson, S.J., the twenty-five-year chaplain for the Visitation Monastery and a close family friend, often played cards at my grandparents' table.

My grandfather was an avid moviegoer. He frequented the downtown Saenger Theatre, where he would slip in at the last minute and sit in the back row. Father Anderson once related that my grandfather became so inspired from watching one particular aquatics flick that he came up with an idea. After the movie, he walked over to an area down from the State Docks, and, according to Anderson, "peeled down and jumped into the water." That night he swam across the Bay and ended up around Battles Wharf. After his ten-hour swim he was back at work the very same day. *The Mobile Press* later learned of the feat and ran a story detailing the longest recorded diagonal swim across Mobile Bay.

Few knew of this man's hidden works of charity. My grandfather was a benefactor of the Protestant Children's Home, donating both a house on Dauphin Street as well as a summer home in Fairhope, just north of the Municipal Pier.

The Mobile doctor was also fascinated with books and literature. He wrote both fiction and nonfiction pieces. His interest in the blood system and the heart resulted in a book, entitled *Low Blood Pressure*. My grandfather even received a handwritten note dated September 2, 1952 from Albert Einstein, commending him on his recently published book.

A breeze rustled through the Spanish moss. The air wisped through my hair and felt soothing against my skin. Morning Mass had ended, and I walked about the monastery grounds, a rosary dangling from my fingertips.

The walls offered a comforting solace from the loud, hustling traffic outside. I could sense the nearly 170 years of constant prayer immersed within the century-old barriers. Hundreds of women had lived here, the first group using only the hardwood floor for a mattress. The place had survived hurricanes, tornadoes, fire, yellow fever epidemics, wars, and economic depressions.

I gazed at the old handmade brick buildings. During the Civil War the Monastery was in constant danger of invasion by both Union and Confederate troops. Warned that the buildings might be used for barracks, an initial order was given to cut down all the grand oaks.

When Mobile was blockaded in 1862, the Sisters survived off sweet potatoes from their garden. They ate the vegetables for breakfast, lunch, and dinner; and even made coffee from the roasted spuds.

Once a day the nuns were allowed a recreational hour. During the War Between the States, they volunteered their free time to prepare bandages for the wounded.

An Academy was established in 1833 and operated until 1952. Young ladies studied English, French, music, art, history, science, math, and, of course, religion.

In the 1950's the Monastery opened its doors to private and group retreats. Today these retreats continue to offer moments of solitude for men, women, and engaged and married couples.

This grand dame of the Port City received her historical honors in 1967. The Historic Mobile Preservation Society placed an engraved plaque on the site. Today the marker is attached to the walls running along Springhill Avenue. This brass plate names the Visitation Convent and Academy as being "renowned as an educational and cultural center in the South." Photographs and sketches of the Visitation Monastery also reside within the United States Library of Congress.

Light passed through the Spanish moss and sparkled off the beads of my rosary. I fingered the green strand, my latest purchase from the Visitation Shop.

The day before I had visited the gift store. Among the various items for sale were religious icons, prayer cards, Bibles, books, baptismal and christening linens, wedding gifts, and the Monastery's famous "Heavenly Hash."

Mother Mary Josepha, another of my grandfather's monastic friends, was the original "Heavenly Hash" candy-maker. Demand for the new treat, a gooey mixture of marshmallows, chocolate, and pecans, quickly grew. But when signs of booming interstate commerce began to take shape, the Sisters put their foot down. The candy operation was immediately cut back, and remains a simple cottage industry even today.

A very different kind of food, unleavened communion bread, was also produced at the Monastery. The breads for the Mobile Archdiocese and diocesan churches in Florida and Mississippi as well as other religious denominations were made here.

The "baking room" was a hub of activity. Each baking day one of the Sisters mixed up a batter of wheat and flour. The batter was carefully placed into individual molds, resembling waffle irons. Engraved within the plates of the ovens were various signs and symbols of Christ.

Once the mixture was baked, each thin wafer, called a "host," was then placed into a humidifier. This process ensured that the host was soft enough to cut without leaving behind splintered pieces or broken crumbs. The hosts were then counted, wrapped, boxed, labeled, and finally mailed to their various destinations. More than a million communion breads were produced annually at the Visitation.

Today the air was clean and unusually dry and filled with the faintest aroma of gardenias. I smiled, instantly recognizing the source of the springtime scent, the gardens of the back interior courtyard. These private grounds are filled with gardenias, wild roses, hydrangeas, and Japanese magnolias.

Surrounding the private gardens is a striking arched walkway. Built in the 1870's, this cloistered walk was a familiar path for my grandfather. Many times on his way to and from the infirmary he would pass by the gardens. I closed my eyes and imagined him inhaling the same floral aromas, eyeing the wild roses growing along the trellises, or admiring the Sacred Heart statue in the middle of the courtyard.

An old Royal Crown Cola thermometer remains mounted to the brick walls of this same courtyard. Steady as ever, the rusted piece from the forties still delivers the precise temperature. Yet, I could envision an inquisitive German scientist and doctor pausing at the thermometer and peering down to check the exact mercury level.

A cat now wandered along the cement, luxuriously brushing its fur against the side parlor door. I remembered back to my own visits when I had sat in that same room listening to the late Sister Bernadette Marie. She would tell tales about my grandfather and little anecdotes about his life.

Sister Bernadette Marie was one of six siblings, half of them entering the Catholic religious life. The Long Island native was a former jogger and swimmer, but contracted polio when she was twelve years old. Her father, also a physician, placed his daughter in a wheelchair and a tutor was brought in.

To cheer her up, a young suitor once brought the recovering teenager some flowers. The boy left laughing and smiling, explaining that the young nun-to-be had actually lifted his spirits.

A kind-hearted jokester, Sister Bernadette Marie's humor was contagious. I can recall one of the final times that I saw her alive. She came limping into the parlor and greeted me with a puppet on her right hand. As she began to move the puppet's hands, we both laughed aloud. It was a boxing nun.

The tower clock boomed out the time. I admired the heaven-kissed white structure, dating back to 1885. Before automation arrived in the 1970's, the clock was set by hand. The Visitation Monastery lays claim to an illustrious array of clock tower women, including Mother Mary Josepha and Sister Bernadette Marie.

Once every week a designated clock tower attendant would scale two flights of stairs. She would arrive at a door, where she would turn a skeleton key and then climb to a third floor. Nineteen decaying steps and one rickety handrail later, she would reach the top of the tower, where she would ever so carefully turn the old metal wheel.

Two large windows faced the north and south. The tower worker bee had a bird's eye view of the grounds below. To keep herself company during her task, Sister Bernadette Marie set up a small altar, complete with statues of the saints.

Along with her clock tower duties, Mother Mary Josepha, of Montgomery, Alabama, was the Superior during the forties and the early fifties. When the clock suddenly stopped running, the Mother Superior called in a horologist. She was informed that it would cost thousands of dollars to repair the old timepiece. Her response was "cat's foot!" meaning "foolishness!" The determined female began working on the metal cogwheel herself, carefully filing away at the surfaces. To the expert's surprise the clock started running, remaining only a minute or two off for many years to come.

To celebrate the glorious occasion, Mother Mary Josepha held a reception, complete with cookies and lemonade. But there was a trick to claiming these goodies, namely scaling the old stairs to the top of the tower.

The clock chimed twelve times, signaling the call for the Angelus. The other retreatants began to move silently into the dining room for lunch. I followed them inside.

Several months ago I received a photograph of my grandfather, a gift from well-known photographer Father Robert L. Anderson, S.J.

I took the photograph over to the Visitation Monastery. We passed the picture back and forth through the bars. Both of the Sisters, my grandfather's last two remaining monastic patients, looked over their glasses and studied the photograph. The women broke into broad smiles and nodded approvingly.

We visited for some time and further stories surfaced about Eric Theodore Doehring. Mesmerized, I sat in the cane-back chair and listened. Shadows of limbs grew longer against the walls. Leaves of oak branches swaying in the breeze began to cast flickering silhouettes along the ceilings. Realizing that the sun was getting lower, I departed.

I headed toward the front door. The squeak of the hinges, the sturdy weight of the oak, and the old tarnished knob felt comforting. I walked down the front steps and took another glance at the photograph. It showed a one-year-old snuggled inside a cotton blanket, half of her face peeping out from underneath. Her right eye peered out in wonder and her wide-open mouth offered a curious pose. The little girl's entire body appeared to rest within the mammoth palms of the man with "hands like hams."

The big heavy lids were closed, a peaceful serenity about them, and soft thin lips dissolved into outstretched cheeks and broad dimples. He closely nestled his puffy cheeks up to his first grandchild's forehead only two months before he died.

As I walked out to my car, the bells chimed four times.

I turned the ignition over and carefully tucked the photograph away, all the while wishing that I could have shared it with a special Army medic, a clock repairer and candy-maker, and a puppeteer who taught me the truth about the one man who had terrified me.

RIVIERE DU CHIEN

Claiborne S. Walsh

There we were, dog days spent swimming
in youthful zest unmindful of degrees;
the humidity hanging so thick you could stab it,
slice it and serve it up wet, steaming hot
on a slab. Damp towels draped and pulled up
around our shoulders as childlike giggles and angst chilled
late summer warmth. Laughing until we forgot limp,
sweat-soaked curls framing faces in the thrill of
midday's first-caught fish. Heat too on: smells
of scales, the increased sound of cicada, touches
of hot boards beneath sensitive soles, wavy images
rising above paved roads to our Nirvana.
Dog days took on new meaning in name back then,
Became a cooling river in August swelter.

THE WATER DOG
S.L. Varnado

The Water Dog or Mudpuppy, 12 inches in length, is a large aquatic salamander found in rivers and lakes of Eastern America. The color varies-often dark brown above, paler on belly with dark spots. A larva throughout life, it has bushy red gills. Although it has a reputation for being poisonous, it is actually harmless. *A Golden Guide to Reptiles and Amphibians.*

In the summer of 1942 we were living at a little mill town called Navco, about five miles out in the country from Mobile, Alabama. Father ran the commissary (or "cumpny sto," as it was called). I attended the sixth grade at Mertz Station Consolidated School. It was my first taste of a "country school," and I had learned through hard experience to adjust to the rigorous standards of "country kids," had undergone the ritual fist fight, had my correct grammar "corrected," and been teased about wearing "knickers" until I talked my mother into letting me wear overall pants (blue jeans). I was slowly changing from a city boy into a country boy.

The war was well under way, the shipyards in Mobile were booming, and the economy was improving after ten years of depression. Mobile was swollen by an influx of people from Mississippi, Louisiana and Florida who had come to take jobs in the shipyards. The older inhabitants of the city evinced an ill-concealed disdain for these newcomers. It was the same attitude Proper Bostonians had taken a century earlier toward the Irish and Italian immigrants. It may have been the way Old Romans felt about the barbarian hordes that swept into Rome.

Mobile was like many similar coastal cities such as New Orleans, Savannah, Charleston and Wilmington: aristocratic bastions of conservative manners, slumbering in the warm memories of a Civil War long forgotten by the rest of the nation. The city fathers, members of the Bourbon Dynasty, had made their post-war fortunes in cotton, lumber, sugar cane and pine products. With a mild condescension and tolerance they ruled a population of middle class whites and good-natured blacks.

But Navco was different. The mill hands ("mill trash" as they were called) had followed the mill trade all their lives. They were ignorant, good-hearted, feisty and poor. The Mill (it was a furniture mill where parts were cut and shipped to Canton, Mississippi for assembly) was their life. It was all they knew. Like bands of nomads they drifted back and forth between Navco and the assembly mill in Canton. They lived in a section known as The Quarters, in rows of unpainted wooden shacks with metal roofs and outdoor toilets. Minimum wage that year was fifty cents an hour. It was a hand to mouth existence, and it created an underlying surliness that formed the background of their lives.

Since my father was manager of the commissary, we occupied a slightly higher rung on the social scale. We lived in a neat little house about two blocks from the commissary and had a car, a radio, and a refrigerator. Although I was friends with some of the mill kids, they felt a slight resentment toward me. They said I was "uppity"—that I thought I was "something." I couldn't figure out exactly what this meant. I read books (*Tom Swift and his Electrical Airplane*), experimented with my chemistry set, and played pool on the pool table I had received on my eleventh birthday. What was wrong with that?

One morning in the summer of 1942, I was sitting on one of the benches outside the commissary listening to Willie Johnson play his harmonica. He worked as janitor in father's store and was taking his lunch break. He had consumed two Stage Planks (gingerbread men coated with vanilla frosting) and a bottle of strawberry soda. His harmonica music consisted mainly of gurgling, liquid sounds that were supposed to resemble a train starting. He stopped after a while and knocked the spit out of his harmonica.

"Pretty good, Willie," I said.

He nodded. "I teach you how to play de blues yo' self, if you want."

"Aw right. When would be a good time?"

"'Bout fo' o'clock. Lessn yo' Papa close de sto' down early."

"Why would he do that?"

"Ain't you heard 'bout de strike?"

I shook my head. "No."

"Folks all talkin' 'bout it. Doan like dat new Yankee manager."

I had noticed a lot of activity that morning in the company street. Groups of idle men drifted around, forming little huddles and talking. It meant nothing to me.

At that moment, a lumber truck passed in front of us and pulled up at The Gate Shack where Mr. Ladner, the guard and check-in monitor, got up out of the chair he was leaning back in and walked slowly up to the cab. He carried a clipboard in his hand. You could just barely hear him.

"Where you from?" he asked the driver.

"Ocaloosa Mill." Mr. Ladner slowly wrote it down. "I reckon you can go ahead, but watch out. If anybody tries to mess with you, just turn around and come on back."

"Mess with me?" the truck driver said, pushing his black felt hat back on his sunburned brow. "Sum bitch mess with me I slap him upside the haid."

"No, you won't do nothing of the kind," Mr. Ladner said firmly. He was a tall muscular man with a scar on his left cheek. He carried a .45 pistol on his belt. "There's talk about a strike," he continued. "You could find yourself in a lot of trouble. Take the timber down to the North Stacks and unload it. And like I say, if anybody gives you any trouble, just turn around and leave."

The driver spat past Mr. Ladner and drove the truck through the gate. The truck was loaded with hardwood logs: maple, oak, and elm. They would be seasoned for a few weeks in the Stacks, sawed into planks, sent to the kiln to dry, then to the planing mill and finally to the cutting mill.

"See what I tol' you," Willie said triumphantly. "White hands got it in for that new Yankee manager. Say dey gun shut de Mill down."

"But I thought people went on strike for more money."

"Not Southern white folk. Southern white folk won't put up with no sass from a Yankee. Mist Fuller, de ole manager, knowed how to treat 'em. Dat new Yankee manager, Mr. Snider, cuss at 'em like he a sergeant in the army."

"Where did you hear all this?"

"Nigger boadin' house. All de niggers talkin' 'bout it. Doan know what to do. White folks actin' pretty mean."

At that moment, Father came to the door of the commissary and saw us. He was a dark-complexioned man with a receding hairline. He wore a starched white shirt, a tie and an apron. "Willie," he said.

"Yassuh."

"If you're finished with your lunch, you need to move those fertilizer sacks in the storeroom."

Without answering, Willie got up reluctantly and headed around toward the back of the store. He was a thin, gangling negro of about twenty-five. He tucked the harmonica in his overall pocket and looked back at me. "You cum 'roun 'bout fo' an' I'll give you yo' fust lessen."

"What's he talking about?" Father asked, ruffling my hair affectionately.

"He says he's going to teach me how to play the harmonica."

"That's all right. Listen, son, don't go down in the mill area today. They say the men are going on strike, and I don't want you to get in trouble."

"Yes sir."

"Tell mother I'll be home about six—unless I have to close the store early."

"Why would you do that?"

"Because of the strike. I don't think it will happen. There's a United States Post Office in the store. They wouldn't close that down."

Mr. Griggs, an energetic, bustling little man, was post master. He wore thick glasses and was usually annoyed about something. He and Father didn't like each other, but I could see that Father was glad the Post Office was in the store.

"You going on home?"

"Yes. I might go see Bernie."

Father went back in the store. I walked down the road to our house and then turned up Columbus Avenue. I knocked at the door of Bernie's house. His father was a "straw boss" at the Mill, so they occupied a higher place in the social hierarchy than the "mill trash." In fact, everybody on Columbus Avenue considered themselves a little better than the hands. The houses were painted and had indoor plumbing.

Bernie answered my knock with his usual sardonic grin. He was dressed in shorts. He was a good-looking boy, with black hair, a large nose and brown eyes. He was Lebanese (or "Assyrian" as people called it) and had a keen sense of humor. He was my best friend, but we were rivals. My serious approach to life sometimes nettled him while his constant hilarity got on my nerves.

"Hi," he said, crossing his eyes (one of his favorite tricks). "Care to play some Polo? I'll have the groom bring my horse around."

"What you doing?" I asked, giving him a serious look.

"Reading the Bible and singing hymns."

"Got any new funny books?" (All the boys in our neighborhood were constantly trading comic books. I had the largest collection, which earned me a certain amount of respect, despite my supposed "uppity" ways.)

"I got a new Mandrake the Magician," he said, "but I'd rather go down in the Mill Quarters. They're having a strike."

"I know. My father told me to keep out of the Quarters."

"My father told me to keep out of the Quarters," he said in a high mimicking voice. "How's he gonna find out?"

I thought about it. "We might get in trouble."

"Well, I'm going." He slipped into a pair of overall pants, a shirt, and a pair of tennis shoes. "You coming?"

"I guess so. Aren't you even going to tell your mother?"

"I'll send her a telegram," he said.

We crossed through his back lot, climbed a fence and cut through the South Stacks. You could see the guard shack through the cross piled timber. Mr. Ladner was arguing with a tall, red headed man who was carefully dressed in a suit and tie. Ladner shook his head and shrugged his shoulders.

"That's Mr. Snider," I said.

"Yep," Bernie replied. "My dad says he's a fool. He don't know from nothin'. Dad says the first thing he should do is get outta that suit and into some work clothes. Then he should buy a plug of tobacco and start chewing."

"Maybe it's not his fault that he doesn't know how to act."

"He better learn fast."

When we reached Mill Street, the Cotton twins met us on their bikes. They were called that because both had absolutely white hair and always acted exactly alike. It was next to impossible to tell one from the other. As usual, they were singing:

"Oh, say can you see, any bed bugs on me;

If you can, take a few, 'cause I got them from you."

"Mighty good singing," Bernie said sarcastically. "You oughta be in the Movies. You could do the Tarzan yell." They stared at him without expression.

"We heard they were having a strike at the Mill," Bernie said.

With their fingers, they pulled their eyes wide apart until they both resembled Chinese.

"Me no know, me no tell,

Me push button and run like hell," they said in chorus.

"We heard they were going to kill Mr. Snider," Bernie said. "Is it true?"

"He's got to die sometime," one of them replied. (I think it was Brierly).

"Where are the police?"

"Kickin' people around, I reckon," said the other.

"Can we go play pool on your pool table?" Brierly asked me.

"I guess so."

"First we gotta find out about the strike," Bernie said, pulling me by the arm.

"How come he don't never cuss?" Sylvester asked, pointing at me.

"Hasn't learned the words," Bernie said. "I'm teaching him."

We walked on past the metal building that was called the Cutting Mill. Groups of idle workers strolled by, deep in conversation. One of them said: "You kids better git to hell outta here." We paid no attention. At the end of the Mill Street next to the planning mill, a large group of men had assembled and were listening to William Moss who stood on a small platform. He was the informal leader of the mill hands. He wore overalls and a pair of glasses. He was talking very loudly, and the men were nodding in agreement. Bernie and I hovered at the back of the crowd.

Suddenly I felt someone push me. I looked around. It was Virgil Moss, William Moss's son. He was a big muscular boy with a slight fuzz on his face. He was a bully, and harbored a special animus against me.

"Ya'll better git on," he said. "My daddy's talkin' to the men. He don't want no sissies listenin'."

"It's a free country," Bernie said. "Who died and made you president?"

"You just git on," Virgil said.

With an impish grin on his face, Bernie pushed me into him. Our heads collided.

"Sum bitch," Virgil said and hit me in the face. I punched him in his stomach. He looked surprised. "Bastard," he said, and pulled me down on the ground. We were rolling around on the oyster shell road when several of the workers pulled us apart. "You kids stop that fightin'," one of them said. "Ain't we got enough trouble already? Git the hell outta here."

Bernie and I ran off. Virgil watched us with a frown on his broad face. "He'll be laying for you," Bernie said with a cackling laugh. "He'll beat your ass."

"I'm not scared of him," I said with false bravado. I was, of course. He made my life a misery. I had spent hours making up fantasies in which I killed him—sometimes with a knife, sometimes a gun.

More and more men were collecting on the Mill Street. I saw the familiar shape of old Mr. Riley walking toward us. He was a semi-retired worker who went around the mill grounds picking up trash with a pointed tool. I used to follow him around, talking to him while he worked. He seemed to like me. We discussed science, and sometimes he got off on religion. He liked to fish, and I often joined him on the Dog River wharf where he would sit for hours with a cane pole, smoking a corncob pipe. Now, however, he seemed different. He was swaying down the street, yelling at the top of his voice. "Hossanah! Glory be to Gawd."

"Drunk as a skunk," Bernie said.

There was a mild round of applause as William Moss finished talking. Just at that moment, Mr. Ladner came driving past us in his green Hudson. Mr. Snider sat next to him with a stern look on his face. His mouth was twitching slightly.

"He's just astin' for trouble," Bernie said.

The car stopped, and Mr. Snider got out. The crowd made way for him. Their numbers had grown to about two hundred. Snider climbed up on the platform and began to speak, but a chorus of "boos" greeted him. He held up his hands for silence, but the booing continued. After a minute or so, he made a gesture of disgust and started to climb down from the platform. At this point, somebody yelled, "Let's git him," and a dozen hands grabbed him. Tossing him up and down, they carried him along the road that led to Dog River. I caught a glimpse of his face, and I could see he was scared. I felt sorry for him. The road ended at a large wooden wharf that jutted out into the river. Once in a while, barges used it to unload logs. Next to the wharf was a large steam pipe that ran from the Kiln to the river. The pipe was red hot. I had touched it once at the urging of some of the mill kids and burned my hand.

Bernie and I hid in a willow thicket where we could watch things. Dog River was about two hundred feet wide at this point. Its banks were mushy and weedy. We watched as the mill hands carried Mr. Snider out on the wharf. He was pleading now. They took hold of his arms and legs and began to swing him back and forth. I glanced up the road and saw Mr. Ladner watching. He shrugged his shoulders and said something to a man standing next to him. The man nodded and walked away.

"One and two and three," the men chanted and released their hold on Snider.

Flailing and kicking, his neatly clad body flew about twenty-five feet out over the river and landed with a tremendous splash. A cheer went up.

"We better git outta here," Bernie said, and we ran back up the road toward home. We were both scared. Along the way we met the Cotton twins.

"What happened?" one of them asked.

"Me no know, me no tell," Bernie replied.

"Can we go play pool on your pool table?"

"Not right now. We got to get home. Then, later on, Willie Johnson is going to teach me the harmonica."

"You gonna let a nigger teach you the harmonica?"

"The word is 'negro,'" I replied. The Cotton Twins stuck out their tongues and rode on.

When I reached the commissary, it was closed. Groups of surly looking mill hands wandered around, muttering to themselves. I saw two police cars and Mr. Ladner talking to some policemen. Later, two more police cars pulled up. Mr. Snider, wet and angry looking, was talking to a big red-faced policeman. About a dozen of the mill hands gathered around. They were shouting and gesticulating. Bernie and I ran home.

"Where have you been?" Mother asked as I entered the house.

"Just messing around."

"I hope you didn't go near the mill."

I said nothing.

"Go wash your hands."

At supper that night Father told how some of the men had closed the store down and how Mr. Griggs had tried to stop them. "One of the men hit him with a watermelon," he said. "Broke his glasses. By the time the police arrived, Mr. Snider was roaring mad. He told the police that the mill hands had tried to drown him. So the police rounded up some of the hands and began to question them. The hands said they weren't trying to drown him. They were just teaching him to swim. The police got to laughing so hard they couldn't make an arrest. 'It's not against the law to teach a man to swim,' one of them said. Mr. Snider was furious. I understand he's quit his job as manager. The hands have agreed to go back to work tomorrow at noon. They said they wanted the morning off to celebrate."

"I think it's ridiculous," Mother said. "They could have killed the man."

"He was out of place," Father said. "He just doesn't understand Southern working people."

"I don't either," Mother replied.

Well, it was just as Father said. By noon next day the mill was rolling again. I dropped by Bernie's house, but he was gone, so I wandered down to the wharf on Dog River. Old Mr. Riley was sitting on the wharf, smoking and fishing. He was over his drunk and greeted me warmly.

"You seen all that monkey business yestidy?" he asked.

I nodded. "Just goes to show you," he said, spitting in the river. "Ain't nobody so crazy as Southern people. They're as crazy as when they started the Civil War. Other folks strike for money. They strike 'cause they don't like a Yankee cussin' 'em. I'm from Ohio myself. Folks up that-a-way got more sense, but they ain't near so comical."

At that moment his fishing line began to move rapidly out into the river.

"Got one!" he said. He pulled hard, but whatever was on the end of his line pulled harder. The tug of war lasted about a minute. Finally, Mr. Riley pulled a strange looking creature out of the river and hurled it back onto the wharf. The thing looked like a huge lizard. It was about a foot long, brown colored with red gills and tiny legs. It flopped around on the wharf. Its tiny little eyes held a look of unbearable hatred.

"Lord, Gawd!" Mr. Riley said. "It's a Water Dog. Ain't seen one of them things in twenty years. Don't touch it."

"Why not?"

"It's deadly poison. Kill a man in five minutes."

"What is it?"

"It's a amphibean. Lives on land or water. One of the most deadliest species of North American wild-life." He took out his pocket knife, and cut the line. The Water Dog flopped back into the water.

"Wonder what it was doing in Dog River?" I said.

"Up to no good," Mr. Riley assured me. "I seen a-plenty of them in Ohio. I had enough fishing fer one day. Them things give me the creeps."

We left together.

from THE STIRRUP LATCH
Mary McNeil Fenollosa as Sidney McCall

It is said that Richmond Hill is actually Springhill. This is the beginning of the chapter entitled "Colonel Jim."

In all residence communities of long standing, there obtains a hint of the primitive and tribal, demonstrated by the tacit acceptance of a chief, a sort of modern "ealdorman," in other words, a leading citizen. There is invariably a Big House, bigger than all others, and in it a man or woman who remains in the foreground of the general mind.

On Richmond Hill this dominant being, though he himself would have been the last to admit it, was James Roy, universally called "Colonel Jim." He was sole dweller in the enormous mansion originally known as "Roycroft," but since termed by its solitary inhabitant, "Stag Harbor." Architecturally it was the Hill's most notable relic of antebellum splendor, with a row of lofty, fluted columns supporting so massive a pediment that one was vaguely reminded of the Parthenon.

The driveway, exactly a quarter of a mile in length, was an avenue of spreading live oaks, set, at the time of planting, more than two hundred feet apart. Under the oaks, well forward, ran continuous lines of azalea bushes. No pruning shears had ever touched them. The upper branches, commingling, sprang to a height of at least fifteen feet, while at the bordering sides, as if in recognition of their office, they had maintained two parallel lines of verdant rectitude. Being by nature lovers of shade, they continued to flourish, even though all other forms of undergrowth had gradually disappeared.

Above them the live oaks made a leafy tunnel, suffused with chill, green light; and in the early spring, just when Ciceley's yellow jessamines were throwing their golden noose, Colonel Jim's azaleas gave forth a cry of answering rapture. They were all of one color, the deep, pulsating rose of a watermelon's heart, freshly cut.

THE BOYINGTON OAK
Kathryn Tucker Windham

This is one of many stories from a haunting collection of ghost tales: *Jeffrey's Latest 13: More Alabama Ghosts.*

In 1979, after Hurricane Frederic lashed through Mobile, destroying buildings and uprooting thousands of the city's fine old trees, many people asked, "Did the Boyington Oak survive? Is that old tree still standing?"

The Boyington Oak did withstand the furious winds of Frederic. Its deep spreading roots held fast, just as they have held against the blasts of scores of other hurricanes since the tree began to grow on the grave of Charles Boyington back in 1835.

That tree, tradition has it, sprang from the young man's grave as proof that he was innocent of the murder of his friend, Nathaniel Frost. As the tale has been handed down, Boyington said to the crowd gathered to watch his hanging, "I'm innocent. I did not commit the murder. And as proof of my innocence, an oak tree with a hundred roots will grow from my grave."

So people watched the mound of earth that marked Boyington's burial place in potter's field, and, strangely enough, a seedling oak began to grow there, began to spread its roots and to flourish. And the people who watched the tree's growth remembered the doomed man's prediction, and they wondered.

Charles Boyington left much to wonder about.

He had no friends when he arrived in Mobile in November of 1833. He came aboard a sailing ship, but no one knows why he chose Mobile as his destination.

It may have been an omen of some kind, an ill-fated omen, that Boyington arrived in Mobile the day after the stars fell on Alabama. Everywhere he went that first day in Mobile, Boyington heard excited accounts of the massive shower of meteors that had illumined the night sky, and he heard muttered predictions, "It's a bad sign."

It didn't seem to be a bad sign for Boyington, not at first. With the help of Captain Arnold, master of the ship that had brought him from New York, Boyington got a job as a printer with the firm of Pollard and Dale. He found pleasant living accommodations at a boardinghouse operated by Mrs. William George, and at that boarding house he found a friend, Nathaniel Frost.

Frost was also a printer, and he, too, was a native of New England. But, unlike robust Boyington, Frost was frail and sickly, suffering from tuberculosis. Boyington appeared to be sympathetic to Frost and even shared a room with him so that he, Boyington, could help Frost at night when seizures of coughing exhausted his puny strength.

On balmy days when Frost felt strong enough (he was able to work only part time), Boyington often took him for walks in the fresh air. They walked slowly and rested often. Frequently they walked out to the city graveyard to read the epitaphs on the grave markers, to admire the work of the stonemasons, and to wander among the trees. If Frost became melancholy and talked of death, Boyington cheered him by reciting a snatch of poetry or by singing a humorous song.

Boyington was an unusually talented young man. Not only did he have a pleasing singing voice, he also wrote almost classical prose, composed stirring poetry, and played the lute, stringed harp, mandolin, and harpsichord well. Those talents combined with his genteel manners, and his imposing appearance (though he was only five feet eight or nine inches tall, his erect bearing made him appear taller) won him quick acceptance in Mobile society.

Only a few weeks after his arrival in Mobile, Boyington was invited to attend a holiday ball at the Alabama Hotel, a fine building at the southeast corner of St. Francis and Royal streets. It was at that ball that he fell in love with a young French woman, Rose de Fleur, daughter of Baron de Fleur. Baron de Fleur had been forced to flee France following a duel in which he killed a count who had powerful social and political ties. At least that was the story told in Mobile.

On the night of the ball, Rose de Fleur wore a dress of pure silk, ivory in color, trimmed with scallops and rosettes of handmade blue lace. A late-blooming red rose, cut from the walled garden at her home, was pinned on a cluster of curls in her deep brown hair. As she danced, her dress caught the lights from the hundreds of candles circling the ballroom, and it shimmered in a kaleidoscope of fleeting colors.

Boyington somehow arranged to be her partner for dance after dance until her father frowned his disapproval, and Rose, reared to give strict and immediate obedience to her parents, danced with other young men. Before they parted, Boyington made plans to meet Rose when she went to the cathedral the next morning for early mass. Though Boyington was not Catholic (he professed to no religion), he became a faithful attendant at those early services. He found the ancient ritual beautiful and moving, but, in truth, his attendance was in no way motivated by religion. Rose was there.

Those meetings with Rose at mass (she was always accompanied by a chaperon) provided Boyington a rare opportunity to be with his love. Her parents were very strict, never permitting Rose to be alone, and they discouraged visits from young suitors. So Boyington used trusted servants to slip love notes and poems to Rose, and those same servants notified him when her stern father was away from home.

On those occasions when Baron de Fleur was away, Boyington met Rose for clandestine strolls along Mobile's tree-shaded streets. Sometimes they walked to the city graveyard, a favorite trysting place for lovers, and sat beneath a huge chinquapin tree to talk and to hold hands (always a chaperon followed them at a discreet distance) and to dream of the future. Each time they met, Boyington became more deeply in love with the French beauty.

The days when he could not be with Rose were torture to Boyington. So consumed was he by his love for her that he could think of little else. He lost his appetite (Mrs. George, his landlady, prided herself on setting a fine table, and Boyington's failure to enjoy his food disturbed her), and insomnia plagued his nights.

During many of his sleepless nights, Boyington wrote tender poems of adoration for Rose, and on other nights he struggled to concoct some plan that would make him financially able to seek her hand in marriage. He had arrived in Mobile almost penniless, and his resources had improved only slightly since then.

Boyington's fellow printers, several of whom also boarded with Mrs. George, teased him cruelly about being "love-sick." He took their teasing good-naturedly until the day when one of them found a crumpled sheet of paper on which Boyington had written a love poem to Rose. The man waited until just before mealtime, when most of the boarders, including Boyington, had gathered in the big hall to await the ringing of the dinner bell, and then in a taunting voice he read the poem aloud. The hall was filled with laughter.

Boyington was enraged. He lunged toward his tormentor and would have struck him had not two men restrained him. Frost spoke sharply to him, urging him to be calm, and Boyington heeded the advice of his friend.

The mild winter, so different from the bitter cold of the New England winters that both Boyington and Frost had known, drifted into spring. The spring of 1834 was lovely in Mobile. The entire city was ablaze with the fresh beauty of budding trees and flowering shrubs, a beauty so perfect and so fragile it seemed to Boyington to have been created solely as a setting for his beloved Rose.

That spring, as had ten thousand springs before it, seemed to promise happiness to all lovers, but for Boyington that promise was a cruel hoax.

In early April, Boyington lost his job. He had no savings, no resources, and, though he tried, he could find no other work. His situation would have been desperate had not his friend Frost helped him.

"Don't get so upset," Frost told him when Boyington screamed out in hopeless bitterness against his bad fortune. "You'll find a job. And until you do, I'll lend you the money to pay your room and board. The future is not as black as it appears to you right now."

But the spring had lost its beauty for Boyington.

He tried to hide his plight from Rose, but she sensed a change in his behavior and in his outlook. And her sympathy only deepened his humiliation and his despair.

One Saturday (it was May 10, 1834) Boyington returned to the boardinghouse shortly before noon after having spent the morning in an unsuccessful effort to find a job. Frost was leaning against the banisters on the front porch whittling. The sun felt warm and good on his back. Boyington watched the skillful manipulation of Frost's knife.

"You can carve almost anything, can't you?" he asked.

"No, I'm actually not very good at carving, but I can make simple things. My grandfather taught me what I know. Whittling helps pass the time. It's soothing. Maybe you ought to try it," Frost replied.

Boyington seemed not to hear him. "Could you carve a little wooden heart for me to give to Rose?" he asked.

"Sure," Frost answered. "That will be easy. Maybe we can go for a walk after dinner, and I'll work on it then."

So after the midday meal, Frost sharpened his knife and selected a small block of walnut from which to carve a heart. Then the two men set out for a walk.

About mid-afternoon, Boyington returned to the boardinghouse alone.

"Where's Frost?" one of the boarders asked. "He didn't get sick, did he?'

"He's all right," Boyington replied. "I just had some things to attend to, so I came on ahead." He hurried to his room.

A few minutes later, he handed Mrs. George a small package and asked that she have it delivered to Rose. Then he left the house.

When the steamship James Monroe left Mobile headed for Montgomery that night, Boyington was on board.

The next morning, Sunday, Frost's body was found beneath a chinquapin tree near the Church Street Graveyard. He had died of repeated stab wounds, wounds inflicted by a sharp knife, to the heart.

Monday's Mobile papers carried this official notice from Mayor John Stocking, Jr.:

> MURDER-REWARD-Whereas a most atrocious murder was committed within the city of Mobile upon the body of Nathaniel Frost; and whereas, suspicion rests on one Charles Boyington as the perpetrator of the horrid act; therefore, I, John Stocking, Jr. Mayor of the City of Mobile, by virtue of authority in me vested by a special resolution of the Board of Aldermen, do hereby offer a reward of TWO HUNDRED and FIFTY DOLLARS in the event of the said Boyington being convicted of said murder.

The notice of the reward was followed by a description of Boyington and the speculation that the object of the murder was likely robbery. The pockets of the deceased man had been emptied of fifty dollars or more, and his fine gold watch (it had a second hand on its face) was missing, the notice said.

The Thursday (May 15, 1834) edition of the Mobile Commercial Register and Patriot carried the announcement that Boyington had been taken into custody aboard the James Monroe, was being held prisoner at Claiborne, and would be returned promptly to Mobile.

A sheriff's posse, men who had chased the steamboat with Boyington aboard up river after he fled Mobile, returned the suspect to Mobile on the steamboat *Currier*, arriving Friday, May 16. He was placed immediately in the city jail.

Boyington staunchly maintained his innocence, but a grand jury indicted him for the murder of Nathaniel Frost. His trial was set for November.

During his months in jail awaiting trial, Boyington had several visits from Rose who came to bring him fruit, flowers, and books and to reassure him that she believed him innocent of the horrible crime. Her visits to the jail were stopped abruptly by her father.

Boyington wrote long letters to Rose in which he proclaimed his innocence and pledged his eternal love to her. He also used his time in jail to compose many poems, several of which were published in the local press.

Rose may have believed that Boyington did not commit the murder, but the jury which heard the case found him guilty, and he was sentenced to die on the gallows. Though the evidence against him was purely circumstantial, it was strong enough to convict him.

The execution date was set for February 20, 1835.

Even after the trial, Boyington continued to declare his innocence. His spiritual advisor, Dr. William T. Hamilton, pastor of the Presbyterian Church, urged Boyington to prepare for eternity by speaking the truth of his actions, but Boyington refused to confess to a crime which he swore he did not commit.

He appealed to Governor John Gayle to spare his life, but the governor declined to intervene in the case.

On the day of the scheduled execution, Mobile's streets were filled with people who had come to witness the hanging. They lined the streets from the jail, on St. Emmanuel Street, out to the present Washington Square where the gallows had been built. Whether by accident or design, the route that Boyington's death precession would follow led past the spot where Frost was slain.

It was the custom in those days for the condemned man to ride to his execution seated on his coffin. However, an exception was made in Boyington's case, and he was permitted to walk behind the cart that bore his coffin. Dr. Hamilton walked beside him.

Boyington was dressed in a plain black suit, and he wore a high silk hat which he doffed to friends whom he recognized in the crowds along the streets. He walked in cadence to the music of the brass band leading the procession, and his expression did not change until he first saw the waiting gallows.

He quickly regained his composure, mounted the platform and began to read a lengthy prepared statement setting forth his innocence. When the sheriff ordered a halt to this delaying tactic, Boyington uttered his now-famous prediction about the oak tree that would grow from his grave as proof of his innocence.

The hanging, witnesses recorded, was gruesome, terribly botched by inexperienced hangmen and by a prisoner who struggled for his life.

The event was marked by unusual incidents. As Dr. Hamilton was speaking the last words of comfort to Boyington, sheriff Toulmin walked over to greet a friend who was sitting on a log near the gallows. Suddenly Sheriff Toulmin fainted. And so did his friend. And at the same instant, the sheriff's horse collapsed in his harness.

Boyington used the confusion resulting from these faintings to make one final effort to free himself from the noose, but his struggle was useless. After about half an hour, his body was cut down and nailed in his coffin. He was buried (Dr. Hamilton and a few other men who had known him supervised the burial) in the northwest corner of potter's field at the Church Street Graveyard. His grave was near the wall on Bayou Street and only about sixty yards from the place where Frost was slain.

Shortly after he was buried, a tiny oak seedling sprouted out of his grave. Hundreds of people came to look at the seedling and to wonder if it indeed was a sign of Boyington's innocence.

Friends of Frost place a marker on Boyington's grave, a marker that read:

CHARLES R.S. BOYINGTON
Hanged for the Murder
of
Nathaniel Frost
February 20th, 1835

That marble marker disappeared long ago. No visible sign of the grave remains (the area was cleared for use as a playground years ago and is now used, unofficially, for parking, but the oak, a strong tree with a hundred deep roots, that grew from Boyington's grave, still stands.

Visitors to the spot who listen as bay breezes rustle the leaves of that massive oak hear a repeated refrain: "I'm innocent—innocent—innocent—"

UNDER THE BRIDGE
Jeffrey Goodman

How many dawns...

Under the girders of a causeway bridge,
You see, in coastal rain, the homeless edge
Back from the storm, yet, hardly feel alone,
As you observe the leaves, wind-torn and blown,
Under the bridge, like spirits lost and dead.
Late weekend traffic thunders overhead,
And when it crashes, you invoke the power
Of sympathy to save a private hour.

Among the homeless, one hides in the leaves
A goody stash he keeps away from thieves,
Like you, he says, who, quickly, need to learn,
If you steal, you drift on. Sheltered, fires burn.
Under the bridge, where nothing much is won,
Roasting a pigeon, tramps build a roach run.
Fleas, maggots, and fruit flies malinger, too:
Yet weather tells a migrant what to do.
As the storm calms, a boy's bicycle frees
One to lunch with friends at St. Anthony's;
Or, at Salvation Army, tries a hex
Nut's damaged grooves on lamps ex-convicts fix.
And one is lingering around the park
Of crack-heads, on DeTonti Square, to mark
Time with trash talk, before the buying hour,
Trying to hawk a tourist a dead flower.

One, with a Spartan nerve no drifter lacks,
One wiser than the strays running in packs,
In packs of mangy, city mutts that chew
A gutter rat, cat, or bird, light as dew,
Is keeping back the rain with a torn sheet;

Pees on the bridge, and, crossing Dauphin Street,
Is talking to himself, that lonely boy,
Double you neither see, nor dare destroy.
He buys for him, today, a Happy Meal,
They ride, at Mardi Gras, the Ferris wheel
Each year that, rising, falls, and, falling, glows,
As he quits it, alone, when the wheel slows.
You know fate's wicked wheel and ride it, too.
You breathe the very air that it spins through.

You listen to the barking of the hounds.
Below the bridge, a gamin's cry resounds;
And when you see him thumb a rainy Bic,
Lighting a joint, with it, his buddies lick,
The cry so moves you, you, on Wallace Drive,
Now feel it bring the evening sun alive.

DORLAN FAMILY CEMETERY

Carol Case

I know that the bones of my ancestors are buried
beside one another in Bayou la Batre and Heron Bay,
that boats bearing their names bob in brackish water
beneath the Southern skies where egret and seagull hover
over white caps, cattails, driftwood and oyster beds,
searching the horizon for piling on which to land.

Several times I've packed and tried to leave this land,
but even from a distance I could feel it buried
in my voice like oysters nestled in salty beds.
It rippled out from me like waves on the bay.
Each time I drifted away, the place seemed to hover
within, forcing me to seek our local bodies of water.

My earliest memories are of family and bay water,
leaping off wharves jutting out from the land,
or watching through windows as rain clouds hover.
I expect one day to be brought home and buried
between blood kin, within walking distance of the bay
where my forebearers' headstones are lined like beds.

Every season the shrimpers head out to the beds
that lie beneath the surface of brackish water.
They spread nets like veils and wings upon the bay,
and get their bearing looking homeward toward the land.
Solitary fishermen still stand astern of their boats and hover.
dipping hook, line and sinker in search of what lies buried

beneath, not so very far from where their breed are buried
and I wonder if, at night, they too dream in their beds
of mothers who always watched the sea, the women who hover
over children playing near the edge of the water,
mothers, wives, whose daily prayers whispered fathers to land
with candles lit to keep the howling hurricane wind at bay.

It's not the land that holds us but the salt air and the bay.
It takes a life time to learn where reefs are buried,
to watch the sunsets as lights appear twinkling from the land,
sleeping out on screened porches, breezes blowing across the beds,
knowing wherever we go, we'll be lulled to our home on the water
to ask a blessing on the boats when heavy rain clouds hover.

Now I'm back home in this place, my feet buried in the sand bed
at the edge of Mobile Bay, and I feel the familiar breezes hover
like an ancestral spirit sending messages across the shallow water.

ON GOVERNMENT STREET
Gail Gehlken

Wisteria roots
growing deep in sandy soil
        send snarled
barrel-gray vines
creeping up and
around poles, live oaks, and
Southern pines

holding tight
to established foundations
        before climbing,
before throwing themselves
from limb to limb
and tree to tree

in curtain-like swags
with flamboyant grace
        never fearing their route
nor forsaking their path.

Like Easter's renewal,
the vines let loose
        their lavender-blue
grape-shaped clusters

bringing spring
        to wash away winter
like resurrection
conquering death.

from AN UNCHARTED INCH

Maurice Gandy

CHURCH STREET CEMETERY

Around infant tombs of brick and mortar,
Few hopeless inches raised
Above the reaching grass,
Monument and urn thud down unheard
In the sodden sand.
Slabs with intricate concern for the soul
Have been granulated by wind and rain—
Records of great pain made glyphs,
Faded as any childhood myth;
To be puzzled over by the vine
In its long, groping climb
After light.

Is this how the children end?
Buried by rubble
Of dreams fallen in?
They lost the road
And they can't go back
And no one will ever know;
Now no one will ever know;

DEAR LORD OF US
ON SOME MORNING GLORIOUS
CLEAVE THIS BRICK AND STONE
EMBRACE THESE TINY BONES
AND GENTLY BEAR THEM
GENTLY HOME.

HARRY AND THE GRAVEYARD CAT

A Story for Children
A Reminiscence for Adults

Genie Hamner

"Hey, y'all, hurry up so we can play Ain't No Boogers Out Tonight before it's too dark!" Harry called at the Whittakers' kitchen window. His grandmother had given him permission to play in the cemetery if Billy's big sister Joan, now fourteen, would play too. All of them preferred Ain't No Boogers to Hide and Seek because it was not played in hot summer daylight—and it was definitely more fun, especially with that possibility of encountering boogers.

Harry crossed the street again to his Gramma Malone's, thinking he might finish his ear of sweet corn after all. Billy would call when they were ready.

Because more children his age played together before bedtime, Harry liked to spend summer nights at his Gramma & Grampa's. They liked it too, especially his grandmother, who knew his favorite foods, favorite books, and favorite games, and had given his big Himalayan cat Jack a home for two years.

"Come on out!" Billy yelled as Harry cleaned his cob. "Dessert later," he told his grandparents as he hurried out to join his friends.

Seven of them rushed together into the cemetery, which was just up the tree-lined lane from his grandparents' house. They were excited about playing outside at first dark. If anyone was scared about playing there, they weren't about to admit it, not even Wes Brewster, the youngest of the group.

First they decided on a spot to serve as base: the tree opposite the entrance to the Toulmin Burying Ground; Harry's grandmother had told him about its graves being moved to the Spring Hill Graveyard after businesses began squeezing its original location. The most frequently used road in the cemetery ran between the Toulmin hedge and the tree, making the tree both accessible and somewhat enclosed—a perfect base.

Joan had to appoint someone to be "it." She asked each one to choose a number and tell it to the person beside him or her. When the numbers were known among the six, Joan announced a number. Billy's brother Allen, nine, became "it," because his number was closest to Joan's choice. Like most of them, he didn't want to be "it," didn't like to be "it," but didn't whine as the younger ones usually did, not even when Joan told him to cover his eyes and count to sixty by ones.

Allen tried counting by tens, pretending he didn't hear all of her instructions, but when she halted him loudly, he began again by ones. Everyone scampered away to find cover. Allen counted as fast as he could, hoping at least someone would be within sight when he sang out, "Ain't no boogers out tonight! Grandpa killed them all last night!" He paused, then shouted, "Coming, ready or not!"

It was still light enough for him to make out figures, but he saw none at first.

Then everyone seemed to move at once, maybe trading places, for all he knew. Which way to run, to tag someone before he reached the tree? Who would be hardest to tag? He knew his brother Billy was wiry and wily. Tagging him would make Allen feel full of star power. He decided to go after little Wes, but to watch out for Billy.

Allen thought he spotted Wes behind a large gardenia bush, but he wasn't positive. It was close to base, so he decided to check it out since he could return quickly. After scanning ground level and seeing feet, he dashed around the bush and chased Wes's older brother Clay as he flew toward the tree. A low darkened old headstone that nearly made him fall almost gave Allen the opportunity to tag him out of the game. "Well, dadgummit," Allen muttered to himself when Clay touched the tree.

Then again he believed he spotted Wes, very far away but sort of dancing from tree to tree in that far southwest corner. Allen knew better than to run that far from base, but he would keep checking. Meanwhile, he heard a calamitous noise as two players apparently ran into each other. They struggled to be quiet, but muffled laughter continued from the spot. He knew he had a chance to tag one or even two, in which case it wouldn't matter if everyone else made base about the same time or immediately after. Allen decided to take a chance.

As he ran to tag either one of them, he realized they were behind the Moorer mausoleum, rather than the enormous live oak nearer to him. Should he keep going? Just then some very small person went flying by him toward the tree; he thought he leaned far enough, quick enough, to tag Carol Whittaker, the baby sister of Joan, Billy, and Allen. He had thought she was Wes, dancing in the distance. Otherwise, he would have known she moved like wind. Well, what now?

At that moment, Harry and Billy came scrambling toward the tree, still struggling with each other to touch base first. It was a crowning moment for Allen, who jumped out and tagged both. Which one did he tag first? Each said it was the other, but Allen settled it. Billy would be "it," he declared, although he wasn't exactly sure which he had tagged first.

As everyone came back together to begin the second game, each had things to report. It seems that Carol had seen a black cat, or thought she had seen a black cat. Everyone had been playing the game too intently to panic about anything, but Carol's vision stirred them. Feeling eerie, jittery, and excited, they united to search for a black cat.

Harry recalled being told about an old lady who used to have a little, old, probably dirty cottage between the cemetery and the reservoir west of it. His father and some of the guys in his group had stalked the place on their way to sneak in the reservoir, and they had reported Mrs. Jones as owner of about thirty cats, plus a whole bunch of what they called "wolf dogs," all as skinny as she was. The wolf dogs usually scared that group away, he'd heard. Harry didn't know how long Mrs. Jones and her cottage had been gone—bulldozed, did they say?—but he wondered if one of her cats's kittens or grand-kittens could still be around as the black cat Carol thought she saw. And if so, were Mrs. Jones's cats fearsome "tiger cats," as the dogs were fearsome "wolf dogs"?

When everyone returned from searching with no new knowledge of the cat, Harry mentioned Mrs. Jones and her menagerie. Actually, all of the children had heard stories about the old lady and her odd life but hadn't paid much attention. Now their curiosity was stirring. They would have to be on watch for Carol's cat, as they began calling it. It seemed a mystery or a fantasy, and the fogginess that was dancing in added to the eeriness.

To alter the mood, they began talking about some of the gravestones they noticed during the game and the search. The oddest was against the back wall about where Mrs. Jones's cottage had been; it was black African granite with gold zigzag stripes marking the four adjoining slabs. Names were carved on two of them. Flowers bloomed beside the wall and around the sides of the mass of granite. During the game, Wes had actually stood near it, unbeknown to Allen.

Clay, who had roamed the cemetery after he had touched base, told the others that they should return sooner the next night, to look for the cat and to see how very old some of the gravestones were. The oldest ones he had seen were Thomas McMillan's—he died in Spring Hill in 1878—and a Mr. Blair's who died earlier than Thomas McMillan and was born in Waxhaws, South Carolina—"Waxhaws!" Clay's laugh set off general laughter with a faint tinge of lingering anxiety.

The group began separating to go home, with the plan to meet earlier and investigate the place more thoroughly the next afternoon, and then play again, with Billy as "it." Heading through the side gate, the last one to leave, Harry was startled but certain he too spotted a black cat.

At four the next afternoon, Harry and Billy began rounding up the group. Joan and Carol were swimming in a neighbor's pool, but the boys could begin their exploring without them. They wouldn't begin playing Ain't No Boogers, however, until the girls came with them after supper.

Harry led the expedition because he claimed to have more relatives buried there than anyone else did. Most of the Toulmins were in the section where the old family had been moved, and others who had moved to Spring Hill had their own separate grave plots. Ain't No Boogers was an old Toulminville game Harry's grandmother had taught him. Her grandmother and others there had played it. Not many people seemed to know about it anymore. But Harry was proud to have introduced the game and to be leader of the explorers.

They met at the black graves, marked Wilkins, on the back wall, being easy to locate. Clay wanted to show them the McMillan and Blair graves he had seen the night before, but on the way, Harry insisted that they go in the Toulmin section and see the oldest one there that they could read. The marker at the entrance said the old graves had been moved in 1964, but the original family burying ground in Toulminville had been established by Gen. Theophilus Lindsey Toulmin about 1828, on his own tract of land, where he had established Toulminville in the first place. The boys' goal then was to find the general's gravestone. There it was! Vandals had damaged it, and time had nearly worn away its message, but a plaque gave his name and then gave his death date as 1866, when he was 70 years old.

"So when was he born?" Wes wanted to know. He was only seven.

"Let's see. I guess it was about 1796," Clay answered, full of his advantage of four years.

"Gee, was he old!" Wes concluded.

By then, Clay was already moving toward the markers he was determined to show the others. But again he was sidetracked, when Billy insisted that they detour left for a quick look at probably the tallest newer marker in the whole cemetery. It was over five and a half feet tall, taller than Joan. Harry remembered this one too. The group marveled at the Celtic Cross at its peak. Then they marveled when they walked behind it and read, "Marl Marcellus Cummings / Born 11 December 1926 / Died 14 January 1992 / Given by his nine children…." Most of the seven knew one of his grandchildren. They stood silently before the handsome stone.

As their reverie concluded, Clay whistled them together and forward. First he reached Mr. McMillan's marker. A tall standing stone on a large rectangular base, it said he was born at Palgown, Newton Stewart, Scotland, July 19th, 1804, and died at Spring Hill, Ala., June 10th, 1878. His wife, buried beside him, with a smaller standing stone, was born in South Carolina and died in Mobile. Standing nearer the Dilston Street fence was John J. Blair's, a grander marker than McMillan's. Atop its square base was a large square pedestal maybe six feet tall, and atop the pedestal was a taller column. Only one or two similar markers were in the cemetery, and one of them was nearby, reading simply "Mary." John J. Blair, whose wife Martha did not seem to have a grave or stone in this graveyard, did indeed come from Waxhaws, South Carolina, where he was born on 12 April 1793, and died 13 June 1844.

"What do you make of these graves bricked up above the ground?" Wes wondered. There were three large ones, side by side, two daughters and one son of John & Martha Blair, and a child's near the McMillans' graves.

"You can see some like it in the other old cemeteries in Mobile. The slabs are like those flat on the ground, you see. But why they were built up, I don't have a clue. This place is too high to worry about floods. Maybe they thought they looked finer that way. But the writing has been worn down worse than most others, and one looks like it has been broken into," Clay responded.

"I'm glad we can't see inside!" Wes declared. "I wouldn't look."

"Yes you would," Clay said. "Or you'd peep through your fingers!"

"You're scaring me, Clay. Stop it," Wes shouted.

Just then, the swimmers, now dry and dressed, ran across Dilston and into the cemetery to join the expedition. Again Harry expected to resume his leadership, and again he was interrupted, not that anyone but Harry cared.

"Look!" Joan shouted. "Look at this standing stone: 'Thomas McMillan Blair, Lieut. 5th Co., Washington Artillery C.S.A., son of John J. and Martha Blair, born at Spring Hill, Ala., Aug. 3, 1839, KILLED AT *Battle of Chickamauga*, Sept. 20,1863.' I can't believe we've found the grave of a Civil War soldier! Just imagine!"

"So what's the big deal," Billy asked. "I'm tired of this old stuff. I'm ready to play. Who cares whether they're named Stewart, or Marston, or Perdue, or Broun, or Gustav Adolph Sengstak, or White-Spunner, or Gaillard, or one of those easy ones—Walker, Tiller, Hunter, Huff, Hunt, Hill, Gates, Green, Gray, Brown, and Still. I think 'Still' would make a fine name for a graveyard, don't you?"

"Well, press my watch, brother!" Joan said. "You must have slipped over here this morning and studied names, my man! You couldn't have done that otherwise. No way!"

"Just who do you think you are, some kind of rat-spy? I'm not telling how I know. Not to you, anyway, Miss Smarty. Think you know it all, don't you?"

When Joan made no reply, Harry took off running around the low brick, vine covered wall with a small sign, "Dawson," hanging on a closed gate, hurrying to the historical marker for the Spring Hill Graveyard before further delay. The plaque said it was established in 1844, Harry told them, and that meant after some of the people, like Mr. McMillan and Mr. Blair, had been born. Maybe Spring Hill didn't exist much sooner than 1844, he guessed, and maybe some of the people buried earliest had helped make the community in the beginning, even before it had its own cemetery and post office. That seemed quite likely, but they would have to check it out with their parents or grandparents.

"I wonder what they looked like back then, and how they dressed, and whether the men wore long curly wigs," Wes said.

"Billy, do you know where they went to the bathroom? I've heard something about 'outhouses,' and 'privets' or 'privies.' I'm just curious," Allen said to his older brother.

"Aw, Allen, you always want to change the subject! For all I know, the men went up to the reservoir and the women went down in the gulley where they say pretty gardens used to be. Let's don't talk about that now," Billy said, thoroughly embarrassing his kid brother.

Before feelings were hurt further, Clay was moving back along the Dawson wall, whistling for the group because he was nearing the oldest live oaks in the cemetery. It didn't take but three or four of those enormous trees to form a canopy over that entire end of the cemetery.

"Wonder how old these trees are?" Allen asked.

"Another of your left turns, Allen," Billy shouted.

"But I want to know too," little Wes said.

So all seven of them rushed to the largest and spread their arms, to see how big around it was. The two ten-year olds Billy and Harry, plus eleven-year old Clay, and nine-year old Allen were able to touch fingertips as they stretched around it. Carol and Wes, both only seven, stood below big brothers, their arms stretching across backs, their hearts throbbing proudly as they made their contributions to their group's effort.

Joan, meanwhile, took in the scene and snickered before saying, "It's a giant, for sure, you mighty boys and girl! Maybe Dad could figure the age by knowing the circumference."

While some observed the expansive canopy of trees, others turned to the Stein markers, noticing how thick and sturdy they were. Thicker than any others in the cemetery. And all alike.

"They must have lived on Stein Street," Allen said with a belly laugh. It seemed obvious enough to make him feel stupid, but others laughed heartily as well, so he felt okay.

"They probably owned a lot of this property—Stein Street as well as the land here for their family cemetery," Clay surmised.

"I've found the marker for Albert Stein! I've found the marker for Albert Stein!" Joan shouted as if she had made a major discovery. "It only gives his name and dates, 1787-1874.

"We studied him in local history," she told them. "He was a civil engineer who came to Mobile around 1840 to redesign the Mobile Waterworks, and they're still in use as he built them, I believe. He used fairly long cypress pipes with beveled ends and other ways of making sure they fit together perfectly, to run the water under city streets, and the water source he used was a spring at the foot of Spring Hill. Before he came to Mobile, I believe he also designed the waterworks for Cincinnati, Richmond, Louisville, Kentucky, and other cities, some large, some small, and achieved special effects with hydraulics in several ports. He was an architect, too. What did he design? Oh, I remember, churches! One that he designed and had built was the first St. Paul's

Episcopal Church, now called the little church or the chapel. That was the church which his family attended. Gee, even though his marker is very simple, he must've been famous in his own day," she concluded, pleased with her find.

"Well, I don't know about the rest of you, but I'm not as enchanted as Joan is. I think I'll scoot home for supper and return for the game," Billy announced, and turned to go. Allen, Joan, and Carol turned to follow him, but something caught Carol's eye.

"I see that black cat again, everybody! I know I do!" By then she was running in the opposite direction, toward graves marked "Greer." As she neared the spot, the cat slipped out of sight and left her looking at a white marble angel. It nearly took her breath away. "Come here now," she ordered in her second-grade voice. "The cat's gone, but here is the prettiest angel in this graveyard. She's the prettiest angel I've ever seen. I want one just like her on my grave someday."

"Oh, Sis. Don't talk like that! That's far, far away," Joan said to her.

"Maybe so, Joan, but remember, that's what I want. I'm not scared to have my place here with all these people who've lived where we live. And I hope children will come play here with each other and with their dogs. I hope they *will* run across *my* gravestone. This is a place for fun and learning, not for crying or being scared. So remember that too, Big Sis." And off they all trotted for their supper.

Billy and Harry were the first ones out again. As they waited for everyone else to arrive, Harry told Billy some stories his grandmother had told him about Mrs. Jones and her wolf dogs, some about how different boys would dare others to go knock on her door and run away fast, or try to sell her a ticket to the Mary B. Austin Play Day lunch.

She also had told him about the thin black cat that his very own cat Jack had become friends with. Several times she saw the thin black cat on her patio, but he would run out of sight if she went outside. He seemed to slink in and slink away or simply disappear. He didn't look like he had come for anything but food. Because he was so thin, sometimes she would put a handful of dry cat food on the patio, hoping he would come for it and she could glimpse him again, but she never did, or not that way.

Then one night when Jack came to the glass door, she saw that the black cat was with him. "When I cracked the door," Harry quoted her as having said, "Jack stepped back as if using his formal manners and let the black cat enter and eat out of his pan. I had never seen anything like it, one cat leading a scaredy cat to food, and the scaredy cat's losing his fear when spotting the food. He settled down and ate his fill, apparently, then he hastened silently out the door and out of sight. This beat all cat stories I have heard. It was beyond odd. Spooky, in a way." She became silent then.

"What happened the next time?" Harry said he had asked her, expecting some even more surprising event.

"He returned only once, when I was out planting," Harry quoted his Gramma as saying. "I'm sure he was hungry, but I didn't stop and bring food out for him. Nor did I watch what he and Jack were doing, since I wanted to finish what I was doing. In just a few minutes, though, when I heard some faint rustling as of leaves and a barely audible, eerie, inhuman sound, I looked swiftly enough to see him dashing away with one of my little green frogs, the ones with the pop-up eyes and canary yellow eye liner. I adored those frogs and their strange voices, so with no thought of the cat's hunger, I chased him away, flailing my arms and screaming like a crazy woman. All but two of my frogs are gone now, and I'm sure that cat took them. What's worse, he didn't eat a one, I don't believe. It was simply in him to kill."

"I asked her if that made it sound more like he descended from Mrs. Jones's cats," Harry said, "but she lifted her shoulders and tilted her palms up and said she couldn't guess. Maybe."

Because he seemed to be quoting exactly what his grandmother had said, Billy felt a blend of excitement and uneasiness. "Tonight, let's look for the cat first," he said.

"Trying to get out of being 'it'?" Harry teased. "I'm not sure we can arrange that. We'll have to take a vote." He was smiling. "I think searching for a black cat at first dark sounds like a fine change from Ain't No Boogers Out Tonight. In fact, that cat might be as much booger as cat, and I believe Carol will agree with me."

"So why don't we fill water pistols, in case we need them?" Harry added, grinning.

"Right on, buddy!" Billy responded as they scrambled for the two small pistols and one larger one Harry had and filled them to the brim with water. Off they went to shout out the full gang and let them return for their weapons, if they owned them.

When all had assembled, Billy announced that since he was "it," he would assume leadership before the game began. "No objections, right? Oh you be quiet, Harry! Now this is the plan. We will search for the cat first. We're prepared, with our water pistols in our pockets, and I say let's spread out in a line from the back of the cemetery down to the Dilston Street fence, with spaces between us, and then all together walk forward as straight as you can. As we move down slowly, stare at everything, trying to discover that skinny cat! Yell out if you do, and everyone else will close in. Okay? Remember, when we reach that Dawson wall, we'll have to shift in closer together, but then spread out again. Okay, now. Forward, MARCH!"

The mood was somber, for they were taking their assignments very seriously. But they were enjoying the staged effect, too. So on they went, no one yelling out, until Carol neared the black granite.

"Yahoo! Scooby-Doo! Spider man! Come to the black markers!" she yelled.

Then came her second yell. "Oops! That was my imagination, I believe."

The group moved on, but not long before Wes—who had fallen behind to look at a ginko tree that began with two trunks until one of them divided into three, making four—called out, saying he thought he now saw the black cat on the black marker. The brigade did an about face and looked carefully until Clay, near the black slabs, assured the rest nothing was there.

"Yes, there is!" Carol said. "There he is! I see him, for sure!" She was moving like wind, fast and silently, and she swept the nearly hidden cat into her arms. "And don't you try to get away from me," she told him somewhat more softly.

At that moment, she saw the soldiers rushing in with their guns up. She pulled herself up into her finest posture, raised her chin and her right hand, and commanded, "Halt in the name of the law! And that means, don't you *dare* aim at this hungry cat. You've probably never been as hungry as this cat is everyday! Put those pistols back in your pockets, and go home for cat food and milk."

As the guys began to take orders from the small girl, in their turning toward home, Carol turned her back for privacy and began to rub the ears of the cat. She could feel each of his bones when she rubbed his back. He preferred ear rubs, and soon began purring. She was too focused on giving him attention to realize what a kind and forceful person she was showing herself to be, but Joan, at a distance, realized.

By the time the boys returned, Carol was ready to complete her self-appointed role. "One or two of us will come everyday to this black place and put food down beside the wall. We will also bring water or milk, and keep a little pan here for it. Does anyone have a better idea? Someone needs to adopt this cat, and it might as well be us."

Everyone was pitching in trying to make a place to care for the cat close to the black stones. Each one seemed really excited and really happy about what was happening.

"What will we name it?" Wes asked. I think we should name it."

"Him," Clay corrected.

"Well, all right, name him."

"I've already decided that," Carol declared as if she were an adult. "The name is 'Booger Jones.' And that's that."

Harry gave her a thumbs up, then everyone did.

And that was that.

* A Mr. Jones and his wife once lived at the foot of the reservoir, in a cottage on property now incorporated into the cemetery. It seems that he was overseer of the reservoir. She continued to live there for years after his death and was known in the neighborhood for keeping many cats and even more dogs. (ELH)

from THE SOUL OF THE CITY

Ethel S. Creighton

The old theater, built by M.N. Ludlow, was one of the first theatres built in Mobile. Many famous artists were heard on its stage, and it figures in a murder case in which a leading lady killed her actor husband.

THE THEATRE

Against the old building
In the filling-station yard
The moonlight makes
Strange shadows,
Deep restless shadows moving with the
Breeze.
Many people stop for oil and gas;
They do no know that in the velvet
Darkness
An orchestra is waiting,
And ballet girls
In tiny skirts,
And all the cast for a great play
Stand by.
The theatre is gone;
Only this old back stage is left
Holding these
Shadows by a
Slender thread.

MOBILE PAST

There go the ships a'sailing by.
Where go the ships, there go I.

—Betty Spence, "Ballad of 'Floating Island'"

GROWING UP WITH HISTORY
Walter Edgar

As I travel around the country giving talks about the South and the American Revolution, one of the questions I am asked most often is "What made you decide to become a history professor?" The short answer is that in 1961 I started out a pre-med student at Davidson College until I hit chemistry class. Then, in response to a question from my worried parents about what I intended to do with my life, I replied that my favorite courses since grammar school had been history and I wanted to become a historian. I'm not sure that my response reassured them, but at least they had an answer.

While I had had some wonderful teachers, it was not they who first turned me on to the subject. For, you see, I grew up in a family where history was something discussed at the dinner table and at family gatherings. History, especially local history, was often the topic of conversation. Whenever we took a trip, I believe we must have stopped at every historical marker. When we did, the adults with us would elaborate on what the marker said. Although I don't remember either my sister or my saying what one of my own children did on a similar historical stop ("If I ever hear someone say 18th century again, I'm going to throw up!") I'm sure we must have thought it on occasion.

The late 1940s and early 1950s—pre TV—meant that on Sundays our family (parents and siblings and one or more grandparents) went for afternoon excursions. Sometimes it was a trip to Bellingrath Gardens to visit my Uncle Bell [W.D. Bellingrath]; sometimes it was to meet at the Government Street home of one of my grandmother's elderly cousins, Amy Triplett Ledyard. In nineteenth century fashion, the house was built almost to the sidewalk. It was a great place from which to watch Mardi Gras parades.

Both Uncle Bell and Cousin Amy were marvelous storytellers. On these visits we children were expected to sit and listen to the conversation—at least part of the time. And for those of us who sat still long enough, we learned a great deal.

But, I didn't need to go visiting to find someone who could tell great stories. My paternal grandfather, Ernest Edgar, Sr., and my maternal grandmother, Serena Abbot Moore, always had a good tale or two for their grandchildren. Big Dad (as we called my grandfather), was a heavy set man with a full head of gray hair. He was an old fashioned gentleman who changed his clothes and hats according to the season. From Easter to Labor Day he always wore seersucker suits and a panama hat. After labor day, it was a dark blue or black three-piece suit and a fedora. Winter or summer, his long-sleeve white shirts were heavily starched.

Big Dad had scores of memories to share. He had grown up in an orange grove in Florida in the last years of the nineteenth century when the state was not far removed from frontier status. Then his father had moved to Mobile and founded the Mobile Pulley Works on Ann Street beyond old Hartwell Field.

Granny Moore, in a quiet but always authoritative voice, could reel off many generations of family history. She didn't simply recite names and dates; she always had an anecdote about each person. Thus forebears were not just names, but living, breathing human beings. And, bless her heart, she didn't keep many family secrets. I'd match her chronicling of various branches of the family tree to any Old Testament writer of "who begot whom."

In talking with me about history, Granny Moore made sure that I needed to understand that history, while important, had its place. Her husband (my grandfather) was from near Claiborne in Monroe County and had been the youngest child of an older couple who had been adults before the Civil War. Granny used to say that all her late mother-in-law did was rock on the porch and lament about how much the family had lost as a result of the war. Granny's admonition was that learning about the past was important, but that you should not try to live in it. She said that many was the time she wanted to go over and pull her mother-in-law out of the rocker and tell her: "quit moaning about what had been. Do something with yourself in the present. Life is for the living." It was a maxim that she herself followed until her death in 1972.

Talking about history is one thing, but exploring the physical reminders of the past made an even greater impression on me. In the late 1940s, we usually made at least one, maybe two, visits a year to Fort Morgan. In those days all of the highways were two lanes and there was no air conditioning in automobiles. Our jaunts started off early so we could beat the heat for at least the first leg of the trip in my mother's black Pontiac. To while away the time we played cow poker—one point per cow on your side of the road. White mules were worth five points and a cemetery could wipe out all of your winnings. When we got to Fish River, traversing the wooden floating bridge which rose and fell with the tides was as exciting as any carnival ride.

Then, as the soil got whiter and the trees more scrubby, we knew that we were approaching the fort. It was then pretty much in a state of neglect with only an elderly caretaker, Hatchett Chandler, and a number of goats roaming the grounds. While most folks today associate the fort with the Civil War, my parents used our outings there to teach us United States history as well.

Less than five years after the end of World War II, there were still sandbag machine gun emplacements at the crossroads leading into the old military reservation. Among the stands of pine trees behind the dunes were spindly wooden watchtowers where observers had searched the Gulf for any lurking German U-boats. Both were reminders that ships had been torpedoed at the entrance to Mobile Bay and that there were always fears of an enemy invasion. The abandoned black-painted hulks of the Spanish-American war batteries were concrete relics of America's rise to world power. Then, there was Fort Morgan itself. Despite the accretions of military occupation during four wars since 1865, much of the old fort remained as it had been during the Civil War. Among the mounted cannon were several that dated back to the eighteenth century and were a legacy of the three European empires that had once held sway over this place we now call Alabama.

It made no difference how many times we went to the fort, or climbed the steep granite stairs to the parapet, or rolled objects down through the hotshot furnace. Each visit always seemed fresh and exciting. In 1951, Mr. Chandler dropped in on our picnic lunch and regaled us with more stories about the area (Isabella deSoto and her oleanders; Old Hickory and Holdfast Gaines; and, of course, the Battle of Mobile Bay). And, being a published author, sold my mother a copy of his book, *Little Gems from Fort Morgan*.

I still have this book in my library and note with interest that the author set aside five cents for each copy sold to benefit the Damon Runyon Cancer Research fund. As of April 1951, he had deposited in the Farmers and Merchants Bank of Foley the sum of $66.00. That mean that he had sold more than 1300 copies—even today that's a bestseller for historians!

But history was not just something we went to see once or twice a year, there was all of downtown Mobile to explore-pre-urban renewal. Below Broad Street, there were still hundreds of antebellum structures. A trip to run an errand downtown could easily turn into a history lesson. Before the coming of the malls, people still shopped downtown. Doctors and dentists had their offices in the VanAntwerp and Merchants National Bank Building. The Saenger and Downtown Theaters showed first-run movies. Downtown Mobile was a wonderful, lively place.

When I got older and was allowed to take the bus downtown alone, I'd sometimes opt to walk part of the way back home because then, the city's built heritage was still pretty much intact. Using Marion Acker's pocket-sized *Glimpses of Old Mobile* as a guide, I searched out much of what remained of the city's built heritage. The gray granite pile of the Robert Mills-designed Custom House and Post Office stood on the corner of Royal and St. Francis. In the 200 block of lower Government Street, there was McGill Institute with a window where a former occupant had used her diamond ring to scratch her initials into a window pane. Closer to the river was the red brick and stone-trimmed LeVert House with its Romanesque arches. The Cawthon Hotel towered over Bienville Square, but its famous roof garden had long since been enclosed. Brick-paved Water Street was lined with warehouses and ship chandleries that occupied rambling nineteenth century buildings. Many of those warehouses, when demolished, supplied the "old brick" for homes in the new subdivisions in the western part of the city.

No trip downtown was complete without a visit to the Haunted Bookshop located on the first floor of the old LaClede Hotel. With its cast iron balconies and slightly seedy appearance, it was the perfect location for a used bookstore. Chats with Mary Frances and Cameron Plummer and Caldwell Delaney opened up a whole new world—that of Mobile-related fiction. As my interest in the city's past grew, it became easy for relatives to know what to get me for Christmas and birthdays—a book about Mobile. And there were lots of titles from which they could choose: Frances Gaither's *Painted Arrow*, Welbourn Kelly's *Alabama Empire*, Frances Parkinson Keyes' *The Chess Player*, Erwin Craighead's *Mobile: Fact and Tradition*, Richebourg McWilliams' *Fleur de Lys and Calumet*, and Caldwell Delaney's *Mobile*. The first Mobile book that I purchased on my own was a copy of Julian Rayford's *Cottonmouth*—from the Haunted Bookshop.

Looking back from the perspective of a half-century, I can see now that my appreciation for history and material culture was an integral part of my education as a small boy in post-World War II Mobile. The war had brought changes to the city, but they were not apparent until nearly a decade later. The Mobile in which I grew up was pretty much the city that had existed between the two world wars—a gracefully aging Southern seaport. It fairly exuded history. That Mobile has long since disappeared, but I'm thankful that I grew up in that place. And, I'm thankful that I had a family for whom history was a living, integral part of modern life…of who we are—not a fossilized specimen in a glass case.

MISS ALICE FRAZER RECALLS THE YELLOW FEVER EPIDEMIC OF 1897

Virginia Greer

It was a hot, muggy season. Heavy rains fell, and the swamps north of Mobile stood swollen with stagnant water. Toward nightfall, the swampy undergrowth took on an eerie, repugnant look, and the ghostly miasma covered the murky waters like an evil spirit. The darkness and the unknown terrors of the swamp seemed to be inexplicably linked with the dread words—yellow fever.

At 256 State Street, the five young children of Dr. and Mrs. Tucker Henderson Frazer were puzzled and mystified. Eleven-year-old Alice Frazer and her younger siblings sensed something unusual was happening within their household that summer of 1897.

"Serious and secret discussions were taking place between my mother and father," recalled Miss Frazer in February 1962. "They were not paying much attention to us either! We could not understand it."

"Finally my mother took me aside and said, 'Daughter, I will tell you what your father and I have been discussing. Don't say anything about it, although it will be known in time. Your father has had a letter from a doctor in Biloxi telling him of a case of yellow fever in Gulfport. He feels that when news of the case reaches Mobile, people will panic and there will be an exodus.'"

"'You are the oldest and I want you to know Father feels it will be impossible to keep yellow fever out of Mobile now that it is near. He wants me to take you and the children and go to relatives in Atlanta. Atlanta will not quarantine against Mobile.'"

Recalling those impressionable memories of her eleventh summer, Miss Frazer continued, "My mother knew that if yellow fever struck Mobile, my father would never abandon his duties as a physician. She refused to leave town."

Already that summer, yellow fever had swept Cuba and areas south in epidemic proportions. Dr. Walter Reed and physicians in Cuba were working on the theory that yellow fever was caused by the bite of a mosquito. Dr. Frazer was an early supporter of Dr. Reed's hypothesis, so when he saw that his wife would not leave Mobile, Dr. Frazer took measures to protect his family. He had screens put over the upstairs bedroom windows at a time when window screens were rare. "The children may play outdoors during the day, but before sunset they are to come indoors and go upstairs," he said.

Close at hand, people in New Orleans began falling victim to yellow fever. This caused great consternation among Mobilians, and Mobile quarantined against New

Orleans. Miss Frazer remembered seeing trains from New Orleans come through Mobile. "People could get on the trains, but no one could get off," she said.

As predicted, the news of cases of yellow fever near Mobile spread, and people crowded on every available train to get out of the city. Those who did not leave by train fled to Cottage Hill and Spring Hill, camping out if need be, to reach higher ground away from the marshes and swamps.

"Mobile was almost a ghost town. The streets were so deserted that the streetcars seldom ran. Too few people. Weeds grew high on State Street," Miss Frazer continued her narrative.

"We rode our bicycles and played outdoors during the day, but before sunset we were indoors, upstairs. There were many yellow fever cases in Mobile. When Father came home at night, we children were not permitted to go near him because he treated yellow fever patients, but we could lean over the banister and call down to him."

Every house with a yellow fever case was required to display a yellow flag on the door as a warning. "There were yellow flags on doors all around us," said Miss Frazer, "and I remember the depressing feeling those long afternoons as tolling bells announced the funerals."

The first case of yellow fever had appeared in Mobile in late August, and the summer heat continued well into the fall. Public schools did not open until "after the first killing frost," Miss Frazer said. "I remember that school opened that year on the first day of December."

Mobilians who had fled the city slowly returned. "We had a great deal of company," said Miss Frazer. "I recall hearing a friend tell my father that Mobile was completely dead and would never amount to anything again. But my father said that when the medical profession discovered the cause of yellow fever, it would be completely blotted out in Southern cities and forgotten about in the next few years."

Not one member of the Frazer household came down with yellow fever. The disease was conquered in 1899, and the words of hope voiced decades ago by a staunch Mobile physician lingered in the ears of his daughter in 1962.

Miss Alice Frazer died in February 1983.

from MAUVILA
Jay Higginbotham

Through the front gates Soto and his horsemen thundered on, against the drooping sun, preceded into the plaza by Juan de Guzmán's foot and crossbowmen who already were beginning to fire the buildings. Juan Páez let loose another fire-arrow, this one striking a hut near the center of the plaza. The arrow lodged in the thatched roof, the fire spreading rapidly; the roof exploded into flames, thick columns of smoke spiraling up and out, then down below. When the smoke reached down into the cabin, the doors sprang open, the Indians burst from their hiding places, coughing and gasping for air.

"At them!" Soto yelled, "*¡Adelante!*" then back came the cries, "*¡Vamos! ¡Valor! ¡Animo!*" as the revived *caballeros*—Pedro de Carrión, Juan de Alvarado and Cristóbal Mosquera—bore down on the bewildered clubmen, slashing them, gouging them with their lances. "Gonzalo Silvestre! Don Antonio Osorio!" Soto cried. "Aim for their faces!"

Headlong the *caballeros* charged into the mass of bodies, thrusting their points in lightning jousts. The Indians screamed, clutching their eyes, leaping about blinded. Guzmán's footmen rushed in for the kill, slaughtering like goats those who remained standing. "That's it!" Soto cried. "That's the way! Kill them all!" He rode up to Juan Páez and shouted, "Now fire the buildings! Fire them all except that one!" He pointed toward the captives' cabin surrounded by warriors, unaware that one of Páez's men from the other side of the plaza had but moments before sent two flaming arrows onto the floor and roof, then he turned to his remaining forces. "Attack that building first," he said, pointing toward the cabin where Tascalusa was thought hiding. "Then we'll rescue our people. Fire it!" he cried again, waving his sword toward Tascalusa's cabin. "Fire it now!"

Juan de Páez and his crossbowmen came forward, aiming the burning arrows first at Tascalusa's building, then at the houses around the plaza. Some of the footmen charged with torches, lighting the roofs and doors. The roofs burst into flames, the rooms filling up quickly with smoke, driving the natives through the doors and windows, emptying the houses. The fire and smoke seemed to enrage the Indians; they rushed the Christians wildly, overrunning two of the horses, tripping and tumbling them to the ground.

The mass of bodies choked the streets, blocking passage, but suddenly a renewed force of horse charged through the east gate led by Alonso Vásquez and the governor's nephew, Francisco de Soto. Raving, they thundered through the streets, heading for the massive wall of flesh clogging the way in front of them, scattering bodies and mangling every clubman they could reach. "Revenge for Don Carlos, you dogs!" Francisco de Soto yelled. He stormed ahead recklessly, thrashing his steed like a mad Moor with the fire of vengeance in his eyes. "*¡Jesús qué Victoria!*" he screamed, his lance striking left and right, piercing the faces of the awe-struck warriors. His companions watched his movements in amazement. With sheer abandon, he dismounted and charged into a flurry of Indians with only his shield and sword, swinging wildly until an arrow came streaking through the air as if shot by a god, plunging through his eyesocket and out the side of his neck. "Aww- wgggghh," he gasped, falling straight back. Aghast, his companions pulled him to the rear, then quickly out the gate.

Soto never saw it; only later did he learn that his nephew had been struck down. For now he was on the other side of the plaza near the north wall, urging his men to attack but realizing the Indians were still numerous.

"Where's Lobillo?" Soto asked, glancing toward the north wall, then at the sun. "It's beginning to get dark now. What's keeping him?"

"The arrows are too thick," Gallegos said, "we can't get through."

"Where are they all coming from?" Soto asked, searching for the sources. Above the trees the sun was seething and sinking, a fiery orange seemingly on the verge of exploding.

"Over there!" Gallegos shouted. He pointed toward a large cabin near the wall.

"Charge it, then!" Soto called out. "Fire it, now!" Hurriedly, the firebrands torched the building, sending hundreds of warriors scurrying into the square. Lobillo rushed his men through the stockade, felling scores of longbowmen, some of whom, having left their arrows behind, turned on the Christians with their bows, welting, cudgeling them until cut down by Lobillo's halberdiers. Torrents of natives were pouring into the streets now, most of the buildings apparently in flames. Mauvila was in chaos, warriors and nobles, hunters and chieftains scrambling about, screaming in bewilderment. "*¡Por Dio!*" Soto muttered, looking around, wondering how things could have come to this. The Indians were everywhere, tearing about, not knowing where to go or what to do. Soto's men cut them down rapidly, but still they came on. "At them!" Soto kept shouting. "Kill the bastards! Kill them all!"

Outside Mauvila, the remaining horses were running down those trying to escape. Scores of natives were climbing the walls, some slipping through the holes cut by the halberdiers, others bolting through the gates. Once past the stockade, they struck for the trees, many maimed and burned, screaming, with their hair on fire. The horses, the dogs, pursued them relentlessly, tracking them down like rabbits, striking at their heads and shoulders. Few of the natives made it to the woods, most collapsing before they reached the trees.

Inside the stockade, the natives began to rally, recovering from their confusion. In desperation, they began to charge, bunching up in great clusters, once more driving the Christians toward the stockade.

"Out through the gate!" Soto yelled, waving his horsemen back, trying to scatter the Indians. "*Nuño de Tovar*," he called out, then together the horses retreated for the entrance, thundering away from the burning houses. "On to the gate!" Soto cried, hoping the Indians would be following. He was yelling at Tovar, at the rest of the horses, urging them back, when he felt a jolt on his left side. "Aaarghhhh," he groaned, grasping his thigh, but the arrow dug deep in his buttock. He kept riding, groaning, gripping the shaft, frantically trying to extract it, but the point would not give way. When he got to the gate, he stopped, feeling the flint digging in his flesh. He tried again to extract it, but it wouldn't budge so he broke off the shaft, wincing and cursing.

Surveying Mauvila, Soto saw the flames shooting higher in every direction. Every building, it seemed, was now on fire, the Indians still pouring into the streets, some joining in the assault against the Christians, others trying to scale the walls. Those joining the attack were quickly cut down, their bodies falling about, piling up in heaps like maggots.

Through the smoke and dust fading in the sunlight, Soto's eyes shot ahead to the building just beyond the council hut, to the cabin where the priests and women were. "Good God…" he groaned. The captives' cabin, he could see, was on fire like the others but he couldn't tell how far the flames had progressed. Whether the captives were still alive or whether the smoke and fire had already consumed them, Soto didn't know, but looking at the blazing roof, the sinking sun, he knew if they could ever be rescued, he would have to move now; though little time was left, though he'd been thwarted at every turn by the mass of bodies obstructing his way, there was still one final chance to save them.

"*Nuño de Tovar*," Soto shouted, holding his sword aloft, the shaft in his buttock still racking him with pain. "*Nuño de Tovar, Alvaro Nieto…*" He called their names again, as they gathered around him at the gate. "We must rescue our people," he shouted, pointing his blade. "We must get to that building now!"

"We can't make it through," Nieto said. "It's impossible. There are too many of them, the horses can't keep their footing."

"I don't care if it's impossible or not," Soto yelled. "It's our only chance to save them, we've got to do it! We've got to do it now, do you hear? Now! *¡San-ti-a-go!*" he cried, turning his horse.

"*¡Señor San-ti-a-go!*" his men echoed, "*¡Santiago y cierra España! ¡Jesús, qui Victoria!*" and off they galloped, shaking their swords and shouting, tearing down the dusty street toward the cabin beyond the council hut. "*¡San-ti-a-go, y a ellos!*"

Hearing the Christians' cries, seeing the *caballeros* thundering toward the buildings, the Indians moved forward, their fear of the horses seeming to vanish. Before, when they'd seen the beasts approaching, they'd scattered at first glance, but now they appeared aweless. Crazed by the smoke and carnage around them, they were less frightened now of being eaten alive by giant ogres than of death by sword and fire. "*Palammi!*" the clubmen screamed, gazing into the setting sun. They rushed out to meet the horsemen, their priests behind them, baring their chests to the sky, begging the gods of the sun to swoop down and save them, devour the oncoming proctors of evil. "*Palammi! Palammi!*" the high priests shrieked, echoed by the warriors plunging to a final applause, a last death charge they believed would annihilate the Christians also.

"At them!" Soto cried. "*¡San-ti-a-go!*"

"My God"—Nuño de Tovar gasped, as the horse neared the mounds of flesh. "This is it! *¡Dios es grande!*" He raised his lance high as if making one last, one defiant thrust before dying, but as he lifted the point and aimed it for the face of the first Indian reaching them, an arrow whooshed through the air, striking the double-pieced shaft, lodging between the pieces, the arrow making a cross with the lance. "*¡Por Dios!*" Tovar cried, gaping at the cross he was holding. "It's a sign—it's a miracle."

Side by side now, plunging toward the wall of flesh, the sun flaring wildly just above the orange horizon, Soto and Tovar, scarcely ten yards apart, felt something strange between them—a presence, pale and incorporeal, just behind and beside them—but they did not turn, they forged on, uplifted by the form they could barely see, a hoary figure on a shining white horse galloping along with them—with all the Christians—into the maw of death, into the fiery midst…

VOYAGE OF THE *CLOTILDA*

The Last Slave Ship?

Jean McIver

The subject of the last slave ship has generated a great deal of conflicting information and misinformation so that developing an accurate account is difficult. After the Federal law abolishing importation of slaves into the United States went into effect, the practice continued, according to some sources, at least until 1862, while other reports have concluded that the last slave ship arrived in Brazil in 1888. Interest in the *Clotilda* developed immediately after the ship landed because the captives were considered contraband and the ship's crew pirates. Further, it was illegal to construct ships to maintain or support the slave trade. The voyage of the *Clotilda* developed from a boat captain's defiance of these Federal laws.

Timothy Meaher, regarded as one of the best and most successful of steam boatmen, was a pioneer in navigating the Alabama River. During 1858 he served as captain of his steamboat, the Roger B. Taney, on a weekly trip between Mobile and Montgomery. The voyage of the *Clotilda*, often identified as the last slave ship to dock on the shores of the U. S. mainland, was conceived on one of these trips. A group of easterners aboard ship were discussing secession from the Union and Federal legislation that made it a capital offense to import Africans for the purpose of slavery. They also discussed the risk involved in breaking these laws and decided that this was reason enough for the slave trade to end. On the other hand, Timothy Meaher assured his listeners of the ease with which a cargo of slaves could be brought into the country, and on a bet of $100,000 Meaher agreed that he could bring in a cargo of Africans within two years.

On returning to Mobile, Meaher made arrangements to acquire the *Clotilda*, gaining the confidence of several prominent slave-holders who promised to purchase some of the Africans if the venture proved successful. Captain William Foster, the *Clotilda*'s builder, was engaged to command the ship. Some sources suggest that the ship set sail in 1858, but a widely accepted date is 1859. However, Captain Foster's notes indicate that the ship sailed from Mobile on March 4, 1860 with a cargo of rice, rum, beef, pork, sugar, flour, dry goods, sundries, bread, molasses, water and $9,000 in gold. The crew of twelve set out for the coast of Africa in rather calm weather, reaching Cuba in 3 1/2 days. But from Mence to Bermuda they encountered rough weather during which the ship was badly damaged. Captain Foster writes:

> From Mence to Bermuda had rough weather. Sprung main boom and other damages: March 17 off Bermuda 60 miles north, encountered a heavy

> gale of wind lasting nine days. With great damage to vessel, having shipped a sea which carried overboard everything on deck except two boats. One fastened on top of midship house, and one on cabin house, also carried away boat davits and half the steering wheel, and split the Rudder head in three pieces: Portuguese "Man of War" chasing us from 8 A. M. to 6 P. M.; squalls all day, and about dark our foresail went out of the boli rope in splinters: the most exciting race I ever saw.

On April 16, when the *Clotilda* reached a port where the crew could stop to repair the ship, they refused until Captain Foster also received clearance from the American Consul to trade on the coast of Africa with a recommendation that he go to an island experiencing famine. The crew resumed sailing on April 22nd, arriving at Whyda May 15 when, as Captain Foster and the crew:

> […] anchored 1 1/2 mile off the shore at 4 P.M. A boat boarded us the same evening to know our business: I told him I wished to exchange commodities and therefore would have to see the Prince and officials […] Having gotten ashore safely. I met with interpreter who kindly congratulated me and gave me in charge of three natives, who put me in a hammock with canopy and carried me into the city of Whyda. Six miles distant: upon arrival I found splendid accommodations for traders. I spent the night in Merchants Exchange. Having breakfasted early I with Cicerone sallied forth to transact my business with the […] ebony Prince, a man of 250 lbs.

Having "agreeably" transacted his affairs with the ebony Prince, Foster selected 125 humans from his estimate of 4000 captives confined in a warehouse, these to be exchanged for $100 per head and commodities. The *Clotilda* left with only 110 because of the crew's fears of capture by steamers they had sighted.

The return voyage to the United States was less eventful, though the trip was marred by a sighting of a man of war, inclement weather and a near collision with a sunken ship. After anchoring off "Point of Pines" Grand Bay on July 9, Captain Foster paid $25 for use of a horse and buggy to take him to Mobile where he engaged a steam tug to tow the *Clotilda* into the Alabama River at Twelve Mile Island. There the captives were transferred to a river steamboat and sent into the canebrake to hide until further "disposal." After sending the captives to the steamer, Captain Foster says, "I burned the schooner to the water's edge and sunk her." A decayed remnant of a ship found in this area is thought to be the *Clotilda* (Captain William Foster, letter to Mr. Donaldson, 25 September 1890, Archives, University of South Alabama, Mobile, Alabama).

In a 1906 article in *Harper's Monthly*, one of the survivors of this voyage, identified as Abacky, was described as "an unfortunate creature" who "related a painful tale of suffering. In slow, soft tones of awful earnestness," says the author, S. H. M. Byers, "she spoke of their peaceful farm and village life in Africa; how they tilled the ground, planting yam and rice; how some of the women traded in products with other tribes—and all was peaceful. Abacky's home was in Ataka, near King Dahomey's land. The peaceful existence there was broken just after daybreak one summer morning when the citizens heard sudden shouts and firing of guns. According to Abacky, "men, women, and children sprang from their beds, only to be killed or captured" by the raiders of "the terrible King Dahomey who had come to enslave the village." The attack was such a surprise that it lasted only about a half hour. I can imagine Abacky's pain as she recounted the fate of the villagers. The young and the strong were chained together by the necks and the feeble and old were left dead or dying in their burning village. While Byers does not provide specific details regarding Abacky's travel aboard the *Clotilda*, he does call attention to a glaring omission in Captain Foster's account—descriptions of conditions in which the captives were forced to live aboard the ship. Byers writes:

> Abacky's story of the [. . .] murderous cruelty of that voyage of weeks and months, as the helpless captives crouched in filth and darkness, chained in the hot hold of the ship, gasping for breath, praying for a drop of water, was related in a way that would have melted stone. After forty years her eyes were burning, her soul inexpressibly agitated, at the memory. ("The Last Slave Ship," *Harper's Monthly Magazine*, 113 (1906): 742-46)

More revealing is the story of Cudjo Lewis, the last survivor of the *Clotilda* captives, who left, through oral transmission to his descendants, a story of his family's creation—the Kazoolas (spelled variously)—which includes an account of his capture and the voyage.This story was recorded by Israel Lewis, III who got it from his grandfather Israel Lewis, Sr., who got it from his father Joseph, a son of Cudjo. Betrayed by Akeniki, a disgraced Kazula male who had been banished from his village, the Kazulas were attacked by the army of Dahome. Caught off guard, the Kazulas soon realized that Akeniki had betrayed them. Cudjo noted that some elderly family members called Akeniki a "dust sucking snake," obviously a strong, negative epithet. Israel Lewis noted that the family members attributed the attack to Akeniki's revenge and were especially upset that a family member had served as a spy.

Cudjo reported that all the young men and women fought with the "spirit of a leopard," but it was in vain because of the surprise attack and also their being outnumbered. The king and queen mother drank an herbal substance concocted by a "secret priest" which made them appear to be dead. So the invaders left them for dead. The invaders "burned houses, grain, food stuffs, animals, poisoned the water and stole wealth they had seen. They killed the elderly and sick but tried to save many young males, females, children and expectant mothers." The captives were forced to walk many days before reaching the water and boarding the *Clotilda*. Capturing his grandfather's dialect, Israel Lewis wrote:

> Wen deh got to dee big wata, deh seened sum ships setting on top of dee wata. Dee slaves wuz put in a large place wid many other African slaves fram many kinds, afta deh walked down a dirty road. Many days went by an deh seened a man wid white skin talking to some Dahomean soldiers. He was callded CAPETAN!! Den Capetan pointed to dee Tarkars an dare frenz. Some soldier fixed dare hands in front an sumting 'tween dare foots an legs. Deh couldn't walk free. Den deh all wuz pointed to step in little wood boats that carried dem all to a big wood sheep. Deh needed help up to the top of the [...] deck an some soldiers or men pointed down to a big dark hole. Deh went. Dare wuz many, many, many who went down in that hold, which looked like night. Most could stand up but dee man at top said 'down, down,' wile pointing a stick or his arm. Womens and chillins up near Capetan, mens in sides an back of dee sheep.
>
> Den, afta manee days an nights down dee bottom, dee night all the time, in dee sheep, Capetan, who looked hara and dara in disa hole ware deh all stayed [...]
>
> Deh landed in Amarika. Dat is wat sum wite mens seh. Sum ob dee Afriky jumped ob dee sheep in sum near woods an bushes an wuz gone. Dee Afriky who stayed wuz lined up an sold to sum wite mens by Capetan Fasta. Sum went to Mount Vernon, Clark, Selma, Tuscaloosa, an Greensboro. But Papa Kudjo, Charlee, Polee, Peter Lee, Orsey, Ellis, Zuma, Kanko, an 'bout twenty-two more stayed an wuz owneded by Capetan Meaher [...]
>
> Afta dee wa, ancestors knowed dat deh want go hohm. Deh 'cided to do all dat deh knowed fur deh families [...]
>
> Wen ao ancestas wuz freed deh builded houses, cherchez. Ones by Papa Kudjo out at dee point. Deh ails wasa baptaiz at Stone Street Baptist Church [...] Lata deh hedded MCT [Mobile County Training School], in Plateau (Israel Lewis, III, "Who Was Cudjo Lewis? [The last living slave of the *Clotilda* 1860], ts. Archives, University of South Alabama, Mobile).

Thus, when the Civil War ended, these Africans hoped to return to the homes from which they had been snatched, but their scrimping (for example, existing mainly on a diet of molasses and cornbread or mush) resulted in their saving little, and these former slaves realized that their dream of returning home would never materialize. This unrealized dream is poignantly illustrated by the headline accompanying Cudjo Lewis's obituary, which appeared in the *Mobile Register* in July, 1935 "FAMOUS EX-SLAVE DIES HERE WITH AMBITION UNREALIZED." Ambition along with other admirable qualities, such as endurance and intelligence, enabled Cudjo and the other Africans to use their skills especially in carpentry, masonry, and farming to create a bearable life in an unknown land, establish the community we now know as Africatown, and contribute to the development of the Mobile community. Consequently, they all bought from Meaher property on which they had lived and farmed. Perhaps because he was the last survivor of the *Clotilda*, Cudjo was often sought out by interviewers, among them Zora Neale Hurston whose article appeared in the *Journal of Negro History* in October, 1927. What emerges is the portrait of a remarkable, witty man with a vivid memory and a sense of history. Through this and other interviews, Cudjo made significant contributions toward the preservation of the African heritage that he had known. He provided revealing glimpses into the daily lives of the people of his native land. There, life was peaceful among these industrious people who survived through agriculture. Among them there was no hunger, no poverty. He further provided information on their marriage customs, religious practices, and the justice system. For a people labeled "savages" and "pagans" by "civilized" Europeans, Cudjo's countrymen possessed a highly developed sense of morals. For example, he told Hurston that murder is always punished by death in the same manner as the victim died. One of the severest tribal laws was against theft, a crime almost unknown, for everyone worked, houses were never locked, and all had plenty. To illustrate his point, he told Hurston,

> 'Suppose [...] I leave my purse. You know the square in Mobile? I talk, I go way and leave my purse on de ground. Every body see it. They say: 'Cudjo forget his purse' Nobody steal it. When I get to de Creek (Three Mile Creek) I feel I see I left it on de square. I say its [sic.] too far to turn back. Today I have no time. I get it tomorrow. Tomorrow I am too busy again, but it stay there. Nobody move it because it belongs to Cudjo. Could I do that in America?'

Another important contribution that Cudjo Lewis made was his eye-witness account of the role of Africans in the slave trade. His description of the destruction of his village and the murder of some of the villagers is not a pretty sight, and it is one thing that African Americans sometimes wish to discount. We are also indebted to him for his description of life for the captives during the "middle passage," the inhumane packing of the people into the hold, the lack of a balanced diet, the difficulty they experienced when trying to walk after they were brought out of the hold. What we learned from Cudjo Lewis and other Africatown settlers who have been interviewed illustrates something about African and African American culture that is often discounted among Western societies. This is the importance of oral tradition, though one quickly recognizes the shortcomings of oral transmission. When Cudjo Lewis's imparted historical information, made up his parables, and told stories recalled from his homeland, he used oral tradition, thereby preserving a history which could have been lost.

As of 1890 the Africatown settlement was generally acknowledged as the only community of its kind in the country, though one might find similarities on the islands off the coasts of South Carolina and Georgia. The Africatown settlers developed a distinct code of government, organized a church, and are credited with establishing one of the oldest public schools for Blacks in the Mobile area. Africatown was regarded as the largest (some think only) community of pure blooded Africans in the United States. The men worked in the mills and their wives helped by planting gardens and fruit trees and becoming vendors of fruits and vegetables. They selected three men to serve as judges and became politically active in the Republican party. Records show that Cudjo Lewis applied for U. S. citizenship on October 23, 1868 but no record has surfaced indicating that his application was approved. Among the Africatown descendants are found teachers, social workers, professionals in all fields, and owners of various businesses. Their many accomplishments are a testament to the courage and endurance of a people who created out of adversity a life and legacy far richer than they dreamed which is today a vital part of the Mobile community.

One may wonder what happened to Captain Foster and Tim Meaher after the *Clotilda*'s return. Legal documents filed in August, 1860 by A. J. Requier, the U. S. Attorney for the Southern Diistrict of Alabama, show that Captain Foster was not charged with slave trading, a capital crime, but with failure to declare his cargo with customs, for which a thousand dollar fine was assessed. In July, 1860, Burns Meaher and John M. Dabney were both charged with purchasing captives "with the intent to hold, sell, or dispose of such negroes, as slaves. "Ultimately neither Captain Foster, John M. Dabney, nor the Meaher brothers, were convicted of any crimes involving the *Clotilda*.

PERSONAL INTERVIEW WITH ELLA DILLIARD

Ila B. Prine

Ella Dilliard's home is 756 Canal Street in Mobile, Alabama. The following is an excerpt from an interview about her childhood during slavery.

Later when she was brought to Mobile she worked for Judge Oliver Semmes for twenty years. Judge Semmes was the son of Admiral Raphael Semmes, and she said he was a blessed, good man. For the past fourteen years she has been working for the Frank Lyons family of Mobile.

Ella lives in a double tenement house, having one room and a small kitchen. The room is full of old furniture and odd things. On the mantle is a lovely old china pitcher that once was owned by Judge Semmes and which Ella prizes very much. The thing that puzzles Ella most among the modern inventions, she said, are the aeroplanes, and the way ice is made. She said:

> "...we never had any ice way back yonder. We had nice, old, open brick wells, and the water was just like ice. We would draw the water and put around the milk and butter in the dairy. It's a mystery to me how they make that ice, but, my goodness! I guess I need not worry my head about things, because I am not here for long. All my family is dead and gone now, and the only companion I have is this here little white hen. Her name is Mary. You see, I bought her last year to kill for Christmas, but I couldn't do it. She is so human; and you ought to see the eggs she lays. I even have a few to sell sometimes. I just keeps Mary in the room at night with me, and she is heaps of company for me."

AN INTERVIEW WITH CECILIA GAUDET

Susan Tucker

Cecilia Gaudet (b. 1897) speaks of divisions within the nonwhite communities. In particular, she speaks of the Creoles of Mobile and her link to these people as a fair-skinned person of African, Native American, and Caucasian descent. The Creoles in Mobile, like the Creoles of color in New Orleans and Charleston, were descended from French, Spanish, and African settlers. They often enjoyed a higher standard of living than did other persons of color. They, like the better-off blacks, often employed domestic help.

When Creoles did enter domestic work, they usually did so as seamstresses, caterers, baby nurses, and midwives. In these positions they could maintain a degree of independence, coming and going into white homes according to a schedule they controlled. Their place was different from that of other nonwhite workers—psychologically, because they were valued for their skills and creativity, and also physically, because their work required them to enter the white home in a specialized capacity, sometimes by the front door and sometimes into rooms generally reserved for family. Seamstresses, for example, had weekly appointments in private homes and might sew anything from underwear to wedding gowns. They generally had drawers reserved for them in the family parlor.

But such work offered more than independence and respect; it was another means by which black women redefined domestic work. By choosing to do this kind of work, married women with children could arrange things so that much of their work could be done at home. When asked, some Creole women I interviewed would say they had never worked, and only much later would I learn that they had actually earned money but had done so at home.

Cecelia Gaudet spoke of these women of color who did these special kinds of domestic work. In the course of her discussion, she identified class divisions within the nonwhite population. Class is very important to her. She asked questions of me designed to see if I was of "the better class."

I had a sense that she did not want to believe that her mother was black and that many years went by before she resolved this conflict in her mind. But she hinted that the advice of her grandmother—"You're either white or black; you're either one or the other"—was helpful in that it made her feel that there was less ambiguity about racial identity than she had previously thought. In recounting this story to me, she also spoke of her early memory of streetcars that had not been segregated.

When I asked her why segregation became more rigid and why the Jim Crow laws were passed and enforced so strictly, she gave me two answers. "There were low-class blacks coming in from the country," she said. And she added, "White people, they want everything their way."

She can also remember having her head shaved when she had typhoid fever and her father's protest that her hair would not come back straight. She showed me a picture of herself with straight hair. In this picture she is eight years old and wearing an organdy dress. The photograph is enlarged and sits in a large gold oval frame. She had a white British gentleman friend carry it out to me as I sat in her living room. She has the antiques of her grandmother and aunt, and probably also much of their ingenuity, strength, and prejudice. Her gentleman friend told me that he was certain that "there is royal blood in her somewhere."

I'm a Spanish War baby! My father he signed up to fight, but he never did go. He was just seventeen years old, eighteen when I was born. My mother and father both was teenagers.

And from right after I was born, I was reared on my father's side. I was raised by my grandmother and my aunt. My grandmother worked with the doctors delivering the babies, and she also worked with sick old people in their home and with other people in their home. And my aunt was a seamstress. She'd go to people's houses and sew. They'd have a room for her—with a machine. And she would make everything—bride's dresses, design them and all, christening gowns with all that lace—and all the slips and panties for girls.

My grandmother she was also one of those Creole cooks. She used to do parties, weddings, christenings, Thanksgivings. She'd go to big fine jobs like that, and sometimes she'd be gone two or three days cooking.

My father he was mostly a bookkeeper and things like that. So my people on my father's side was pretty well-to-do. And I was the first grandchild and the first great-grandchild, so they just gave me everything. They didn't buy anything—they made all my clothes because they didn't want any of the other children to have anything like it. And when I was young, they had a horse and a buggy and a nurse!

I was with my father's family because see, my daddy crossed over!* My mother was colored, and I was born out of wedlock. But they took me, my grandmother and them. I was the first grandchild, and my grandfather used to say he might not live to see the other ones, because he was in bad health, and he wanted it fixed in the courthouse where I would carry his name. So I carried his name. This was up in the country. And my grandfather died. That left my grandmother and her children—four boys and in the middle, a girl. And me. So my aunt was for coming to Mobile, because they were very smart. My grandfather had educated them all, and my aunt she said they had better opportunity to fulfill what they knew in Mobile.

Up there, everyone knew who they were… and they could, in the city, go either way, 'cause they were all fair.

So she came to Mobile, and they all followed, with me. I was two. My aunt was about nineteen then, and people would swear that I was her child—my aunt's child. Said that she had me out of wedlock. She said, "No, it's not my child." Says, "It's my brother's child," says, "But I love her like my child."

So it was very funny, when she was on her dying bed… I was married and all that. It was in 1930. I went to her bed, and I said, "Auntie, I want you to tell me the truth." She said, "What is it, baby?" I say, "Are you my aunt or are you my real mother?" She say, "Why you ask me that?" I say, "I don't know." I say, "They all told me you wasn't." I say, "But was they telling me the truth?" She say, "Baby, I'm not your mother." Say, "I'm your aunt." I guess it must have always been something I wasn't quite sure about. See, now down the bay here in Mobile, the Creoles lived in the south part of town. We didn't live down there, but my uncle lived down there. The Creoles—they weren't white, they weren't black. They didn't mix with either group, least some of them didn't. Some of those Creoles they didn't even ride the streetcar. They'd walk because they didn't want to set in the back. And they'd have their own schools, or they'd not go.

But like it was all mixed up—the races, for many people. My grandmother was Indian and French, but now, she didn't want to be distinguished as Indian or Creole. She said, "They're ain't but two sets," she said. "You're either white or black; you're either one or the other." But her children, if they wanted, could pass for anything. Me, I was the darkest thing in my house. But I didn't know the difference. Honest to goodness, I didn't know I was black until I was nine years old. That was the age when I learned about colored and white and all.

I had just had the typhoid pneumonia, and I was laying there on the porch. It was in the first neighborhood where we lived that wasn't all fair. The children was there in the street dancing the holy man dance, and that tickled me to death. It tickled me so bad I laughed out. So they called up the banisters. The darkest little girl I ever saw, she said, "Come on down and play with us." And I was so shy. But finally, I made up my mind to go over there and play with them. But it took me a month before I did. I was shy, and I saw they were black children. They were the first ones I'd ever heard say nigger. And I was dark, And then I just realized. Now my grandmother she told me then it didn't matter how dark or light you were.

Cutting the holy man, they called it—that dance. It was just a dance where you crossed your legs and twirled around. I can't remember exactly I just remember the one that did it the best, she was bowlegged, and that tickled me to death!

But anyway, we had a nice life. We got along nice. They always had a good living. And they sent me and my cousins to the private school for blacks, Emerson

Normal and Industrial Institute. It was run by northern white people for the most part. And the teachers had to be a graduate before they could teach and a missionary in a foreign country before they could come down here. And all the teachers lived in big dormitories, and they weren't allowed to go on the streets by themselves. Like the nuns used to be, they had to go two by two.

I started work when I was fourteen years old. This lady had had a baby that my grandmother was helping with. And she asked my grandmother could I come out there and stay with the other children. I made a dollar a week all summer. I worked with the same people until I graduated.

Then I worked for Dr. Standish and them. He was a doctor, a prominent doctor. A friend got me to work for them—a colored girl. They had raised her up and married her off. They raised her. Seem like her mother had died when she was working there, and they took her. She slept right in the room with Miz Standish. And she married right in their parlor, and she used to work for them. Folks used to have separate bedrooms in those big houses. And rumor always was he had another woman, and Miz Standish kept this girl in with her to make sure he wouldn't come in to her. Well, but she married off, the girl who worked there did. And then when she began to have children, it got to the point where it was too hard on her, and she recommended me.

And now they were rich. Miz Standish, she was fast rich. She showed me the picture of her place, where she was from. She had one of those big old antebellum homes with big columns. Said they had the big cotillion balls and things there back in those days.

Oh, she was fast rich! And she was hell to work for, but she was nice to me. She was crazy about me. She picked me. She bragged across the street to the lady that she had the two best-looking people working for her. That was me and the cook.

And for her big parties, boy, she had me so thrilled! She bought the clothes for me to wear. She liked to show me off. She had me a beautiful black dress. It was shining, and she had the apron—it was just lace. And the most beautiful lace cap. I was a picture. And my hair was eighteen inches long then and very thick, and she used to like me to wear it in a plait. She took pictures of us, and she liked to show us off.

And the doctor he was very nice. I helped him in the little office he had set up in the house. And he said I was born for a nurse. When I left there, he wanted to put me in school. He said he would pay all my expenses, and he'd buy me a lot where I could build me a house. He said, "If you stay, I'll fix things for you."

But now, couldn't nothing stop me from going to Chicago. My cousin that I was raised with was in Chicago. My aunt she was going to be with him. But she had a very good position here where she was sewing, and she said she felt like what I was doing wasn't much, so they got me to go ahead. I was supposed to go up there to look for a place.

I was there in Chicago for three years. I worked making lampshades, and then I beaded. They were wearing beaded dresses then, and I did that. And I met my husband there and married him. He was a Mobilian, too, but I didn't know him until I moved to Chicago. There were lots of Southerners in Chicago. See, when World War I was, that's when they had the free transportation for people to go north. And they liked to scalped Mobile. All that the army didn't have, the steel mills and Chicago did.

Well, I liked Chicago, but my husband didn't. The weather didn't take to him. But both of us, we liked the opportunities up there. And the white people up there—there were some more willing to let black people get along and try things out just like whites, although, now, the streetcars and trolleys were segregated and some hotels you couldn't go in. And then the neighborhoods was segregated, most of them.

But people could get more jobs there, and that started the people leaving Mobile. If you look at the obituaries of the Negroes today, you can see they are scattered from here to there. There's nobody home; children just scattered every which way. They did better by leaving Mobile, them that could. Even those who thought they had good positions here could do better there.

My husband was a boner up there for Swifts. But he heard from his sister that they were losing some of their property here. So we came back in 1924. I got a job working at housekeeping for a gentleman. He had lost his wife, and he had a sister there. She was an old maid, but they were rich, and she never didn't know nothing about housekeeping.

She and his two children and him, they fell in love with me. He said I was a perfect housekeeper and cook. I was like their mother. I stayed there until I bought me a place in town. They lived too far out, and my husband said it was too hard on me to go out there.

Then, for a good while, I just did work here and there. This family I'd worked for some before, her son got typhoid pneumonia. I nursed him. Then, her daughter she got grown and married, and whenever she wanted something special done, then she'd come around me—for serving parties. And when these babies in white families were born premature, well, I nursed them.

I took a little girl—she wasn't but six years old—and I raised her because I didn't have no children of my own that lived. So I took care of her and sewed at home and sold vegetables, flowers, chickens, eggs. And sometimes I'd go out and serve parties or weddings.

But I worked a long time. And I'm going to tell you, now, the majority of people here in Mobile worked. And the majority of them made their living working for white people or washing and ironing for them. Everybody couldn't be teachers, and that was the only thing for them to do. They had to work for white people as cooks, housekeepers, maids.

And it's some people that just done it for a lifetime. It was the only job they had. They done it for a lifetime, from young people till they got old for the same family. They raised the people's children, and they raised the children's children, like that.

And there were a lot of washwomen. Now my sister-in-law did hand laundry. She was a beautiful hand laundress. She went to people's houses and did some on the yard. She used to do it at her house too. She did beautiful work.

But, oh, the pay was so small! I know some people say they got $1.00 a bundle, some said 50 cents and 75 cents. And if they got $1.50, I think that was big money! When I was a child, you could see them carrying the clothes on their heads in baskets—bundled on their heads.

I stopped work when my husband got very sick. It got too much on me. And I said, "Shoot, why should I work?" I worked all my life, and he was getting three checks from retiring. So I came down at sixty-two.

I miss work, in a way. Everywhere that I went, people liked my work and they just turned me loose. They didn't bother me. I never did work for nobody mean. Some people had a hard time because some people was poor, and I wasn't and I was always treated nice.

I tell 'em all: I don't regret a day that I lived. I was raised nice and my people… people left 'em money. I won't say they were rich, but they were good livers, and I didn't know nothing about no hard times. I didn't know nothing about being real poor. I say, God just blessed me. But it never went to my head.

And I guess it didn't, because of my grandmother. Everybody said she was more like a virgin! She cared for everybody. She would take our clothes, our material, and make a shirt for a poor little child. And poor people would come by our house. My aunt always had people to come there and do wash and things for her, and when they'd leave there, she'd just have them loaded down, with things she'd given them.

There was a priest that came down there. He'd come eat supper with us. And he said we acted more like the holy family than anyone anywhere he went! Say when he come there, we'd all come in, and say, we'd act more like the holy family! But that's the way we were raised.

*Crossed over means to have crossed between the races in some way. For example, it could mean "passing" as white or black, marrying someone of another race, or, as here, having a child by someone of another race.

from GULF STREAM

Mary Stanley

from Book One: ADELE

The road twisted suddenly and grew progressively better as it lifted toward Silver Hill. Adele paused. With a quick furtive look backward upon Sand Town lying like a hot, ragged fringe, she swung the basket down from her head to her side. It was heavier carrying it so, and as she went forward a little line of sweat gathered along her upper lip. She was grateful for the shade of the cool oak-bordered lanes of Silver Hill.

The fence lines were thick grown with mock orange and privet, and sprayed over and about with jasmine and Cherokee rose. Through the green tangle she now and again caught glimpses of the white houses, their green blinds shut against the afternoon sun, their brick-edged gardens thick with japonica, sweet olive, and azalea bushes. Her infrequent trips to Bayport, the city that lay at the foot of Silver Hill, filled her with astonishment and a keen, excited feeling of unreality, but the gracious, brooding beauty of the Hill with its air of serene surety flooded her with a sense of peace, an assuagement of all her poor blind groping after beauty...

But to Adele it seemed a splendid thing as she turned into the side gate and made her way up to the back door, along a brick walk, hedged high and thick on both sides with yaupon. Crêpe myrtle bushes, great splotches of watermelon pink against the white of the house, spilled a mass of crinkled flowers across the walk to flow against the steps of the back porch in a rosy wave of color. Adele knocked at the door of the kitchen and the high-pitched voice of Viney, the cook, answered her.

The mass of bodies choked the streets, blocking passage, but suddenly a renewed force of horse charged through the east gate led by Alonso Vásquez and the governor's nephew, Francisco de Soto. Raving, they thundered through the streets,

BALLAD OF "FLOATING ISLAND"

Betty Spence

Mary Eoline Eilands, 1845-1937, Mobile's legendary "Floating Island" kept a half century waterfront vigil awaiting the return of her sea-faring lover.

On the morning Mary was to wed,
she learned at the wedding door
her sweetheart's ship had run aground
off some ill-fated shore.
Like a part of the earth breaking away
to form its own peculiar shelf
Mary's poor heart broke away...
an island unto itself.
There go the ships a'sailing by.
Where go the ships, there go I.

Wearing her bridal dress and veil
she went faithfully each day
down to the waterfront to ask
what ships were in the bay.
Keeping vigil beyond belief,
her presence at the docks
struck fear in the heart of stevedores
who swore she was bad luck.
There go the ships a'sailing by.
Where go the ships, there go I.

From her home on St. Emanuel
she made her daily rounds.
Folk say she walked with a floating step
that appeared to know no bounds.
First to the Cathedral to pray, then
to Smith's for day-old bread.
There were throw-away fish at the docks
And over-ripes at the banana shed.
There go the ships a'sailing by.
Where go the ships, there go I.

When her wedding dress wore out
and her golden hair turned gray,
Mary Eilands wore long, black skirts,
Fashion come what may.
Mindless of whispers at her back,
children calling names,
deep oceans of sorrow kept alive
consecrated altar flames.
There go the ships, a'sailing by.
Where go the ships, there go I.

With a swagger of a moon-drunk tide
driven by discontent
"Floating Island" lived out her days
in wild bewilderment.
Hers was the plight of all who give
so fully to another;
the awful loss of one so loved
is the loss of the other.
There go the ships a'sailing by.
Where go the ships, there go I.

FOR ALL SEASONS
Celestine Sibley

NOVEMBER

As a teen-age reporter working part-time for *The Mobile Press,* I caught the infection of covering election night when Franklin D. Roosevelt won his first landslide victory. The paper occupied an old church building on St. Michael Street in those days, along with an auto parts store and some other enterprises which were built early on into the thick walls of the old sanctuary. As the youngest and least experienced hand available, I was assigned to take returns over the auto parts store's telephone, which had been borrowed for the occasion. The excitement was in the newsroom, of course, since the national returns poured in there. The AP teletype machines clacked out those from all over the country. And as fast as they came in, they were flashed onto a screen on a building across the way. Crowds milled about the street, watching and cheering. Meanwhile, it was very quiet in the auto parts store. My phone was the last to be rung, only when all others were busy. Finally somebody brought me word that I could leave my post and join the throng on the roof of an adjacent building, watching the dark-lettered slides spell out victory for Mr. Roosevelt on the white sheet across the street. By the time I got there, a victory celebration was in full swing and a torchlight parade was strutting down the street to the music of not one but several bands playing "Happy Days Are Here Again."

It seemed to me then—and I suppose ever since—that those old enough to vote and bring about an event so personal and so vital as choose a president were enormously lucky.

There have been many election nights since then, all of them exciting, some of them terribly moving. I have sat up with the defeated almost as often as with the victorious. I have been out on the campaign trail with candidates and to polling places where votes were being counted by weary election officials. Once in the mountains, I was looking for the vote counters in a remote cove and was told that they had taken the votes down on the river bank to count them.

"They always count them on the river bank," a friend told me. "All six of them."

There are many more voters in that precinct now, and they no longer take the ballot box to the river bank to examine its urgent contents by the illumination of moonlight and moonshine. Nor is the newspaper the center of returns—gathering any longer. Time was when so many people trooped into the newsroom to see how the election was going that they had to rope off an area where the reporters and editors could work uninterrupted. Candidates and their wives and children came in to make their victory statements and sometimes to grin bravely and concede defeat. Campaign workers and random voters milled about. We drank bad coffee out of paper cups and fought fatigue sometimes until dawn, and it seemed major and history-making.

Now computers have taken over the tabulation of votes, which the wizards from our bookkeeping department once handled. And television stations dispense them, so there are no longer eager crowds standing shoulder to shoulder in the streets with up-lifted faces, waiting suspensefully. You can roll up your hair and put cold cream on your face and get in bed and learn how it's going.

But it's still exciting that "first Tuesday after the first Monday in November of every even-numbered year."

ELIZABETH GOULD RECYCLES THE PAST

Mickey Cleverdon

Elizabeth Gould was an architectural historian who taught at the University of South Alabama from 1966 to 1975. She is the author of *Nineteenth Century Mobile Architecture: An Inventory of Existing Buildings (1974); From Fort to Port: An Architectural History of Mobile, Alabama, 1711-1918 (1988);* and *From Builders to Architects: The Hobart-Hutchisson Six (1997).*

Out of the practice room she bikes beyond
The wood of Fountainebleau to woo the Romanesque, suspend
Gravity in cadence of pier and arcade, modulate nave
And transept, learn by heart rib and groin, resolve
Autun's wild bestiary and the sweet oxen of Laon.
Back home the Harvard gallants hung a sign
To honor her arrival: "No mad dogs, children, women welcome here."
No matter. Beyond all that we cheer
Her still free-wheeling drive to keep alive
The solid structure of our dark past, survive
As heirs to her discriminating eye, echoes
Of a vision left behind...the music follows.

MOBILE NATURALISTS

For me Mobile was a place of vibrant life—not of spirits, however, nor of people, and certainly not of relatives, but of butterflies.

—E.O. Wilson, from *Naturalist*

from THE TRAVELS OF WILLIAM BARTRAM
William Bartram

We now approached the bay Mobile, gently ascending a hilly district, being the highest forest adjoining the extensive rich low lands of the river; these heights are somewhat encumbered with pebbles, fragments and cliffs of fusty ferruginous rocks; the stones were ponderous and indicated very rich iron ore; here was a small district of good land, on the acclivities and bases of these ridges, and a level forest below, watered by a fine creek, running into the Mobile. From hence we proceeded, again descending, and travelled about nine miles generally over a level country consisting of savannas, Cane swamps, and gently rising knolls, producing *Pinus taeda, Nyssa sylvatica, Quercus rubra, Fagus castenea, Fraxinus,* with other trees. Arrived at Taensa, a pretty high bluff, on the Easter channel of the great Mobile river, about thirty miles about Fort Condé, or city of Mobile, at the head of the bay.

Next day early in the morning I embarked in a boat, and proceeded for Mobile, along the banks of islands (near twenty miles) which lay in the middle of the river, between the Eastern and Western shores of the main; the banks of these low flat rich islands are well cultivated, having on them extensive farms and some good habitations, chiefly the property of French gentlemen, who reside in the city, as being more pleasant and healthy. Leaving these islands, we continued ten or twelve miles between the Eastern main and a chain of low grassy islands, too low and wet for cultivation; then crossed over the head of the bay, and arrived in town in the evening.

The city of Mobile is situated on the easy ascent of a rising bank, extending near half a mile back on the level plain above; it has been near a mile in length, though now chiefly in ruins, many houses vacant and mouldering to earth; yet there are a few good buildings inhabited by French gentlemen, English, Scotch and Irish, and emigrants from the Northern British colonies. Messrs. Swanson and M'Gillivray, who have the management of the Indian trade carried on with the Chicasaws, Chactaws, Upper and Lower Creeks, etc. have made here very extraordinary improvements in buildings.

The Fort Condé, which stands very near the bay, towards the lower end of the town, is a large regular fortress of brick.

The principal French buildings are constructed of brick, and are of one story, but on an extensive scale, four square, encompassing on three sides a large area or court yard: the principal apartment is on the side fronting the street; they seem in some degree to have copied after the Creek habitation in the general plan: those of the poorer class are constructed of a strong frame of Cypress, filled in with brick, plastered and white-washed inside and out.

July 31st, 1778, the air very hot and sultry, thermometer up at 87, we had excessive thunder, and repeated heavy showers of rain, from morning until evening.

Not having an immediate opportunity from hence to Manchac, a Critish settlement on the Mississippi, I endeavoured to procure a light canoe, with which I designed to pursue my travels along shore to the settlements about Pearl river.

August 5th, set off from Mobile up the river in a trading boat, and was landed at Taensa bluff, the seat of Major Farmer, to make good my engagements, in consequence of an invitation from that worthy gentleman, to spend some days in his family; here I obtained the use of a light canoe to continue my voyage up the river. The settlement of Taensa is on the site of an ancient town of a tribe of Indians of that name, which is apparent from many artificial mounds of earth and other ruins. Besides Mr. Farmer's dwellings, there are many others inhabited by French families, who are chiefly his tenants. It is a most delightful situation, commanding a spacious prospect up and down the river, and the low lands of his extensive plantations on the opposite shore. In my excursions about this place, I observed many curious vegetable productions, particularly a species of Myrica (*Myrica inodora*): this very beautiful evergreen shrub, which the French inhabitants call the Wax tree, grows in wet sandy ground about the edges of swamps; it rises erect nine or ten feet, dividing itself into a multitude of nearly erect branches, which are garnished with many shining deep green entire leaves of a lanceolate figure; the branches abundance of large round berries, nearly the size of bird cherries, which are covered with a scale or coat of white wax; no part of this plant possesses any degree of fragrance. It is in high estimation with the inhabitants for the production of wax for candles, for which purpose it answers equally well with beeswax, or preferably, as it is harder and more lasting in burning.

from FISH TO FLOWERS

Rosemary Parker Butler

On the banks of a winding river known as Fowl River—named so by the French as there were so many birds on its banks when they arrived in the 1700s—is a beautiful estate known worldwide as Bellingrath Gardens. Fowl River winds along the river banks of Mobile County, Alabama. Tourists from home and abroad make regular treks to the estate, considered by many to be the "charm spot" of the deep South. Few people, however, know that another tourist attraction existed in the spot that has historical ties to the present day Bellingrath Gardens.

A major destination point for area sportsmen, more than a century ago, was a popular fishing camp built on the river where the Bellingrath Gardens estate now stands. Official courthouse records prove that location to be the same area where visitors now come to view the beautiful Bellingrath house and gardens.

On March 30, 1786, Spanish Governor Favrot sold to one Daniel Ward a plantation fronting on Fowl River. The Spanish census of 1786 recorded an elderly woman living there named Julia Villars, noted as a free mulatto (mixed blood). As time passed, the records show that the great, great, granddaughter of Villars, Clemencia Parker, would, almost a century later, be an owner of this property.

This piece of property remained unclaimed after the United States assumed this area from Spain in 1813.

On October 23rd, 1840, Edward Parker, a mulatto, freeman, applied to purchase the property. Edward Parker, born in Maryland, was a seaman who regularly sailed into this area from the northeast coast and later remained in the area. The application #8857 was filed at the old land office at St. Stephens, Alabama. He received a certificate that stated "according to the provision of the act of Congress of April 23, 1820, full payment having been made, the United States of America granted a patent to S.W. 1/4 Sec 13, 7S 2W to Edward Parker, signed by John Tyler, President of the United States.

Edward Parker and his wife, Lavinia, settled on the land and immediately began purchasing other nearby parcels. They had one son, Francis Joseph Parker, who later married, Clemencia La Lande, the great, great, granddaughter of Julia Villars who had resided there in 1786.

Edward Parker and his son, Francis, established a fishing camp there that came to be known as Parker's Place. Their wives, Lavinia and Clemencia, cared for their guests. Accommodations were built to serve the many white overnight guests who came from around the country to fish and hunt. Parker's Place was considered by many to be a sportsman's paradise. When the Bay Shore Railroad came to the area in 1899, a main station was built on the property.

One of the many guests who enjoyed fishing and hunting at Parker's Place was Walter D. Bellingrath. He brought with him other overnight guests.

In March 1913, Francis Parker died. His widow and heirs then began to sell off the property as shown in Mobile County Probate records.

W.D. Bellingrath purchased two parcels in 1916 and two more in 1927. Thus began the change from fish to flowers.

W.D. Bellingrath continued to honor the Parker memory by preserving a large oak tree on the property said to be over 500 years old. In 1940, he had the branches braced and 27,000 pounds of concrete poured in its trunk. He named the tree the Parker Oak, and it was so noted in the Bellingrath Gardens brochures until the old oak was lost after Hurricane Frederick.

Bellingrath Gardens is a tribute to two men, one who used the land for those who found pleasure in pursuing fish and fowl in their native habitat, and the other who provided pleasure for those who delighted in beholding the beautiful wonders of nature. Fauna or Flora—a Paradise either way.

BELLINGRATH GARDEN

Eka Budianta

Camelia bushes, a solitary swan
on the blue lake near the shore
I am at your side, Eva, I am at your side
can't you hear my poem?
The house you asked for, I erected here
In my dreams and wanderings.

A small wooden bridge, a toy boat in the park
do you still need my love?
I carry the land in my soul
my blood feels its fire.
To the wounded doe, I gave back life
and set free in my dreams and longing.

In Bellingrath Garden, Mobile, Alabama
my people have lost their queen.
Only their king is visible, throwing leaves into the pond
with the bout of turbulence passed.

EL RÍO E BAHIA DEL ESPÍRITU SANTO: SENSE OF PLACE

Charles Bernard Rodning, M.D.

river rollin'
by itself
to the sea

Mobilians are literal or figurative descendants of Native American, European, Mediterranean, and African immigrants to a geographically and ecologically unique locale of the North American continent—the Mobile Delta. The Tercentenary of Mobile justly celebrates that cultural and historical heritage (Higginbotham, 1987, 1991) but, perhaps more importantly, affirms a connection between humankind and their environment. The Delta gives Mobilians a sense of place—a glorious creation to be nurtured and protected.

HISTORICAL PERSPECTIVE:

The three hundred years of historical time that Mobilians have experienced and recorded pales by comparison to proto-historic and geologic time scales. Archaeological excavations have revealed evidence for habitation of the Mobile Delta by Native American populations—Cherokee, Chickasaw, Choctaw, Creek—and their ancestors for millennia prior to Spanish exploration and French colonization (Brown, 2002). The abundant flora and fauna of this deltaic region undoubtedly attracted early explorers (hunters-gatherers) and settlers (farmers). The sands, silts, and clays deposited by deltaic floodwaters enabled agricultural and aquacultural development to flourish. The mazes of intermingling waterways provided naturalistic routes for transportation and trade. *El Río e Bahía del Espíritus Santo, [The River and Bay of the Holy Spirit,* as the Spanish first recorded it cartographically (Fernández de Orviedo y Valdés, 1852)], also gave oceanic vessels access to a harbor and a northern interior.

The Mobile Delta is a unique and paradoxically robust and fragile ecological niche. It is composed of sediments deposited by the Alabama River system at its juncture with the Atlantic *Golfe de México* (Shepard, 1960). Herodotus (circa 484-circa 425, B.C.), the Greek philosopher, geographer, and historian, first used the term delta to describe the Nile riverine-oceanic interface. During his geographical explorations and research for what would become the first great historical narrative and critical analysis of the ancient Occidental world (Herodotus, circa 445

B.C.), he observed that the land bounded by the diverging distributary branches of the Nile River and Mediterranean Sea was deltoid in shape, and used the fourth letter of the Greek alphabet Δ to describe it.

hellish heat—
  not even a dragonfly
jostlin' cattails

SCIENTIFIC PERSPECTIVE:

The Mobile Delta has varied in size, shape, structure, and composition predicated upon geologic, climatologic, and hydrologic conditions.The very existence of a delta represents a balance between riverine (flow and deposit of stream-borne sediments) and marine (wave energy, wind intensity and direction, coastal currents, tidal action, and offshore slope) processes. The presence of any delta is a consequence of a river emanating from a drainage basin, which deposits sediment more rapidly than can be dispersed by coastal oceanic waves or currents, and is perforce a dynamic dispersal mechanism. Climate also substantially influences runoff and sediment transport from that drainage basin. In sub-tropical climates such as southern Alabama, rainfall is abundant throughout the year, but increases substantially during the rainy season. Consequently, annual water and sediment discharge is quite continuous and constant, but increases during heaviest rainfall, and the channels of the Mobile Delta accommodate the increased riverine flow readily (Shepard, 1960).

moonlit shadows
    across fallow fields—
silvery bright

The Mobile Delta is stratified into four components—alluvial, upper deltaic, lower deltaic, and subaqueous deltaic plains. That part of the Mobile River confined by valley walls, such that flow is restricted from lateral dispersion, is its alluvial plain. It is the conduit by which water and sediment derived from the drainage basin are transported to the sea. At some point downstream the plain broadens, and the river channels diverge dichotomously. That area is the apex of the delta and the beginning of the upper deltaic plain. Those components lie at an elevation above the effective intrusion of tidal water and are formed entirely by riverine processes. Areas between channels support broad freshwater marshes, swamps, or shallow lakes. Farther downstream the lower deltaic plain is periodically inundated by tidal waters, and landforms that develop there result from the interaction of riverine and marine processes. Areas between the brackish channels range from bays, marshes, and mangrove swamps to tidal flats and beach ridges. Seaward the subaqueous deltaic plain forms entirely below sea level and constitutes a prominence on the continental shelf. Marine processes are dominant there, and its importance cannot be underestimated, because it is the foundation for the landward exposed portion of the delta. Bordering the channels of the upper deltaic plain are slightly elevated landforms referred to as natural levees, which develop as a result of the deposition of sediment during floods. As floodwaters surge over the channel banks, water velocity decreases and causes deposition of the coarser suspended sediment near the channel margins.

yellow crocuses
sproutin' through
muddy footprints

Sediment dispersal occurs predominantly by two mechanisms. During low river stage, transported sediment remains within the channels throughout its traverse and is not dispersed laterally until it reaches the river terminus. During such times river-current velocities are generally low, and marine currents and waves redistribute the sediment laterally along the deltaic front. The coarser grained sediments are concentrated by waves near that juncture, whereas the finer grained sediments are dispersed laterally along the deltaic coastline. When flooding occurs water and sediment inundate the natural levees, alluvial plain, and adjacent interdistributary area. Silts and clays are thus introduced rapidly into areas that normally have very low rates of sediment accumulation. That process is a major factor in aggrading of the subaqueous deltaic plain. River-currents are appreciably higher than those which prevail during low-river stage and overpower marine currents and wave action. Sediments are dispersed much farther seaward during flood season. Silts, and occasionally sands, are transported across the shoals and are deposited along the deltaic front or steeper sloping portion of the subaqueous deltaic plain. Such dispersal of sediments is the mechanism by which the delta grows seaward (prograding).

Those dispersal patterns and sorting of sediments results in a well-developed depositional sequence both horizontally and vertically. In the upper deltaic plain, fine-grained silts and clays are deposited by the river along with the organic material that accumulates in situ in the interdistributary areas. Immediately seaward in the lower deltaic plain, sands and silts accumulate and are constantly redistributed and resorted by marine processes. Farther offshore, the fine-grained sediments, predominantly clays, accumulate beyond the deltaic front. Thus, the horizontal sequence of deltaic sediments is a gradation from silts, clays, and organic material in a landward direction; coarser sands and silts in the mid-deltaic plain; and finer grained marine clays offshore. In the vertical axis clays and organic sediments are deposited at the highest (topset), sands and silts at the intermediate (foreset), and marine clays at the lowest (bottomset) water depths.

blackbirds settlin'
on a gnarled oak—
under a sickle moon

HUMANISTIC PERSPECTIVE:

Stewardship of the Mobile Delta must be our legacy. Mobilians must achieve a realistic and realizable balance between exploitation and preservation of our deltaic environment to sustain it and to sustain our community. Humankind and their environment are interdependent. Wendell Berry, an eminent contemporary essayist, novelist, and poet has emphasized the imperatives of humankinds' connection to land, sea, and neighborhood. He has proposed a "sympathetic mind" that values compassion, gratitude, humility, loyalty, and mercy, as a means of retaining or restoring a sense of place.

Water is an apt and vivid metaphor for resolution of the dichotomy that exists between exploitation and preservation. Consider that Oriental philosophic and artistic traditions refer to a "mind like water" as an ideal model for the human spirit. Shih-t'ao (1641-1720), a Buddhist monk and the most famous of the Individualist Chinese painters of the early Chi'ing Period (Seventeenth Century), in his monograph *Hua-yü lu (Comments on Painting)* proposed these perspectives. Water effortlessly flows by its own law; is clean and pure in essence; spreads its benefits in ponds, streams, lakes, rivers, seas, and oceans; teems with biological life; and demonstrates its strength in tides and crashing waves. Water conforms effortlessly to its circumstance—waterfalls, flowing rivers, still backwaters—and responds immediately to its environment—freezes, melts, evaporates, cleanses, disperses, dissolves. What the author was conveying is that a mind as clear and reflective as water is a mind receptive and responsive to a source of energy and insight inclusive of, but also beyond, the senses—to an intuition, to an understanding, to a wisdom, to an enlightenment, to the "Way." Such a mind recognizes an interdependence, interrelationship, and interweaving among all phenomena. Certainly this implies an alignment with one's source and a maintenance of one's true essence, but it also acknowledges a need to be adaptive and responsive to one's circumstance and environment at each moment—acknowledging a need to be adaptive and responsive to the present in terms of space and time (Aria and Eng Gon, 1992; Csikszentmihalyi, 1990).

Like water, courageous and virtuous individuals, he wrote, "follow their own true nature and do what they do for its own sake." By adopting a "mind like water," Mobilians will be able to observe objectively, to discern acutely, to learn efficiently, to act effectively, and to conserve prudently; and will be able to avoid rigid posturing, forswear arrogance, and shun slavish consumerism and abject adherence to dogma. They will experience a heightened sense of awareness or epiphany and an acute perception of reality or "thusness" as they are about their endeavors. They will be able to articulate their innermost passions and their outermost public declarations, and they will be able to serve as strong advocates for themselves, their families, their neighbors, and their sanctuary—*El Río e Bahía Espíritu Santo.*

last pen stroke—
crossin' moonlit shadows
on the chime of windbells

REFERENCES:

Aria B and Eng Gon R: *The Spirit of the Chinese Character. Gifts from the Heart.* San Francisco: Chronicle Books, 1992.

Brown IA (Editor): *Bottle Creek: A Pensacola Culture Site in South Alabama.* Tuscaloosa, Alabama: University of Alabama Press, 2002.

Csikszentmihalyi M: *Flow: The Psychology of Optimal Experience.* New York: Harper & Row, 1990.

Fernández de Orviedo y Valdés, *Gonzalō Historia General y Naturel de las Indias, Islas y Tierra-ferme del Mar Oceano.* Volumes I and II, Madrid, 1852.

Herodotus: *Historiē* (circa 445 B.C., Rawlinson G, Translator). Everyman's Library, London: J. M. Dent & Sons, Limited, 1949.

Higginbotham PJ: *Old Mobile: Fort Louis de la Louisiane,* 1702-1711. Tuscaloosa, Alabama: University of Alabama Press, 1977, 1991.

Shepard FP (Senior Editor): *Recent Sediments, Northwest Gulf of Mexico.* Austin, Texas: Guidebook Series, Bureau of Economic Geology, University of Texas, 1960.

THIS JUNGLE

Diane Garden

— MOBILE, ALABAMA

I can't believe we've moved
to this city built on a swamp.
Everything's growing so fast
we have weeds that are waist high,
so we need a scythe to forge
through as if we were on a safari,
and we have bushes within bushes—
honeysuckle trailing from gardenias,
nandina in ligustreum, oak in holly—
azaleas up to the windows, popcorn
trees lifting up our stepping-stones,
privet climbing up Hannah's window.
The little mermaid on her light catcher
looks as if she's swimming through
seaweed. The buildings are dripping
lace like Spanish moss from the oak
trees. Part of me likes Mobile, but
part of me's afraid of this jungle,
of this air that's moist, of creatures
swarming like sperm, of all this green
that's so alive—of all this fertility.

BONES AND ONIONS ON THE ROAD FROM BEAVER MEADOW TO MOBILE

Vernon Fowlkes, Jr.

My son Thomas brushes and scratches
in the leafy dirt, uncovering the light
brown bones of some unknown
animal. He wonders if we've discovered
the remains of a hushed-up country
murder. When the dog-collar surfaces
out of the loam, he knows
these bones once answered
to a name. He raises a jawbone—

I smell the wild onions
we gathered earlier
with my father down the hill.
Their pungent fragrance rises
from the brown bag, mixes
strangely with the earthy
smell of this old death. It's then
I feel the Old Woman conjured here—
"Sprig of onion, bone of dog ..."
the incantation might go—
She rides lightly in the grassy,
oniony aroma. She would wrap
herself 'round this desecrated
skeleton, walk the earth again,
if we would let her.

We bag the bones, ride up the road
through Beaver Meadow, Chunchula,
Oak Grove. Before we turn back
to Mobile, my father points out
the old Davis place. This is where
the dance was when your grandmother rode
the handcar from Smithtown

on the dummy line. Again,
we catch the ghostly scent
of onions as we picture her
in her long dark dress and button-up
shoes, cranking that rattling rail
car along the tracks. In our own
car, the bones that would be
hers clatter a clanking rhythm behind us.

from CHINA MARINE
E.B. Sledge

I AM NOT THE MAN I WOULD HAVE BEEN

Looking back over those momentous events of fifty years ago when I was a Marine evokes strong emotions. The years immediately after the war were the hardest. As Paul Fussell remarked, the combat veteran not only has to survive the experience, he has to learn to live with it the rest of his life. He was so right. For the first twenty-odd years after my return, nightmares occurred frequently, waking me either crying or yelling, always sweating, and with a pounding heart. Some nights I delayed going to bed, dreading the inevitable nightmares. Old comrades wrote me that similar troubles drove many of them to drink and to the ensuing misery of alcoholisrn, which they beat with sheer self-discipline.

Science was my salvation! During many of those years, I was a graduate student in biology—first earning my M.S. degree at Auburn, then my Ph.D. at the University of Florida. It was like an intellectual boot camp; standards were high. I found quite by accident that after a day of concentrating intensely on some difficult problem in biology or biochemistry, the war nightmares did not come that night. I also found that a conversation about the war with a veteran was a likely cause for nightmares—unless I applied my mind to some fact of biology or biochemistry before bedtime. An hour's intense concentration on science resulted in a peaceful night's sleep. Often I would listen to records of some of the intricate keyboard music of J. S. Bach or the orchestral works of W. A. Mozart, and my mind was put completely at peace. Eventually, I managed to conquer the curse of combat nightmares.

In later years some memory of the war has flashed through my mind nearly every day. Old buddies tell me it has been the same with them. However, if my thoughts become too worrisome, I apply the above formula, which acts like oil on troubled waters even though nightmares rarely visit me anymore. But if one does not watch himself, depression can become a problem too. Needless to say, I read as little about World War II and watch as little film about it as possible.

The war left me with a deep appreciation for the simple things in life. Putting on a pair of clean, dry socks is one of the greatest luxuries I know. A shave, a warm shower, and sleeping in a sheeted bed are, too. When it is raining, especially on an autumn day, I look out the window at the falling drops and my thoughts sometimes drift back to those awful days on Okinawa—Snafu and I bailing out a muddy foxhole with an old helmet, shivering in a torrential cold rain, and both of us cringing as each Japanese shell came screaming into the corpse-strewn area to explode with a deafening crash. I quickly bring the focus of my mind back to the present and thank God I do not have to suffer such hardship and misery again. And, oh, what a blessing to be relieved of constant terror!

My love of the outdoors was strangely affected by the war—the way I looked at my surroundings was altered. My view of the outdoors had taken on more of an analytical perspective of its features as military terrain—likely areas for the placement of various foxholes, the company 60mm mortars to cover defilades, the light machine guns so as to achieve crossfires along the company front, fields of fire, and possible avenues of enemy attack or ambush. This change in outlook was intense in the early years home, but I cleared my mind of it by concentrating on plant and animal species present or probable. But the old combat view of things still creeps in sometimes after more than fifty years.

My feelings about one of my prewar hobbies, hunting, were completely changed by my combat experience. Father and I had hunted quail, mourning dove, and squirrels primarily. He had taught me a great deal about the habits of wild game and the outdoors, and I had been thrilled with our trips afield. He was a fine shot with either a rifle or shotgun and taught me well.

After my return home, he and I went on a dove hunt west of Mobile. The field was owned by one of Father's patients, who permitted only Father and his guests to hunt there. This particular trip was my first and last dove hunt after the war, so I remember it vividly.

Although Father owned fine automatic shotguns, .20-, .16-, and .12-gauge, my gun of choice for doves was a single-shot .410. It did not have a long range or as big a shot pattern as the larger gauges, but I either hit the bird or missed it—fewer cripples. Doves fly rapidly and are beautifully streamlined in flight. I had to learn to shoot at a rapidly flying dove so that it was in the middle of the fairly small shot pattern. As the gun held only a single shell, the shot either bagged the bird or he was out of range in a split second. Gunners with larger caliber automatics often banged away at the same bird with all three shells and missed. On hunts consisting of several gunners, I was invariably advised (when a young teenager) to get a bigger shotgun for doves. "You can't hit anything flying fast with that pea shooter." As boys were taught then, "Respect your elders—and no sassy backtalk." I always grinned and said, "Yes, sir."

After dove hunting with Father and taking his advice, my .410 rarely missed. In those days, as I recall, a box of shotgun shells held twenty-five shells, and the game limit on doves was fourteen birds per hunter. I practiced hard, carefully selected my shots, and usually got my limit by firing fifteen shells, with ten shells left over. Father was very proud of my marksmanship, hitting a fast-flying dove was a difficult shot for anyone.

Many times when the hunt was over at sunset and we unloaded our guns and then put our birds in separate piles before dividing up the game equally, the hunters who had been on a stand near me would stare at my number of birds and say, "Boy, where did you get all them birds (doves)? I hardly heard you shooting more than a dozen times and I shot up 2 boxes of shells to get my limit!" I would grin and say I was just lucky. Father would wink at me and smile with pride. I always competed with myself, choosing my targets carefully, firing, and following through—trying to get my limit with as few shells as possible. I never just banged away like some hunters.

On the first dove hunt with Father after the war, I put only fifteen shells in my game bag and left the remaining ten in the box in the car. I didn't tell Father, but I wanted to see if my years of rifle shooting in the Marine Corps had spoiled my ability as a wing shot. I knelt beside an old fence overgrown with vines and knee-high broom sage on the edge of the cornfield. Father moved farther along the fence and secreted himself in a similar manner. The sun was just rising; it was a cold bright day. Some doves came flashing over to alight in the field and feed on spilled corn kernels. I was amazed at how streamlined and fast they were. Father was shooting sparingly—he was an even better shot than I was. Every time he shot, I saw a dove fold its wings and pitch to the ground. When I fired at my tenth bird, he folded his wings like all the others and slanted rapidly down, hitting the ground with a thump. I felt my shell compartment and counted five shells. Ten shots and ten kills—hadn't forgotten my wing shooting technique after all.

I had, as usual, marked where the last dove fell. I went out to pick it up. This bird was still alive—it was lying on its side with its head erect, and I knew he was badly injured because I could see him gasping for air. Slowly I picked up the dove, my hand was wet with blood. I looked at the dove's head. The bright sun shone clearly on the beautiful dark brown eyes bordered by the pale blue fleshy eyelids as the bird gasped for air. "My Lord! You poor thing—and you couldn't even shoot back!" When a dove hunter held an injured bird, the procedure to prevent further suffering was to grip the bird's body and hit its head hard against the gunstock, killing the bird instantly. This I did, bagged the dead bird. I pressed the ejector lever on my gun; the empty shell ejected. Ten shells, ten doves.

I slowly walked out of the field to the old hunting car parked nearby. I laid my gun on the grass and sat on the running board of the old Ford. I fought hard to hold back the tears as they ran down my face—my mind's eye still clearly seeing those beautiful brown eyes bordered by those fleshy pale blue eyelids. Father came hurrying over to my "stand" by the fence and called me. I called to him and he came over to the car. He was concerned as to why I left the field, but when he saw the tears, he said, "What's the matter, Fritz?" I mumbled, "I just can't kill 'em anymore, Pop! I can't bear to see 'em suffer. I'm sorry, but I'm through with hunting!"

"You do not need to apologize to me or anyone. If that's the way you feel, you've earned the right to do as you please about hunting and it's nobody's business but yours." He suggested we have some hot chocolate, for I was shivering. Finally, he put his hand on my shoulder and said, "How many shells and how many birds?"

"Ten and ten" I replied.

"Well, well, you always were damn good! Now you're even better. But maybe it's time to quit, you don't have anything else to prove about wing shooting—and it'll relieve the dove population, I'm sure," he laughed. That wonderful, kind doctor who I was so lucky to have as a father knew the war had changed me more than I realized. After all, during World War I, he was considered an expert at treating shell-shock cases from France.

Some time later I discussed my feelings about hunting with Father. The depth of his understanding amazed me. "You've just seen too much suffering, Fritz, why don't you take up bird watching as a hobby—and nobody gets hurt." I took his advice and never shot another dove but banded them for the Conservation Department and fed them in my yard all year round.

I had one other experience as a hunter (my last) shortly after I returned home. A long-time friend and patient of Father's, Mr. Augustine Meaher, invited me on a deer hunt at his hunting preserve known as "The Promised Land." Gus owned several thousand acres of deep forest along the Mobile and Tensaw Rivers (the Tensaw was an Indian tribe that had occupied the area in the sixteenth and seventeenth centuries). His property had been a huge ancestral plantation after settlers removed the Indians west, but no farming had been done there since the Civil War, and the area was covered with trackless forests harboring deer, black bear, and countless game and nongame species. It is a fascinating area and a biologist's paradise.

Gus had a successful business in Mobile and used the area primarily for deer hunting—sometimes inviting ten to twelve guests. I had no desire to shoot a deer, but Father asked me to go because Gus extended the invitation to both of us; Father had a spell of flu and could not make the trip, so I accepted the invitation. Actually, it was considered quite a privilege to be invited on one of these trips because they were fabulous affairs—like a sporting event in the nineteenth century—with at least a dozen servants and a fine pack of deer hounds, numbering about fifteen to twenty dogs. Every living thing—servants, hounds, and guests—was a certifiable character, with a nickname that always seemed to fit the individual. This was primarily because Gus had a wonderful sense of humor. Throughout the entire day, he carried on an endless, witty banter with the servants, guests, and even the hounds. In addition, he was one of the most well-read people I ever knew. It was fascinating to hear him discuss the history of The Promised Land, what was known about the local Indians and their trading customs in the earlier years.

Gus picked me up before daylight and we drove to Mount Vernon, a little town north of Mobile. Then it was off through woodland roads to the riverbank, where we loaded our gear in several boats for the crossing to the hunting camp. Frost covered everything in the pale light of dawn. The head boatman, Jim (who was a Negro preacher, burial-insurance agent, and one-time deputy sheriff as well as Gus's foreman around the property), squared everybody away in the boats and saw to the life preservers. At this point the river was about one hundred yards wide and sometimes rather choppy.

We crossed the river and unloaded. Gus rode in a World War II jeep and drove each of us to his stand. Each hunter got out of the jeep, and Gus instructed him where to expect a deer running in front of the drive (hounds followed by their handlers). Gus was no-nonsense when he told each hunter not to leave his stand until called for and to remain still and quiet once the hounds began baying and the drivers began shouting "Whoop, whoop" to start the deer. (A hunter wandering around the woods could be shot by an inexperienced person who fired at any movement instead of at a certain, clear target. This sort of thing had never happened on Gus's place, and he made as certain as he could that it never did.)

After everyone was on his stand (which reminded me of sentry duty), the drive began. The drivers shouted and whooped, and when the hounds picked up a deer trail, they began baying. The baying of a hound is a wonderful sound. It bears no resemblance to a hound barking but is a sustained, deep-throated "whoop, baroop, ooop," and each hound's voice can be recognized by the owner or drivers. When a dog struck a hot trail, its voice became excited and the syllables closer together. When a hound found an older trail, he usually announced it with a periodic "baroop," then silence for possibly several minutes, then "baroop," and so on.

What was music to me was terror to the harried deer, which ran and bounded away as fast as it could run. I heard the hounds to my front getting excited as they approached. One sounded "baroop, baroop." Then I heard the deer bounding through the underbrush. It sounded like several men crashing through the area. I peeped around the tree I was standing by and saw a medium-sized deer with spike antlers bounding toward me with what looked to be twenty-foot leaps. As the buck entered a small clearing, I stepped out and aimed just in front of the heart area. The buck saw me and rolled his big terrified eyes so that I could see the whites. Just as I began squeezing the trigger, he jumped into the next bounding motion. I aimed, led the deer with the front sight, squeezed off the shot, and "followed through" as he was in the air. The shotgun roared and the buck was dead before he crashed into a thicket at the edge of the clearing.

I looked at that beautiful, graceful animal driven into my ambush by the hounds and thought, "Is this sport?" I felt like I had shot a cow in a pasture. Several hounds ran up to the deer, sniffed it, and then milled around, totally uninterested in the dead deer. They had been bred to trail the game, not eat or attack it. Someone yelled, "Did you shoot a deer, Gene?" I answered "yes," and within a few minutes several drivers and other hunters were milling around and commenting on the probable age and weight of the buck. The hounds milled around, wagging their tails and panting. Several men congratulated me, and I was the least excited of them all. If I had made the shot with a rifle, it would have required skill—but to lie in wait as a terrified deer ran for his life right into an ambush, where it was unlikely he could escape a spread of buckshot rather than one rifle bullet, hardly seemed like sport. At lunch I told Gus deer hunting with a shotgun was not for me. So he said for the afternoon hunt he would have Jim take me by boat to a spot where thick woods came down to the riverbank and deer frequently swam across. I could take my rifle because the deer drive that afternoon would be in another area and drivers and hounds would not be in any danger of my firing.

Jim took me in the large skiff downriver about a mile and turned into a small growth of cane where the water was shallow. He wished me luck and told me what time he would pick me up. I took up my stand in a patch of cane with the river to my back and a small pond to my front at the forest's edge. The trees were large and visibility was good for quite a distance. Soon I heard the afternoon drive begin, the hounds far away to my right. My area was quiet except for a beautiful pair of wood ducks playing and searching for food in the pond. An occasional squirrel ran down one tree and up another. Suddenly, I heard loud sloshing like several people were walking in shallow water. Two beautiful does appeared, walking briskly through the water as they exited the woods and stopped at the far edge of the pond about thirty yards away. They kept looking toward the area of the drive and moving their ears to capture every sound possible. More loud sloshing of water, and two does and a large buck came up to the first does and stopped. They finally looked in my direction. I remained still, and since the wind was blowing toward me, the deer could not pick up my scent. They stood motionless, staring at me and standing in the clump of cane. They seemed more concerned with the baying of the hounds than with me, though.

Because of the way I held my rifle, I could see my wristwatch, so I timed the action, or inaction, of the deer. One of the does picked up an acorn at the edge of the pond and ate it. The buck was large and had a fine set of antlers, the eight points gleaming in the light. Slowly I raised my rifle and sighted in on his chest—no, he was too fine a creature to kill. I had murdered one of his kind that morning, so I did not need the venison. Slowly, I lowered my rifle. The buck remained motionless—his instincts probably told him no shape such as he saw in the cane was natural. Deer, like most mammals, have very poor sight, except for detecting motion, and are primarily colorblind.

For fifteen minutes we stared at each other. A shot in the air would send them springing away into the woods. But a shot would frighten them, which I had no desire to do. The deer seemed more curious than afraid. They kept sniffing the air, which apparently bore no scent of danger. I had on waterproof boots but was beginning to get cold. Finally, I needed to move a little. I knew that as soon as I did, they would bolt. So I whistled softly. Every big ear quickly turned in my direction. I whistled softly again. All the deer slowly lowered their ears, turned, went sloshing onto higher ground, and ambled into the woods, looking back at me once or twice. The whole episode is one of my most cherished memories.

When Jim picked me up in the boat, he asked if I had seen a deer. I said no, not wanting to tell him I had seen five. When we returned to camp, several people asked what I had seen, and I reported a few squirrels and some wood ducks. If I had told those eager hunters what really had happened, they would have elected to throw me into the river.

Gus didn't allow any drinking during hunting hours. So after the guns were all unloaded and put into their cases, the bottled spirits were brought forth and the partiers had a ball; each of the weary hounds went to the fenced yard, jumped up on the raised platforms, and went into his barrel for a nap. The platform was raised as protection against high water as well as alligators—which have a special appetite for dog flesh.

We recrossed the river after much conviviality and scattered to our homes. So ended my last deer hunt, with the memory of that beautiful buck and his harem down the river. I have wondered how long he survived.

I am not antihunting as long as it is managed by wildlife experts. Most game animals outproduce their food supply, and since civilization has destroyed most of the natural predators, starvation results unless populations are controlled by game management overseeing proper hunting practices. But the terrified eyes of that spike buck I shot are something I'd like to forget. I have felt the same terror when being shot at—so hunting is not for me.

World War II gave me a convenient measuring stick for duty, courage, terror, friendship, patience, horror, endurance, compassion, discomfort, grief, and pain that has remained with me daily. The English poet Robert Graves said World War

I affected him in much the same way. Anyone who has not suffered the prolonged fear and limitless fatigue that was the combat infantryman's lot might find this difficult to comprehend.

Over fifty years later I look back on the war as though it were some giant killing machine into which we were thrown to endure fear to the brink of insanity—some fell over the brink—and physical fatigue to near collapse. Those who survived unhurt will never forget—and cannot forget—the many friends lost in their prime and the many articles of civilization ruthlessly destroyed.

As I look back, some facts are quite clear: Japan's sneak bombing of Pearl Harbor destroyed many American lives, ships, and planes. We had no choice but to destroy Imperial Japan. The A-bomb ended that war. It saved millions of American lives by preventing a murderous invasion of Japan and the probable destruction of a suicidal Japanese population. The Japanese soldier was a bloodthirsty foe imbued with the Code of Bushido (Code of the Warrior) and yamata damasbii (the fighting power of Japan). If we had not defeated an army that thought it was unbeatable, who knows how many American cities might have shared the horrid Rape of Nanking. (Skeptical revisionists may laugh if they wish.)

In looking back, I am still amazed I escaped the killing machine. Why I never fell killed or wounded in that storm of steel thrown at us countless times still astonishes me. I am proud of the number of the enemy I fired on and hit with my mortar, rifle, or Tommy gun—and regret the ones I missed. There is no "mellowing" for me—that would be to forgive all the atrocities the Japanese committed against millions of Asians and thousands of Americans. To "mellow" is to forget. Each man who survived, I am certain, was plucked from the mire of death by the Almighty—and in this I feel humble and grateful. Socrates said, "Know Thyself." I do. The war taught me.

AN AUTUMN PALETTE
Vivian Smallwood

Autumn comes briefly to this coastal town
Where lagging summer wears her welcome out
And spring and winter play at hide-and-seek.
With barely time to button up her smock,
She spreads her brushes and her paints about
And splashes at the canvas of the week.
And what a world of browns she has in stock!
Drab brown of water oak, the silver-brown
Of reeds beside a honey-colored creek.
Amber of grasses drying in the sun,
Nut-brown of hickory, bronze of sycamore,
Sienna, russet, copper-color, dun—
Who would have thought there were so many browns?
She leaves untouched the live oak and the pine,
Camellia, boxwood and the lank wild cherry,
But suddenly and joyously she flings
A wealth of red and gold on fading things.
Crepe myrtles blaze along the boulevard,
The tallow trees are miracles of light,
And every dogwood holds its flock of leaves,
With scarlet wings already poised for flight.

From *Window to the South*

THE GARDEN SPOT

Charles McNair

My annual end-of-winter accomplishment—a 20-foot-square patch of dirt scratched free of grass and weeds—lies beside the house today, bare as the cover of an old black book.

In this little garden spot, seeds sleep in new beds, dreaming Cinderella stories. Soon they'll be graceful yellow squash with swans' necks, fat tomatoes hung in the sky like planets, and red peppers fierce as spurs on fighting roosters.

Since my college days, I've put in a spring garden wherever I happened to live. Something about the warming air in March, the first blossoms, that first crocus doing a push-up in the yard, fills me with a gardener's instincts. I yearn to take part in what the world itself is doing—seeding, putting down roots, creating. Never mind that this ambition melts away with the searing temperatures of summer. By August, every year, my victory garden is usually an embarrassment, a resort for rabbits grown fat and happy on lettuce, a haven for garden spiders and wild weeds.

Still, for a few glorious weeks in spring, the garden space is a plot of promise. In these days, friends can find me down on my prayer bones sculpting the earth with bare hands, living out one of the timeworn rituals of Southern life.

The finest thing I ever produced in a garden was a tremendous fairy-tale forest of sunflowers, close by Mobile Bay. In this part of Alabama, soils are sinfully lush, the earth so rich that a homeowner's most earnest battle is to keep plant life off the windows and out of the garage. Whole bayside neighborhoods can fill up in a year with baby pecan and oak trees, set out by thrifty squirrels. In spring, azaleas and gardenias hypnotize Sunday drivers and lure them off the road, while kudzu spins webs for slow pedestrians. Anything grows. You get the idea that dogs even bury bones with high hopes.

Gardeners soon discover, though, that there are hungry creatures for every healthy plant in these semitropics. I learned the hard way: Nematodes hollowed my tomatoes; aphids turned my eggplants into ruined Tennessee Williams mansions. Caterpillars chomped up my potato blooms, then romped down the vines to play tag all summer in a rooty funhouse.

By some miracle, my sunflowers proved invulnerable to these scourges. All summer they sucked the baywater up and up, all the way to their steering-wheel-sized heads. They lorded it over the bayside. Van Gogh never had a canvas big enough for these flowers. They towered on ankle-thick stalks to 8 and 10 feet in height, their blooms scanning the blue afternoon skies like a colony of satellite dishes.

As I admired these fabulous plants, I began to notice how a scarlet cardinal came each afternoon to inspect the flowers, cocking his head to one side and dreaming of the day when thousands of seeds would ripen and fall. June bugs used the blooms as a heliport, harmlessly zooming on and off, their green and ruby bodies buzzing.

I charted the legendary motion of sunflowers, imagining that, why yes, they really did swivel on their necks from east to west to follow the sun all day, drinking the light.

And one wonderful night in June, I sat on my porch with a glass of iced tea and watched lightning bugs dance up to the sunflowers, land and linger then fly away again, carrying brighter little pieces of yellow light into the dark.

Fine and simple lessons, I thought: a man's mind grows wide with a garden.

I have had the good fortune through the years to see lovely spring gardens in several parts of the world outside my native Alabama. In Paris during March, raised beds of lettuce and chive float like shaggy green rafts in rainy courtyards. South of Naples, some gardens grow vertically; the great curtains of grapevine shade rows of chamomile and herbs. In Yugoslavia, oxen trudge across the landscapes, their heavy heads nodding yeah, yeah, as they drag a plow through a patch of peanuts.

In my own little Alabama garden spot, I find a theme common to all this worldwide breaking, entering, and bringing forth: No matter where there is a garden, its essence lies in one simple, satisfying combination—here is a person, and here is the earth.

Caught by the full moon rising into a greening treeline this March, I leaned on my shovel at the end of a planting day. A passage from an old book with a rich black cover floated into my mind: And the Lord god planted a garden eastward in Eden; and there he put the man whom he had formed.

I like to imagine that at the end of that first spring day, the Lord himself, bone-weary and satisfied, leans against his shovel, too. The moon shone down. The earth breathed coolness up into his feet. He saw new green plants and black soil and decided it really was very good.

And perhaps He made himself the same quiet promise every gardener makes each spring to the world: I'll keep faith and I'll work hard; this place will grow beautiful in time.

Originally published in *Southern Living* magazine as a Southern Journal selection, March 1991.

JUBILEE
Ben Erickson

It was a moonless night, and the ebbing tide was almost dead low. The bay was smooth and glassy, with not even the hint of a breeze to stir the humid summer air. The old man held the floundering light while he and the boy waded through the knee-deep water. The lamp gave off a constant hiss as the pressurized gas ignited around the fragile ashen mantles. Its brilliant white light illuminated the water in front of them, magnifying and throwing every feature on the bottom into sharp relief.

They walked slowly, so as not to cloud the already murky water, sliding their feet along to avoid stepping on a buried stingray. Moving the lamp from side to side, the man scanned the water in front of him, searching for the indistinct outline of a flounder lying camouflaged on the bottom. Their luminous beacon attracted a menagerie of small fish that moved when they moved and stopped when they stopped, like a traveling circus of miniature marine performers. Needlefish were also attracted by the light. Shooting through the water like bottle rockets, the slender fish startled the boy from time to time as they collided harmlessly against his bare legs.

The boy gripped the long wooden handle of the gig loosely in his fingers. As they walked he dipped the metal tip underwater, never tiring of watching its single sharp point appear to bend magically in the refracted light. A empty wash tub floated behind him, tethered to his belt by a frayed manila rope.

"Have you ever seen a jubilee?" his grandfather asked, without taking his eyes off the water.

"I've heard of them, but I've never seen one," the boy said, chasing a minnow with the tip of the gig.

"Well, this stretch of Mobile Bay is about the only place you'll find them," he told him.

The boy reached down with the gig and touched a crab the size of his hand that was frozen in the light. The point clinked metallically on its hard shell, causing the crab to extend its claws in self-defense as it backed out of the circle of light.

"You really need to live on the bay to see a jubilee, not just visit once in a while during summer vacation," he said, glancing over at the boy. "They don't happen very often, and when they do it's usually late at night after everyone's asleep. Yes sir, they're an amazing thing to behold."

The old man suddenly stopped and pointed at the bottom a few feet in front of them. "Do you see him?" he asked.

Sighting down the bony index finger of his grandfather's outstretched hand, the boy could just make out the dim outline in the sand.

"Ease forward, until you're close enough," he whispered in the boy's ear, as if the fish could hear him through the water.

The boy did as he was told and stood poised to strike.

"Now, do just like we practiced," the voice over his shoulder said. "Remember how the water bends the light, and aim for where he really is, not where your eyes tell you."

The boy calculated the difference between reality and illusion then thrust the gig downward. The bottom in front of him erupted in a cloud of silt, obscuring everything. He held tight to the gig as it vibrated in his hands, pinning his prey to the bottom. Soon the struggling lessened.

"That's it," the old man said. "Now, slide one hand under him."

Still holding the gig firmly with one hand, the boy slid his other one down the handle until he could feel the cold skin of the fish. Sliding his upturned hand beneath it, he felt the hard steel of the gig slip between his outstretched fingers.

"Got it," he said, his mouth barely above water.

"Good. Now, lift him up and put him in the tub."

He cradled the still quivering flounder into the washtub, then let it slide off the gig. The fish lay gasping in the bottom of the empty tub. Its skin was a mottled patchwork of greens and browns, with both eyes staring up at them from the top of the pancake thin body.

"Nice work," his grandfather said, giving him a congratulatory pat on the shoulder.

They resumed their slow pace through the water. The hissing of the lamp blended with the sound of mosquitoes buzzing around the boy's ear. By now he had grown so used to their high-pitched whine, that he didn't even bother waving them away anymore. Another crab appeared at the edge of their ever changing circle of light, and once more the boy reached out and touched it with his gig. This time there was no answering clink.

"Soft-shell," the old man said. "Best eating around. Pick him up and put him in the tub for me."

"How?" he asked. "I don't have a net."

"You don't need one," his grandfather replied. "Just use your hands."

"But it'll pinch me," the boy said, hiding his free hand behind his back at the mere thought of it.

"He just shed his shell, and the new one hasn't had time to harden yet," he told him. "He couldn't hurt you if he tried."

Reluctantly, the boy reached down into the water and touched the crab with his bare hand, then jerked it back. When there was no reaction, he fished it out and held it up to the light. It looked like any other crab, except that the shell was as pliable as rubber. He touched the claws, and even they bent uselessly.

"Crabs have to shed their shells when they grow too big for them, just like a snake shedding its skin," the old man said. "Trouble is, they're helpless when it happens. So they do it at night in shallow water, where there's less chance they'll be seen. Before long the new shell will harden and their armor will be restored. Put him in there, and I'll cook him when we get back," he said, motioning to the washtub. "You fry them up whole and can eat almost everything."

The boy put the crab in the tub next to the flounder, and they continued wading through the night.

"I can still remember my first jubilee. I couldn't have been but six or seven at the time, not much younger than you are now," his grandfather said, sizing up the boy at his side. "Back then if somebody happened on one, they'd let everyone on the bay know about it. Bells would ring and people would beat pots and pans all up and down the Eastern Shore. Lights would come on in houses, and word would spread like wildfire."

He looked over at the shore, ignoring the glare from the yard lights that now lined the bay and pictured it as it had once been.

"Yes sir, I can still hear them like it was yesterday..."

"Jubileeee! ... Jubileeee!"

The disembodied voice ran along the shore calling loudly in the dark, accompanied by the sound of a cooking spoon beating time on a pot. Passing the unlit house, it continued down the narrow strip of sand, growing fainter and fainter until it finally faded out all together.

The sound filtered through the open upstairs window and tickled at the back of the sleeping boy's consciousness, like a feather under his nose. When he had gone to bed, the oppressive heat had caused him to kick off the covers. Now, hours later, he was huddled in a tight ball against the cool night air. As the house around him began to awaken, he stirred restlessly. Doors opened and muffled voices drifted up the staircase to his room. Softly at first—just a distant tap-tap-tap of the spoon on the pan—then growing louder and louder, the unseen voice approached again in the darkness, as the runner made his return trip down the beach.

"Jubileeee! ... Jubileeee! ... Jubilee at Point Clear! ... Come and get 'em while they's still there! ... Jubileeee! ... Jubileeee!"

The boy's eyes opened like released window shades, and in an instant he was wide awake. Rolling out of bed, he looked out the window that faced the bay. In the dim light reflected off the water, he could just make out the receding flash of the pan and the gleam of an unbuttoned white shirt on dark skin. Pulling on his clothes, he opened the door to his room and bounded down the staircase.

His mother was already in the kitchen, piling buckets and croaker sacks on the table. Through the back screen door, he could see his father hooking their old mare to the wagon.

"I'll take them out to him," he said, gathering up the containers.

His mother watched as he struggled to carry more than his small arms could hold. Barely able to see over his burden, he bumped and clanged his way out the back door and down the steps.

His father turned at the sound. "Well, look who's up!" he said. "I guess you heard all that racket on the beach?"

"Can I go? Please!" he asked.

"It's mighty late for a boy your age to be out."

"I'll do everything you tell me. Please!" the boy pleaded.

His father eyed him critically. "Well, I wasn't going to wake you," he said, pausing for dramatic effect. "But since you're already up, I suppose so."

A broad grin split the boy's face at the invitation. His father took the armful of containers from him and put them in the back of the wagon. Reaching down, he lifted the boy up onto the seat, then climbed in after him.

His mother appeared at the door with a fruit jar full of iced tea and a paper bag. "Just in case you men get hungry," she said, handing it to them.

"Don't wait up," his father said, giving her a peck on the cheek. "We'll be back by morning. Come on now, Molly," he called to the horse as he slapped the reins.

The mare seemed to sense their excitement and started down the drive at a brisk trot. Turning out onto the main road, they were swallowed up by the night.

Trees and bushes overhung the narrow shell road that paralleled the bay. Even though the boy had traveled it hundreds of times before and knew it like the back of his hand, the darkness changed everything. Mysterious shadows formed in the dim light from the kerosene lanterns as they swung back and forth on their hooks, inspiring visions of highwaymen or pirates lying in wait around every bend in the winding road. Moving closer to his father's side, he narrowed his eyes until they were reduced to slits he could barely see through. His father whistled a cheerful tune and didn't seem the least bit concerned at their peril, but with every new pair of eyes that stared back at him from the edge of the road, the boy feared the worst. Each time they materialized into the familiar shape of a raccoon or possum, he breathed a small sigh of relief.

Soon they were joined by other wagons, as people from miles around heard the news, and the air was filled with the rumble of wheels on the rough road. When they reached the point of land that jutted out into the bay, the wagons pulled single file off the main road and down a sandy track that led to the shore.

Lights were on in the hotel that straddled the point, and the balcony facing the bay was lined with guests that had been roused in the middle of the night to witness the unusual spectacle. They leaned out over the porch railings, watching with curiosity as the scene unfolded below. The beach glowed with bonfires and lanterns, and laughter mingled with the chattering of excited voices.

His father stopped the wagon by the side of the road and climbed down. Taking the croaker sacks from the back, he removed one of the lanterns from its hook, and together they walked down to the water's edge.

The pungent smell of the bay was even stronger than usual, and the boy's eyes grew wide as the lantern lit up the shoreline. Flounder, stingrays, and other bottom dwellers of all sizes and shapes flapped helplessly in the shallow water. There were so many that in places they were piled two or three deep. Crabs crawled over them in an effort to escape, some pulling themselves all the way out of the water in the process. It was almost impossible to set foot in the bay without stepping on something. Looking down the beach, he could see lights scattered for a quarter mile in either direction.

"You've read in the Bible about manna falling from heaven?" his father asked.

"Yes, sir."

"Well, this is manna brought up by the sea."

"What makes them do it, Papa?" he asked, puzzled.

"I guess the powers that be tell them to."

"But there must be a reason?"

"No one knows, son. I guess it's just one of life's little mysteries," he said. "Now hold the light for me while I fill these sacks."

He gathered up more than they could eat, then carried the burlap bags up the beach to the wagon with the boy following behind him. The brackish water of the bay seeped through the porous cloth, leaving a wet trail in the sand. By the time he hoisted the last of the heavy sacks over the side of the wagon, the changing tide had already begun to pull what remained back out into the depths of the bay. Many of the other wagons were leaving, and the hotel guests had long since vanished from their porches to retire for the second time that night.

Taking the paper bag and jar from the seat, they walked over to join the group of men sitting around a bonfire on the beach. Examining their weathered faces in the reflected firelight, the boy recognized them as fishermen, crabbers, and shrimpers who were regulars at his father's store. They would often stop by to chat and spend a hot summer afternoon on the benches and chairs that lined the store's shady porch, accompanied by the popping of the tin roof as it expanded in the sun. Often they would entice his father to join them on fishing trips to try and lure a mighty tarpon from the bay.

The men made a fuss over the boy, rumpling his hair and asking him what he wanted to be when he grew up.

"A fisherman," he replied without hesitation.

They burst into hoots of laughter.

"Well I guess he takes after you, Bill," one of the men said, nudging his father. "You've never been able to leave the fish alone."

The laughter died down, and they found a vacant spot in the circle around the fire. Overhead, the stars twinkled brightly against the dark sky. A flask was passed from hand to hand to take the chill out of the night air, and stories were told as they stared into the dancing flames. Their voices rose and fell in the glow of the flickering embers, then drifted upward, suspended on a cloud of rising smoke.

They told stories about the bay, while it lapped against the shore just a few yards away. Over the years their tales had grown and changed in the telling and retelling, until they had been transformed into something else all together.

The boy put his head on his father's lap and listened to the men talk as he looked up at the night sky. If he stared long enough, the tiny points of light above him appeared to move against the vast blackness. Around him, the voices wove in and out of his consciousness.

"So I was out in my boat—you know that little sixteen-footer I had built over at Hawkins yard—checking traps, and it was getting on near dark. I'd just dumped the last one when I heard a boom right behind me as loud as thunder, and a splash soaked me to the skin. Before I could turn around, a wave hit the boat broadside, knocking me clean off my feet. As I picked myself up from the bottom of the boat, I saw something circling around me in the gloom not far away. Squinting hard, I could just make out the gray back cutting through the water. Its dorsal fin stuck up at least three feet in the air, and I realized that I was looking into the eyes of the biggest hammerhead shark these parts have ever seen. Before I could decide what to do next, the brute's massive tail took another swipe at my boat and splintered the transom like kindling. I started taking on water fast and…"

One bright star in particular seemed to pulsate as the boy watched. He imagined it as a lighthouse on some distant celestial shore, guiding the other stars on their way. The sound of the men talking droned on around him.

"It was a slow afternoon, and the fish had long since given up on biting. I must have dozed off, because the next thing I know there's a roaring sound, like I was standing right by a waterfall. When I opened my eyes, the first thing I saw was a dark cloud hovering above me. I sat up in my boat and looked out, and as close as from me to you was a waterspout. Its funnel was black and evil looking, and I could see fish as big as my arm caught in it and sucked up as quick as a cat..."

Out of the corner of his eye, the boy saw a shooting star streak across the sky. He followed its phosphorescent trail until it disappeared as if it had never existed.

"When she stopped dead in the water, I figured my net had hung on a snag. Then, so help me, she started moving backward, picking up speed as she goes. Water began sloshing over the stern as I made my way aft, grabbing a knife as I went. The bay behind me was bubbling and churning like a thing alive. I go to sawing on the port line, and it popped like a piece of piano wire, knocking the knife clean out of my hand. That put all the pressure on the starboard side, and she started heeling over..."

A star low in the western sky far out over the bay attracted the boy's attention. As he watched, it twinkled from red to green and back again. Just like the lights on a ship, he thought, as the soft sounds of the bay lulled him to sleep.

"I guess we was running about ten miles out in the gulf when I saw a line of squalls moving our way. So I told the boys to pull in the lines, and I turned us back toward home. On the way in the wind began to pick up, and the barometer started to drop. We were about halfway there when all hell broke loose. I couldn't see more than fifty feet in front of me, and the wind was blowing so hard that the water was covered in foam. I finally made it to the channel by the grace of my compass and dead reckoning alone. I was about to try and take her through the pass blind when the rain slacked up for a minute, and I could see breakers all the way across it. So I spun the wheel hard about, trying to head back out to sea to ride it out, when a rogue wave come out of nowhere and hit us broadside..."

As the fire burned down, the sky began to lighten in the east. An early morning breeze ruffled the water, sending the smoke swirling across the beach. One by one the men stood up, stretched, and headed for home.

Gently picking up the sleeping boy, his father carried him back to the wagon. When he lifting him up onto the seat, he opened his eyes.

"Where are we?" the boy asked.

"Going home, buddy," his father told him. "I've got to open the store, and you and your mother have fish to clean and crabs to boil."

"Oh," he replied, squinting through sleep swollen eyes.

Turning the wagon around on the sandy track, his father clicked his tongue, and they headed back down the road toward home. It wasn't the excitement of a night outing that motivated the mare's pace this time, but a vision of the barn with fresh hay in her stall. The rocking of the wagon soon had the boy fast asleep again, nestled against his father's side.

By the time they turned down the lane to the house, the sun had risen and was peeking through the leaves of the live oaks. Opening his eyes, the boy looked around him. The morning breeze played in the branches, causing the limbs to sway. Their rhythmic movement sent flecks of light skittering across the ground in constantly changing patterns, like a shower of shooting stars flung across the night sky.

"Yes sir, that was a long time ago," the old man said, looking toward the distant point of land, its shape outlined by the lights from the hotel. "A lot has changed since then."

"Do you think we'll have a jubilee tonight?" the boy at his side asked, poking his gig at a clump of grass growing on the bottom of the bay.

"No one knows," he said, mirroring his father's words from so long ago. "Like many things in life, they tend to show up when you aren't expecting them and leave long before you're ready for them to go."

"Like me?" the boy asked, looking up at him.

"Yes," his grandfather said with a smile, "and like your grandmother, too."

They walked on in silence.

"Mama says I look like her," the boy said finally.

The old man stopped and searched his face in the lamp's glow, then reached out and brushed his hair back from his forehead.

"Yes, I guess you do at that," he said. "I can see her in your eyes."

The boy looked away self-consciously, pretending to examine the lifeless flounder in the tub.

"I can't remember her," the boy said, guilt filling his voice.

"You were little then," he replied. "Memories fade."

"But you remember the jubilee? You told me everything about it," he said. "I can't even see her face anymore."

"Do you remember how she used to rock you on her lap?"

The boy thought a minute, then nodded.

"What about that time you stepped on a catfish fin, and she bandaged it up and made you her special homemade gumbo?" he asked.

The boy nodded again.

"You remember more than you think you do," his grandfather told him.

"Will I remember you?" the boy asked, a look of concern on his face.

Before the old man could answer, a shooting star streaked across the sky in front of them. For a brief moment, it was brighter than everything else combined.

"You'll remember," the old man said, as the light from the falling star began to fade.

from NATURALIST
E.O. Wilson

"TO DO MY DUTY"

In the spring of 1941, my grandmother Mary Emma Joyner Wilson, known to her family as May, died in Mobile of a heart attack in the house where she had been born in 1868, married, attended a private school run by her mother, raised four sons, and stayed the remainder of her life. Since 1916, when her husband died, she had lived in the company of her bachelor son, Herbert. During all those seventy-three years she had seldom journeyed beyond the edge of the city.

My father brought Pearl and me to live in the large rambling structure that he and Herbert inherited from my grandmother. The house had a long history, at least for the young state of Alabama. Built by May's grandfather in 1838, it was for a few years the only house on Charleston Street, though located only a dozen blocks from Bienville Square and the commercial heart of the old city. Here then, if anywhere, were the roots of my peregrine family.

Alabama's seaport was a small town in the early 1800s when my father's forebears arrived, a junior version of New Orleans complete with muddy streets, balcony grillwork, creole cooking, and epidemics of yellow fever. In 1815, two years after American troops took it from the Spanish on orders from President Madison, Mobile was nothing more than fourteen city blocks grouped in a large square north of Fort Charlotte. By the 1830s and 1840s the town was growing rapidly, but many of the streets, including Charleston, still led down to what an early map labeled "low and miry land"—mud banks-lining the Mobile River estuary. The Hawkinses, Joyners, and Wilsons could ride there by carriage in a few minutes and walk over long wharves to reach the ferry slips. Often, no-doubt, they just went to fish and net blue crabs lured with soup bones. The wildlands south of the city still existed in a remnant condition. Large stretches of hardwood and pine forest extended south all the way to Cedar Point, the southernmost tip of mainland Alabama on the west side of Mobile Bay. Beyond that, across Mississippi Sound, a mostly uninhabited Dauphin Island formed a line along the horizon.

When my father was a teenage boy, just before the First World War, he was able, he told me, to step out the front door of the Charleston Streethouse, stroll down the road a mile or two with a .22 rifle under his arm to the wooded terrain now occupied by Brookley Airport, and hunt quail, rabbits, or whatever else took his fancy. When I was the same age in the 1940s, I often rode my bicycle around

Brookley to reach uninhabited woodland and pitcher plant and pine savanna along the Dog and Fowl Rivers. I sometimes paused to eat sandwiches and drink Royal Crown Colas on the two-lane wooden bridges spanning these two streams. Around midday an hour or more might pass without the approach of a single automobile. I leaned on the wooden rails in reverie, looking deeply into the slow-moving and limpid water for glimpses of gars and soft-shelled turtles. Today this land is thickly settled, and heavy traffic rumbles all the way down to a bridge running from Cedar Point to Dauphin Island.

My father was proud of his family history. The Hawkinses and Joyners had emigrated from New England to the Mobile Bay area not long after it became American territory; one, my great-great-grandmother Mary Ann Hawkins, was born there in 1826. They prospered as marine engineers, pilots, and ship owners. My great-grandfather James Eli Joyner, who married Mary Ann's daughter Anna Amelia, operated a ferry that serviced the Baldwin County shore out of Mobile. One November day in 1870 his ship caught fire and sank close to Mobile, and he drowned while attempting to swim ashore. His young wife was holding my grandmother May in her arms on the porch of the Charleston Street house as she gazed at the distant plume of smoke, not realizing that it meant she would be a widow. To make ends meet thereafter, she opened a private school in the house, the first in Mobile. I own her pendant containing a portrait of her mother, as well as the heavy gold watch chain with dolphin catch taken from her husband's body.

In the War Between the States virtually every able-bodied male on both my father's and mother's sides fought for the Confederacy. Of the two paternal great-grandfathers, James Joyner served for the duration of the war as artilleryman and teamster; the other was a special case, the undoubted star of all my forebears as far back as I have been able to trace them: William Christopher Wilson.

Black Bill, as his friends called him, was a man whose blood I like to imagine coursing through my veins, even though after three generations I carry only one-eighth of his genes. He was born William Christopher O'Connor in 1816 in a family of Dublin printers, whose customers I was told included the Bank of England. He must have been a rebel of considerable fire. His parents wanted him to train for the Episcopal ministry, but he yearned for a life at sea. So he left home as a teenager, took a job as a cabin boy on a ship bound for Baltimore, and changed his name to Wilson en route when a passenger by that name died.

In Baltimore he proceeded to take a Jewish bride named Maria Louise Myers, daughter of Jacob Myers and Sarah Solomon Myers, late of Germany. The newlyweds soon moved to Mobile to seek their fortune. Black Bill—his name came later from the color of his long beard and not from a Black Irish complexion—found employment as a bar pilot. He advanced to master's status and eventually acquired his own boat, with which he guided merchant ships through the treacherous shallows between Fort Morgan and Fort Gaines. In the early 1840s he became a founding member of the Mobile Bar Pilots Association, a guild still in operation today. He moved his family to Navy Cove on Fort Morgan Peninsula, where the sails of approaching merchantmen could first be sighted on the Alabama coast as they approached across the open Gulf.

In 1863, when Admiral Farragut blockaded Mobile Bay, Black Bill and his fellow pilots used their fast ships to run supplies in from Havana. Often pursued, Wilson was finally cornered on a small island outside the harbor. Instead of being simply thrown in irons, he was brought before Farragut and his staff, who made an offer: if Wilson would lead the fleet into Mobile Bay so that it could move swiftly past the guns of Fort Morgan and Fort Gaines without running aground on the shoals, he would receive a large monetary reward and be resettled with his family somewhere in the North. He refused, crying, according to his own account, "I'd see the whole Yankee fleet damned in hell before I'd betray my country!" Not exactly the famously historical flourish of Farragut's authenticated "Damn the torpedoes! Go ahead!" that followed soon afterward (or it might have been "Damn the torpedoes, full speed ahead!" or, most likely and least euphoniously, "Damn the torpedoes, Jouett, full speed!"), but good enough for a southern family in a city in which, even into this century, a sign of respect to an older man was to call him "Cap'n," Oddly, William Christopher Wilson was still an Irish citizen at the time of his capture and remained so. And he never legally changed his name to Wilson. Had I known that as a young man, I might have changed my own back to O'Connor, the sound of which has a nice swing around the apostrophe and a pleasing consonantal bark at the hard C, in contrast to the whispery syllables of Wil-son.

Black Bill was sent off to a succession of federal prisons in New York and Maryland for the remaining two years of the war, and Farragut and his men soon got what they wanted anyway. They captured another Mobile bar pilot who was at that time fishing for a living off the coast at nearby Pascagoula, the legitimate pilot business having been pretty well closed down. His name was Martin Freeman (no relation to my mother's people of the same surname, who were then living in northern Alabama) He and other fishermen were armed and prepared to resist a Yankee invasion, but one salvo from the Union guns offshore changed their minds. Freeman agreed to pilot the fleet, and on August 5, 1864, when a double column of monitors and wooden frigates charged into the bay, he was coolly riding the main top of the flagship Hartford. Members of Black Bill's family watched from their Navy Cove house as Federal shells burst on nearby Fort Morgan. Among Freeman's rewards after Mobile had been captured was the Congressional Medal of Honor, making him—I hope I do not put too heavy a spin on it after 130 years—the only traitor ever to receive America's highest military honor.

When we arrived in Mobile in 1941, the old house was dilapidated and the surrounding neighborhood in decay. Most of the men in the Wilson clan had either died or dispersed, leaving behind widows and spinster daughters sprinkled about the city. We addressed them all as either Aunt or Cousin, depending on their blood ties and age. These survivors were of surprising interest to my father, who at this point turned out to be a family historian seized by nostalgia and a yearning for reflected glory. On Sunday afternoons we visited these living monuments of the treasured past—Aunt Nellie, the younger Cousin Nellie, Aunt Vivian, and Cousin Mollie—in their respective parlors. I kissed each on the cheek and sat on a chair to one side until I could slip away without notice. The reminiscing droned on, a recycling of the stories and sketches of the late Grandma May, Aunt Hope, Aunt Georgia, Aunt Sarah, and all their stalwart departed husbands and brothers and sons, and what happened in the lamented War Between the States, and the many things families did in Old Mobile. Occasionally we visited Magnolia Cemetery, where our forebears and their multitudinous relations and friends lay at rest. Pearl and I stood patiently by as my father located graves, checked dates, and reconstructed lives and genealogies.

I had no interest in this world of ghosts. I considered my father a bore and my great-aunts and cousins an ordeal. For me Mobile was a place of vibrant life—not of spirits, however, nor of people, and certainly not of relatives, but of butterflies. At twelve years of age, I had arrived with a burning desire to collect and study butterflies. I was keenly aware that the city is on the edge of the subtropics and home to many species not found in Washington, D.C.

At every opportunity I charged out on my balloon-tired, single-gear Schwinn bicycle, pumping my way down Charleston Street to the rubble-strewn weedlots of the riverfront, west to the scattered pine-and hardwood copses of Spring Hill, south on the Cedar Point road as far as Fowl River, and east across the Mobile-Tensaw delta on old U.S. 90 to Spanish Fort in Baldwin County. I greeted the sight of each new species of butterfly with joy, and when I caught my first specimen, I thought myself a big-game hunter with net. The zebra and golden-winged Julia, northernmost representatives of a group that abounds in tropical forests; the goatweed butterfly, bright orange-red with a swift erratic flight, hard to net; the little fairy sulfur, average-sized dog face sulfur, outsized cloudless sulfur, all tropical looking with the flamboyant flashing of their yellow wings; giant swallowtail (and what a thrill to see how different it looked in life from the common tiger swallowtail of the North); zebra swallowtail in the shadowed woods; great purple-hair-streak, a stunning iridescent gem I first spotted resting on a weed in a vacant lot; and the large Brazilian skipper, which I reared from translucent gray-green caterpillars feeding on canna lilies in our backyard—all these I added to my butterfly life list.

During the next two years, before we hit the road again, as it seemed inevitably we must, my interest in natural history soared. I went looking for pileated woodpeckers rumored to nest at Spanish Fort, and on the way saw my first wild alligators, in the marshes of the Tensaw estuary. I scoured the riverine hardwood forests for holly trees and orchids. I built a secret outdoor shelter partly from the stems of poison oak and paid for it with an agonizing rash over a large part of my body (afterward I could identify *Rhus quercifolia* at a hundred paces). I hunted reptiles: stunned and captured five-lined skinks with a slingshot, and learned the correct maneuver for catching Carolina anole lizards (approach, let them scuttle to the other side of the tree trunk and out of sight, peck to see where they are sitting, then take them by grabbing blind with one hand around the trunk). One late afternoon I brought home a coachwhip snake nearly as long as I was tall and walked into the house with it wrapped around my neck. Pearl send me back out with instructions to release it as far from the house as could be traveled round-trip during the remaining daylight hours. I owned a machete and used it to chop my way trough tangled undergrowth, imagining myself to be in the jungles of South America. One day I misjudged the downward stroke and slashed my left index finger to the bone. Blood streamed down my arm on the long bicycle ride home. Pearl let me keep the knife, nonetheless, figuring I'd learned the hard way to be more careful.

When America entered the war in December 1941, the tempo of life in Mobile picked up sharply. Tanker traffic in and out of the harbor increased, and over-flights of B-17 bombers and other warplanes became commonplace. Poor rural whites—peapickers we derisively called them—and blacks poured into the city looking for work. Jobs were plentiful and labor was short. One anecdote making the rounds at the time involved a white woman who stopped a local Negro woman (to use the idiom of 1942) near her house, saying that she was looking for domestic help. The other responded: "Why, so am I." If you were white you were supposed to gasp with amused surprise. Change was in the air.

...In June 1942 Ellis MacLeod came down from Washington to stay with me for the summer. We visited my favorite haunts, shared again our old fantasies, and renewed our intention to become entomologists. That fall after he returned home, I set out to collect and study all the ants in a vacant lot next to the Charleston Street house. I still remember the species I found, in vivid detail, enhanced by the knowledge acquired in later studies: a colony of the trap-jawed *Odontomachus insularus*, whose vicious stings drove me away from their nest at the foot of a fig tree; a colony of a small yellowish-brown Pheidole. Possibly *Pheidole floridamus*, found nesting beneath an amber-colored whiskey bottle in midwinter and which I kept for awhile in a vertical observation nest of sand between two glass plates. And colonies of imported fire ants, unmistakably *Solenopsis invicta*, were there. The vacant lot discovery was the earliest record of the species in the United States, and I was later to publish it as a datum in a technical article, my first scientific observation.

My energies and confidence were gathering. By the fall of 1942, at the age of thirteen, I had become in effect a child workaholic. I took a job with backbreaking hours of my own free will, without adult coercion or even encouragement. Soon after the start of the war there was a shortage of carriers for the city newspaper, the *Mobile Press Register*. Young men seventeen and over were departing for the service, and boys aged fifteen to sixteen were moving up part-time into the various jobs they vacated. On the lowest rung of unskilled labor, many paper routes came open as the fifteen-and sixteen-year-olds moved up. Somehow, for reasons I do not recall, an adult delivery supervisor let me take over a monster route: 420 papers in the central city area.

For most of that school year I rose each morning at three, slipped away in the darkness, delivered the papers, each to a separate residence, and returned home for breakfast around seven-thirty. I departed a half-hour later for school, returned home again at three-thirty, and studied. On Monday nights from seven to nine I attended the meeting of my Boy Scout troop at the United Methodist Church on Government and Broad streets. On Sunday mornings I went to service at the First Baptist Church. On Sunday evenings I stayed up through "Fibber McGee and Molly" on the radio. On other nights I set the alarm soon after supper, went to bed, and fell asleep.

Four hundred and twenty papers delivered each morning! It seems almost impossible to me now. But there is no mistake; the number is etched in my memory. The arithmetic also fits: I made two trips to the delivery dock at the back of the Press Register building, each time filling two large canvas satchels. When stacked vertically on the bicycle front fender and strapped to the handlebars, the bags reached almost to my head and were close to the maximum bulk and weight I could handle. The residences receiving the papers were not widely spaced suburban houses but city dwellings, apartment buildings with two or three stories. It took perhaps a maximum of one hour to travel back and forth to the Press Register dock, load the papers twice, and make two round trips in and out; the delivery area was only a few minutes' ride away. That leaves three and a half hours for actual on-the-scene work, or an average of two papers a minute—during which I reached down, pulled out the paper, dropped it or threw it rolled up for a short distance, and passed on, moving faster and more easily after one satchel was emptied.

The supervisor collected the week's subscription money from the customers on Saturday, twenty-five cents apiece, so I didn't have to work extra hours that day and had time to continue my field excursions. I made thirteen dollars a week, from which I bought my Boy Scout paraphernalia, parts for my bike, and whatever candy, soft drinks, and movie tickets I wanted.

At the time it did not occur to me that my round-the-clock schedule was unusual. I felt fortunate to have a job and to be able to earn money. It was the kind of regimen I had learned to expect as normal from my brief experience at the Gulf Coast Military Academy. I still assumed, without any real evidence, that the same level of effort would be required of me as an adult. And what of my father and Pearl, asleep in their bed as I headed out in the predawn hours in all kinds of weather? Pearl, who came from a hardscrabble life in rural North Carolina, seemed well pleased that I showed the kind of spunk it takes to survive. And the feelings of my father, who never worked that hard in his life—who can say?

But the labor over long hours did not really matter; I had discovered the Boy Scouts of America. All that I had become by the age of twelve, all the biases and preconceptions I had acquired, all the dreams I had garnered and savored, fitted me like a finely milled ball into the socket of its machine when I discovered this wonderful organization. The Boy Scouts of America seemed invented just for me.

The 1940 *Handbook for Boys*, which I purchased for half a dollar, became my most cherished possession. Fifty years later, I still read my original annotated copy with remembered pleasure. Richly illustrated, with a cover by Norman Rockwell, it was packed with useful information on the subjects I liked the most. It stressed out-door life and natural history: camping, hiking, swimming, hygiene, semaphore signaling, first-aid, mapmaking, and above all, zoology and botany, page after page of animals and plants wonderfully well-illustrated, explaining where to find them, how to identify them. The public schools and church had offered nothing like this. The Boy Scouts legitimated Nature as the center of life.

There were rules, uniforms, and a crystal-clear set of practical ethics to live by. If I jog my memory today by raising my right hand with the middle three fingers up, thumb and little finger down and crossed, I can still recite the Scout Oath:

> On my honor I will do my best
> To do my duty to God and my country
> And to obey the Scout law;
> To help other people at all times;

To keep myself physically strong,
Mentally awake and morally straight.

And the Scout law: A Scout is trustworthy, loyal, helpful, friendly, courteous, kind, obedient, cheerful, thrifty, brave, clean, reverent. Finally, there was the Scout Motto, *Be Prepared.*

I drank in and accepted every word. Still do, as ridiculous as that may seem to my colleagues in the intellectual trade, to whom I can only reply, "Let's see you do better in fifty-four words or less."

The work ethic was celebrated from cover to cover. There was a clearly marked Boy Scout of America route to success through virtue and exceptional effort. In the chapter titled "Finding One's Life Work," I read: "A Scout looks ahead. He prepares for things before they happen. He therefore meets them easily." Never be satisfied, the instructions warned. Just to wait and hope and accept whatever comes is the road to failure. Reach high, strive long and hard toward honorable goals, and keep ever in mind Longfellow's invocation:

The heights by great men reached and kept, were not attained by sudden flight; but they, while their companions slept, were toiling upward in the night.

I found something else the public schools never offered, a ladder of education to be taken at your own pace, better fast than slow, with each new step successively harder. I saw the whole challenge of scouting as a competition I would enjoy and surely win. The Scout program was my equivalent of the Bronx High School of Science.

I plunged into the new regimen. In three years I advanced to Eagle Scout with palm clusters, the highest rank, and was made junior assistant scoutmaster of my troop. I earned forty-six merit badges, almost half of those available in the organization. I happily crunched through the programs for subjects as diverse as Bird Study, Farm Records and Book-Keeping, Life Saving, Journalism, and Public Health. I pored over the requirements of all the badges at night to see which one I could best do next. My heart sang when I first read the prescription for Insect Life, beginning: "To obtain this merit Badge, a Scout must: 1. go into the country with the Examiner and show to him the natural surroundings in which certain specified insects live, and find and demonstrate living specimens of the insects, telling of their habits or of the nature of their fitness for life in their particular surroundings."

All the time I attended to my schoolwork in an adequate but desultory manner. The subjects were relatively easy, and I maintained passing grades. But most of the curriculum seemed dull and pointless. My most memorable accomplishments in my freshman year at Murphy High School in Mobile was to capture twenty houseflies during one hour of class, a personal record, and lay them in rows for the next student to find. The teacher found these trophies instead, and had the grace to compliment me on my feat next day in front of the class. I had developed a new technique for catching flies, and I now pass it on to you. Let the fly alight, preferably on a level and unobstructed surface, such as a restaurant table or book cover. Move your open hand carefully until it rests twelve to eighteen inches in front of the sitting fly's head. Bring the hand very slowly forward, in a straight line, taking care not to waggle sideways; flies are very sensitive to lateral movement. When your hand is about nine inches away, sweep it toward the fly so that the edge of the palm passes approximately one or two inches above the spot where the fly is resting. Your target will dart upward at about the right trajectory to hit the middle of the palm, and as you close your fingers you will feel the satisfying buzz of the insect trapped inside your fist. Now, how to kill the fly? Clap your hands together—discreetly, if you are in a restaurant or lecture hall.

Scouting also proved to be the ideal socializing environment for an undersized and introverted only child. Our gangs were the Scout patrols, groups about the size of an army squad, several of which made up the larger troop. We automatically became members of one when we joined the Scouts, and we were esteemed or criticized on our own merits according to Scout rules. I never met a bully in the Scouts, and relatively few braggarts. The questions before each boy were: Can you walk twenty miles, tie a tourniquet, save a swimmer in Red Cross lifeguard exercises, build a sturdy sapling bridge with nothing but ax and rope? For me the answers were yes, yes, yes!

Scouting added another dimension to my expanding niche. I became a teacher. In the summer of 1943 I was asked to be the nature counselor at Camp Pushmataha, the Boy Scout summer camp near Citronelle used by the Mobile Area District. At fourteen, I was the youngest counselor, with no experience at instruction, but I quickly figured out what interested other boys, what would get them talking about natural history and make them respect the subject: snakes. Several volunteers and I built cages and searched the surrounding woods for as many different kinds of snakes as we could find. Somehow in the process I learned how to capture a poisonous snake. Pin its body with a staff as close to the head as you can manage, then roll the staff forward until the head is pressed firmly to the ground and the neck clear, grasp the neck closely behind the posterior jaw angles, and lift the whole body up. Few boys would touch a snake of any kind, so when one was discovered the word was brought to me by yelling messengers: "Snake! Snake!" And off I would go to perform my derring-do, which I followed with a brief lecture on the species discovered. In a short time we had a row of cages filled with a partial representation of the rich fauna that inhabits the Gulf States. I worked like a zoo director, talking to visitors about the diversity of species. I could then segue into discourses about the insects and plants of Greater Pushmataha. I had become a successful natural history instructor.

But before long my inexperience and reckless pride did me in. It happened one afternoon when I was cleaning a cage containing several pygmy rattlesnakes, my star attractions. The adults of this cryptically colored species (*Sistrurus miliarius*) grow to no more than fifty centimeters in length. They are less deadly than their larger cousins found in the same region, the diamondback and canebrake rattlesnakes, but they are still poisonous and moderately dangerous. In a moment of carelessness I moved my left hand too close to one of the coiled rattlers. Like a quarrel sprung from a crossbow, it uncoiled and struck the tip of my index finger. The two fang punctures felt like a bee sting. I knew I was in trouble. Off I went with an adult counselor to a nearby doctor in town, who administered the old-fashioned first-aid treatment as quickly as he could: deep X-shaped scalpel incisions centered on each of the fang punctures, followed by suction of the blood with a rubber cup. I knew the drill; I had learned it when I earned the merit badge for Reptile Life. I didn't cry during the operation, which was performed without anesthesia. I held my hand steady and cursed loudly nonstop with four-letter words, at myself for my stupidity and not at the innocent doctor or the snake, in order to keep my mind off the procedure. I knew a great deal of off-color language at fourteen and must have surprised the adults helping me. The next morning I was sent home for convalescence. I lay gloomily on a couch for a week, holding my swollen left arm as still as possible.

It was a bad time for herpetology at Camp Pushmataha. When I returned to resume my duties, I found that the camp supervisor had wisely disposed of the pygmy rattlesnakes. I was forbidden to touch any more poisonous species, and nothing more was said.

CONTEMPORARY MOBILE

Possibility holds your hand, guides you blindly through the rushing waters.

—Patricia Foster, *The Big Pond*

THE BIG POND
1962, Mobile, Alabama
Patricia Foster

"It's easy to be a big fish in a small pond," Daddy says, sitting beside us, his coffee cup full to the brim, a handkerchief wadded up in a snarl by his plate. Mother listens as she does dishes at the sink. "The difficult thing is to be a big fish in a big pond," Daddy continues, looking into the depth of his cup as if there might be a prophecy floating there. That's another thing entirely." And he gazes out the window at the pine trees knotted together, bordering our yard. Squirrels sprint frantically across the lawn, digging at leaves, then standing stock still to eat until Sheba, the neighbor's dog, rushes out from the bushes, lunging towards them, scaring them away. For a moment I think Daddy seems sad as if, like Sheba, the prize has just been frightened off.

As he talks, I see myself walking in Mama Dot's woods in the blueness of evening, running through a thicket of oaks and pines until I'm lost in a maze of leaves. The Big Pond must be like this, without boundaries or constraints, a place of nervous mystery. The Big Pond, I believe, demands the logic of the heart.

"The Big Pond is in a city," Mother says, turning from the dishes she's rinsing in the sink. I've never wanted to live in a small town, but your father—"

"I'm going to live in New York," my sister Jean pipes up, grabbing a muffin Mother's left out on the table for us to eat. But I sit very still, trying to imagine such a place, a city with lights and noise and hordes of people where the indefinable Big Pond exists. All I see is a girl standing on the edge of the highway, ignored and vulnerable, while a stream of cars rush by. The only person I know who might have another opinion about the Big Pond is Mama Dot, and I plan to ask her at my next lesson.

But that never happens. No longer do we go to Mama Dot's house in Fairhope, bumping across Fish River bridge where the river fans out in a watery harp, to the woods and solitude. No longer do we sleep after recitals on the beach, our hair sun-dried and stiff from brackish water, our toes coated with sand, little piles of shells near our pillows so we can see them first thing when we wake up. We've lost this paradise by the sudden, unsettling diagnosis of Uncle Kenny's tuberculosis. "He's got to go to a sanatorium," Mama Dot announces, running her hands through her thick grey hair, her eyes tense with worry as she looks out at the rose garden where tea roses bloom in flames of scarlet and mauve.

Mama Dot will no longer take pupils, will spend her time helping Uncle Kenny get well while we pursue another teacher. For two years we've been driving once a week to Mobile for dancing lessons at Mrs. McDonald's Dance Studio on Government Street, and now we're introduced to Mrs. Bair, who's landed in Mobile from Connecticut, a fact that makes me wary of her. Just being from Connecticut—so close to New York—I know she's cultured, which means the possibility of malice towards us, for the South is behind in everything, especially the arts. "Why do you need all that fancy fooling around on the piano?" someone in our town will ask, and Mother's face grows hard with impatience. "They're taking lessons so they can appreciate good music," she'll say, but we know it's an uphill fight, for culture in our town summons up water ballets, accordion solos, and the asafetida bags the doctors joke about on the records my father orders.

"I want you girls to have talents," Mother repeats as we drive the endless miles to Mobile, past flooded farmland and the swampy creeks where catfish burrow in the mud and mosquitoes breed in drowsy pockets. "I don't want you to be ashamed the way I was, going to college without the least bit of refinement." Refinement means music and dancing, something to put down on my college applications under the heading OTHER INTERESTS. It's a requirement, I know, for the Big Pond.

When we arrive at Mrs. Bair's driveway three kids in torn, raggedy clothing circle the yard, leaping and squatting, playing a childhood game. As we get out of the car, the oldest girl, who seems about eight, straightens, then turns an absurd scowling face to us as if we're interrupting the most important moment of her life. "Who are *you*?" she asks with a fierce grimace, her lips pinched together at the sides. "And what do you *want*?" She has a slash of dirt across her cheek and stares at us with the fierce pride of an oldest child. She carries a stick, and points it at the baby who waddles around, gurgling happily, then squats on the concrete. His diaper smells. "Pick him up," she says to her sister, who's no more than five or six years old. Inside the red brick house—which is surprisingly ordinary with overgrown shrubs and plain screen doors—we hear the sounds of a piano, the arpeggios of a scale, the muted voices of people talking, then the beginning of a sonata, soft and suddenly beautiful.

"We've come to take music lessons," Mother says as if she's talking to an adult. The baby, seeing us, toddles towards us, then plumps back down on the concrete and grins, waving his arms. Behind us traffic churns. The new leaves on the trees flutter in the breeze.

"With my mother?" the girl asks, unrelenting in her stare. She points her stick at us.

"Yes," we say in chorus. For a moment I think we might curtsey.

"Well, you can't see her yet. She's with another student." And then she turns away, tapping her stick in the air with all the authority of a conductor arousing the French horns to triumphant sound. When she twirls suddenly it's with that same grim, patronizing glare. "Do you have any *cookies*?" Mother looks at us, but we shake our heads, having eaten all of our animal crackers and drunk our cokes on the ride to Mobile. We eat everything very fast, barely making it to Magnolia Springs before we're digging our fingers into the crumbs, licking our palms.

"But you could go get us something," Jean says, seizing the opportunity. "You could go to that pastry shop on Dauphin Street and buy us elephant ears."

"Yeah!" the little girl shouts with glee. "Yeah, yeah, buy us some elephant ears!" And now she's all smiles and happiness, jumping up and down, waving her stick in the air. She comes very close to us, almost purring with tenderness, staring at my mother with sudden adulation in her eyes. "Will you buy one for *each* of us? We need to have one of our own so we don't have to share." Behind her, the baby cries, "Mama! Dadda!" and rocks happily on the ground. The other little girl stands beside him, not smiling, silently rubbing the sides of her feet on the concrete.

Mother nods. "But you'd better take care of your little brother. He needs his diaper changed."

The little girl turns to him dispassionately. "He's hungry, aren't you Zack? You want some el-ey-phant ears!" Hearing her, Zack tightens his fists and sucks noisily on his grimy thumb. "But hurry," the little girl turns back to Mother, pointing her stick at us, "So they can eat theirs before their lesson."

At first I'm stunned by these children. How can a lady from Connecticut have such dirty children? Their dark hair is matted to their foreheads and tangled around their ears; their clothes are limp with heat and sag in the back; they're ribbed with dirt like the Butterfield kids who receive Christmas baskets from the church every year, who have lice and worms. And what's more, they don't act ashamed. They don't seem to know it's too late to go barefoot, impolite to ask for free food. Already I can tell they're greedy and impatient, demanding and insistent.

It's only when Mrs. Bair, our new teacher, steps out of the house, that the girl becomes quiet, gazing at her mother with absolute adoration. "*Ma-ma*," she calls. "*Ma-ma* … look. *Look*!" And she does a cartwheel on the concrete, her skinny legs opening up like rusty scissors, then crumpling as she falls in a heap to the ground. "Wait! I have to do it again." But I don't watch her anymore. I'm staring at our new teacher. After the spartan beauty of Mama Dot, with her old khaki shorts and orthopedic shoes, her prominent cheekbones and seering gray eyes, Mrs. Bair looks absurdly dramatic. Her very long blonde hair, pulled back into a loose ponytail, only heightens the pasty whiteness of her face, her cranberry lipstick, her blue eyeliner, the black sheath and clingy white pants that wrinkle around her ankles. She's wearing flip-flops and dangly earrings. Her face, keen and pockmarked, looks wintry with indoor life. Everything about her seems incongruous, misplaced. I feel the beginning of dread. What can she know of the Magnolia River, of the blind fish that swim in Devil's Hole? What can she know of lying dizzy in the sun, watching a wasp buzz back and forth in its senseless drone beneath the shadow of the eaves? Mama Dot understood these things, would jump up after your lesson, rushing outside to find the woodpecker she heard just as you were finishing the Grieg.

"Come in," Mrs. Bair says, her eyes flickering blueness, intensity, a severity I don't want to know. To avoid her gaze, I study the pockmarks on her face, the tiny indentations that embellish the slash of skin from cheek to ear. She opens the screen door, then turns to her daughter. "Sherry, you bring the kids inside. You can have milk and crackers at the kitchen table."

The little girl startles to attention, her feet planted on the ground. "We can't! We're waiting for the elephant ears."

Only then does Mrs. Bair smile. "Okay, but come inside once the elephant ears arrive." She turns to me and says quietly, "Sherry is a genius. She already plays Beethoven and Schumann, but she's fickle and wants her own way." She doesn't look at Sherry as she says this, but studies my face which I'm careful to keep expressionless as if I hear about geniuses every day.

Sherry is a genius. All the way home from Mobile that thought burrows inside my brain. I see Sherry parading around the yard, indomitable, autocratic, her smartness overriding everything else, leading her effortlessly towards the Big Pond. Already these advantages weigh heavily in my mind. To be a genius is to be allowed privileges, authority, to be born with something that nobody else has. My mother, I assume, is almost a genius, though this has never been verified and only gives her prerogative in the naming of others. Of course, we never refer to genius, only to people who are "very *smart*."

"Oh, she's very smart," Mother will say about Lucy Polk, a high school senior who won the national science award for growing her own penicillin for the science fair. "She'll do something in the world." I always see Lucy in her room, silent and secretive, growing penicillin in a test tube in her underwear drawer, getting up in the middle of the night to check on its progress. We imagine her picture splashed across the newspapers after she's made a life-saving discovery, and then our whole town will be famous. In the early part of my life, my brother's praised for having a photographic memory, though I can't remember him announcing a thing he's learned, and yet when I see him, I think *memory*, as if it's a little halo surrounding his head. Genius is what mother would like for us, but I can't help thinking that all my wishing and hoping to be smart is distracting me from something I need, something that's much closer, right next to my bones. Years later, still full of longing, I stop a man in the midst of passionately undressing me. "Do you like my mind?" I ask with something close to desperation. My voice is taut, beseeching, and he pauses above a button, then smiles. "Yes," he says softly, without touching me. Relieved, I let my dress fall in one fell swoop to the floor.

The next week Sherry's playing the piano when we arrive, sitting atop two pillows on the chair, leaning into the piano, her elbows held out like tiny wings. She looks like an urchin, her hair hanging forward, snarled in knots, but she seems absorbed, in a trance, an expression of guilty pleasure on her face. She's playing something by Schumann, and then suddenly when she messes up, she yanks her hands free and says, "That wasn't my fault," and starts over. It's only when she hears Mother come into the room—"*Oh, I'm sorry. I thought we were late*"—that she stops abruptly and turns around. "What did you bring me?" she asks, her face lighting up, her eyes zeroing in on Mother's purse for the white pastry bag. "Did you go to Dauphin Street and get elephant ears?"

"Sherry," Mrs. Bair interrupts. "That's enough. You're being rude. Now get up. Your lesson's over."

"But I want to do it again," Sherry says and begins playing, scooting up closer to the piano, her hands flying across the keys. Now she's banging out the piece, no longer absorbed, merely hurrying, determined to finish.

When she finishes, she gets up quickly, wiping her hands on her dress. "I wrote all the diatonic triads for major keys on my board," she says to Mother with that flush of enthusiasm of a child praised for progress reports. "Didn't you bring me *anything*?"

Mother looks embarrassed. "I'm sorry, but we had to hurry," and Sherry's face clenches up as if she might cry until her sister waltzes in.

"You're supposed to be copying the alphabet," she says to the girl, hands on her hips. "Now get out of here. This is MY room," then she lurches forward with a windmill of fists.

"Girls!" Mrs. Bair catches Sherry, who then tries to climb up into her mother's lap, her legs circling her thighs, her hands grabbing at her dress.

"Ma-ma!"

But Mrs. Bair won't allow it. "*Ma-ma!*" She pushes Sherry away, peeling off her fingers. "Stop that. Go outside and play or go to your rooms."

Sherry's head droops and she looks at her feet. "I hate you," she whispers but

Mrs. Bair is already absorbed in some new thought, putting away Sherry's music, dropping the pillows onto the couch. And in the secret hardness of my heart, I'm overjoyed that Sherry is bereft.

That spring we go three days a week to Mobile, leaving right after school, my sister and I running to mother's car in the line-up, getting in, throwing our books to the floor, ready for whatever snack Mother's prepared. We settle into the rhythm of the car, driving through the outskirts of Foley, past Kaiser's potato fields and the tin sheds full of gladioli, into the blood red sun of a spring afternoon.

Imagine that you are me. Riding with your mother and sister beside weed-choked ditches, through farmland and fields and into the watery swamps that lead into Mobile Bay. You feel the slight dip and leap of the car when it crosses the first of many bridges, a sense of subtle pleasure that the car is rising like a bird in the air. You are needy of such pleasures for this trip is a familiar one, taken during rain and sleet and sun, with gulls flying over the bay, occasionally an egret or a heron swooping onto a grassy island, landing with a great flap of wings. You tell yourself not to think, not to feel, that this is just another day in a group of endless days of music and dancing and school. Your sister seems happy to be a part of it. Your mother drives with the concentrated zeal of the driven. Only you hold back, uncertain, dreading Sherry, the eight year old genius! You too want to prance and pout, but feel like yourself only before sleep, in that wide, clean space of drowsy trance. It's your one moment of pleasure, slipping free of your body, the sky drifting in the darkness of your eyes. More than anything you wish you could tell someone, "*this is me*" but it would sound too goofy to explain. Better to stop thinking. Better to put yourself on hold, to stare with squinting eyes at the bay, hoping that today IT will appear as it does in your dreams, a watery animal, half fish, half lizard, covered with shimmering scales that glitter like diamonds in the sun. IT came to you one night in a dream, appearing suddenly on your doorstep, droplets of water sparkling with wetness as it landed with a hiss outside your door. And when you opened the door, you knew that IT had come to protect you, had arrived just in time to kill your enemy, the snake, lying sleek and black and coiled on the bottom step.

Closing your eyes, you let the cloud-covered sun warm your body until slowly you become smaller, tighter, your neck elongating, your body shifting shapes. When you open your eyes, you're no longer a girl going to music lessons, but a creature crawling out of water into air, pure and bright and whole.

I'm not ready for my lesson. Sitting in the Bair's kitchen at the table with the salt and pepper and the little jars of jam, I try to finish my assignment. I'm supposed to transpose a melody from the key of C into the key of E and though the book lies in my lap, I'm distracted, edgy, remembering the rush of spring air on my face, the staccato flash of red and pink azaleas, and suddenly all I want is a vanilla ice cream cone with chocolate syrup dripping off the top. I don't want to do my assignment. I don't want to be here. I spy Jean's bag on the table and quickly rifle it, hoping she has the same exercise as me. But I don't find anything but her school books. I see papers on the table and pick up each piece. On one, chords range in all the major keys. Some have been erased and redrawn, but they're large and black and easily visible. SHERRY is written at the bottom of the page. I'm looking hard at this sheet when Sherry strides in and with a sudden swipe, yanks it out of my hand.

"Cheater," she says, wagging the paper at me.

"Am not," I glare. "I was only looking." And yet some tiny part of me feels guilty, implicated. Culture is still foreign to me, this awkward apparatus I'm supposed to carry like a house on my back. Even playing Chopin's Fantasy Impromptu, I think only of sand and sun and dirt. More than anything, I want to walk out into the land, to hide alone in the woods and wake restless to the morning's heat. I see the piers jutting out into the bay and feel the roughness of the pilings beneath my feet, the smell of dampness, the water glassy smooth like a mirror shrouded in fog. I stare at Sherry with sudden defiance. If she quits, she'll be labeled eccentric, impetuous, a genius who didn't live up to her potential; if I quit, I'll just be a quitter, nothing more. I don't know how long I stand there staring at her until out of the corner of my eye I see the faintest glitter, the hint of brilliance. I get up, dropping my lesson to the floor.

"Where are you going?" Sherry yells. "You've got to finish your lesson." Her bright eyes follow me to the door, stabbing me with reproach. "You can't just drop it on the *floor*!"

But I don't look back as I run out the door.

To release yourself from duty is a voluptuous surprise, vetoing the sturdy promise of a shield, protection from hostile forces, furtive encroachments, insults and betrayal. Instead there's nothingness. Nothingness and the possibility of everything. Possibility holds your hand, guides you blindly through the rushing waters. This, after all, is the dream of fairytales, the benevolent mentor, the rescuing prince, the fairy godmother.

"Come back!" Sherry calls. "Come back!"

But I sit quietly on the bumper of Mother's car and kick pebbles into the street, defying the Big Pond with every whack.

[illegible] up a [illegible] in the [illegible] Kleenex [illegible] through the book, [illegible] by [illegible] distracted, [illegible] remembering [illegible] on my face, the [illegible] red and pink [illegible] vanilla ice cream [illegible] with [illegible] off the [illegible] my assignment. I don't [illegible] bag in the table [illegible] has [illegible] but I don't find anything but her schoolbooks. I see paper on the table and [illegible] up each piece. [illegible] range [illegible] Some have been [illegible] that they're large and black and easy visible [illegible] written [illegible] the bottom of the page [illegible] the sheet where [illegible] strokes [illegible] in my hand.

[illegible] the [illegible]

[illegible] And yet [illegible] part of me [illegible] is still [illegible] arguments for sup[illegible] planning [illegible] More than anything I want to [illegible] of the [illegible] to hide [illegible] I see [illegible] putting out [illegible] the [illegible] and the smell of [illegible] smooth [illegible] I stare at Sherry with [illegible] quick [illegible] her [illegible] and [illegible] the [illegible] know [illegible] and there [illegible] out of the [illegible] the [illegible] hint of [illegible] up, dropping [illegible] to the floor.

"[illegible] are you doing?" Sherry yells. "You've [illegible] You can't [illegible] drop it on the floor!"

"But I don't [illegible]"

[illegible] is [illegible] tiny [illegible] around [illegible] strong [illegible] and [illegible] and [illegible] the possibility of [illegible] possibility [illegible] blindly [illegible] water. [illegible] all, is the dream of [illegible] revolve [illegible] [illegible] the [illegible]

"[illegible] me back."

But [illegible] quickly [illegible] Martha's car and [illegible] down the Big Pond [illegible]

from J A P S
Tom Franklin

In November of our senior year, Benny's dad was diagnosed with lung cancer. He died in his own bed. Benny quit school and took a bag-boy job at the Jackson IGA to help make house payments. The same thing happened a million times, to a million guys. Glad it wasn't me, I took off to the University of Alabama and got a Bachelor of Arts degree in English. The few weekends I spent at home I'd call Benny but his mother always said he was working or sleeping. She took messages but he never called back. That made him easier to forget. I would hear things, though. Irma Smith told my mother that Benny was smoking two packs of cigarettes a day. "You think he would've learned," Irma said.

After college I lucked into a nine-buck-an-hour job at a sandblasting plant in Mobile, and all the poetry I could explicate was lost in the roar of the sandblasters. I rented a two bedroom house in Hillsdale, a university housing project, for one-sixty-five a month and paid off my Toyota. I applied for credit cards and fell in love with Carly, who I met at a poetry reading at the public library. She appreciated Walt Whitman and W.H. Auden and Robert Penn Warren. And me. She taught second grade at a private school and we were both twenty-four. She moved in after nine weeks.

Benny who?

My parents lost it. They said Carly and I were living in sin. There wrote me this long letter saying I was damned unless I gave my heart to Jesus. I wrote back and instructed them to check with Carly—she had my heart.

A month later I got laid off. But that was okay. I took some graduate courses at the University of South Alabama with my unemployment checks. My poetry, I decided was wonderful. Plus I spent more time with Carly—including a June week at the Gulf in her uncle's condo—but suddenly she decided that this wasn't the right time in her life for a major relationship. Let's just be friends for awhile, she said. Who know what'll happen a year from now?

Crickets were buzzing outside my bedroom window the night she left. I went after them with a pool cue. Couldn't find my .357 with the ivory grips. I threw my typewriter in the commode and made it fit with an axe.

I was alone for the first time, Carly gone, my parents ignoring me. The Japs attacked that night and every night after. You'd think I was a fried Vietnam vet the way I'd wake up sweating, screaming, feeling my eyes.

School let out for the summer break. I spent days cutting lawns at ten bucks a pop, nights trying to stave off the REM war flicks. I got really tanned, but couldn't stop thinking of Carly. In the Hong Kong Restaurant on Old Shell, where they listed the Chinese animal years on the backs of menus, I noticed that she and I were born in the years of the boar and dog, respectively, and were "compatible for marriage." I called her and some guy answered. I told him I'd just brained his mother with a tire tool, and hung up. The Japs hit hardest that night, and I jumped awake, sweaty, with a cold fist around my stomach. I wet my face in the bathroom sink, went and sat in a folding chair in the front yard and listened to the electronic bug killer frying. At three-twenty-six a.m. I heard a long, thick crackle, and walked back to the carport and found a singed bat flopping around under the bug grill.

MY SOUTH TODAY

Marilyn Schwartz

I grew up in Mobile—in the old South—during the Cold War with the U.S.S.R. Back then, Communism was the great threat. My piano teacher, Miss Mary, warned me to be ever vigilant. This woman was so anti-Communist that she wouldn't buy a cookbook she coveted because it contained a recipe for borscht. I'm afraid I didn't take Miss Mary too seriously when she said if we didn't watch closely, one day the Russians would march right down Government Street.

But oh, Miss Mary, you were so right!

Two years ago, a major Russian exhibit, "Nicholas and Alexandra," was proudly displayed at Mobile Civic Center. People from all over the country came to view this important exhibition. This was definitely the New South. People from St. Petersburg, Russia, were being feted in a wonderful collaboration of two cultures.

Miss Mary is no longer with us, so she didn't see all this come about. I asked one of her friends what Miss Mary would have thought if she had seen people speaking Russian at The Dew Drop Inn restaurant.

"She would be delighted," said her friend. "Nicholas and Alexandra would not bother her; they weren't Communists."

I have friends up North who argue with me about a New South. They don't think anything is new and exciting.

"How can you expect the South to be taken seriously," a friend of mine on the East Coast wanted to know, "when your big claim to fame is beauty pageants? Southern Belles are an anachronism in the new millennium." Mind you, this is from a man who has never been south of New Jersey.

Well, I hardly think so. Southern women are known to be tough and strong. Sure, we still have a lot of beauty queens. But we also have plenty of doctors, lawyers, politicians, and even Marines. It's just that some of the beauty queens also happen to be Marines.

In the New South, just like the Old South, women are taught to work hard and compete. The same training goes into campaigning for the Presidency as it does in vying for the title of Miss America.

In fact, I have always maintained that if Bob Dole had been trained as Miss Georgia, he'd be President today.

SOMETHING ABOUT BRIDGES

Brewster Milton Robertson

"The weather looks promising," the distinguished-looking man remarked, squinting at the sky as he put her small suitcase and hanging bag on the back seat. Sockless in high-mileage loafers, wash-faded jeans and a venerable tweed jacket, he always radiated a certain charisma, ever the widely-celebrated artist.

His luggage must be in the trunk. She mused fretfully.

"Do you think I'm dressed all right?" she asked anxiously. She was wearing a simple khaki shirtwaist dress under her good navy jacket. At her neck was a red, white and blue scarf.

"Relax, kiddo. It's your big day. You look just perfect."

"About last night...I said some things I didn't mean...I can be such a bitch. I'm not that egotistic. I owe you a lot..."

"Don't be silly. I've known for a long time you're too good to keep all to myself." He lightly kissed her nose before he handed her into the car.

"No...I meant it just now. I'd be nothing without you. I owe you...everything, really."

"You're too young to worry so much. You'll do just fine. Don't sweat it." He patted her arm as he pulled the car away from the curb into the early morning traffic.

"Not so young...thirty-two next month."

"Oh, c'mon...career-wise you're a baby." He shot her a look. "Hammer Gallery handles you now...I was almost forty when an important gallery took me on."

"I'd still be a nobody if you hadn't made them take a look."

"Don't underrate yourself...you've got your whole life ahead of you."

"Uhm-m-m... "

Surely his luggage is in the trunk.

She busied herself with the radio, as he negotiated the traffic. On the outskirts, the traffic thinned. Distractedly, she sorted through his cassettes...

Kristofferson, Gordon Lightfoot, Willy Nelson.

"Oh! I didn't know that you liked Linda Ronstadt?"

"She's OK...have you seen her lately?. She's gotten rather heavy..."

I must be more careful about my weight...he keeps himself so fit.

Slipping a tape in the slot, she kept browsing through the case.

The Beatles?...

Springsteen?...oh, right! He bought that one for me...

Aha! Whitney Houston.

"Why haven't you switched to CDs?"

"Then what would I do with my tapes? I've invested a lot in that collection."

Sometimes he pouts just like a little boy, she was reminded, observing the protruding line of his lower lip.

"Hmm-m-m…I never thought of that." She winced.

Go easy, he's very sensitive about his age.

"It is a nice collection." She went back to browsing tapes and found a Judy Collins. Switching cassettes, she listened to *Both Sides Now and Someday Soon.*

The Kingston Trio. Sinatra. Chet Atkins…

And, Segovia…Segovia?

At the last refrain of *Someday Soon*, she slipped *Sinatra* in the deck. When she looked up, she was surprised to find they were already out of the little city. The narrow road was winding through the rolling, heavily-wooded delta. Beside the road, splashes of warm sunlight and blue sky reflected off the unspoiled surface of a torpid, darkly-emerald river.

"I love the delta. It's so beautiful."

"Look there, just ahead. You don't see those old dinosaurs around much anymore...they're disappearing fast." He pointed as they approached an old iron bridge across the river. "When I was a kid, bridges like that were everywhere. That was long before the Interstates."

"Looks like it could use a coat of paint." Squeezing his thigh, she was suddenly taken by a little erotic frisson—it was wonderful, just to be with him.

"Those old bridges are always in need of paint. The struggle between iron bridge and rust is inexorable. Look close there on the girder. See the orange paint underneath the silver where it's chipped? When they were new, they primed 'em all with that orange paint…'red lead,' my daddy use to call it. Mostly nowadays they paint 'em silver…"

"*Inexorable*, huh?" She mimicked his careful speech. "I just hope it doesn't collapse and dump us in the river." She giggled.

He glanced across and smiled.

"Don't worry…these bridges go on forever. When I was a boy old relics like this were…*ubiquitous*."

"Ubiquitous? C'mon, why don't you just say, 'everywhere?'…nobody ever uses ubiquitous in conversation…"

"Ubiquitous was what they were…the proud engineering standard on roads and highways…*everywhere*." He grinned.

They were crossing the bridge now and he rolled down the window to sniff the country air. There was a heady suggestion of honeysuckle…with a musky redolence of mud and saltmarsh.

"Well, I must admit this one looks sturdy enough up close," she conceded.

"Oh, this old boy'll probably be here for awhile yet. I still see 'em around... still going strong. One of the first watercolors I sold was of an old iron bridge like this." He looked wistfully in the rearview mirror. "Later, when I was making money, I bought that painting back. Cost me a fortune. But I had it printed...I issued it in a signed edition. Made my money back and then some."

"I've seen it. It's powerful painting...a masterpiece, really!"

"Water looks deep back there...make a good swimming hole."

"I hadn't thought of that."

"Funny...every time I see one of those bridges, it reminds me that my mama made me wear corduroy knickers when I was a little kid."

"Knickers?"

"You know, like Payne Stewart...that golfer that was killed in that weird air crash. Knee britches, kinda like Gainsborough's Blue Boy. Way back then, they were the vogue in the snooty women's magazines. We lived in the country, but those prissy magazines ruled my mama's life..."

"But, corduroy? My, God...just thinking about it makes me itch..."

"Oh, that wasn't the worst part. In rural Virginia where I grew up, practically every male my age wore overalls."

"Overalls? You mean like jeans?"

"Well...yeah, but in the country we called 'em overall pants."

"How strange? How old were...when your mother made you wear the knickers?"

"Wore 'em 'til I was almost eight. Those damn sissy knee britches got me into a lot of fights as a kid. Everybody at that country school was older and bigger'n me."

"I'll bet you were a plucky little lad." She teased. "Did you like to fight?"

"Not me...I've always been more the lover..."

"Hmmm...I can certainly believe that..." She squeezed his arm again and sneaked a sidelong glance. *The spitting image of that British actor.* She gave an involuntary shiver.

"Your mother should have been more understanding...let you wear your precious jeans...your overall pants...besides, what does all this have to do with iron bridges?..."

"Oh?...well, you see that was just it...the worst part..."

"What?"

"I didn't own any jeans. Not a pair. My mama frowned on overalls. Our swimming hole was on a river near an old iron bridge a lot like that one back there. In the country, if you don't have any overalls to cut off in the summer, what does a poor boy wear to go swimming?"

"Beats me? I read *Huckleberry Finn*. I thought country boys just went skinny-dipping..."

"Well...yeah, that's right. We did sometimes..."

"Hm-m-m? What about the girls?" She looked up at him now, suddenly interested.

"Skinny-dipping?...well...some of 'em...sometimes...but not in the daytime ...and never at the regular swimming holes."

"Oh?...tell me more."

"What makes you think there's more?" He laughed.

"All right, have your secrets. But, if your mother was so big on those fashion magazines and wouldn't let you run around in jeans, I would've thought she'd buy you all the latest rage in bathing trunks?"

"Ordinarily, maybe...but you have to understand. We were poor...well, maybe not actually poor. But money was tight. Besides, in the end it was those fashion books that did me in. My mama thought the Singer sewing machine company had an answer for everydamnthing. Would you believe that she bought a pattern and tried to sew me some swimming trunks?"

"What's so wrong with that?"

"It was awful. She made 'em out of the floweredy material from a cotton hog-feed sack."

"Floweredy?"

"Uhm..." He nodded absently.

"A flower-printed hog feed-sack?"

"Yeah...swear to god. Most country folks back then raised hogs, and the hog feed companies put the stuff in these cotton bags printed with flower prints. The neighborhood was full of dresses and blouses made of that material ... now that I think about it, it probably wasn't all that bad for the ladies. Some of that stuff was kinda early *Laura Ashley*. Those country women got a lot of mileage out of those hog-feed sacks. Made 'em into underwear too."

"Lingerie? Well, I'm not at all surprised you'd know that." She giggled again.

"Oh, in those days everybody hung their clothes out on clotheslines to dry. Victoria had no secrets back then." He looked over and winked.

"Well?...*Laura Ashley*'s not bad...sounds kinda sexy to me."

"Uh? Maybe? It was okay for the ladies, I guess. But for boy's swimwear?... trust me...in those days, cut off overalls was where it was!"

"Poor thing...I bet those trunks weren't all that bad."

"They were awful. I was mortified. They were way too long...longer than Michael Jordan's basketball shorts. And, with heavy-puckered elastic in the waist? I swear, those britches looked for all the world like old Mrs. Smith's homemade bloomers that flapped on the clothesline behind her house every Monday morning. I'll never forget the first day my mama made me wear those sissy britches. They were all covered with orange and navy-blue daisies. I was seven. I wanted to die."

The image brought a laugh.

"I'll bet you were cute…"

"Listen, this was serious. I was big for my age and a damn good swimmer. I was struggling to live down those sissy knickers. And, I was already sneaking off to where the big kids swam in the deep water around a group of giant boulders jutting out into the river. Nobody ever touched the bottom in that hole. My mama would've killed me if she'd known. She thought I was going to the regular swimming hole up the river by the iron bridge. All the local mamas took the little kids up there beside that old iron bridge."

"You ought to be ashamed; seven years old and already sneaking around behind your mother's back."

He nodded thoughtfully and smiled a little boy grin. "Yeah, anyway, all this is ancient history. I'm really quite a bore. It was just that seeing that old bridge took me back." Idly, he patted her knee. "Mobile won't be long now. The University's not far. Department Chairman. Has a nice ring, don't you think?"

"It's not official yet." She tried to smile. "Will you go in with me?"

"No. They're looking for Chairman material. We wouldn't want them to think you're a baby."

Guess I had that coming.

Rolling down the window, the breeze felt good in her hair. The honeysuckle was a fairy breath.

"Well…don't just leave me hanging. What happened? With the swimming trunks, I mean?"

"Oh. Uhmm…when I showed up that first day in all my flowery glory, there was a bunch of girls sunning themselves on that big old high boulder. It was flat on top. And, of course, there were always a lot of the older boys just standing around taking in the girls. I confess, I had eyes for a girl named Maryanne. Her mother was a teacher. She went to school in town. She already had curves. I can still see her clear as day…"

"Forget the curves." She slapped his knee. "What about the swimming trunks?"

"Oh…yeah. There was this smartass kid, Bobby Gearhart. He was at least a year older than me, but in my grade. He took one look and started in right away. 'Is them your Grandma's bloomers you got on?' he sneered. He was always trying to show off in front of the girls."

"Oh, crude! I hope you ignored him."

"Ignore him? I wanted to kill him," he paused, remembering. "Bobby was one of the few boys in my grade who wasn't bigger or stronger than me. But he had three older brothers who rode the same school bus. Ordinarily, on the basis of simple numbers, I was totally intimidated by all those older Gearharts…Bobby knew it, too."

"That's not fair..."

"Nothing's ever fair. In those days I was younger than everybody in my grade at that country school. I was a sensitive sort...a real sissy. I still have a real problem with the appropriate expression of my aggressions."

"Oh...you're not...you don't! Nothing like that, sometimes you're much too outspoken."

He wrinkled his nose and made a face.

"OK...you're putting me on—just finish the story."

"Anyway, that day, all in all, I made perhaps the most eloquent statement of my true feelings that I've ever made."

"Oh? What?... "

"I hit the little son of a bitch smack-dab in the nose."

"Oh, my! You...you didn't?" She giggled. "Did his brothers beat you up?"

"They weren't there. Besides, at that moment it wouldn't have mattered... sometimes the intrinsic value of some things transcends the risk of minor adversity. I knew his brothers would jump me at the bus stop later on, but I was too mad. I didn't give a damn." He threw back his head and laughed out loud. It made a satisfying sound.

"Didn't he try to fight you back?"

"Neah. I really clobbered him. He didn't know what to do...just went off bawling and smearing blood across his face with the back of his hand. He disappeared up this steep path to a little dirt lane that led up to where the main road crossed the old iron bridge. Look. See how steep this bank is? See all the trees?" He nodded toward the edge of the road where it dropped sharply down to the river. "The path up to that dirt road was really like an irregular staircase worn through the thick undergrowth, with tree roots serving as steps. Remember going down the escalator at the MARTA station at Peachtree Center in Atlanta? Or, the METRO in D.C.? That old path was like that. It tunneled up through the leafy tangle of trees and vines. But, when Bobby left, my troubles were just starting. He'd hardly had time to reach the top when Turkey Wright came strutting out of the woods at the bottom. Turkey was a real bully...he was always chewing tobacco. The girls were there and like any good bully, Turkey was always looking for a chance to show off."

"Chewing tobacco? My word, you were seven...how old was he?"

"Oh, nine, maybe. They started early where I grew up. Anyway, he took one look at those sissy britches I was wearing and walked right over and spit tobacco close by my bare foot."

"Ooo-o, gross...he was just looking for trouble..."

"Yeah...but I could tell he was a little tentative. He didn't push up real close like he usually did. I figured that seeing all that blood on Bobby's face must have given him food for thought. Still, you gotta understand that both physically and culturally, I was totally out of my league in that crowd when I was seven. In a lot of ways it presented an unbridgeable gap. Of course I had no inkling on that day, standing there in those godawful floweredy britches, that some gaps just aren't worth the bridging anyway. But…I guess to tell the truth…I was just plain scared to death."

He fell silent, obviously thinking it over.

He cleared his throat.

She touched his hand.

When he spoke again, his voice had hoarsened a little. "Anyway … Turkey didn't move any closer, but he looked sideways at the girls and puffed out his chest. Then he circled slowly around me looking at those floweredy feedsack pants. Finally he sneered: 'Where's your brassiere?'"

He let out a little chuckle, remembering.

"What a bully…what did you do?"

"I wanted to pick up a rock and bash in his head…but he was at least two years older and four inches taller than me. That was a sizeable difference." He cleared his throat again. "Anyway, it's probably just as well there weren't any rocks around."

She nodded.

"I knew better, anyway. I wasn't into lost causes. I had already figured out the thing about discretion and valor—the hard way! It had a lot to do with survival. Even at that age, I could out-swim most of 'em…and I was the only one at the whole Fort Lewis School who could make a decent dive. Only a few boys would even dare to hold their noses and jump feet first from off that high boulder. I had seen an exhibition at the picture show. Knees straight, feet together, toes pointed: *kersplish*! I simply stood up tall and looked to make sure the girls were watching and made a clean dive, floweredy drawers and all, into the water. I was the only one around who had ever had enough nerve to dive off that rock. At that moment it was the best response I could make…my *pièce de rèsistance.*"

"Good for you. I guess that ended the teasing about the swimming pants?" She clapped her hands together.

"Not really…but after that, I didn't care so much. Time has a way of changing things. Believe it or not, my fame for diving off that rock did get me new respect. Of course, that day, in my moment of humiliation, I had no inkling that over the next four years diving off that rock would fade into insignificant kidstuff. By the time I was eleven, I would dive from the top rail of that old iron bridge. Three rails and ten feet higher than Doug McDaniel had ever dared. Doug was a local legend. He was in his twenties. He was married and worked for the Virginian Railroad."

"You mean this man and you were diving off a bridge like that one back there?"

"Yeah, but where Doug always dove from the lowest girder several feet below the roadbed—wasn't more'n about fifteen feet above the river when the water level was normal. On Saturdays there was always a crowd that came out from town. Doug was something of a local sensation."

"And you came along and dove off the top railing? How high?"

"Twenty-something feet more or less…maybe more…"

"My God! How old? Eleven? Weren't you terrified?"

"Sure. Scared to death. I'd been laying in bed at night for months fantasizing before I finally got up my nerve. Finally, one day, on impulse, I just climbed right up and sailed headfirst off the high rail, right over the top of his head. I even surprised myself. Doug couldn't believe it either. Pride forced him to climb right up there after I'd done it. He had been the star attraction for years. Doug was a local tough… always getting into fights. He had his gang around him all the time. When his gang saw me dive and they saw Doug climb up they came running over to the riverbank. There were whistles and cheers. The crowd egged him on. They were yelling, 'Attaboy, Doug. Don't let the kid show you up.' You know…stuff like that."

"Eleven years old? I imagine that got everyone's attention."

"Yeah. It still kinda takes my breath away when I remember how I felt the first time I looked down from that height. When he climbed up there, he raised his fist in sort of a shaky gesture of bravado. Almost lost his balance on that skinny little rail. I can still see him, as I looked back up at him from the river. He turned white as a sheet and had to grab the guy wire. For the moment old Doug had more of the spotlight than he wanted."

The image made her snigger.

"Anyway, he just stood there trying to get up his nerve. I climbed right out of the water and walked straight back up, onto the bridge. There was only this one spot just above a little channel between two rock ledges in the riverbed. It was the only place that a man, or even an eleven-year-old boy, could safely dive from that height. We're not talking about a game of misses…you had to hit that narrow channel right on the button. It was only about four feet wide…even less at the very bottom."

"Weren't you terrified?"

He gave her an appreciative look.

"Yeah, I guess I was. I remember he asked me, 'Did you hit bottom, kid?' I said, 'Neah. Just turn your hands up so that they flatten as soon as you hit water. Makes you stay shallow. It's okay. Go ahead, there's nothing to it.' I tried to act like I wanted him to. But I didn't really. I really wanted the glory all to myself."

"You're a born troublemaker…you know that?" She gave his leg a squeeze, tracing a naughty little pattern on the inside of his thigh with her finger.

He gave her hand a squeeze.

"Doug said, 'I'm a lot heavier than you,' I can still hear the strain in his voice. I knew he was scared, so I warned him again about being real careful to go shallow. I couldn't resist doing a little 'psych' job on him."

She shook her head, trying to imagine him at eleven. Had he ever been afraid? "You were a real devil, even back then."

"Not really, but I grew up a lot that day. First time I remember having that feeling of power that only comes when you discover that you're better than you know yourself to be. Remember how you felt the first time you saw your work hanging in the window of that fancy gallery in Fairhope? Do you understand what I'm saying?"

She nodded. Up high, a hawk flew in lazy circles. Below, a formation of pelicans flew low above the river swirling beside the narrow road. In the distance, an almost-imagined rumble of thunder came from somewhere near Mobile Bay.

Just ahead, a sign read: MOBILE 11 mi.

Nervously, she turned up the tape as Kristofferson crooned, "*Loving her was easier than anything I'll ever do again...*"

She felt herself tensing up again.

Get a grip. He'll see what a wimp you really are.

She caught her breath and turned the music down.

"So, what happened?"

"Well, I didn't wait on him. I was still shaking, but I climbed right up there and dove again before he had a chance to go. The first time I had been totally occupied with conquering my fear and making dead sure I didn't ram the bottom. I hadn't paid much attention to how it looked. This time I gave great attention to execution. Knees straight, feet together, toes pointed: *kersplish*! I stayed with it all the way so I could pull it in clean, and I rammed the rocky bottom a little harder than I wanted. I scraped my hands but I didn't care. I knew damn well I'd nailed it that time."

He paused remembering, then cleared his throat before he spoke again.

"When I surfaced, I turned and tread water and looked back up and gave him this nasty-nice smile that said, 'See? Nothing to it.' He hollered down at me, 'You went in awful. Did you get bottom, kid?' His voice cracked a little. I held up my hands so he could see the trickle of blood seeping out of the little abrasions. I said, 'Yeah, a little, but I always like to make it look good for the girls.' I was still trying to psyche him out."

"You really were a born hellion..."

"No...just a kid. But when I climbed up the bank and made my way through the crowd, there were a lot of 'ooohs' and 'aaahs.' I loved it. I was licking the blood off my hands to keep from staining my floweredy pants. To tell the truth, I guess I might have strutted just a little for the ladies."

There was a twinkle in his eye...a suggestion of an impish eleven-year-old boy at the corners of his mouth and eyes.

He looks that way when we're making love.

The image brought a sweet aching to her chest.

"I'll always remember standing there enjoying my moment in the sun. Old Doug was still up there on the rail alone, trying to muster his courage. But at that point it required more than courage...I'd added style to the game. Doug had no finesse. He knew it. He stood up there a long time before he finally shook his head and climbed back down. I can still see him walking slowly back across the bridge. His rowdy drinking buddies were gathered around their pickup trucks and cars parked in the field across the road from the swimming hole. One of them said, 'C'mon Doug, what's the matter?' Doug just grumbled, 'The water level's down...it's too shallow for me the way it is now. I'm a lot heavier than the kid. I'll do it right after the next rain.' It was a lame excuse. I kinda felt sorry for him. Still, Doug McDaniel had a mean reputation. Nobody dared confront him." He paused and cleared his throat.

"That was some day. I remember Turkey Wright showed up late. He came over to me and said, 'I heard about the show. You gonna dive again?' It was odd, but at that moment I realized that over the four years since the day on the high rock, I'd passed him two grades in school and grown taller by a head. When I looked around for Doug, he was sitting all alone. I knew I'd won, but my moment had passed. I didn't have the heart to rub it in. I just told Turkey, 'Not today,' and walked on home without diving again that afternoon."

Again, he fell silent.

Kristofferson sang, "*...for the good times.*"

When he spoke again, his voice seemed distant, almost as if he were talking to himself. "Later on that same week, after we had had a heavy rain, I caught sight of Doug alone at the bridge one afternoon. The river level was high. His truck was parked on the other side. I watched him climb up to the top rail. He sat up there for a long time. He was still in his denim work clothes. Finally he climbed back down, got into his truck and drove off. He never knew I saw him..."

"Did McDaniel ever get the nerve to dive from that top rail?" she asked after a moment.

"No. Doug quit coming around the swimming hole after that. I don't think he dove off the bridge again that summer ... not even from his old spot from the beam below the road bed level."

"I guess you'd outgrown the homemade swimsuit by then."

He glanced her way and grinned and shook his head.

"No. That's the funny part. The rest of my glorious eleventh summer, just before I would launch myself through the summer air into the river below, I would sometimes see Turkey Wright in the crowd on the riverbank. Turkey and the Gearharts in their cutoffs no longer made my life miserable. By then I didn't want to wear cut off overalls anymore. My mama's floweredy bloomers had become my colors."

"*Bravo*..." she cheered and clapped her hands again.

"And, would you believe it, I began to see a lot of floweredy feedsack swimming britches about."

"Oh, no! That's just too wild. I guess that really fed your poor starved ego." She threw back her head and laughed.

"Yeah. But by then it wasn't so important anymore. By then, I was more interested in Maryanne. She was almost fourteen and liked me a lot. She thought I was twelve. I was getting right big for my age, and I never told her any different."

"Oh? And what about the corduroy knickers?"

"Oh, they were already history. My daddy finally came to my rescue. He put his foot down. Gave me two pairs of overall pants for Christmas when I was in the second grade. My eleventh summer was my last at the old iron bridge. I learned to shoot a basketball and took my act to town."

"All for Maryanne, huh?"

He smiled and shrugged. "Maybe. Anyway, by then I didn't want to bash in Turkey Wright's head anymore. And I'd skipped a grade and was already starting high school. I was pretty good at basketball and I still liked to dive. In high school and college, I tried to get serious about diving. I had a coach who thought I might do all right. I worked pretty hard until I hit my head on the board doing a reverse dive. After that it was never the same again. I didn't quit, but I never quite got over that—I lost some of my nerve. I was okay, I guess, but I never won anything...not really...still?...I had some moments. In October of fifty-three in Seoul City Stadium with Dr. Sammy Lee, the two-time winner of the Olympic Gold for platform diving...we put on a little exhibition for the Koreans. But the truth was that Sammy was really the whole show. The war had finally ended and Sammy was my friend. That day, I was just glad to be alive. Pretty much I've always been just a damned show-off I guess..." He shook his head sheepishly.

"Don't ever stop..." she whispered and took his hand and pressed it to her cheek. Then she turned it over and kissed his palm.

Through the trees, she could see the gates to the University up ahead. Against a cloudless deep blue sky, the soaring spire of the famous campus chapel loomed closer.

She was quiet for a moment. Then she spoke, "You know, nowadays I see flowered britches much too long, with puckered elastic, just like your mother made you in all the surf shops in the fanciest of resorts. They call 'em Baggies or Jams... or some such thing...sell them for a small fortune at the classy men's stores that advertise in GQ."

"Yeah. I know…and I still hate 'em. In my estimation, they'll always be just plain tacky."

"There's just no accounting for taste. But you have to hand it to your mother, she was light years ahead of her time."

He turned into the wide drive.

"Well, it's your big day…so much for country boys, corduroy knickers…and old iron bridges…" he said.

"I'll never look at bridges the same." She gave him a loving look. "Whatever happened to Turkey Wright and Doug McDaniel?"

"I've often wondered…"

"How about the fair Maryanne?" She pulled down the sun-visor mirror.

Lipstick looks OK, I guess.

"In high school, for a while, I thought I might marry her." He chuckled.

"What happened?"

"She took an interest in sewing machines … "

Her laugh was cut short as they approached the rust-tinged-limestone facade of the austere old administration building. The sculptured gothic window arches frowned a forbidding scowl.

"This Department Chairman thing, it's really the big time, isn't it?" It really wasn't a question. She was very nervous now.

"Top of the heap…" He pulled up and parked. "Don't worry, kid, you'll knock 'em dead."

"Well, I just might at that." She gathered herself and sat up straight and stretched like a cat while he came around the car.

When he opened her door, he leaned across and got her briefcase.

"Right on time. I'll walk you to the door," he said and locked the car door behind them. "You're on your way…sky's the limit now." He made a gesture at the impressive campus.

She reached out and took his hand. "Don't you understand? I don't ever want to go any place without you…I just happen to love you…quite a lot," she half-whispered and tugged his sleeve.

He stopped and looked at her, puzzled.

He crinkled his nose. "I love you too, kiddo…quite a lot. So?…" He shrugged, questioning.

"So? So didn't you pack anything? I thought…" She held her breath, searching his face.

"Oh! My duffel's in the trunk." He bent to kiss her nose.

To hide her blush, she pretended to busy herself with the strap on her handbag.

Hugging his arm tightly, she raised her chin high as they started up the wide brick walk.

"Now...will you please tell me again?" She beamed. "That part about that feeling of power that only comes when you discover that you're better than you know yourself to be."

TRANSITIONAL OBJECTS

Janet Nodar

Miss Ida opened the glass door that sealed the air conditioning into her house and stepped onto the screened front porch. The gray-painted floorboards felt slick beneath her nyloned feet. Two silhouettes were waiting patiently for her on the steps. Beyond them, the tree-shrouded street was still in the clotted warmth of a summer evening in Mobile.

"Hello!" called a young female voice. "Mrs. Hannahan?" Miss Ida peered through the screening. She suspected a sales pitch. The girl wore a white shirt and a khaki skirt. Her brown blunt-cut hair was pulled back with a silver barrette. She carried a woven handbag. Next to her was a stocky young man in belted gray shorts and a striped shirt. A burgundy 4-wheel drive, presumably theirs, was parked in Miss Ida's lumpy driveway. Miss Ida didn't know these two, but she knew their look; they matched the other couples remodeling her midtown neighborhood, organizing street parties, filling the yards with bright plastic toys.

"We don't want to bother you," the girl said. "Is this a good time? We're not selling anything, I promise." She smiled. Her lips were a bright, slick pink, her brown eyes round and inquiring.

"What can I do for you?" Miss Ida asked.

"My name is Ashley Potter, and this is my fiancé, Trey Graham. We're from Pascagoula. I'm researching my family tree. My mother's family was from Mobile. My great-grandmother may have lived in your house when she was little." The girl illustrated her sentences with wide gestures, pointing at herself and the young man next to her, waving a hand vaguely westward, towards Pascagoula, opening her arms like a celebrant when she said 'your house.' "If this is the right place, we'd like to take a photograph."

"We bought it from the Dowlings thirty-nine years ago, when our children were small." Miss Ida undid the screen door's hook and the couple came up on the porch. They were not as young as she'd first thought.

"Tyler David Graham the Third," Trey said, in a surprisingly insubstantial voice.

They shook hands.

"Ida Maureen Hannahan," Miss Ida said. "The house was built in 1896. When would your great-grandmother have lived here? Who was she? Who are your parents, Ashley?"

"My grandmother was born in 1902. Her name was Mary Catherine Davidson. She married an Ingraham. My mother is a Mary Catherine, too, called Katie. My dad is George Potter; he's originally from Kentucky."

"Davidson—that's right," Miss Ida said. "Doctor Davidson built this house. Three doctors' families have lived here; we're the third." She knew the outlines of the house's history. In fact, she knew the outline of the block's history. She was not unusual; so did everyone else on Decatur Street. "And I think I knew an Ingraham family, years ago. I myself grew up on Spring Hill Avenue. I was born next to the Bragg-Mitchell mansion; our house is gone now, though."

Ashley opened her purse and took a photograph out of a white envelope. In it, a woman wearing gloves and a long pale skirt stood in front of a bungalow, her face turned stoically against the sunlight. The black and white picture had a flat pen-and-ink look. The house was quite familiar, although no burglar bars defended the downstairs windows, and there were no screens across the front porch.

"It's my house!" Miss Ida said.

"That's what we thought!" Ashley said, nodding rapidly, so close that suddenly Miss Ida could smell her slightly sour breath. Miss Ida stepped back, gently.

"My mother told us she thought it was on North Decatur," Ashley said. "We drove up and down and finally realized your house was the one in the picture. Such a long time ago. Look how small the oak trees were." Now, their branches shaded the house and their roots disrupted the sidewalks.

"Can this be your great-grandmother?" Ida asked, pointing at the sunlit woman.

"My mother says it isn't. It could be a cousin." Ashley put the photograph back in her purse.

"Would you all like to come inside out of the heat?" Miss Ida was already perspiring though her dress, and her head hurt a little. Trey's forehead was beaded with sweat.

"Yes, ma'am," Ashley said.

They sat on the velvet Victorian sofa in Miss Ida's front parlor. Miss Ida scanned the room and found it orderly enough. ShaNeece had dusted on Wednesday. The evening light touched the rugs from Persia, the bell-curved mahogany clock Ida had inherited from her grandfather, the enamel box filled with Confederate uniform buttons.

The house was usually neat, now. Bill was no longer around to dump his pockets out just anywhere. Children made forts with the furniture or left water rings on the mahogany only on the occasional Saturday. Miss Ida had begun to take solitude and sole possession for granted. The well-appointed, formal rooms were like a part of her person, intimate as her knees. They comforted her. They defined her. Miss Ida was a Mobilian, held in place by memory and history, by this space and these objects, things that had been polished by grandparents, worn by aunts, cherished by uncles, things intended for her children.

"What a lovely home," Ashley murmured.

"I'll just get us all a cold drink," Miss Ida said to them. She went to the kitchen and poured glasses of sweet iced tea. She sliced a lemon and arranged the slices on a china plate. Without a break in her rhythm, as if this was also part of her preparations, she poured a shot from the bottle of sherry in the cupboard, drank it, bit into one of the lemon slices, and rinsed her mouth out with water. She spread a fine linen square on a silver serving tray and arranged the glasses, the plate of lemons, three tea spoons, tiny lace napkins.

"Miss Ida? Can I help you?" Ashley had followed her. "Let me carry that for you." Ida nodded, although it annoyed her a just a hair, the girl walking through the house like that. Ashley looked around the kitchen.

"This is wonderful!" she said.

"What is?" Ida asked.

"All these old appliances! Everything's right out of the fifties. And this old sideboard." Ashley clasped her hands together, as if to keep herself from clapping.

"Old appliances are fashionable now?" Ida said. Ashley cut her eyes at Ida and picked up the tray. She walked unsteadily through the house. Miss Ida winced as the glasses clinked. The girl was not as polished as Ida had first thought. She had a febrile air. She lacked grace. Miss Ida felt a bit sorry for her. She pitied people who did things incorrectly. All they needed was instruction, really. After all, no one was born knowing how to waltz or eat a lobster. She wouldn't say anything to Ashley, of course. Miss Ida generally reserved her efforts for her family, particularly her daughters and her daughter-in-law.

Trey, head canted, was examining the books shelved beside the fireplace. Ashley thunked the tray down on the coffee table. The spoons jittered. She chose a glass, wrapped a napkin around it, and crossed the room, away from Miss Ida.

"Those are my husband's books," Ida said. "He was the reader in our family."

"And where is your husband today?" Trey asked. Again, Miss Ida was surprised at his bodiless voice. Ashley frowned at him; she'd already realized Miss Ida was a widow. Trey didn't seem too bright, really.

"My husband passed away two years ago," Ida said.

"I'm sorry," Trey said, embarrassed.

"That's all right. Please don't worry about it."

Ashley put her nose practically on the simpering porcelain shepherds and shepherdesses on the mantel.

"Those are gifts from my children," Ida said.

"Beautiful," Ashley said. She tripped on a brass vent cover set into the floor and caught herself on a small polished table with her free hand. "Oops; didn't spill," she said, reddening. She looked closely at the vent cover, which was worked in a vaguely plant-like art-nouveau design, and said, "I've seen these brass plates on display stands in antique stores."

"Surely not," Miss Ida said.

"I mean it," Ashley said. "We're looking for an old house in Pascagoula. You can't find this sort of thing in a new house. They just don't do this kind of work anymore."

"Oh, no," Miss Ida said, a bit smugly, as if the work's virtue somehow reflected her own. "Not with people like they are nowadays."

Ashley and Trey nodded as if they agreed with her. They looked at each other. Trey raised his eyebrows. Ashley put down her tea glass and then wiped it off with her lacy napkin. She opened her purse and got out thin white latex gloves, a pair of scissors, and a roll of duct tape. Trey grasped Miss Ida's forearms and lifted her to her feet.

"We're not going to hurt you," Ashley said, putting on the gloves. "Put your hands behind your back, please." Miss Ida obeyed, passive as a daffodil. She did not quite understand what was happening.

"I'll open the gun cabinet," Trey said in his feathery voice, gripping Miss Ida firmly while Ashley worked. He did not look at Miss Ida; he might have been holding a door.

"You get her jewelry."

"What a good idea," Ashley said. Trey looked at her sullenly. "Move the car to the back of the house first. We can't go back and forth out the front."

Trey half-carried Miss Ida to her bedroom and propped her against her pillows like a stuffed animal. The TV remote, her reading glasses, the cut-glass decanter, her crocheting, were still placed neatly on the little table by the bed, just the way she'd left them that morning. She heard a car start outside. She heard the back door bang. She heard Ashley and Trey rooting through her home. About eleven o'clock, a neighbor noticed Miss Ida's open drapes and lit-up house and came to check on her. She was still on the bed, crying with frustration, hungry. Her hands and feet ached.

Trey and Ashley had smashed the gun cabinet and taken Bill's guns. They'd stolen his coin collection in its old-fashioned blue folders. They'd taken the antique clock and the Persian rugs and the lustreware. They'd taken Miss Ida's jewelry and the sterling flatware that had been her mother's. They'd taken her grandmother's porcelain. They'd taken her silver salvers, her platters, her chafing dishes, her Empire tea service, her VCR, the television, the answering machine. They'd taken Bill's stereo, and the gold-rimmed liqueur glasses he'd bought for Ida in Venice. Ashley had taken the tray Miss Ida had used to serve the tea.

A paramedic patiently sponged the duct tape goo off Miss Ida's wrists and ankles. He wanted to take her to the hospital, but Miss Ida declined. "No thank you," she said. "I really don't feel that it's necessary." She could not stop trembling. The paramedic poured her a shot from the bedside decanter. She drank it gratefully. She was ashamed of herself. Ida Maureen had always assumed that she would act heroically in adverse circumstances, but she had not. Bill's death, her parent's deaths, the miscarriage she'd suffered between Victoria and Renata—although she had faced these events bravely, they simply had not prepared her for Ashley and Trey.

Ida showed the police where Ashley had stumbled and caught herself on the table. They found two useful fingerprints. Sergeant Haston, who seemed to be in charge, interviewed her in the parlor. He was a solidly built black man with a bristly black and silver mustache. He wore a gray pin-striped suit. After she changed and brushed her hair and put on lipstick, Miss Ida served him a glass of tea, even though it was by this time very late and tea wasn't really appropriate. Making coffee just seemed too difficult. Miss Ida used the metal spoons she normally reserved for picnics, since Ashley had taken the good ones. She knew people who would have thrown the glass and spoon away, after a black person drank out of it, but she was not like that. She didn't think she'd ever had a black person who didn't work for her in her parlor before, but she was not prejudiced.

"I feel so stupid," she said to the Sergeant. "They fooled me completely.

The way they looked. Even the names they used were right."

"It's not your fault, Mrs. Hannahan," Haston said. He sipped his tea once, to be polite, and set it down and didn't touch it again. "That's the advantage con artists like these two have; they rely on the decency of regular folks."

"That girl is a natural-born liar," Ida said. "All that hooey she gave me about her mother's family." There was no record of Ashley or Trey or their families in Pascagoula, of course.

"Well, her prints are on the national computer now," he said. "She can't BS her way out of that, no matter where she goes. We'll get them both eventually.

"These two probably have regular clients for the things they steal, in a big city like Atlanta or New Orleans. And they probably don't live in Mobile, since they let you see them. I'm afraid there's probably not much chance you'll get your things back," Haston said, "but we can always hope." It wasn't as tragic as all that, anyway, he seemed to think. Miss Ida was fully insured. Her injuries were minor. Sergeant Haston didn't say these things, of course, but she could tell that was what he thought.

"Mama, you need to move!" her children said when they arrived. They'd told so before; now, she just had to see that they were right. "Sell the house. It's too big for you. We told you it wasn't safe, you living here all by yourself." She'd make a fortune now that midtown prices had gone so high. She could buy a neat little condo, or she could travel, or she could come and live with one of them.

Miss Ida didn't want to move, though. The robbery had made a fool of her. It had made a fool, somehow, of her life. She wouldn't leave, not like this. However, she did spend the rest of the weekend at Renata and Jim's. They went to church with her on Sunday morning. Miss Ida was the center of attention, mentioned in the sermon as well as the prayers.

In the car on the way home, she apologized to her daughter. "They took your legacy," she said. "All those things really belonged to you and Victoria and Bill Junior. I'm so sorry."

"Oh, Mama," Renata said. "You're okay. That's what matters." She looked straight at her mother and tears welled in her eyes. They embraced. Renata meant what she said, but Miss Ida knew that later her daughter would think about the missing silver, the lost coins, and she would cry again. In particular, the children regretted the loss of their father's treasures. Ida felt that she had let them down. Miss Gina Brubeck had lived in a musty Victorian mansion across Decatur from Miss Ida's house her entire life. When she died, her descendants picked through her leavings, and then Hoppy Brubeck, her great-grandson and the executor of her will, held an estate sale. The sale had been on the Saturday before Miss Ida was robbed. Antique dealers had begun circling the block at 6 a.m. It was quite possible, Miss Ida thought, that Ashley and Trey had found the sunlit, World-War-I-era photograph of her front yard among Miss Gina's doilies and paperbacks and battered furniture. If, that is, they'd been in Mobile.

Miss Ida called Hoppy at Second Magnolia Bank, where he was a loan officer. "Waall, I remember a gal who was fascinated with a box of old pictures," Hoppy said. "She uses them to make shadowboxes. I sold her the whole caboodle for three dollars."

"Was there a photo of my house in there?"

"It's possible. I pointed out a couple of the places in the pictures. She said she likes Midtown. She asked about the houses, which had old families in them and so on."

"Did you call mine "Dr. Hannahan's house?"

He snorted. "That's what it is, ain't it?"

"What did she look like?"

"Shoot, she was downright memorable. Short blond hair, blue eyes, nice figure. She was wearing one of them short little t-shirts; showed her tummy. She had a ring through her belly-button. I asked her if she was engaged." Hoppy snorted again, apparently still pleased with his joke.

Ashley's brown hair hadn't looked like a wig, but then Ida hadn't examined it closely, either. Contacts could make blue eyes appear brown; makeup could turn a rough-looking girl into a potential Junior Leaguer, at least temporarily. It seemed possible that Hoppy's photo-buyer was Ida's robber. Hoppy didn't remember seeing anyone who resembled Trey, although that didn't prove anything, since Trey didn't have the sort of figure Hoppy tended to notice.

Miss Ida's alarm went off at 6 a.m. the next Saturday. She dressed in a knit pantsuit with red and blue flowers appliquéd at the neckline. While she drank her coffee, she highlighted the likeliest garage and estate sales listed in the *Press-Register*.

"Antiques" could be anything, Miss Ida discovered; chipped blue enamel wash bowls, Elvis clocks, Barbies, metal-rimmed linoleum kitchen tables, costume jewelry from almost any era. They certainly didn't have to be Louis XIV chairs, or the ornate tea services and gilded porcelain she'd grown up with.

Miss Ida consulted the various Kovel's antique guides. She also read several police officer's autobiographies and books on detecting. She usually sat in her unremarkable car and observed the people going back and forth from the sales for a half hour or so before she shopped. She learned to bring snacks and a thermos of coffee. Gradually, she lost interest in the decanter by her bed, the bottle stashed in the kitchen cupboard.

At a moving sale on Tuthill Lane, five weeks after the robbery, Ida saw the girl Hoppy had told her about, getting out of a shiny white TransAm. She was alone. Her hair was short, impossibly white-blond, and slicked to her skull as if greased. She wore black jeans and a tight black t-shirt that left her midriff bare. A silver ring did indeed adorn her belly button. It was Ashley; Miss Ida knew by the surge of triumph that coursed through her body. She folded her newspaper and got out of her car.

Ashley leafed through some chintz draperies and blew the dust off a book. Miss Ida examined some overpriced glassware. Ashley jiggled the drawers in a rattan dresser. Miss Ida turned absently and smacked right into her.

"Oh, dear, excuse me," Miss Ida said fussily, smiling. Ashley's eyes were toothpaste blue and round with surprise; she stared at Miss Ida.

"Are you all right, dear?" Miss Ida asked.

Ashley released some air. "Fine," she said, her voice straining at calm.

"I can't quite read this label," Miss Ida said. "Old eyes, you know. Do you mind?" She handed Ashley a glass with a tiny sticker on the bottom.

Ashley upended the glass. "Toscany." She gave it back.

"Thank you so much," Miss Ida said, holding the glass loosely.

"It's not an antique. You can buy those at Service Merchandise for less," Ashley said.

"Oh, dear," Ida said. Ashley shrugged and walked away. Miss Ida paid $2.00 for the glass, and $3.00 for a child-sized Lone Ranger place setting.

"I didn't see that Lone Ranger," said a man holding a box of picture frames and books behind her. He sounded suspicious, as if Miss Ida had tricked him somehow. Deep wrinkles corrugated his forehead. He went to lots of sales; Miss Ida saw him frequently, but he'd never spoken to her before, in spite of her friendly smiles.

"It was right over there," she said.

He studied her. "I'll give you five for it."

"No, thank you," Miss Ida said.

"Ten."

"Done." Miss Ida gave him the set. He gave her some damp bills. The plump woman presiding over the garage sale regarded them with a betrayed look on her face.

"Do you know that girl?" Miss Ida asked him, nodding in Ashley's direction.

"I see her around. Her name's Cynthia something," he said. "I'd keep an eye on her if I was you."

"Why?" asked Miss Ida.

"She's got her little tricks," he said darkly.

"Like what?"

He shook his head, finished sharing. "I'm not saying anything else."

The next Saturday, Miss Ida saw Ashley, or Cynthia, at an estate sale and then again at the big flea market in West Mobile. They nodded but didn't speak. Ashley watched Miss Ida potter through the items for sale; Miss Ida ignored her.

A few weeks later, Miss Ida accepted a free glass of lemonade at the Azalea Trail Antique Mall's Fall Extravaganza. She stood under a green awning, next to Ashley, and sipped. Shade felt cool; the humidity was low. Miss Ida wore a shorts outfit in pastel plaid, and earrings that precisely matched the dominant pink. Ashley wore a flowered sun dress that terminated just south of her rear end. She'd decorated her eyelids with black eyeliner, and black roots showed in her hair.

"Well, hello dear," Miss Ida said. "How are you?"

"Fine." Ashley turned away, as if reluctant to be trapped in conversation with an old woman. She had the nerve to be rude. Miss Ida was pleased. The girl thought she was safe. Misleading Ashley had turned out to be only the slightest variation on the manners Miss Ida had been putting on and taking off like a transparent shield her entire life. She introduced herself.

"I'm Cynthia Roper," Ashley said, smiling slightly.

"You must enjoy the treasure hunt. I see you so often." Cynthia Roper, Cynthia Roper, Miss Ida repeated internally; she didn't want to forget before she had a chance to make a note.

"Uh-huh."

"Unusual for a young person. Are you from Mobile?"

"I grew up in Theodore, but that's long behind me," Cynthia said, glancing sidelong at Ida and then studying the shoppers as if she was looking for someone. Miss Ida did not allow any surprise to show on her face. Theodore was a redneck enclave on the southern fringe of Mobile, a country crossroads almost dissolved into the suburban sprawl. Cynthia did not look like a girl from Theodore. She promptly explained why: "I've been living in Atlanta; I was into the art scene. It's a whole different world. But I had to come home because of some family things."

"Ah," Miss Ida said, nodding. Family things. Perhaps the Atlanta police were after her. "What kind of work do you do?"

"Oh, this and that," Cynthia said.

"Do you have a boyfriend?"

"Unh-unh."

"Things aren't like they were when I was young. All we thought about was getting married."

Cynthia smiled at her patronizingly. She stretched, arching her back, her breasts suddenly sharply outlined under her dress, hinting at a sexual life Miss Ida couldn't even imagine. "I'm fancy-free," she said. "I don't like to be tied down."

"You young people," Miss Ida said mildly.

"I'll bet you're an Old Mobilian, aren't you?" Cynthia said. "Mardi Gras, making your debut, all that."

"Well, I suppose," Miss Ida said, surprised. "My family's been here a long time." Miss Ida hadn't been a debutante; that was only for the well-to-do daughters of the oldest Spring Hill families. However, she had been Queen of her father's mystic society ball when she was nineteen.

"So has mine, but nobody thinks we're anything special. Not that I care. I don't think that stuff is so wonderful." Word by word, Cynthia's young voice grew harsher, as if it was being grated through her larynx. "Those women. They're all just alike. They look me up and down, and then all of a sudden I'm invisible. 'Who's your father? Where'd you go to school? What was your sorority?' They think they're the center of the universe. They don't have a clue. They don't know anything about fashion, about what's hip, what matters." Her hands dramatized her words; with "what matters," she jabbed her fingers into the air as if she was arguing with her own bruised pride.

Miss Ida breathed in and out, wearing a look of gentle inquiry like a mask.

"I don't care a bit about it," Cynthia said.

"That's obvious," Miss Ida said lightly.

Cynthia looked at her sharply. She tossed her lemonade in the trash and walked away. She didn't speak to Miss Ida again that day, but the next Saturday, when they met at a garage sale on Monterey Street, she went out of her way to be friendly. By then, Miss Ida had found Cynthia's address in the phone book and seen her house, a tiny mildewed cottage on a narrow street near Washington Square. The black shutters framing the windows were missing some slats. Red geraniums bloomed on the undulant porch.

Clearly, this was the point at which Miss Ida should have entered official channels. She should have contacted Sergeant Haston, or told her children, or something. It wasn't that she had a plan. She didn't even know what she wanted, except that she wanted something personal. She wanted Cynthia to know that she hadn't fooled her, to know that Miss Ida had outfoxed her, that Miss Ida could do something about her.

It was Sunday. Miss Ida skipped church. She knocked on Cynthia's front door. Cynthia was wearing a Dallas Cowboys night shirt and a pair of greasy glasses; her eyes were a muddier blue without her contacts. She gaped at Miss Ida, surprised.

"I just wanted to get your opinion about something," Miss Ida said.

"How did you know where I live?" Cynthia asked.

"It's in the phone book."

Cynthia shrugged and opened the door for her. The living room was draped with clothing; the house smelled like mildew and gas. She didn't apologize for the mess. The dining room held a surprisingly good cherry table and chairs. Beyond it was a boxy kitchen. The bit of counter top that Miss Ida could see was crowded with boxes of food, dirty plates, dirty glasses. Miss Ida fussed in her purse and pulled out a little porcelain bird.

"It's not valuable," Cynthia said, looking at it for only a second before she gave it back.

Miss Ida caught her foot on something invisible and stumbled. She cried out, as if in pain, and plopped down on the stained white couch.

"What's the matter? Here, sit down," Cynthia said gracelessly. "Want some coffee? Sugar and cream?"

Miss Ida nodded. Cynthia went in the kitchen and ran water. A family portrait sat on the end table. It revealed a different Cynthia, one with a simpler air and long brown hair that curled demurely around her face. Beside her sat a younger sister with a wide, unselfconscious grin. Two blank-faced boys and a matriarch with a bulldog chin stood behind them.

"Where's the restroom, dear?"

"Down the hall, last door."

Ida hobbled toward the bathroom. She looked through an open door and saw a big bed, a knot of candy-colored sheets, a clutter of shoes and nylons and sweaters. A baby doll, not a collector's item, sat propped on the dresser. Her hair was gummed to her scalp. Her face was gray with dirt. Her feet twisted freakishly under the shreds of a faded pink gown. She had been part of some child's life. Miss Ida walked briskly back to the living room with the doll in her hand.

"What are you doing?" Cynthia asked, gaping. She'd set mugs on the coffee table. "You went in my room!"

"Is this yours?"

"It was my sister's." There was an exposed note in Cynthia's voice; the doll meant something to her.

Ida tugged on the doll's head. It twisted off easily. She dropped the head on the floor. The doll's body was full of matted yellow fluff.

"Stop that!" Cynthia said, standing up.

Ida pulled at the doll's arm; it tore free. Cynthia snatched the doll out of her hands. She picked up the doll's head. "You crazy old bitch!"

"You are trash," Miss Ida said. "Pure unadulterated trash. I wouldn't wipe my feet on you. I wouldn't let you clean my toilet. You make me sick."

Cynthia stared at her.

"How stupid you are," Ida said. "Remember when you tripped on the brass vent cover in my parlor and caught yourself on the desk? You left a lovely set of prints. Ashley."

Cynthia came up out of her chair. Miss Ida ran toward the front door, but Cynthia yanked her back. Miss Ida tore free and ran blindly into the tiny kitchen. She fumbled with the back door's deadbolt. Cynthia shoved her from behind, smashing her into the door, and then hooked her fingers into Miss Ida's hair and pulled her back through the kitchen. Miss Ida grabbed an iron skillet off the stove, twisted sideways, and smacked it solidly into Cynthia's ear. Cynthia stumbled; her grip slackened. Ida hit her again. Cynthia fell down. Miss Ida called 911.

Ida enjoyed testifying. Her attorney son-in-law helped her prepare. The bruises were gone, and her scalp had stopped hurting. She was in the tabloids:

"Granny Gets The Goods!" Trey, discovered living quietly near Miami, plead guilty. He testified against Cynthia, too. Her bulldog mother came to court every day, and once or twice the brothers, but Ida never saw the younger sister. After her conviction, Cynthia was extradited to Georgia. There, she and Trey both testified against the dealers who'd bought their stolen antiques.

One day, soon after the trial was over, a scrubbed yuppie couple stopped to watch Miss Ida's realtor pound a For Sale sign into her front yard. They cooed over the hardwood floors and rolled their eyes when they saw the kitchen, and bought the house for eight times what Miss Ida and Bill had paid for it. When Miss Ida locked the door the last time she felt unexpectedly buoyant, like a leaf on water. Although she was in fact wearing a sensible pantsuit, it was almost as if she'd dissolved away a hard outer shell, to be left with only her true pink and naked self.

Miss Ida continued to buy and sell things, even though the hunt for Ashley was over. She enjoyed exercising her newfound skill. Sometimes pieces reminded her of her lost candlesticks, her mother's silver, but they were never the missing pieces. She handled them appraisingly; they were just objects; they could not tell her anything about herself. Sometimes she felt regret inside her, like a slow leak. Even if she could have gotten her real things back, she couldn't replace her life. Sometimes, she almost wished she had not spoken so harshly to Cynthia.

SOMEWHERE INSIDE
(After George Ella Lyon)
Jessica Jones

I am from a place
with fig trees and kudzu,
rich with curling vines of wisteria
and whiffs of budding gardenias.

I'm from notes of Dolly Parton and Kenny Rodgers
and from people who believe
that no dream is impossible.

I'm from large family reunions
and sweet potato casserole

...from makeshift stages
and clouds of hairspray
sequins and glitter and bobby pins.

I'm from Gipetto's workshop
and Care Bear stares
and from ears that hang low and wobble.

I'm from plaid skirts and white shirts
and Uncle Remus Tales
...from dress-code violations
And from strong, proud women.

From awake forever in a sweet unrest
from wherefore art thou, Romeos,
from I should know where God and man is,
and from drinking with thine eyes.

From peach cobbler to French pedicures
and Pinocchio to Romeo,
where I'm from is really a dream.
It's Mobile, Alabama;
it's MeeMaw's backyard.
It lives inside of me.

CONTRIBUTOR'S NOTES

Hank Aaron (Hammerin' Hank) was born in Mobile on February 5, 1934. He played for the Atlanta Braves and the Milwaukee Brewers and clubbed 755 roundtrippers over a 23-year career.

Rachael Alex is an undergraduate studying creative writing and anthropology at the University of South Alabama. Her work is previously published in the 2011 and 2012 volumes of *Oracle Fine Arts Review*. She is the editor-in-chief of *Oracle 2013* and editorial intern at Negative Capability Press. Her awards include the 2010-2011 Steve and Angelia Stokes Scholarship for Undergraduate Fiction, the 2011-2012 Stokes Scholarship for Undergraduate Nonfiction, and the Katharine Lawrence Richardson Memorial Scholarship.

Robert Bahr has sold more than 600 articles to magazines such as *Boy's Life, Playboy, Popular Mechanics, Prevention, Smithsonian, Sports Illustrated, Writer's Digest,* and *T.V. Guide.* He has also written 14 books, most of them for major New York publishers. His collection of short stories, Indecent Exposures was released by Factor Press in 1993.

Whitney Balliett (1926-2007) was the jazz critic for *The New Yorker* and author of fifteen books. *His Collected Works: A Journal of Jazz, 1954-1999,* was published in November 2000.

William Bartram (1739-1823) is best known for his *Travels*, a book that includes his journey to Mobile. He is one of the first spiritual naturalists and the first to use the term "sublime" to describe nature.

Eka Budianta is an Indonesian poet who visited Mobile in the spring of 1987. During this time he lectured and read his poetry at Spring Hill College.

Patricia Crosby Burchfield grew up in Baldwin County, Alabama. In 1967, she received a B.A. degree in English and Mathematics, in the Charter Class of the University of South Alabama. She holds an M.A. degree in Special Education for Gifted students, also from the University of South Alabama, and an M. Ed. in Mathematics Education from Auburn University. Her first published work, a short story, "The Lost Valentine," written when she was eight years old, appeared in the *Mobile Press-Register* on the Children's Page, edited by Disa Stone.

Rosemary Butler, a career social worker, has broken racial barriers in several state and local institutions. She has been appointed to national, state, and local positions by Governors George Wallace and Fob James, and by President Lyndon Johnson.

Truman Capote (1924-1984) was born in New Orleans, but grew up in Monroeville, Alabama. He is the acclaimed author of *Breakfast at Tiffany's* and *In Cold Blood.*

Carl Carmer was a popular author of memoir, nonfiction, and novels during the 1940s and 1950s. His most recognized book is the autobiographical *Stars Fell on Alabama.*

Carol Case is a poet and graduate of the University of South Alabama where she was the recipient of the 2002 Steven and Angelia Stokes Scholarship in poetry.

Mickey Cleverdon is the author of *Questions of Form*, which featured woodcuts by her husband, John. It was published by Slo Loris Press in December 1999. In June, 2002, they were part of a group show "2x2" at the downtown Mobile Museum of Art, with a series of paintings and poems based on "Women of Character" which included the Elizabeth Gould poem and portrait. During November 2002, she and the artist Jo Patton presented a show of poems and paintings, "Wharfs and Words," at the Eastern Shore Art Center in Fairhope, Alabama.

Ethel S. Creighton is the author of *The Soul of The City.*

Evelyn Dahl wrote the gripping novel, *Belle of Destiny*, that centers around Octavia LeVert and was published in 1958. Dahl also became president of the Alabama Writers' Conclave and started the Mobile branch of the Pen Women.

Frank Daugherty is a native of Mobile, a graduate of Duke, Tulane, and Yale universities. He also studied German literature in Munich and Berlin. He is the author of *Isle of Joy* and Director of the ESL program at the University of South Alabama.

Elizabeth Doehring, a second generation Alabama author and award-winning writer, is a voting member of the National Book Critics Circle and Alabama Writers Forum. Business writer for the history collection book, *Mobile Bay: Yesterday, Today & Tomorrow,* Doehring's works have also appeared in national magazines such as *Bookpage, Paste, and Spirituality & Health.* Her works have also been published in American newspapers such as the *Denver Post, Miami Herald, St. Petersburg Times, Atlanta Journal Constitution,* and for the past ten years with *The Mobile Press-Register.* In Europe Doehring writes for the *Sligo Champion.*

John Dos Passos (1896-1970) was born in Chicago, IL. He studied at Harvard and was an ambulance driver in the later years of WWI, out of which came his antiwar novel, *Three Soldiers* (1921). His best known work is the trilogy on U.S. life, *USA* (1930-1936).

Cammie East was born in Mobile to Mary Francis and Cameron McRae Plummer, proprietors of the late and lamented Haunted Book Shop. She graduated from Julius T. Wright School for girls, attended Wellesley College, and earned a degree in history from the University of South Alabama. She joined the staff of the *Mobile Register* in 1974.

Walter Edgar, a native Mobilian, is Neuffer Professor of Southern Studies at the University of South Carolina. He is the author or editor of ten books about South Carolina and the American South, including the bestsellers, *South Carolina: A History and Partisans And Redcoats*.

Ben Erickson grew up in Mobile where he graduated from the University of South Alabama. Mr. Erickson is an award-winning furniture maker who has written numerous articles and reviews for woodworking magazines. His first novel, *A Parting Gift*, was published by Warner Books in May 2000.

Mary McNeil Fenollosa (1865-1954) was born in Mobile to William Stoddard and Laura Sibley McNeill. She was married to Ernest Fenollosa, curator of Oriental art at the Boston Museum of Fine Arts, December 28, 1895. Her well-known books are *The Dragon Painter*. Boston: Little, Brown, 1906; *The Stirrup Latch*. Boston: Little, Brown, 1915; and *Truth Dexter*. Boston: Little, Brown, 1906.

Patricia Foster is the author of *All The Lost Girls* and editor of *Minding The Body* and *Sister To Sister*, as well as co-editor of *The Healing Circle*. A graduate of the Iowa Writer's Workshop, she is currently a professor in the M.F.A. Program in Nonfiction at the University of Iowa.

Vernon Fowlkes, Jr. was born and grew up in Mobile. He attended Louisiana State University where he graduated in Creative Writing in 1977. He has done graduate work in Creative Writing at the University of South Alabama. His poetry has appeared in *The Southern Review, Negative Capability, Willow Springs,* and *Elk River Review*. He lives in Mobile.

Tom Franklin was born and raised in south Alabama, where he worked as a heavy-equipment operator in a grit factory, a construction inspector in a chemical plant and a clerk in a hospital morgue. He received an M.A. from the University of South Alabama and an M.F.A. from the University of Arkansas. He is the author of *Poachers*. His new novel, *Hell At The Breech* was published by HarperCollins.

Frye Gaillard is the Writer-in-Residence at the University of South Alabama. He received his bachelor's degree in history from Vanderbilt. His works include *Cradle of Freedom: Alabama and the Movement that Changed America, Watermelon Wine: The Spirit of Country Music,* and the *Books that Mattered: A Reader's Memoir*.

Maurice Gandy teaches full-time at Bishop State and part-time at the University of South Alabama. He is the author of *An Uncharted Inch.*

Diane Garden is the author of *The Hannah and Papa Poems* (Negative Capability Press) and *Measures to Movements: Poems Inspired by Artworks* (2012). She has published poems in *The Jewish Spectator, Presence Africaine, MidAmerica* and other magazines.

Gail Gehlken teaches in the Mobile County School System. She has won six Alabama State Poetry Society Awards and a 2002 Hackney Literary Award.

Jeffrey Goodman is a former Stanford poetry fellow. He teaches English and Creative Writing at the Alabama School of Math and Science in Mobile and has published two books of poems, *After the War* and *A Strung Bow,* as well as a number of critical and scholarly papers on both the poetry of Renaissance and on modern poetry. He has lived in Mobile since 1991.

Rob Gray is the author of two books of poems, *DREW: Poems from Blue Water* and *I Wish That I Were Langston Hughes,* both from Negative Capability Press. He has taught at several universities and is currently at the University of South Alabama. He lives in Mobile, AL with his wife, Kim, and two children, Liam and Emma.

Virginia Greer is a past reporter for the *Mobile Press Register* where she earned awards for her work in medical and mental health reporting. Her writing has appeared in numerous magazine and newspapers. She is the author of three books: *Give Them Their Dignity, The Glory Woods and Emergency.* Ms Greer is included in Who's Who in Alabama, Who's Who in the South and Southwest, and Foremost Women in Communication.

Winston Groom is the author of *Better Times Than These, As Summers Die, Only,* the acclaimed *Forrest Gump,* and *Storm in Flanders.*

John Hafner is Professor Emeritus of English and American Literature at Spring Hill College. A native of Mobile, his academic degrees are from Spring Hill College (B.S.), Marquette University (M.A.), and the University of Wisconsin-Madison (Ph.D.). He has published a short story, several poems, travel articles, and scholarly articles in assorted magazines and journals. He serves on the boards of the Alabama Humanities Foundation, the Alabama Writers' Forum, and the Art Off Centre project of the Centre for the Living Arts.

Carolyn Haines, a native of Lucedale, Mississippi, is the author of short stories, fiction, and nonfiction. She graduated from the University of Southern Mississippi with a journalism degree and worked for daily newspapers for nearly a decade before turning to fiction. She earned an M.A. in English from the University of South

Alabama and was granted a writing fellowship in 1998 from the Alabama State Council on the Arts. She writes a Mississippi Delta mystery series for Delacorte. She is also the author of *Summer of the Redeemers, Touched,* and *My Mother's Witness.* In 2010, she was named recipient of the Harper Lee Award.

Genie L. Hamner, University of South Alabama English Professor Emerita, grew up on a farm in Wilcox County. Three of her grandparents grew up in Mobile, or Toulminville, which was established on the land that her maternal ancestor General Theophilus Lindsey Toulmin purchased in 1825. Having left the state for a Ph.D. at UNC-Chapel Hill, she has lived in Spring Hill/Mobile a mere thirty-five years.

Corey Harvard has served as editor-in-chief of *Oracle Fine Arts Review* and associate editor of *Sonnetto Poesia.* His latest work can be found in *Sense Magazine, Oak Bend Review,* and *Pirene's Fountain.* On his free time, he writes and performs music around Mobile.

Paul Hemphill was born in Birmingham, Alabama. He graduated from Woodlawn High School and received a B.A. degree from Auburn University. The author of eleven novels, he is a prolific journalist, sportswriter and novelist, much of which is about the blue-collar South and its working-class denizens.

Jay Higginbotham is founder of the Mobile Municipal Archives. Author of eighteen books, he has received five literary awards, including the Gilbert Chinard Prize and the Alabama Library Association Award. *Fast Train Russia*, was first published in the USSR in 1981, and the American edition (Dodd, Mead, 1983) was enthusiastically received in such publications as *The New Yorker, Christian Science Monitor, Kirkus Reviews,* and the *Library Journal.* He has written for the *Encyclopedia Britannica* and is listed in the *Dictionary of International Biography.*

Roy Hoffman was born and raised in Mobile and graduated from Tulane University. After working in New York City for twenty years as a journalist, speechwriter, and editor, he returned to Mobile in 1996 to write full-time for the *Mobile Register* while continuing to develop his fiction. He is the author of *Almost Family*, (Dial Press, 1983; University of Alabama Press, 2000) that received the Lillian Smith Award for fiction, and *Chicken Dreaming Corn*, (Hill Street Press, 2003), set on early 20th C. Dauphin Street. His essay "On the Dock of the Bay," from *Preservation* magazine, is reprinted in the anthology, *A Certain Somewhere: Writers on the Places They Remember* (Random House, 2002). He is on the regular, visiting faculty of the Brief-Residency M.F.A. in Writing Program at Spalding University in Louisville, Kentucky.

Ariel Williams Holloway (nee Lucy Ariel Williams) was born March 3, 1905, the third child and only daughter of Dr. and Mrs. H. Roger Williams, a practicing physician and druggist in Mobile. She received a B.A. degree with a major in music from Fisk University in 1926 and a B.A. in Music from the Oberlin Conservatory of Music in 1928. She married Joaquin M. Holloway in September, 1936 and was appointed Supervisor of Music in the public schools of Mobile in1945.

D. Holt worked with R. Wells to write the song titled "Mobile."

Annie Shillito Howard (1884-1997) graduated from Judson College in 1902. She taught school and worked for the Commerce Department for 32 years.

Norman Jetmundsen, Jr. is a native of Mobile. He attended Davidson and Murphy High Schools. He graduated from the University of the South in Sewanee, TN with a B.A., where he majored in English. He then obtained at J.D. from the University of Alabama School of Law, and a M.Litt. from Oxford University.

Peter Jenkins is the author of *A Walk Across America, Looking For Alaska,* as well as *Close Friends* and *Along The Edge of America.*

Earle C. Jones is the lyricist of the song titled "On Mobile Bay."

Jessica Jones graduated with her B.A. and M.A. from the University of South Alabama. She has taught ESL at USA and reading enrichment programs for the Institute of Reading Development. She currently works as special publications director at *Gulf Coast Newspapers*, and won this year's Alabama State Poetry Society spring awards: first place in the national Spring Contest and second place in the state Persona Contest.

Steve Joynt was born in Richmond, Virginia. He received his Bachelor's degree from the University of Virginia and a Master's degree in journalism from Columbia University, New York. He lives in Mobile with his wife Nancy Kent Godwin and works as an assistant city editor at the *Mobile Register.*

Yvonne Kalen moved to Mobile in 1972 and has since been engaged in community activities, among them the Arts Patrons League where she served as President, the Symphony Committee, Friends of the Library, Theatre Guild, Friends of the Ballet, and Mobile Arts Council. She also served as a board member for two museums, and for the Odyssey Program of the University of South Alabama.

Jack Kerouac (1922-1969) was born in Lowell, MA. He is the author of *The Town and the City* (1950) and the subsequent *On The Road* (1957). Other works include *The Subterraneans* (1958) and *Big Sur* (1962).

Celia Lewis has lived in the Church Street East Historic District in Mobile for over thirty years, where she and her husband, Mack Lewis, have been involved with historic preservation both as a passion and a livelihood. She has conducted poetry workshops for middle-school children, founded a student literary magazine, and is publisher and co-editor, with the late Bob Woolf, of *Rette's Last Stand: The Poetry of Everette Maddox* (Tensaw Press, 2004). She holds a master's degree from Spring Hill College.

William March (1893-1954) was born in Mobile, attended Valparaiso University in Indiana, and studied law at the University of Alabama. He served in the Marine Corps during World War I and was awarded the Distinguished Service Cross, the Navy Cross, and The Croix de Guerre with Palm. After the war, he took a job with the Waterman Steamship Corporation, and worked there for eighteen years before turning to writing as a career. March is the author of *Company K; Come in at the Door; The Little Wife and other Stories; The Tallons; Some Like Them Short; The Looking Glass; Trial Balance; October Island;* and *The Bad Seed.*

Jean McIver served as the Director of African-American Studies at the University of South Alabama, a professor of English, and a co-editor of the anthology *Black Alabama.*

Charles McNair, a native of Dothan, Alabama, lived in the Mobile Bay area for several years in the 1980s. He worked as a jeweler, taught English as a Second Language to Saudi Arabian students at the University of South Alabama, and served as features editor of the *Azalea City News*. His novel, *Land O'Goshen*, was nominated for the Pulitzer Prize in 1994.

Henry Valentine Miller (1891-1980) was born in New York City. With money from his father, intended to finance his college education, he traveled throughout the USA and Alaska. In 1930, he moved to France for nine years and published *The Tropic of Cancer* (1934) and *The Tropic of Capricorn* (1938). Other books include *Black Spring* (1936) and *The Air-Conditioned Nightmare* (1945). *The Rosy Crucifixion* trilogy was published in 1965.

Mary Murphy worked in the Pharmacy Department at the University of South Alabama and served as an adjunct instructor in the English Department. She received her M.A. degree from the University of Southern Mississippi. Her articles on healthcare have frequently been published in *Sense* magazine.

Albert Murray was born on May 12, 1916 in Nokomis, Alabama and grew up in Mobile. After graduating from Mobile County Training School, he earned his B.S. degree at Tuskegee Institute and an M.A. at New York University. His publications include

The Omni-Americans: New Perspectives on Black Experience and American Culture, Stomping the Blues, South To A Very Old Place, The Hero and the Blues, From the Briarpatch: On Context, Procedure, and American Identity, The Blue Devils of Nada: A Contemporary American Approach in Aesthetic Statement; novels: Train Whistle Guitar, The Spyglass Tree, The Seven League Boots; poetry: *Conjugations and Reiterations; and Trading Twelves: The Collected Letters of Ralph Ellison and Albert Murray.*

J. Franklin Murray, S.J. taught English at Spring Hill College for many years. He served as departmental chairman and, later, as academic vice president. In addition to acting as official host for visiting celebrities, he guided several generations of students through the pleasures of literature.

Harry Myers was born in Mobile. He was a professional engineer, the head of a prestigious engineering organization, and the recipient of numerous professional awards and civic honors. In addition to a successful engineering career, his accomplishments include, sculpture, writing poetry, and photography.

Janet Nodar has lived in Mobile since 1985. She's published non-fiction and fiction, and attended graduate school at the University of South Alabama, teaching English composition, finishing a novel, and raising a family.

Raymond Oliver is a former Mobilian who published poetry in *Negative Capability*.

Linda Busby Parker is a writer living and working in Mobile. Her first novel, *Seven Laurels*, won the James Jones First Novel Award and the Langum Prize for Historical Fiction. Linda has served as a Fellow in Fiction at Bread Loaf Writers' Conference and as a Tennessee Williams Scholar in Fiction at the Sewanee University Writers' Conference. She teaches fiction writing at the University of South Alabama and in a Continuing Education program at Middle Tennessee State University. Linda has published short pieces in *Writer's Digest, Big Muddy, and Confluence.*

P.T. Paul is a graduate of the creative writing program at the University of South Alabama. Her award winning thesis, a mixture of poetry and prose, was published by Negative Capability Press as *To Live and Write in Dixie*.

Edgar Allan Poe (1809-1849) is an American poet, author, critic, and editor of the Romantic Movement. His works include "The Tell-Tale Heart," "The Raven," "Ligeia," and "The Fall of the House of Usher."

Ila B. Prine was a writer dedicated to writing about and interviewing slaves of the South.

Julian Lee Rayford (1908-1980) a native Mobilian, buried in Church Street Cemetery, hitch-hiked across the continent four times "trading his chants for bread." He is the author of *Cottonmouth*, other stories, and nonfiction and worked as a reporter for the *Mobile Press-Register.*

Michelle Richmond grew up in Alabama and earned an M.F.A. from the University of Miami. She teaches writing in San Francisco.

Tut Altman Riddick was born in Mississippi but grew up in York, Alabama. She studied at Huntingdon College, Livingston University, and received a B.A. degree from the University of Alabama. Following college, she moved to Mobile where she became involved with civil rights and worked to establish a coffee house, a day care center, a playground, and a quilting club to foster community relations. In addition to mosaics, painting, sculpture, and photography, she has published numerous books of poetry.

Walter Rideout, (1918-2006) retired professor of English from the University of Wisconsin-Madison, worked on a biography of Sherwood Anderson.

Mary Riser received an M.A. degree in Creative Writing from the University of South Alabama where she taught literature and writing as an adjunct professor. She is Chair of the Fairhope Film Society and author of *Forming Habits*, a collection of short stories.

Brewster Milton Robertson, a member of the Southern Book Critics Circle, was twice nominated for the Pushcart Prize and Best American Essays. His work has appeared in *The Chattahoochee Review, Publisher's Weekly, USA Weekend, the LA Times, BookPage, Apostrophe,* and other magazines. He is on the faculty of Florida International University Writer's Conference at Seaside, Florida.

Charles Rodning graduated from Gustavus Adolphus College (B.S. magna cum laude, Biology, Chemistry), the University of Rochester School of Medicine and Dentistry (M.D.), and the University of Minnesota Health Sciences Center (Ph.D., Anatomy). He has published medical / surgical literature on clinical scientific, economic, ethical, historical, and humanistic topics. He has published *Tradition of Excellence: A Pictorial History of Surgical Education at the Mobile General Hospital and College of Medicine / Medical Center, University of South Alabama, Mobile, Alabama.*

Father Abram Ryan (1838-1866) was Poet Laureate and Poet-Priest of the Confederacy. He was pastor of St. Mary's Church, Mobile.

Joseph Sackett moved south in the mid-1990s following a fast-paced career in tactical aviation. He has, since settling in Mobile, written four books, taken dozens of photographs, and published 360 newspaper, magazine, ezine, and newsletter articles. Insightful and humorous, *Mobile, Mobilians and Southern Ways* is a delightful collection of several of his previously published works.

Andrew Saunders was born in Mobile as were his mother and grandparents on her side back to 1834. Educated in the sciences at Loyola in New Orleans, he has, for thirty-seven years, pursued a business career unrelated to his education or his primary interests. He is president of Saunders Engine Company, a regional marine services firm.

Jack Shearer was born in Virginia and reared in Alabama where he attended Murphy High School in Mobile. He graduated from Birmingham Southern and went to Northwestern where he obtained a theological degree. He was an ordained minister. He later obtained a Ph.D. at Kennedy Western University. He studied with Masters and Johnson and worked as a sex counselor. He founded the Pastoral Counseling Center of Mobile. He is the author of *Love Treatment for Human Sexuality*. He was president of the Haunted Bookshop and HB Publications in the 1990s. He is currently retired and working on a novel.

Marilyn Schwartz, (1943-2012) a native of Mobile, newspaper columnist for the Dallas Morning News, is the author of *A Southern Belle Primer or Why Princess Margaret Will Never Be A Kappa Kappa Gamma.*

Celestine Sibley, (1914-1999) was best known for her charming slice-of-life columns for the *Atlanta Journal Constitution* and her 25 books. But at her heart, Sibley was considered first and foremost a hard journalist.

Eugene B. Sledge (1923-2002) was born in Mobile. He grew up in a Georgia Cottage on Springhill Avenue. During WWII, he enlisted in the Marine Corps, and saw heavy combat on the islands of Pelelliu and Okinawa. After the war he was stationed in China. Upon his return to the states, he took a Ph.D. in Biology and taught at the University of Montevallo for many years. In 1981, his war memoir, *With the Old Breed* was published and is now considered the classic infantryman's account of close combat. Prior to succumbing to cancer in 2002, Sledge had completed a manuscript on his China experiences, *China Marine*, published by the University of Alabama Press.

John S. Sledge was born in Gainesville, FL in 1957 and spent his formative years in Montevallo, AL. He has deep Gulf Coast roots, however, as his father was a native

Mobilian and his mother spent her girlhood in New Orleans, at one time living in the Pontalba Building. Sledge took an MA in historic preservation from Middle Tennessee State University and worked in Georgia and Tennessee prior to moving to the Eastern Shore in 1985. Since that time he has worked as an architectural historian for the Mobile Historic Development Commission. He is also the *Mobile Register's* Books Editor, a position he has held since 1996.

Vivian Smallwood, (1912-1994) was born in Vinegar Bend, Alabama. She lived most of her life in Chickasaw, Alabama and was the recipient of numerous poetry awards. She is the author of *Window to the South* and *And Finding No Mouse There.*

Betty Spence studied poetry writing at the University of South Alabama and has published poetry in such magazines as *Elk River Review, New Laurel Review, Negative Capability,* and *Mobile Bay Monthly*. She has taught creative writing for the Eastern Shore Institute of Learning and for various city of Mobile community programs.

Mary Stanley is Marie Sheip's pen name. She lived in Spring Hill where she wrote her novel, *Gulf Stream.*

Susan Tucker is Curator of Books and Records at the Newcomb College Center for Research on Women, Tulane University. Educated at Tulane and the University of Denver, she is a Certified Archivist, who since the late 1970s, has specialized in manuscripts, oral histories, and books related to the lives of women in the nineteenth and twentieth centuries. She is the author of *Telling Memories Among Southern Women* and numerous essays on the history of scrapbooks, photograph albums, and the papers of women.

S.L. Varnado, an emeritus professor at the University of South Alabama, lived in Mobile as a boy during WWII. He has written for several magazines, had a book published by the University of Alabama Press, and written a column for the *Mobile Register.*

Sue B. Walker is the Stokes Distinguished Professor of Creative Writing at the University of South Alabama, the publisher of Negative Capability Press, and a published playwright, critic, poet, and fiction writer. She served as Poet Laureate of Alabama from 2003-2012.

Eugene Walter (1921-1998) was born and raised in Mobile. He served as Air Force cryptographer in Alaska and the Andrean Islands in WWII, lived in New York in the late '40s. In Paris, in 1951, he joined Princess Caetani as assistant on her polylingual literary review, *Botteghe Oscure* and later helped found *The Paris Review*. His work includes *Jennie, The Watercress Girl, The Likes of Which, Love You Good, See You Later,* and *The Byzantine Riddle.*

Claiborne Walsh, a native Mobilian, attended Spring Hill College before working in advertising in Mobile, New Orleans, and Savannah. She was Director of the Eastern Shore Art Center and co-chaired The Grand Festival of Art and its Outdoor Art Shows. She has been published in various anthologies and magazines.

R. Wells worked with D. Holt to create the song titled "Mobile."

Kathryn Tucker Windham (1918-2011) grew up in Thomasville, Alabama and graduated from Huntingdon College. She was a writer for *The Alabama Journal, The Birmingham News,* and *The Selma Times-Journal.* She has received Associated Press Awards, the Alabama Library Association's non-fiction award, an honorary degree from Huntingdon College and the 1985 "Living for America" award. She is nationally recognized storyteller and a frequent commentator for National Public Radio's "All Things Considered."

E.O. Wilson was born in Birmingham, Alabama in 1929. He received his B.S. and M.S. in biology from the University of Alabama and, in 1955, his Ph.D. in biology from Harvard. He is the author of two Pulitzer Prize winning books, *Oh Human Nature* (1978) and *The Ants* (1990) as well as the recipient of many fellowships, honors, and awards, including the 1977 National Medal of Science, the Crafoord Prize from the Royal Swedish Academy of Sciences (1990), the International Prize for Biology from Japan (1993), and, for his conservation efforts, the Gold Medal of the Worldwide Fund for Nature (1990) and the Audubon Medal of the National Audubon Society (1995).

ACKNOWLEDGEMENTS

First Edition

The editors would like to thank the following for their help, without which this book would not be possible: Ron Walker for keeping the committee members fed and the meeting running smoothly; Elisa Baldwin, Michael Thomason and Carol Ellis at the University of South Alabama Archives for their knowledge of historical Mobile and assistance with the vast collection of photographs and written work; Charlotte Chamberlain and the staff at the Mobile Public Library Local History and Genealogy for help with research; Spring Hill College's archivist, Dr. Charles Boyle, and librarian, Nancy Bolton; Ann Irvine for calling in ideas; Father James Dorrill for his input; Jan Sauer and the librarians at the University of South Alabama Library; President and Mrs. Gordon Moulton for their support of the literary arts; Nicole Ervin Amare for obtaining legal advice; Debby Dwyer for consistently valuable advice; Kim Bancroft Wood for editing assistance; Bert Hitchcock of Auburn University; Nan Altmayer; Jack Shearer; Joaquin Holloway, Jr.; Phyllis Feibleman; Virginia Greer; Don Parker; Billie Goodloe for help and suggestions; and especially to the late Rhoda Heile Hafner whose inspiration will always be an integral part of this text.

Revised Anniversary Edition

The editors would like to thank Dr. Steven Trout, chair of the Department of English at the University of South Alabama, for his support of creative writing and providing opportunities for interns to work on projects such as this.

PERMISSIONS

Every effort has been made to trace the ownership of copyrighted material and to make full acknowledgment of its use. If errors or omissions have occurred, they will be corrected in subsequent editions upon notification in writing to the publisher.

The editors wish to thank the following for their kind permission to publish the excerpts from the following:

Selection from *A Walk Across America* by Peter Jenkins. pp. 243-248. © 1979. Reprinted by permission of the author.

Selection from *As Summers Die* by Winston Groom. Prologue. Reprinted by permission of the author. © 1980 by Summit Books.

Selection from *China Marine*.

Selection from *The Looking Glass* by William March. pp.76-77. Reprinted by permission of Harold Ober Associated Incorporated. Copyright 1943 by Little, Brown and Company.

"Miss Alice Frazer Recalls the 1897 Yellow Fever Epidemic" by Virginia Greer from *Mobile Talk About A Town*. © 1985 by Virginia Greer. Reprinted by permission of the author.

"November" by Celestine Sibley, as reprinted from *Seasons*, used with the permission of Peachtree Publishers.

Selection from *On The Road* by Jack Kerouac. pp. 138-139. © 1955, 1957 by Jack Kerouac; renewed © 1983 by Stella Kerouac, renewed © 1995 by Stella Kerouac and Jan Kerouac. Used by permission of Viking Penguin, a division of Penguin Putnam, Inc. Books.

"My Dream of Mobile" by Henry Miller, from *The Air-Conditioned Nightmare*. © 1945 by New Directions Publishing Corp. Used by permission of New Directions Publishing Corporation.

"Boyington Oak" by Kathryn Tucker Windham from *Jeffrey's Latest 13*. © Reprinted by permission of the author.

Selection from *I Had A Hammer* by Henry Aaron with Lonnie Wheeler. pp.5-8. © 1991 by HarperCollins Publishers. Reprinted by permission of the author, Lonnie Wheeler.

"Cecilia Gaudet" by Susan Tucker from *Telling Memories Among Southern Women*. ©1988 by Susan Tucker. Reprinted by permission of the author. Published by arrangement with Pantheon Books, a Division of Random House, Inc.

PERMISSIONS

Selection from *The Seven League Boots* by Albert Murray. pp. 271-275. © 1995 Pantheon Books. Reprinted by permission of the author.

"Evelyn Waugh" by Father Franklin Murray from *The Motley*, Spring, 1972. Published by Spring Hill College. With permission.

"All Dressed Up and No Place to Go" by © Whitney Balliett, originally published in *The New Yorker*. 1970.

Selection from *The Naturalist* by E.O. Wilson. © 1994 by Island Press. Reprinted by permission of the author.

"Good Old Boys" by Paul Hemphill from *The Atlanta Journal*, 1969. Used by permission of the author.

"The Garden Spot" by Charles McNair, March 1991. p. 112. © *Southern Living*. Reprinted by permission.

Courtesy of the *Mobile Register* © 1997, © 2000, © 2002. All rights reserved. Reprinted with permission. Roy Hoffman, Sue Walker, Carolyn Haines, Steve Joynt.

"My South Today" by Marilyn Schwartz. © 2002. *Southern Living*. Reprinted with permission.

"Measuring Life" by Rachael Alex. c. 2011. *Oracle Fine Arts Review 2012*. As Rachael Fowler. Reprinted with permission of the author.

"Two Blocks and Twenty Bucks" by Corey Harvard. © 2012. *Sense* magazine. Reprinted with permission of the author.

"On Mobile Bay" by Earl C. Jones. Permission granted by W.S. Hoole Special Collections Library.